This 4th Edition of the Student Text for *12th Grade Expository Reading and Writing Course—Semester One,* is printed with permission from the California State University (CSU) system. It is to be used for instructional purposes only by Los Angeles Unified School District (LAUSD) teachers and students. The right to use these materials is not transferable without permission from the CSU system and LAUSD.

June 2009

CSU **The California State University**

The *Expository Reading and Writing Course: Semester One* was developed by the California State University (CSU) Expository Reading and Writing Task Force, chaired by John R. Edlund of California State Polytechnic University, Pomona. It was edited by Dixie Abbott, Janet Lundin, Katina Oliphant, and Faye Ong of CDE Press working in cooperation with Nancy Brynelson of the CSU Center for the Advancement of Reading and the members of the task force. It was prepared for printing by the staff of CDE Press; the cover and interior design were created by Cheryl McDonald, and typesetting was done by Jeannette Reyes. It was published by the California State University Press, The California State University, Office of the Chancellor, 401 Golden Shore, Long Beach, CA 90801-4210. It was distributed under the provisions of the Library Distribution Act and *Government Code* Section 11096.

ISBN 978-0-9818314-0-4

Contents

Preface...v
Acknowledgments..vii
Introduction..x
Course Description..xv

Module 1:   Fast Food: Who's to Blame?
Module 2:   Going for the Look
Module 3:   The Rhetoric of the Op-Ed Page: Ethos, Pathos, and
             Logos
Module 4:   The Value of Life
Module 5:   Racial Profiling
Module 6:   Juvenile Justice
Module 7:   The Last Meow
Module 8:   Into the Wild

Preface

The California State University (CSU) is pleased to present this publication. Developed as a part of the CSU's Early Assessment Program, these materials are the basis of an approved college-preparatory course in English that may be taught in the junior or senior year of high school. The Early Assessment Program was established to allow students to measure their readiness for college-level English and mathematics in their junior year of high school and to offer opportunities for those students to improve their skills during their senior year.

The Expository Reading and Writing Course (ERWC) was initially designed as an alternative curriculum for students in grade twelve who had not demonstrated readiness for college-level English courses. The reach of the curriculum, however, now extends far beyond grade twelve. As a result of the professional development workshops provided for the ERWC and the CSU Reading Institutes for Academic Preparation, almost 200 schools now offer the course in grade eleven or twelve. In addition, teachers of English and other subject areas use the ERWC materials and strategies within their existing courses in many creative ways. Evaluation studies conducted by the CSU indicate that teacher participation in these professional development programs and use of the course materials have improved results for students in English–language arts during their high school years and as they enter the CSU system.

The ERWC is the culmination of many years of development, classroom piloting, and evaluation for which the course has gained both statewide and national attention. It is the result of the dedication of the CSU Expository Reading and Writing Task Force and the input of hundreds of high school teachers, students, specialists, and administrators who have offered suggestions for its improvement over several years. Collaboration was the hallmark of the course's development. Collaboration is also the hallmark of the course's delivery to thousands of teachers through workshops sponsored by county offices of education and CSU campuses statewide.

We wish to thank all of the individuals and groups who have contributed to the success of this effort, most notably the members of the Curriculum and Instruction Steering Committee of the California County Superintendents Educational Services Association for their cooperation and leadership in promoting and conducting ERWC professional development. And we offer our heartfelt gratitude to the CSU faculty and high school educators of the CSU task force for their vision, creativity, intellect, hard work, and commitment to the development and dissemination of the ERWC. The work of these individuals makes it possible for all students to enter the world of college and careers with the academic literacy needed to think, read, and write effectively and, ultimately, to contribute to California's future.

GARY W. REICHARD
Executive Vice Chancellor and Chief Academic Officer
The California State University

Acknowledgments

The Expository Reading and Writing Task Force

John R. Edlund,* Task Force Chair, Professor of English, and Director of the University Writing Center, California State Polytechnic University, Pomona

Nancy Brynelson, Co-Director, California State University, Center for the Advancement of Reading

Margaret Buchan,*† Principal, Troy High School, Fullerton Joint Union High School District

Roberta Ching,* Professor of TESOL (Teachers of English to Speakers of Other Languages) and Chair of the Learning Skills Center, California State University, Sacramento

Kim Flachmann,* Professor of English and Director of the Writing Program, California State University, Bakersfield

Jennifer Fletcher, Assistant Professor of English, Division of Humanities and Communication, California State University, Monterey Bay

Mary Kay Harrington,* Professor of Composition and Director of the Writing Skills Program, California State Polytechnic University, San Luis Obispo

Carol Jago,* Teacher of English, Santa Monica High School, Santa Monica-Malibu Unified School District

Mira-Lisa Katz,* Associate Professor of English Education, Department of English, Sonoma State University

Peter Kittle, *† Associate Professor of English and Director of the Northern California Writing Project, California State University, Chico

Marcy Merrill, Associate Professor of Language and Literacy, Department of Teacher Education, California State University, Sacramento

Norman Unrau, Professor Emeritus of Curriculum and Instruction, Charter College of Education, California State University, Los Angeles

Sid Walton, *† Teacher of English (retired), Oakland Technical High School, Oakland Unified School District

Alison Warriner,* Professor of English and Director of Writing Programs, California State University, East Bay

Marsha Zandi,* Curriculum Specialist, Sweetwater Union High School District

*Original members
†Inactive members

The California State University
Office of the Chancellor

Allison Jones, Assistant Vice Chancellor, Student Academic Support

Beverly Young, Assistant Vice Chancellor, Teacher Education and Public School Programs

Nancy Brynelson and **Douglas Fisher,** Co-Directors, Center for the Advancement of Reading

Carol Rogala, Administrative Support Coordinator, Center for the Advancement of Reading

Authors

Roberta Ching, California State University, Sacramento

Fast Food: Who's to Blame?
Going for the Look
Juvenile Justice
The Last Meow

John R. Edlund, California Polytechnic State University, Pomona

Left Hand of Darkness
The Rhetoric of the Op-Ed Page: Ethos, Pathos, and Logos

Kim Flachmann, California State University, Bakersfield

Justice: Childhood Love Lessons
Racial Profiling

Mary Kay Harrington, California Polytechnic State University, San Luis Obispo

Into the Wild
The Politics of Food

Mira-Lisa Katz, Sonoma State University

Bring a Text You Like to Class
Language, Gender, and Culture
Rhetorical Reading and Rhetorical Writing: Theoretical Foundations

Peter Kittle, California State University, Chico

The Value of Life

Cathy Kroll, Sonoma State University

Language, Gender, and Culture

Rochelle Ramay, Corning High School, Corning Union High School District

The Value of Life

Alison Warriner, California State University, East Bay

Bullying at School: Research Project

The Task Force would like to thank our newer members: **Jennifer Fletcher,** for the new section in the Assignment Template, Revising Rhetorically, and for revisions and edits to The Value of Life; **Marcy Merrill,** for the new section in the Assignment Template, Introducing Key Concepts, and for vocabulary activities throughout the modules; and **Norman Unrau,** for sharing his wisdom, insight, scholarship, and vast experience. In addition, the Task Force would like to thank **Deborah Wilhelm** of California Polytechnic State University, San Luis Obispo, for compiling and analyzing the sample student essays included in the modules. Finally, the task force would like to gratefully acknowledge **Nancy Brynelson** for contributing her invaluable insights, experience, and institutional wisdom and for working tirelessly to prepare these materials for publication.

Introduction

The materials you now hold in your hands are the final product of the Expository Reading and Writing Task Force. As a part of the California State University's (CSU) Early Assessment Program (EAP), this task force was charged with creating a course to help prepare students for the reading and writing demands of the first year in college. When our small group of CSU faculty and high school teachers and administrators met for the first time on August 20, 2003, the original plan was to collect the best practices from developmental courses throughout the CSU and package them for use by high school teachers. However, the high school members immediately argued that this would not work because every assignment had to be closely aligned with the English–Language Arts Content Standards for California Public Schools and the real problem was critical reading, not writing. From this unanticipated beginning we learned to listen, collaborate, adapt, and share. Together we developed an assignment template and 14 assignments or modules that, taken together, comprise a full year of lessons: the Expository Reading and Writing Course (ERWC). However, it turned out that completing the course was only the beginning.

To implement the course, we recruited high school and CSU faculty to become workshop facilitators, and we held a series of leadership conferences to structure and organize professional development for the ERWC. To date, roughly 3,000 teachers have attended ERWC workshops. The full course has been adopted by almost 200 schools, and the materials are used in hundreds more. We have an online community (http://writing. csusuccess.org/) where teachers can download and share materials and help each other teach them. Perhaps most importantly of all, we have met many teachers and made many friends. Due to feedback from teachers, we added more sophisticated vocabulary development activities to all modules and a text-based grammar supplement for the modules in Semester One. We have listened to our colleagues and friends.

In addition to the EAP goals of helping students meet the standards of the English Placement Test and the literacy expectations of college and university faculty, the course materials are designed to embody the following key principles of an effective expository reading and writing curriculum:

1. The integration of interactive reading and writing processes;
2. A rhetorical approach to texts that fosters critical thinking;
3. Materials and themes that engage student interest and provide a foundation for principled debate and argument;
4. Classroom activities designed to model and foster successful practices of fluent readers and writers;
5. Research-based methodologies with a consistent relationship between theory and practice;
6. Built-in flexibility to allow teachers to respond to varied students' needs and instructional contexts; and
7. Alignment with English–Language Arts Content Standards.

The modules in this binder are just a beginning. Teachers are already creating new assignments based on the assignment template and these principles.

Each module is a sequence of integrated reading and writing experiences that will take from one to three weeks to teach. The modules, many of which include informal writing throughout the process, move from pre-reading activities, through reading and postreading activities, to formal writing assignments. Along the way, students learn to make predictions about texts, analyze both the content and the rhetorical structures, and properly use materials from the texts they read in supporting their own written arguments.

Included in this binder are the approved course description, an overview of the theoretical foundations of the course, the assignment template, teacher and student versions of each module, the reading selections, and sample student essays. The reading selections are also offered in a separate student reader so that teachers can use the online versions of the modules and still have access to the readings. The assignment template is the organizing principle for all of the assignments. It helped the developers sequence the activities and maintain a consistent format and approach. We encourage you to use the template to develop your own assignments and share them with us and with other teachers. In the future, our online community Web site will serve as a repository for new assignments.

We encourage schools to consider adopting the ERWC as one of the college-preparatory options for their students in grade eleven or twelve. Approved by the University of California to satisfy the "b" subject require-ment for English, the ERWC may be adopted as a full-year course or as a one-semester course in either grade. The CSU is authorized to grant ap-proval to schools that wish to adopt the course. If your school is interested in this option, more information is available at www.calstate.edu/eap/englishcourse. Schools have found a variety of ways to implement the course materials within existing English courses as well. We are heartened by the results of four years of evaluation studies on the benefits of the ERWC. In schools with large numbers of teachers participating in professional development for the ERWC, we have seen increases in the proficiency gains of students entering the CSU and increases in the gains on the California Standards Test for English–Language Arts for students in grade eleven. More information on the evaluation studies is available at www.calstate.edu/teacherED/reports/index.shtml.

When we started this project, we knew that there was a chance that our work could have a big effect on the way English is taught in California schools. I can say now that without a doubt, it has. However, when we started out, our success was basically a bottom-up, grassroots effect. Teachers liked the way students interacted with our materials, and they made suggestions, talked to other teachers, and brought people on board. Some teachers even brought binders to principals and district literacy coordinators and walked them through assignments. Teachers made this happen. However, there has also been amazing cooperation and collaboration among the CSU Chancellor's Office, the California Department of Education, the California County Superintendents Educational Services Association, the University of California, the California State Board of Education, the Intersegmental Coordinating Committee, the California Academic Partnership Program, the California Postsecondary Education Commission, and many other policymakers connected with secondary and postsecondary education in this state. We thank them all, with special thanks to the Center for the Advancement of Reading, without which these materials would not be in your hands today.

Thanks so much for your interest in this project. We hope that you and your students enjoy working with these materials.

JOHN R. EDLUND, CHAIR
CSU Expository Reading and Writing Task Force

LAUSD Acknowledgments

The Expository Reading and Writing Task Force

Maria Ablaza ◆ Willie Ackerman ◆ Jeff Alpert ◆ Wendy Bader ◆ Michael Battin ◆ Laurie Bollman-Little ◆ Marianne Brandt ◆ Mark Brow ◆ Christina Burian ◆ Rachel Caban ◆ Bobby Canosa-Carr ◆ Ellen Cohen ◆ Jennifer DaCosta ◆ Jerre Delaney ◆ Laurie Dix ◆ Loretta Dix ◆ Ron Espiritu ◆ Judy Fisher ◆ Arzie Galvez ◆ David Garcia ◆ Doña Guevara-Hill ◆ Lilia Grava ◆ Frank Guzman ◆ Louis Hernandez ◆ Edward Jacobson ◆ Sharon James ◆ Torray Johnson ◆ Jency Kanichirayil ◆ Beth B. Kennedy ◆ Jason Kinsella ◆ Lonee Lona ◆ Lynda Markham ◆ Frankie McGee ◆ Ryan Morse ◆ Karla Ponbida ◆ Sharon Read ◆ Karin Rinderknecht ◆ Renee D. Rodriguez ◆ Amber Setrakian ◆ Robin Share ◆ Nydia Velez Therminy ◆ Alicia Vazquez ◆ E. Lynn Walton ◆ Walter Weronka ◆ Derek Willard.

Expository Composition

B Requirement

(Semester Course – Grade 12)
Prerequisite: American Literature & Composition/Contemporary Composition

230205   EXPOS COMP

Course Description

The major purpose of this semester course is to provide experiences in writing that are characterized by logical and coherent organization, clarity of expression, and suitability in style, usage, and the conventions of writing. The student is required to read closely within and across expository and informational genres (e.g., essays, biographies, critiques, précis, and newspaper and magazine articles) for literal and implied meaning and to demonstrate through classroom discussion, oral presentation, and written expression an understanding of the text(s). Emphasis in this course is on expository reading and writing and the essential skills of editing, although the course provides some practice in other domains of writing.

The curriculum of this semester course was developed by a collaborative group of California State University and high school faculty to help students meet the expectations of college and university faculty, meet the California English-Language Arts Content Standards, and develop literacy skills critical to lifelong participation to the worlds of work and community. Students will read one full-length work, engage major research, and participate in multiple readings and discussions of varied genres through a recursive sequence of integrated reading and writing assignments. The interactive reading and writing assignments, many of which include informal writing throughout the process, move from pre-reading activities, through reading and post-reading activities, to formal writing assignments. Students learn to make predictions about texts, analyze both the content and the rhetorical structures, and properly use materials from the texts they read in supporting their own oral and written arguments. The modules in the sequence of lessons in Expository Composition provide a recursive approach to the teaching of reading and writing that aims to support students' developing abilities to negotiate a variety of complex texts of different genres that students will encounter in college and the diverse communities where they live and work.

Students are expected to write and revise a minimum of eight academic compositions within the twelfth-grade year, including timed writing pieces and developed compositions. The *California Reading/Language Arts Framework* states that students in the twelfth grade are expected to read two million words annually on their own, including a good representation of classic and contemporary literature, magazines, newspapers, and online articles. Students will apply and refine their command of the writing process, writing conventions, and rhetorical strategies of narration, exposition, persuasion, and description to produce texts of at least 1,500 words each. Expository Composition fulfills a B requirement of the UC/CSU Subject Area Requirements.

Focus Standards

Reading

Grade 12

R 2.1 Analyze both the features and the rhetorical devices of different types of public documents (e.g., policy statements, speeches, debates, platforms) and the way in which authors use those features and devices.

R 2.2 Analyze the way in which clarity of meaning is affected by patterns of organization, hierarchical structures, repetition of the main ideas, syntax, and word choice in the text.

R 2.3 Verify and clarify facts presented in other types of expository texts by using a variety of consumer, workplace, and public documents.

R 2.4 Make warranted and reasonable assertions about the author's arguments by using elements of the text to defend and clarify interpretations.

R 2.5 Analyze an author's implicit and explicit philosophical assumptions and beliefs about a subject.

R 2.6 Critique the power, validity, and truthfulness of arguments set forth in public documents; their appeal to both friendly and hostile audiences; and the extent to which the arguments anticipate and address reader concerns and counterclaims (e.g., appeal to reason, to authority, to pathos and emotion).

R 3.3 Analyze the ways in which irony, tone, mood, the author's style, and the "sound" of language achieve specific rhetorical or aesthetic purposes or both.

R 3.9 Analyze the philosophical arguments presented in literary works to determine whether the authors' positions have contributed to the quality of each work and the credibility of characters. (Philosophical approach)

Writing

Grade 12

W 1.3 Structure ideas and arguments in a sustained, persuasive, and sophisticated way and support them with precise and relevant examples.

W 1.4 Enhance meaning by employing rhetorical devices, including the extended use of parallelism, repetition, and analogy; the incorporation of visual aids (e.g., graphs, tables, pictures); and the issuance of a call for action.

W 1.9 Revise text to highlight the individual voice, improve sentence variety and style, and enhance subtlety of meaning and tone in ways that are consistent with the purpose, audience, and genre.

W 2.2 Write responses to literature:
   a. Demonstrate a comprehensive understanding of the significant ideas in works or passages.
   b. Analyze the use of imagery, language, universal themes, and unique aspects of the text.
   c. Support important ideas and viewpoints through accurate and detailed references to the text and to other works.
   d. Demonstrate an understanding of the author's use of stylistic devices and an appreciation of the effects created.
   e. Identify and assess the impact of the perceived ambiguities, nuances, and complexities within the text.

W 2.3 Write reflective compositions:
   a. Explore the significance of personal experiences, events, conditions, or concerns by using rhetorical strategies (e.g., narration, description, exposition, persuasion).
   b. Draw comparisons between specific incidents and broader themes that illustrate the writer's important beliefs or generalizations about life.
   c. Maintain a balance in describing individual incidents and relate those incidents to more general and abstract ideas.

W 2.4 Write historical investigation reports:
   a. Use exposition, narration, description, argumentation, or some combination of rhetorical strategies to support the main proposition.
   b. Analyze several historical records of single event, examining critical relationships between elements of the research topic.
   c. Explain the perceived reason or reasons for the similarities and differences in historical records with information derived from primary and secondary sources to support or enhance the presentation.
   d. Include information from all relevant perspectives and take into consideration the validity and reliability of sources.
   e. Include a formal bibliography.

Listening and Speaking

Grade 12

LS 1.4 Use rhetorical questions, parallel structure, concrete images, figurative language, characterization, irony, and dialogue to achieve clarity, force, and aesthetic effect.

LS 1.5 Distinguish between and use various forms of classical and contemporary logical arguments, including:
   a. Inductive and deductive reasoning.
   b. Syllogisms and analogies.

LS 1.6 Use logical, ethical, and emotional appeals that enhance a specific tone and purpose.

LS 1.12 Identify logical fallacies used in oral addresses (e.g., attack ad hominem, false causality, red herring, overgeneralization, bandwagon effect).

SA 2.1 Deliver reflective presentations:
   a. Explore the significance of personal experiences, events, conditions, or concerns, using appropriate rhetorical strategies (e.g., narration, description, exposition, persuasion).
   b. Draw comparisons between the specific incident and broader themes that illustrate the speaker's beliefs or generalizations about life.
   c. Maintain a balance between describing the incident and relating it to more general, abstract ideas.

SA 2.2 Deliver oral reports on historical investigations:
   a. Use exposition, narration, description, persuasion, or some combination of those to support the thesis.
   b. Analyze several historical records of a single event, examining critical relationships between elements of the research topic.
   c. Explain the perceived reason or reasons for the similarities and differences by using information derived from primary and secondary sources to support or enhance the presentation.
   d. Include information on all relevant perspectives and consider the validity and reliability of sources.

SA 2.3 Deliver oral responses to literature:
   a. Demonstrate a comprehensive understanding of the significant ideas of literary works.
   b. Analyze the imagery, language, universal themes, and unique aspects of the text through the use of rhetorical strategies.
   c. Support important ideas and viewpoints through accurate and detailed references to the text or to other works.
   d. Demonstrate an awareness of the author's use of stylistic devices and an appreciation of the effects created.
   e. Identify and assess the impact of perceived ambiguities, nuances, and complexities within the text.

Representative Performance Outcomes and Skills

In this course, students will know and be able to:

- Read a wide variety of complex informational and expository texts, organized around topics or issues.
- Demonstrate an understanding of the elements of discourse (e.g., purpose, speaker, audience, form) when completing expository and persuasive writing assignments.
- Identify, analyze, discuss, describe, and use appeals to *pathos*, *ethos*, and *logos* and other rhetorical strategies that writers employ to craft an argument.
- Analyze the content, complexity, and structure of the language employed to convey a writer's perspective.
- Demonstrate control of grammar, diction, and paragraph and sentence structure and an understanding of English usage.
- Critique the power, validity, and truthfulness of arguments set forth in public documents; their appeal to both friendly and hostile audiences; and the extent to which the arguments anticipate and address reader concerns and counterclaims.
- Examine models of effective academic, professional, and business writing and speaking: college application essays, introductory and business letters, résumés, and interviews.
- Develop presentations by using clear research questions and creative and critical research strategies (e.g., field studies, oral histories, interviews, experiments, electronic sources).
- Reflect appropriate manuscript requirements in writing.

Assessments

- Teacher-created quizzes and tests
- Essays and other student-written texts
- Oral presentations

- Released university English placement tests

District Adopted Standards-Based Curriculum

- LAUSD *English/Language Arts Instructional Guide Essential Tools*, Grades 11-12

- Required: *Expository Reading and Writing Course, Student Texts and Materials*, Semester 1

- Required: *Expository Reading and Writing Course, Teacher Texts and Materials*, Semester 1

Recommended Texts and Instructional Resources

- District approved standards-based textbook and corresponding district-approved novel(s) and complete works

- Supplementary texts (contemporary essays, newspaper and magazine articles, editorials, reports, memos, voting materials and assorted public documents, and other non-fiction texts)

- *Focus on English,* California State University English Placement Test, Office of the Chancellor

Other Instructional Resources

- *Reading/Language Arts Framework for California Public Schools*

Expository Reading and Writing AB **B Requirement**

(Annual Course – Grade 12)

Prerequisite: American Literature and Composition/Contemporary Composition or American Authors AB

230231 **ERWC A**
230232 **ERWC B**

Course Description

The major purpose of this year-long course is to prepare students for the literacy demands of college and the world of work. Through a sequence of fourteen rigorous instructional modules, students in this yearlong, rhetoric-based course develop advanced proficiencies in expository, analytical, and argumentative reading and writing. The cornerstone of the course—the assignment template—presents a process for helping students read, comprehend, and respond to non-fiction and literary texts. Modules also provide instruction in research methods and documentation conventions. Students will be expected to increase their awareness of the rhetorical strategies employed by authors, and to apply those strategies in their own writing.   They will read closely to examine the relationship between an author's argument or theme and his or her audience and purpose, to analyze the impact of structural and rhetorical strategies, and to examine the social, political, and philosophical assumptions that underlie the text. By the end of the course, students will be expected to use this process independently when reading unfamiliar texts and writing in response to them. Course texts include contemporary essays, newspaper and magazine articles, editorials, reports, biographies, memos, assorted public documents, and other non-fiction texts. The course materials also include modules on two full-length works (one novel and one work of non-fiction). Written assessments and holistic scoring guides conclude each unit.

Students are expected to write and revise a minimum of eight academic compositions within the twelfth-grade year, including timed writing pieces and developed compositions. The *California Reading/Language Arts Framework* states that students in the twelfth grade are expected to read two million words annually on their own that will transition them into adult reading. They will also apply and refine their command of the writing process, writing conventions, and rhetorical strategies to produce texts of at least 1,500 words each. Expository Reading and Writing Course fulfills a B requirement of the UC/CSU Subject Area Requirements.

COURSE SYLLABUS

Scope and Sequence

This year-long English course, developed by a collaborative group of California State University and high school faculty, is designed to help students meet the expectations of college and university faculty, meet the California English/Language Arts Content Standards, and develop literacy skills critical to lifelong participation to the worlds of work and community. These modules, many of which include informal writing throughout the process, move from pre-reading activities, through reading and post-reading activities, to formal writing assignments. Students learn to make predictions about texts, analyze both the content and the rhetorical structures, and properly use materials from the texts they read in supporting their own oral and written arguments. The modules in the sequence of lessons in Expository Reading and Writing provide a recursive approach to the teaching of reading and writing that aims to support students' developing abilities to negotiate a variety of complex texts of different genres that students will encounter in college and the diverse communities where they live and work.

The instructional modules are organized by semester. Most modules include multiple text selections on a topic, often representing different genres and perspectives. Course texts include contemporary essays, newspaper and magazine articles, editorials, reports, biographies, memos, assorted public documents, and other non-fiction texts. Two modules include full-length works—a work of non-fiction in semester one and a novel in semester two. Modules include instruction in critical reading, analysis of rhetorical strategies, vocabulary, grammar, research methods, documentation conventions, and analytical writing based on information learned from and in response to the assigned texts. The cornerstone of the course—the assignment template—provides consistent structure and content for each module by presenting a process for helping students read, comprehend, and respond to non-fiction texts.

ERWC Instructional Modules Semester One

Assignment 1: Fast Food: Who's To Blame?

"Fast Food—Who's to Blame?" is based on four newspaper articles and a set of letters to the editor written in response to one set of the articles about the issue of fast food and its role in contributing to childhood obesity. As the first assignment in the Expository Reading and Writing course curriculum, it serves as an introduction to the approach to teaching expository reading and writing utilizing accessible readings and an engaging topic.

Assignment 2: Going For the Look

"Going for the Look" is based on a single newspaper article about a lawsuit accusing companies of hiring sales associates based on appearance. The article incorporates a variety of brief arguments on both sides of the issue, making it a good assignment for introducing students to rhetorical analysis. It concludes by offering the option of having students write a sample Early Placement Test timed essay (persuasive) or an out-of-class text-based essay (argumentative).

Assignment 3: The Rhetoric of the Op-Ed Page - Ethos, Pathos, and Logos

This assignment sequence introduces the Aristotelian concepts of ethos, logos, and pathos and applies them to a rhetorical analysis of an op-ed piece by Jeremy Rifkin about animal behavior. The culminating writing assignment is a letter to the editor in response to the Rifkin article.

Assignment 4: The Value of Life

This assignment asks students to synthesize their understanding of Hamlet's "To be or not to be" soliloquy, an excerpt from Lance Armstrong's "It's Not About the Bike," an article by Amanda Ripley on the aftermath of 9/11, and a life insurance tool, "The Human Life Value Calculator." Students are asked to add their voices to the discussion by creating a well-developed response to these sources (text-based academic essay).

Assignment 5: Racial Profiling

This assignment teaches students how to read and respond to an argumentative essay by Bob Herbert on racial profiling. First, students practice several reading strategies as they deepen their understanding of the Herbert essay; then, students learn how to write their own argumentative essay on a similar topic.

Assignment 6: Juvenile Justice

"Juvenile Justice" is based on four newspaper articles about whether juveniles who commit serious crimes should be tried and sentenced as adults. The articles include an opinion piece, a summary of brain research, a report of juvenile competence to stand trial, and an article about a Supreme Court case. Students must evaluate the rhetorical stances of different authors and synthesize their arguments in a text-based academic essay (argumentative).

Assignment 7: Into the Wild (Appendix)

Students read, write, and discuss the non-fiction, full-length work, *Into the Wild*, by Jon Krakauer, published in 1996. Engaging students in this biography/story, based on Karkauer's investigation of Christopher McCandless, a young idealistic college graduate, allows them to think deeply about human motivation and begin to understand something of the complexity of maturity. Students conclude the assignment by writing a text-based academic essay on one of a number of themes Krakauer presents.

ERWC Instructional Modules Semester Two

Assignment 1: Bring a Text You Like to Class

This assignment sequence builds on texts that students bring in to share with the class and serves to introduce the second semester. Throughout this sequence students work on externalizing their existing textual skills and knowledge and discovering ways that they can bring their current reading expertise from outside of school to bear on texts in school that they have never encountered before. A sample of music lyrics by a group called Black Eyed Peas is included as an example of the kinds of texts students may bring. An article on hip-hop music as a tool of resistance in youth cultures around the world is also included as an example of the kind of follow-up text that teachers may use to complement the texts brought in by students.

Assignment 2: Language, Gender, and Culture

The "Language, Gender, and Culture" assignment invites students to explore how language use embodies cultural values and gender-based communication styles. This assignment draws on readings in sociolinguistics and literature. The students conclude the assignment by writing a text-based academic essay.

Assignment 3: Left Hand of Darkness

The Left Hand of Darkness is a classic science fiction novel by Ursula K. Le Guin. Embedded in the literary narrative are field reports, folk tales, and other genre-bending texts, which allow students to extend the analytical and pedagogical techniques of the assignment template to a full-length literary work. For the culminating task, students write an extended argumentative essay.

Assignment 4: The Politics of Food

This assignment is based on two articles on the production and consumption of food. The articles were written over ten years apart and have similar concerns: the health and well-being of humans. These two authors have different ways of pointing out the same issues, ultimately asking the students to consider the worlds of science, agriculture, and politics. Students conclude the assignment by writing a text-based academic essay on one of several possible questions.

Assignment 5: Justice: Childhood Love Lessons

This assignment presents an argumentative essay by bell hooks about methods of childhood punishment and the relationships between discipline and expressions of love. Students are then asked to write a persuasive essay in response.

Complete Standards Set Attached

Representative Performance Outcomes and Skills

In this course, students will know and be able to:

- Analyze and apply organizational patterns, arguments, and positions advanced in expository texts.

- Write coherent and focused texts that convey a well-defined perspective and tightly-reasoned argument that demonstrates awareness of audience; reflect appropriate manuscript requirements in writing.

- Demonstrate the purpose and the stages of progression through the writing process.

- Combine the rhetorical strategies of narration, exposition, persuasion, and description in writing reflective compositions, responses to literature, and expository compositions.

- Make warranted and reasonable assertions about the author's arguments, critique the validity of arguments and their appeal to audiences, and critique the extent to which the arguments anticipate and address reader concerns and counterclaims.

- Demonstrate an understanding of the elements of discourse (e.g., purpose, speaker, audience, form) when completing expository and persuasive writing assignments; revise and edit writing for formal and informal publication.

- Deliver polished formal and extemporaneous presentations that combine traditional rhetorical strategies of narration, exposition, persuasion, and description.

- Identify, analyze, discuss, describe, and use appeals to *pathos*, *ethos*, and *logos* as well as other rhetorical strategies that writers employ to craft an argument.

- Analyze the content, complexity, and structure of the language employed to convey a writer's perspective.

- Demonstrate control of grammar, diction, paragraph and sentence structure, and an understanding of English usage.

- Examine models of effective academic, professional, and business writing and speaking: college application essays, introductory and business letters, résumés, and interviews.

- Develop presentations by using clear research questions and creative and critical research strategies (e.g., field studies, oral histories, interviews, experiments, electronic sources).

Assessments

- Teacher-created quizzes and tests

- Essays and other student written texts

- Oral presentations

- Released university English placement tests

District Adopted Standards-Based Curriculum

- LAUSD *English/Language Arts Instructional Guide Essential Tools*, Grades 11-12

- Required: *Expository Reading and Writing Course, Student Texts and Materials*, Semesters 1 and 2

- Required: *Expository Reading and Writing Course, Teacher Texts and Materials*, Semesters 1 and 2

Recommended Texts and Instructional Resources

- District approved standards-based textbook and corresponding district approved novel(s) and complete works

- Supplementary texts (contemporary essays, newspaper and magazine articles, editorials, reports, memos, voting materials and assorted public documents, and other non-fiction texts)

- *Focus on English,* California State University English Placement Test, Office of the Chancellor

Other Instructional Resources

- *Reading/Language Arts Framework for California Public Schools*

Grade Twelve
English-Language Arts Content Standards

Reading

R 1.0 Word Analysis, Fluency, and Systematic Vocabulary Development
Students apply their knowledge of word origins to determine the meaning of new words encountered in reading materials and use those words accurately.

Vocabulary and Concept Development
R 1.2 Apply knowledge of Greek, Latin, and Anglo-Saxon roots and affixes to draw inferences concerning the meaning of scientific and mathematical terminology.
R 1.3 Discern the meaning of analogies encountered, analyzing specific comparisons as well as relationships and inferences.

R 2.0 Reading Comprehension (Focus on Informational Materials)
Students read and understand grade-level-appropriate material. They analyze the organizational patterns, arguments, and positions advanced. The selections in *Recommended Literature, Kindergarten Through Grade Twelve* illustrate the quality and complexity of the materials to be read by students. In addition, by grade twelve, students read two million words annually on their own, including a wide variety of classic and contemporary literature, magazines, newspapers, and online information.

Comprehension and Analysis of Grade-Level-Appropriate Text
R 2.3 Verify and clarify facts presented in other types of expository texts by using a variety of consumer, workplace, and public documents.
R 2.4 Make warranted and reasonable assertions about the author's arguments by using elements of the text to defend and clarify interpretations.
R 2.5 Analyze an author's implicit and explicit philosophical assumptions and beliefs about a subject.

Expository Critique
R 2.6 Critique the power, validity, and truthfulness of arguments set forth in public documents; their appeal to both friendly and hostile audiences; and the extent to which the arguments anticipate and address reader concerns and counterclaims (e.g., appeal to reason, to authority, to pathos and emotion).

R 3.0 Literary Response and Analysis
Students read and respond to historically or culturally significant works of literature that reflect and enhance their studies of history and social science. They conduct in-depth analyses of recurrent themes. The selections in *Recommended Literature, Kindergarten Through Grade Twelve* illustrate the quality and complexity of the materials to be read by students.

Structural Features of Literature
R 3.1 Analyze characteristics of subgenres (e.g., satire, parody, allegory, pastoral) that are used in poetry, prose, plays, novels, short stories, essays, and other basic genres.

Narrative Analysis of Grade-Level-Appropriate Text

R 3.2 Analyze the way in which the theme or meaning of a selection represents a view or comment on life, using textual evidence to support the claim.

R 3.3 Analyze the ways in which irony, tone, mood, the author's style, and the "sound" of language achieve specific rhetorical or aesthetic purposes or both.

R 3.4 Analyze ways in which poets use imagery, personification, figures of speech, and sounds to evoke readers' emotions.

R 3.6 Analyze the way in which authors through the centuries have used archetypes drawn from myth and tradition in literature, film, political speeches, and religious writings (e.g., how the archetypes of banishment from an ideal world may be used to interpret Shakespeare's tragedy *Macbeth*).

R 3.7 Analyze recognized works of world literature from a variety of authors:

    a. Contrast the major literary forms, techniques, and characteristics of the major literary periods (e.g., Homeric Greece, medieval, romantic, neoclassic, modern).

    b. Relate literary works and authors to the major themes and issues of their eras.

    c. Evaluate the philosophical, political, religious, ethical, and social influences of the historical period that shaped the characters, plots, and settings.

Literary Criticism

R 3.9 Analyze the philosophical arguments presented in literary works to determine whether the authors' positions have contributed to the quality of each work and the credibility of the characters. (Philosophical approach)

Writing

W 1.0 Writing Strategies

Students write coherent and focused texts that convey a well-defined perspective and tightly-reasoned argument. The writing demonstrates students' awareness of the audience and purpose and progression through the stages of the writing process.

Organization and Focus

W 1.1 Demonstrate an understanding of the elements of discourse (e.g., purpose, speaker, audience, form) when completing narrative, expository, persuasive, or descriptive writing assignments.

W 1.2 Use point of view, characterization, style (e.g., use of irony), and related elements for specific rhetorical and aesthetic purposes.

W 1.3 Structure ideas and arguments in a sustained, persuasive, and sophisticated way and support them with precise and relevant examples.

W 1.4 Enhance meaning by employing rhetorical devices, including the extended use of parallelism, repetition, and analogy; the incorporation of visual aids (e.g., graphs, tables, pictures); and the issuance of a call for action.

W 1.5 Use language in natural, fresh, and vivid ways to establish a specific tone.

Research and Technology

W 1.6 Develop presentations by using clear research questions and creative and critical research strategies (e.g., field studies, oral histories, interviews, experiments, electronic sources).

W 1.7 Use systematic strategies to organize and record information (e.g., anecdotal scripting, annotated bibliographies).

W 1.8 Integrate databases, graphics, and spreadsheets into word-processed documents.

Evaluation and Revision

W 1.9 Revise text to highlight the individual voice, improve sentence variety and style, and enhance subtlety of meaning and tone in ways that are consistent with the purpose, audience, and genre.

W 2.0 Writing Applications (Genres and Their Characteristics)

Students combine the rhetorical strategies of narration, exposition, persuasion, and description to produce texts of at least 1,500 words each. Student writing demonstrates a command of standard American English and the research, organizational, and drafting strategies outlined in Writing Standard 1.0.

Using the writing strategies of grades eleven and twelve outlined in Writing Standard 1.0, students:

W 2.2 Write responses to literature:

    a.   Demonstrate a comprehensive understanding of the significant ideas in works or passages.

    b.   Analyze the use of imagery, language, universal themes, and unique aspects of the text.

    c.   Support important ideas and viewpoints through accurate and detailed references to the text and to other works.

    d.   Demonstrate an understanding of the author's use of stylistic devices and an appreciation of the effects created.

    e.   Identify and assess the impact of perceived ambiguities, nuances, and complexities within the text.

W 2.3 Write reflective compositions:

    a.   Explore the significance of personal experiences, events, conditions, or concerns by using rhetorical strategies (e.g., narration, description, exposition, persuasion).

    b.   Draw comparisons between specific incidents and broader themes that illustrate the writer's important beliefs or generalizations about life.

    c.   Maintain a balance in describing individual incidents and relate those incidents to more general and abstract ideas.

W 2.5 Write job applications and résumés:

    a.   Provide clear and purposeful information and address the intended audience appropriately.

    b.   Use varied levels, patterns, and types of language to achieve intended effects and aid comprehension.

    c.   Modify the tone to fit the purpose and audience.

    d.   Follow the conventional style for that type of document (e.g., résumé, memorandum) and use page formats, fonts, and spacing that contribute to the readability and impact of the document.

W 2.6 Deliver multimedia presentations:

    a.   Combine text, images, and sound and draw information from many sources (e.g., television broadcasts, videos, films, newspapers, magazines, CD-ROMs, the Internet, electronic media-generated images).

    b.   Select an appropriate medium for each element of the presentation.

    c.   Use the selected media skillfully, editing appropriately and monitoring for quality.

    d.   Test the audience's response and revise the presentation accordingly.

Written and Oral English Language Conventions

The standards for written and oral English language conventions have been placed between those for writing and for listening and speaking because these conventions are essential to both sets of skills.

LC 1.0 Written and Oral English Language Conventions

Students write and speak with a command of standard English conventions.

LC 1.1 Demonstrate control of grammar, diction, and paragraph and sentence structure and an understanding of English usage.

LC 1.2 Produce legible work that shows accurate spelling and correct punctuation and capitalization.

LC 1.3 Reflect appropriate manuscript requirements in writing.

Listening and Speaking

LS 1.0 Listening and Speaking Strategies

Students formulate adroit judgments about oral communication. They deliver focused and coherent presentations that convey clear and distinct perspectives and demonstrate solid reasoning. They use gestures, tone, and vocabulary tailored to the audience and purpose.

Comprehension

LS 1.1 Recognize strategies used by the media to inform, persuade, entertain, and transmit culture (e.g., advertisements; perpetuation of stereotypes; use of visual representations, special effects, language).

LS 1.2 Analyze the impact of the media on the democratic process (e.g., exerting influence on elections, creating images of leaders, shaping attitudes) at the local, state, and national levels.

LS 1.3 Interpret and evaluate the various ways in which events are presented and information is communicated by visual image makers (e.g., graphic artists, documentary filmmakers, illustrators, news photographers).

Organization and Delivery of Oral Communication
LS 1.4 Use rhetorical questions, parallel structure, concrete images, figurative language, characterization, irony, and dialogue to achieve clarity, force, and aesthetic effect.
LS 1.5 Distinguish between and use various forms of classical and contemporary logical arguments, including:
   a.   Inductive and deductive reasoning.
   b.   Syllogisms and analogies.
LS 1.6 Use logical, ethical, and emotional appeals that enhance a specific tone and purpose.

Analysis and Evaluation of Oral and Media Communications
LS 1.12 Identify logical fallacies used in oral addresses (e.g., attack ad hominem, false causality, red herring, overgeneralization, bandwagon effect).
LS 1.13 Analyze the four basic types of persuasive speech (i.e., propositions of fact, value, problem, or policy) and understand the similarities and differences in their patterns of organization and the use of persuasive language, reasoning, and proof.
LS 1.14 Analyze the techniques used in media messages for a particular audience and evaluate their effectiveness (e.g., Orson Welles' radio broadcast "War of the Worlds").

SA 2.0 Speaking Applications (Genres and Their Characteristics)
Students deliver polished formal and extemporaneous presentations that combine traditional rhetorical strategies of narration, exposition, persuasion, and description. Student speaking demonstrates a command of standard American English and the organizational and delivery strategies outlined in Listening and Speaking Standard 1.0.

Using the speaking strategies of grades eleven and twelve outlined in Listening and Speaking Standard 1.0, students:
SA 2.1 Deliver reflective presentations:
   a.   Explore the significance of personal experiences, events, conditions, or concerns, using appropriate rhetorical strategies (e.g., narration, description, exposition, persuasion).
   b.   Draw comparisons between the specific incident and broader themes that illustrate the speaker's beliefs or generalizations about life.
   c.   Maintain a balance between describing the incident and relating it to more general, abstract ideas.
SA 2.3 Deliver oral responses to literature:
   a.   Demonstrate a comprehensive understanding of the significant ideas of literary works (e.g., make assertions about the text that are reasonable and supportable).
   b.   Analyze the imagery, language, universal themes, and unique aspects of the text through the use of rhetorical strategies (e.g., narration, description, persuasion, exposition, a combination of those strategies).
   c.   Support important ideas and viewpoints through accurate and detailed references to the text or to other works.
   d.   Demonstrate an awareness of the author's use of stylistic devices and an appreciation of the effects created.
   e.   Identify and assess the impact of perceived ambiguities, nuances, and complexities within the text.
SA 2.4 Deliver multimedia presentations:
   a.   Combine text, images, and sound by incorporating information from a wide range of media, including films, newspapers, magazines, CD-ROMs, online information, television, videos, and electronic media-generated images.
   b.   Select an appropriate medium for each element of the presentation.
   c.   Use the selected media skillfully, editing appropriately and monitoring for quality.
   d.   Test the audience's response and revise the presentation accordingly.

SA 2.5 Recite poems, selections from speeches, or dramatic soliloquies with attention to performance details to achieve clarity, force, and aesthetic effect and to demonstrate an understanding of the meaning (e.g., Hamlet's soliloquy "To Be or Not to Be").

Advanced Composition   **B Requirement**
(Semester Course – Grade 12)
Prerequisite: American Literature & Composition/Contemporary Composition

230207   ADV COMP

Course Description

The major purpose of this semester course is to provide advanced and enriched experiences in expository writing characterized by logical and coherent organization, integration of advanced rhetorical strategies, clarity of expression, and suitability of style, usage, and conventions. Student will read within and across expository and informational genres (e.g., essays, biographies, critiques, précis, and news and magazine articles) for literal and implied meaning and to demonstrate through classroom discussion, oral presentation, independent research, written expression, an understanding of the text(s). Advanced Composition extends and enriches the curriculum of Expository Composition by connecting major themes to contemporary issues explored in expository and informational text and through in-depth analyses across multiple texts and genres. Emphasis in this course is on expository reading and writing and the essential skills of revision.

Students are expected to write and revise a minimum of eight academic compositions within the twelfth-grade year, including timed writing pieces and developed compositions. The *California Reading/Language Arts Framework* states that students in the twelfth grade are expected to read two million words annually on their own, including a good representation of classic and contemporary literature, magazines, newspapers, and online articles. Students will apply and refine their command of the writing process, writing conventions, and rhetorical strategies of narration, exposition, persuasion, and description to produce texts of at least 1,500 words each. Advanced Composition fulfills a B requirement of the UC/CSU Subject Area Requirements.

Focus Standards

Reading   **Grade 12**
R 2.3 Verify and clarify facts presented in other types of expository texts by using a variety of consumer, workplace, and public documents.
R 2.4 Make warranted and reasonable assertions about the author's arguments by using elements of the text to defend and clarify interpretations.
R 2.5 Analyze an author's implicit and explicit philosophical assumptions and beliefs about a subject.
R 2.6 Critique the power, validity, and truthfulness of arguments set forth in public documents; their appeal to both friendly and hostile audiences; and the extent to which the arguments anticipate and address reader concerns and counterclaims (e.g., appeal to reason, to authority, to pathos and emotion).
R 3.2 Analyze the way in which the theme or meaning of a selection represents a view or comment on life, using textual evidence to support the claim.
R 3.3 Analyze the ways in which irony, tone, mood, the author's style, and the "sound" of language achieve specific rhetorical or aesthetic purposes or both.
R 3.9 Analyze the philosophical arguments presented in literary works to determine whether the authors' positions have contributed to the quality of each work and the credibility of the characters.

Writing   **Grade 12**
W 1.3 Structure ideas and arguments in a sustained, persuasive, and sophisticated way and support them with precise and relevant examples.
W 1.4 Enhance meaning by employing rhetorical devices, including the extended use of parallelism, repetition, and analogy; the incorporation of visual aids (e.g., graphs, tables, pictures); and the issuance of a call for action.
W 1.9 Revise text to highlight the individual voice, improve sentence variety and style, and enhance subtlety of meaning and tone in ways that are consistent with the

purpose, audience, and genre.

W 2.2 Write responses to (expository text):
a. Demonstrate a comprehensive understanding of the significant ideas in works or passages.
b. Analyze the use of imagery, language, universal themes, and unique aspects of the text.
c. Support important ideas and viewpoints through accurate and detailed references to the text and to other works.
d. Demonstrate an understanding of the author's use of stylistic devices and an appreciation of the effects created.
e. Identify and assess the impact of perceived ambiguities, nuances, and complexities within the text.

W 2.3 Write reflective compositions:
a. Explore the significance of personal experiences, events, conditions, or concerns by using rhetorical strategies (e.g., narration, description, exposition, persuasion).
b. Draw comparisons between specific incidents and broader themes that illustrate the writer's important beliefs or generalizations about life.
c. Maintain a balance in describing individual incidents and relate those incidents to more general and abstract ideas.

W 2.4 Write historical investigation reports:
a. Use exposition, narration, description, argumentation, or some combination of rhetorical strategies to support the main proposition.
b. Analyze several historical records of single event, examining critical relationships between elements of the research topic.
c. Explain the perceived reason or reasons for the similarities and differences in historical records with information derived from primary and secondary sources to support or enhance the presentation.
d. Include information from all relevant perspectives and take into consideration the validity and reliability of sources.
e. Include a formal bibliography.

Listening and Speaking

Grade 12

LS 1.4 Use rhetorical questions, parallel structure, concrete images, figurative language, characterization, irony, and dialogue to achieve clarity, force, and aesthetic effect.

LS 1.5 Distinguish between and use various forms of classical and contemporary logical arguments, including:
a. Inductive and deductive reasoning.
b. Syllogisms and analogies.

LS 1.6 Use logical, ethical, and emotional appeals that enhance a specific tone and purpose.

LS 1.12 Identify logical fallacies used in oral addresses (e.g., attack ad hominem, false causality, red herring, overgeneralization, bandwagon effect).

LS 1.13 Analyze the four basic types of persuasive speech (i.e., propositions of fact, value, problem, or policy) and understand the similarities and differences in their patterns of organization and the use of persuasive language, reasoning, and proof.

SA 2.1 Deliver reflective presentations:
a. Explore the significance of personal experiences, events, conditions, or concerns, using appropriate rhetorical strategies (e.g., narration, description, exposition, persuasion).
b. Draw comparisons between the specific incident and broader themes that illustrate the speaker's beliefs or generalizations about life.
c. Maintain a balance between describing the incident and relating it to more general, abstract ideas.

SA 2.2 Deliver oral reports on historical investigations:
a. Use exposition, narration, description, persuasion, or some combination of

those to support the thesis.

    b. Analyze several historical records of a single event, examining critical relationships between elements of the research topic.

    c. Explain the perceived reason or reasons for the similarities and differences by using information derived from primary and secondary sources to support or enhance the presentation.

    d. Include information on all relevant perspectives and consider the validity and reliability of sources.

SA 2.4 Deliver multimedia presentations:

    a. Combine text, images, and sound by incorporating information from a wide range of media, including films, newspapers, magazines, CD-ROMs, online information, television, videos, and electronic media-generated images.

    b. Select an appropriate medium for each element of the presentation.

    c. Use the selected media skillfully, editing appropriately and monitoring for quality.

    d. Test the audience's response and revise the presentation accordingly.

Representative Performance Outcomes and Skills

In this course, students will know and be able to:

- Engage in discussion to prepare oral and written arguments.
- Read a wide variety of complex informational and expository texts and genres, organized around themes, topics, or issues.
- Demonstrate an advanced understanding of the elements of discourse (e.g., purpose, speaker, audience, form) when completing expository and persuasive writing assignments.
- Analyze an author's implicit and explicit philosophical assumptions and beliefs about a subject.
- Connect ideas and issues in informational and expository texts to universal themes and additional independent research.
- Identify, analyze, discuss, describe, and use appeals to *pathos*, *ethos*, and *logos* and other rhetorical strategies that writers employ to craft an argument.
- Analyze the content, complexity, and structure of the language employed to convey a writer's perspective and the extent to which it reflects the genre.
- Demonstrate advanced control of grammar, diction, and paragraph and sentence structure and an advanced understanding of English usage.
- Examine models of effective expository academic, professional, and business writing and speaking: application essays, introductory and business letters, résumés, and interviews.
- Develop presentations by using clear research questions and creative and critical research strategies (e.g., field studies, oral histories, interviews, experiments, electronic sources).
- Reflect appropriate manuscript requirements in writing.

Assessments

- Teacher-designed quizzes and tests
- Essays and other student written texts
- Oral presentations and discussions

District Approved Texts and Instructional Resources

- LAUSD *English/Language Arts Instructional Guide Essential Tools*, Grades 11-12
- District approved *Expository Reading and Writing Course, Student Texts and Materials*, Semester 1
- District approved *Expository Reading and Writing Course, Teacher Texts and Materials*, Semester 1
- Supplemental District approved standards-based instructional materials and resources (contemporary essays, newspaper and magazine articles, editorials, reports, memos, voting materials and assorted public documents, and other non-fiction texts)

Other Instructional Resources

- *Reading/Language Arts Framework for California Public Schools*

Fast Food: Who's to Blame?

Module 1

Fast Food: Who's to Blame?

Teacher Version

Reading Rhetorically

Prereading 1
   Introducing Key Concepts 1
   Getting Ready to Read 2
   Surveying the Text 2
   Making Predictions and Asking Questions 4
   Introducing Key Vocabulary 5

Reading 9
   First Reading 9
   Rereading the Text 9
   Annotating the Text 10
   Looking Closely at Language 10
   Considering the Structure of the Text 11
   Revisiting Key Vocabulary 12

Postreading 14
   Summarizing and Responding 14
   Thinking Critically 15

Connecting Reading to Writing

Writing to Learn and Using the Words
   of Others 17

Writing Rhetorically

Prewriting 18
   Reading the Assignment 18
   Getting Ready to Write 19
   Formulating a Working Thesis 20

Writing 21
   Composing a Draft 21
   Organizing the Essay 26
   Developing the Content 27

Revising and Editing 27
   Revising the Draft 27
   Editing the Draft 28
   Reflecting on the Writing 29

Evaluating and Responding 30
   Grading Holistically 30
   Responding to Student Writing 30
   Using Portfolios 31

Rubric 32

Reading Selections

"It's Portion Distortion That Makes America Fat" 33
"If You Pitch It, They Will Eat" 37
"The Battle Against Fast Food Begins in the Home" 42
"Don't Blame the Eater" 44
Letters to the editor in response to "Don't Blame
   the Eater" 46

Student Version

Activity 1: Getting Ready to Read 49
Activity 2: Surveying the Text 49
Activity 3: Making Predictions and Asking Questions 50
Activity 4: Introducing Key Vocabulary 51
Activity 5: Assessing Key Vocabulary 51
Activity 6: First Reading 53
Activity 7: Rereading the Text 53
Activity 8: Annotating the Text 53
Activity 9: Looking Closely at Language 54
Activity 10. Considering the Structure of the Text 54
Activity 11: Revisiting Key Vocabulary 55
Activity 12: Refining Key Vocabulary 56
Activity 13: Summarizing and Responding 56
Activity 14: Thinking Critically 58
Activity 15: Reading the Assignment 58
Activity 16: Getting Ready to Write 59
Activity 17: Formulating a Working Thesis 59
Activity 18: Composing a Draft 60
Activity 19: Organizing the Essay 64
Activity 20: Developing the Content 65
Activity 21: Revising the Draft 66
Activity 22: Editing the Draft 66
Activity 23: Reflecting on the Writing 67

Sample Student Essays

On-Demand Writing Assignment and Scored
   Student Essays 69

It's Portion Distortion That Makes America Fat

The Sacramento Bee, January 5, 2003
by Shannon Brownlee

1   It was probably inevitable that one day people would start suing McDonald's for making them fat. That day came last summer, when New York lawyer Samuel Hirsch filed several lawsuits against McDonald's, as well as four other fast-food companies, on the grounds that they had failed to adequately disclose the bad health effects of their menus.

2   One of the suits involves a Bronx teenager who tips the scale at 400 pounds and whose mother, in papers filed in U.S. District Court in Manhattan, said, "I always believed McDonald's food was healthy for my son."

3   Uh-huh. And the tooth fairy really put that dollar under his pillow. But once you've stopped sniggering at our litigious society, remember that it once seemed equally ludicrous that smokers could successfully sue tobacco companies for their addiction to cigarettes.

4   And while nobody is claiming that Big Macs are addictive—at least not yet—the restaurant industry and food packagers have clearly helped give many Americans the roly-poly shape they have today. This is not to say that the folks in the food industry want us to be fat. But make no mistake: When they do well economically, we gain weight.

5   It wasn't always thus. Readers of a certain age can remember a time when a trip to McDonald's seemed like a treat and when a small bag of french fries, a plain burger and a 12-ounce Coke seemed like a full meal. Fast food wasn't any healthier back then; we simply ate a lot less of it.

6   How did today's oversized appetites become the norm? It didn't happen by accident or some inevitable evolutionary process. It was to a large degree the result of consumer manipulation. Fast food's marketing strategies, which make perfect sense from a business perspective, succeed only when they induce a substantial number of us to overeat. To see how this all came about, let's go back to 1983, when John Martin became CEO of the ailing Taco Bell franchise and met a young marketing whiz named Elliott Bloom.

7   Using so-called "smart research," a then-new kind of in-depth consumer survey, Bloom had figured out that fast-food franchises were sustained largely by a core group of "heavy users," mostly young, single males, who ate at such restaurants as often as 20 times a month. In fact, 30 percent of Taco Bell's customers accounted for 70 percent of its sales.

8   Through his surveys, Bloom learned what might seem obvious now but wasn't at all clear 20 years ago—these guys ate at fast-food joints because they had absolutely no interest in cooking for themselves and didn't give a rip about the nutritional quality of the food. They didn't even care much

about the taste. All that mattered was that it was fast and cheap. Martin figured Taco Bell could capture a bigger share of these hard-core customers by streamlining the food production and pricing main menu items at 49, 59 and 69 cents—well below its competitors.

9   It worked. Taco Bell saw a dramatic increase in patrons, with no drop in revenue per customer. As Martin told Greg Critser, author of *Fat Land: How Americans Became the Fattest People in the World,* when Taco Bell ran a test of its new pricing in Texas, "within seven days of initiating the test, the average check was right back to where it was before—it was just four instead of three items."

10   In other words, cheap food induced people to eat more. Taco Bell's rising sales figures—up 14 percent by 1989 and 12 percent more the next year—forced other fast-food franchises to wake up and smell the burritos. By the late '80s, everybody from Burger King to Wendy's was cutting prices and seeing an increase in customers—including bargain-seeking Americans who weren't part of that original hard-core group.

11   If marketing strategy had stopped there, we might not be the nation of fatties that we are today. But the imperatives of the market place are growth and rising profits, and once everybody had slashed prices to the bone, the franchises had to look for a new way to satisfy investors.

12   And what they found was . . . super-sizing.

13   Portion sizes had already been creeping upward. As early as 1972, for example, McDonald's introduced its large-size fries (large being a relative term, since at 3.5 ounces the '72 "large" was smaller than a medium serving today). But McDonald's increased portions only reluctantly, because the company's founder, Ray Kroc, didn't like the image of lowbrow, cheap food. If people wanted more french fries, he would say, "They can buy two bags." But price competition had grown so fierce that the only way to keep profits up was to offer bigger and bigger portions. By 1988, McDonald's had introduced a 32-ounce "super size" soda and "super size" fries.

14   The deal with all these enhanced portions is that the customer gets a lot more food for a relatively small increase in price. So just how does that translate into bigger profits? Because the actual food in a fast-food meal is incredibly cheap. For every dollar a quick-service franchiser spends to produce a food item, only 20 cents, on average, goes toward food. The rest is eaten up by expenses such as salaries, packaging, electric bills, insurance, and of course, the ubiquitous advertising that got you in the door or to the drive-through lane in the first place.

15   Here's how it works. Let's say a $1.25 bag of french fries costs $1 to produce. The potatoes, oil, and salt account for only 20 cents of the cost. The other 80 cents goes toward all the other expenses. If you add half again as many french fries to the bag and sell it for $1.50, the non-food expenses stay pretty much constant, while the extra food costs the franchise only 10 more pennies. The fast-food joint makes an extra 15 cents pure profit, and

the customer thinks he's getting a good deal. And he would be, if he actually needed the extra food, which he doesn't because the nation is awash in excess calories.

16   That 20 percent rule, by the way, applies to all food products, whether it's a bag of potato chips, the 2,178-calorie mountain of fried seafood at Red Lobster or the 710-calorie slab of dessert at the Cheesecake Factory. Some foods are even less expensive to make. The flakes of your kid's breakfast cereal, for example, account for only 5 percent of the total amount Nabisco or General Mills spent to make and sell them.

17   Soda costs less to produce than any drink except tap water (which nobody seems to drink anymore), thanks to a 1970s invention that cut the expense of making high-fructose corn syrup. There used to be real sugar in Coke; when Coca-Cola and other bottlers switched to high-fructose corn syrup in 1984, they slashed sweetener costs by 20 percent. That's why 7-Eleven can sell the 64-ounce Double Gulp—half a gallon of soda and nearly 600 calories—for only 37 cents more than the 16-ounce, 89-cent regular Gulp. You'd feel ripped off if you bought the smaller size. Who wouldn't?

18   The final step in the fattening of America was the "up sell," a stroke of genius whose origins are buried somewhere in the annals of marketing. You're already at the counter, you've ordered a cheeseburger value meal for $3.74, and your server says, "Would you like to super-size that for only $4.47?" Such a deal. The chain extracts an extra 73 cents from the customer, and the customer gets an extra 400 calories—bringing the total calorie count to 1,550, more than half the recommended intake for an adult man for an entire day.

19   When confronted with their contribution to America's expanding waistline, restaurateurs and food packagers reply that eating less is a matter of individual responsibility. But that's not how the human stomach works. If you put more food in front of people, they eat more, as studies have consistently shown over the last decade.

20   My personal favorite: The researcher gave moviegoers either a half-gallon or a gallon bucket of popcorn before the show (it was *Payback,* with Mel Gibson) and then measured how much they ate when they returned what was left in the containers afterward. Nobody could polish off the entire thing, but subjects ate 44 percent more when given the bigger bucket.

21   The downside, of course, is that 20 years of Big Food has trained us to think that oceanic drinks and gargantuan portions are normal. Indeed, once fast food discovered that big meals meant big profits, everybody from Heineken to Olive Garden to Frito Lay followed suit. Today, says Lisa Young, a nutritionist at New York University, super-sizing has pervaded every segment of the food industry. For her Ph.D., Young documented the changes in portion sizes for dozens of foods over the past several decades.

22   M&M/Mars, for example, has increased the size of candy bars such as Milky Way and Snickers four times since 1970, Starbucks introduced the

20-ounce "venti" size in 1999 and discontinued its "short" eight-ounce cup. When 22-ounce Heinekens were introduced, Young reported, the company sold 24 million of them the first year, and attributed the sales to the "big-bottle gimmick."

23   Even Lean Cuisine and Weight Watchers now advertise "Hearty Portions" of their diet meals. Everything from plates and muffin tins to restaurant chairs and the cut of our Levi's has expanded to match our growing appetites, and the wonder of it all is not that 60 percent of Americans are overweight or obese, but rather that 40 percent of us are not.

24   Where does it end? Marketers and restauranteurs may scoff at lawsuits like the ones brought this summer against fast food companies, and they have a point: Adults are ultimately responsible for what they put in their own mouths.

25   But maybe there's hope for us yet, because it looks as if fast-food companies' "Omnipresence"—the McDonald's strategy of beating out competitors by opening new stores, sometimes as many as 1,000 a year—"has proved costly and self-cannibalizing," says author Critser. With 13,000 McDonald's units alone, most of America is so saturated with fast food there's practically no place left to put a drive-through lane. Now, fast-food companies are killing each other in a new price war they can't possibly sustain, and McDonald's just suffered its first quarterly loss since the company went public 47 years ago.

26   The obvious direction to go is down, toward what nutritional policymakers are calling "smart-sizing." Or at least it should be obvious, if food purveyors cared as much about helping Americans slim down as they would have us believe. Instead of urging Americans to "Get Active, Stay Active"—Pepsi-Cola's new criticism-deflecting slogan—how about bringing back the 6.5 ounce sodas of the '40s and '50s? Or, imagine, as Critser does, the day when McDonald's advertises Le Petit Mac, made with high-grade beef, a delicious whole-grain bun and hawked by, say, Serena Williams.

27   One way or another, as Americans wake up to the fact that obesity is killing nearly as many citizens as cigarettes are, jumbo burgers and super-size fries will seem like less of a bargain.

If You Pitch It, They Will Eat

The New York Times, **August 3, 2003**
by David Barboza

1 The McDonald's Corporation wants to be everywhere that children are.

2 So besides operating 13,602 restaurants in the United States, it has plastered its golden arches on Barbie dolls, video games, book jackets, and even theme parks.

3 McDonald's calls this promotion and brand extension. But, a growing number of nutritionists call it a blitzkrieg that perverts children's eating habits and sets them on a path to obesity.

4 Marketing fast food, snacks, and beverages to children is at least as old as Ronald McDonald himself. What's new, critics say, is the scope and intensity of the assault. Big food makers like McDonald's and Kraft Foods Inc. are finding every imaginable way to put their names in front of children. And they're spending more than ever – $15 billion last year, compared with $12.5 billion in 1998, according to research conducted at Texas A&M University in College Station.

5 "What really changed over the last decade is the proliferation of electronic media," says Susan Linn, a psychologist who studies children's marketing at Harvard's Judge Baker Children's Center. "It used to just be Saturday-morning television. Now it's Nickelodeon, movies, video games, the Internet, and even marketing in schools."

6 Product tie-ins are everywhere. There are SpongeBob SquarePants Popsicles, Oreo Cookie preschool counting books, and Keebler's Scooby Doo Cookies. There is even a Play-Doh Lunchables play set.

7 While the companies view these as harmless promotional pitches, lawyers are threatening a wave of obesity-related class-action lawsuits. Legislators are pressing to lock food companies out of school cafeterias. And some of the fiercest critics are calling for an outright ban on all food advertising aimed at children.

8 "The problem of obesity is so staggering, so out of control, that we have to do something," says Walter Willett, a professor of nutrition at the Harvard School of Public Health. "The vast majority of what they sell is junk," Mr. Willett says of the big food makers. "How often do you see fruits and vegetables marketed?"

9 The increase in food marketing to children has closely tacked their increase in weight. Since 1980, the number of obese children has more than doubled to 16 percent, according to the federal Centers for Disease Control and Prevention (CDC).

10 School districts in New York and Los Angeles have responded by banning the sale of sugary beverages and snacks in school vending machines.

11   Most big food companies, despite some promises to offer healthier foods and in some cases to limit marketing in schools, deny that they are to blame for the epidemic of excess weight. They insist that sedentary behavior, a lack of exercise, and poor supervision and eating habits are responsible.

12   Food companies say their commercials don't encourage overeating, that the foods they advertise are meant to be "part of a balanced diet," and that some foods are meant to be only occasional treats.

13   "We talk about offering carrot sticks," says Karlin Linhardt, the director of youth marketing at McDonald's. "And we have parents come in and say, 'We offer them carrot sticks at home. When we come to McDonald's we want a treat, french fries.'"

14   Why would companies take aim at children so energetically? Because they, increasingly, are where the money is.

15   "It's the largest market there is," says James McNeal, a professor of marketing at Texas A&M and an authority on marketing to children. "Kids four to twelve spend on their own wants and needs about $30 billion a year. But their influence on what their parents spend is $600 billion. That's blue sky."

16   In toy stores, children can become accustomed to food brands early by buying a Hostess bake set, Barbie's Pizza Hut play set, or Fisher-Price's Oreo Matchin' Middles game. And, for budding math whizzes, there is a series of books from Hershey's Kisses on addition, subtraction, and fractions.

17   Schools are also a major marketing site. With many school districts facing budget shortfalls, a quick solution has come from offering more profitable fast food from outlets like McDonald's, KFC, and Pizza Hut.

18   Some schools have contracts to sell fast food; others have special days allotted for fast food. The Skinner Montessori school in Vancouver, Wash., for instance, has "McDonald's Wednesdays" and "KFC Fridays."

19   There are McDonald's McTeacher's Nights in Jefferson City, Mo., and Pizza Hut Days in Garden City, Kan.

20   "It's awesome. They love it," Tracy Johnson, director of nutrition for the 7,500-student school district in Garden City, Kan., says of the Pizza Hut food. "We also serve vegetables. We try to make it into a healthy meal."

21   According to a survey by the CDC, about 20 percent of the nation's schools now offer brand-name fast food.

22   Vending machines now dominate school corridors. Coca-Cola and Pepsi-Cola have "pouring rights" contracts in hundreds of schools nationwide.

23   Lawyers and consumer advocates have harshly criticized educators for "commercializing the schools" and sending poor dietary messages to children.

24   "It seems very clear it's a breach of duty," says John Banzhaf, a professor of law at George Washington University in Washington and one of the lawyers pressing for class-action lawsuits against big food companies. "Schools get paid a kickback for every sugary soft drink or burger sold."

25   Some food companies heatedly defend their promotions and their products. "I think our communication with children is appropriate; we're not shoving it down their throat," says Ken Barun, director of healthy lifestyles at McDonald's, adding, "To make a general statement that McDonald's food is unhealthy is wrong."

26   Industry officials concur. "These foods and beverages are safe, and consumers—in some cases parents—have to be the one to make the decisions about how much should be eaten," says Gene Grabowski, a spokesman for the Grocery Manufacturers of America, which represents the nation's biggest food companies. "The industry is trying very hard to be responsible in the way it markets these foods."

27   Still, legislators and school districts are rethinking school marketing. There are more than 30 bills before state legislatures around the country proposing to ban certain snacks and beverages from school vending machines, according to the Commercialism in Education Research Unit at Arizona State University in Tempe.

28   Television, of course, remains the most powerful medium for selling to children. These days there is no shortage of advertising opportunities with the emergence of the Walt Disney Company's Disney Channel; Nickelodeon, which is owned by Viacom; and the Cartoon Network, a unit of AOL Time Warner's Turner Broadcasting.

29   Marketers know that children love animals and cartoon characters, and industry observers say they have used that knowledge not just to create new shows but to produce a new generation of animated pitchmen.

30   Some critics say children often can't differentiate the programs from the commercials and that food companies and producers of children's shows have helped blur the line by creating characters that leap back and forth, from pitchman to program character.

31   SpongeBob SquarePants has his own show. But he also sells Kraft Macaroni & Cheese, Popsicles, Kleenex, DVDs, skateboards, fruit snacks, and dozens of other products.

32   In fact, a series of big marketing alliances has bound food companies and television show producers like never before. Disney, for instance, has teamed up with McDonald's on movies and product tie-ins. Disney and Kellogg collaborate on a line of cereals that includes Disney Chocolate Mud & Bugs. And Nickelodeon has struck marketing deals with the Quaker Oats Company and General Mills Inc.

33   "The programs have become advertising for the food, and the food has become advertising for the programs," says Professor Linn of Harvard.

34   During Nickelodeon's "SpongeBob SquarePants" 30-minute cartoon last week, more than half the commercials were about food. The spots showed that children who consume "Go-gurt," the new yogurt-on-the-go, loved skateboards and danced on the walls.

35   A child who poured milk on his Post Honeycomb cereal was transformed into the raffish Honeycomb monster named the Craver. Children walked into walls after seeing other youngsters' tongues tattooed with Betty Crocker's Fruit Roll-Ups. And two others reveled in having so much sugar on their Kellogg's Cinnamon Krunchers cereal that even the tidal wave of milk that washed over their treehouse couldn't wipe off the sugary flavor.

36   But do these commercials really resonate with children? Marketing experts say yes; the children do, too. Nicky Greenberg, who is six and lives with her parents in Lower Manhattan, often spends her afternoons watching Nickelodeon. She can sing the theme song from "SpongeBob SquarePants," and she says her parents buy her Kellogg's Cinnamon Toast Crunch because she loves the commercials.

37   "On the commercial," she says, "There's a captain that goes on the submarine, and there's an octopus, and three kids. And then the girl says, 'Just taste this, pirate.' And the pirate says, 'Ayyy, yummy!'"

38   The reaction was no different last week at a supermarket on the South Side of Chicago.

39   Tatanisha Roberson, who is eight, was riding on the front of a shopping cart pushed by her mother, Erica, twenty-four, heading toward the cereal aisle.

40   The question was posed: What kind of food is Tatanisha interested in? "Anything that comes on the TV, she'll get," her mother said, rolling her eyes. "Rugrats Fruit Snacks; Scooby Doo Fruit Snacks; Flintstones' Jell-O."

41   In private, some company executives complain that when parents go to the grocery store they don't buy healthy products that are offered. Professor McNeal at Texas A&M says the companies are a scapegoat.

42   "I don't think they should be singled out," he says. "Mom blames everyone but herself. There's an abdication of the parents' role. You've got 70 percent of moms who are working, so when they're home they try to please their kids."

43   The big food companies say they follow a set of guidelines for television advertising enforced by the Children's Advertising Review Unit, which was set up and financed by advertisers to regulate themselves.

44   The companies say their ads don't show overeating or make false health claims.

45   Officials at the Children's Advertising Review Unit acknowledge that they don't look at the collective message food companies send to children. "We're not nutritionists," says Elizabeth Lascoutx, a spokeswoman for the unit. "We're not in the position to say this food item cannot be part of a healthy diet."

46   Sensing a backlash to advertising and promotion, especially in schools, Kraft said last month that it would end all in-school marketing efforts. And General Mills, the maker of Cheerios, says that in-school marketing is wrong.

47   "We just view it as inappropriate," says Tom Forsythe. "There's no gatekeeper; they're a captive audience."

48   Some marketing deals have come under pressure. For example, last week, the British Broadcasting Corporation said it would no longer allow its children's television characters to be used in fast-food sponsorships with companies like McDonald's after consumer groups criticized the public broadcaster for helping promote junk food.

49   Some companies deny that they even market to children. Both Coke and Pepsi insist that they direct their products only to teenagers and adults. And Yum Brands, which operates KFC, Pizza Hut, and Taco Bell, says it does not market to children or have operations in schools.

50   But sometimes the evidence would seem to contradict those statements. Coke signed a multimillion-dollar global marketing deal tied to the Harry Potter character in 2001, and many schools, like the one in Garden City, Kan., have contracts to serve food from Pizza Hut.

51   Amy Sherwood, a spokeswoman for Yum Brands, says, "That must be a local deal with the franchisees and those schools because we don't do that on a national level."

52   Kari Bjorhus, a spokeswoman at Coke, said, "We absolutely don't market to children. Our feeling with Harry Potter is it really appeals to the whole family."

53   Yet with regulators, lawmakers, and others mounting campaigns that seek to make big food companies look like big tobacco companies, which have been sued over marketing campaigns geared toward youths, something is bound to change, industry experts say. The World Health Organization and even Wall Street analysts are calling on big food companies to rein in their marketing campaigns and change the way they do business.

54   "The food industry will have to review its marketing practices and transform itself, in our view, regardless of potential regulation or litigation," Arnaud Langlois, an analyst at J.P. Morgan, wrote in a report last April.

55   There is a need to set specific standards on what is marketed to children, according to Professor Willett at Harvard. "We don't sell children guns, alcohol, or drugs, but we do allow them to be exploited by food companies."

56   Even some influential marketing experts are beginning to think their clients might come around.

57   Dan Acuff, a leading children's marketing consultant, says that when profits are at stake, companies listen.

58   "If it's going to hit the bottom line, they'll listen," he says. "You'd like them to have a conscience, but conscience and bottom line are not in the same paradigm in the corporate world."

The Battle Against Fast Food Begins in the Home

The Sacramento Bee, December 17, 2002
by Daniel Weintraub

1   A public health group called last week for Governor Gray Davis to declare childhood obesity a state emergency and take immediate steps to reduce it. But while the California Center for Public Health Advocacy proposes some worthy ideas, the foundation might be aiming at the wrong target.

2   Parents, not state government, are in the best position to fight the epidemic of overweight children in our schools.

3   It is parents—not the government, not the fast-food companies, not the video-game manufacturers—who are responsible for teaching kids healthy eating and exercise habits. Can they use some help? Sure. But they are the ones who need to step up to the plate, so to speak.

4   Child fitness is getting more and more attention these days, and rightly so. But the danger in well-meaning studies and, even more, in lawsuits against the fast-food industry, is that they send a message to parents and kids alike that obesity is somebody else's fault.

5   It's not. It's the fault of parents who let their kids eat unhealthy foods and sit in front of the television or computer for hours at a time. The sooner we face up to the fact as a society, the sooner we are going to be able to do something about it.

6   Last week's report from the Center for Public Health Advocacy took data already published by the state Department of Education and crunched it to make it more relevant to politicians. The center presented the data by state Assembly district, so that members of the Legislature could see where their communities ranked on the fat index.

7   Statewide, the center said, 26 percent of schoolchildren are overweight. The numbers ranged from a low of 17 percent in wealthy Orange County Assembly district to a high of 36.8 percent in an inner-city Los Angeles district. More boys (32 percent) than girls (21 percent) were overweight. And more minorities than white children were overweight, though the study's authors said the data didn't allow them to draw any conclusions as to why that was so.

8   The center blamed the problem on the increasing consumption of fast food and soft drinks, larger portion sizes in restaurants, the availability of junk food on campus, advertising of junk food to children and their families, and the lack of consistent physical education programs in the schools.

9   The authors recommended that the state enforce an existing law requiring an average of at least 20 minutes per day of physical education,

implement a state law outlining nutritional standards for elementary schools, and ensure that water fountains are present and working on every campus.

10   Many of the report's long-term recommendations focused on the fast-food industry: hearings to examine the impact of advertising on kids; a study to examine the prevalence of fast-food restaurants and convenience stores near schools; and incentives for communities that ban fast-food outlets near schools or that ban advertising for junk food on campus.

11   Of the 20 recommendations put forward by the center, only one focused on parents. The authors suggest that schools be required to provide parents with fitness test results on their children and information about the importance of daily physical activity for learning and lifelong good health.

12   But none of the center's other ideas are likely to do much good until parents understand and accept their role in fighting the problem. We have laws against parents leaving a loaded weapon where their children can find it and use it to hurt themselves or others. But no one seems to want to tell parents that they need to protect their children from unhealthy foods and from sloth.

13   It's not easy, especially when both parents are working or there is only one parent in the home. Fast food is fast. It can also seem cheap, at least before you start adding the fries and sodas and desserts. And a television or video game can be like an opiate that quiets a restless child so a weary parent can get some rest of his own.

14   My own home is by no means a fast-food-free zone or a shrine to physical fitness. But we've tried to take a few modest steps to give our kids a fighting chance. We don't stock soda in the kitchen or serve it regularly at home; it's a treat saved for special occasions.

15   We try to cook as many meals at home as possible on the theory that even the least-healthy home-cooked meal is probably better for our children than the healthiest fast-food serving. We limit television time and encourage our boys to get out of the house, either to participate in organized sports or to ride their bikes, skateboards, or roller blades.

16   If the health-care foundations did more to encourage these kinds of simple policies in the home, they might make some progress against the purveyors of fat and cholesterol, whether they are pushing their wares on the street a block from the school, in the cafeteria, or even in the classroom. Before we start talking about banning fast food, let's do more to encourage personal responsibility.

Don't Blame the Eater

The New York Times, **November 23, 2002**
by David Zinczenko

1   If ever there were a newspaper headline custom-made for Jay Leno's monologue, this was it. Kids taking on McDonald's this week, suing the company for making them fat. Isn't that like middle-aged men suing Porsche for making them get speeding tickets? Whatever happened to personal responsibility?

2   I tend to sympathize with these portly fast-food patrons, though. Maybe that's because I used to be one of them.

3   I grew up as a typical mid-1980s latchkey kid. My parents were split up, my dad off trying to rebuild his life, my mom working long hours to make the monthly bills. Lunch and dinner, for me, was a daily choice between McDonald's, Taco Bell, Kentucky Fried Chicken, or Pizza Hut. Then, as now, these were the only available options for an American kid to get an affordable meal. By age 15, I had packed 212 pounds of torpid teenage tallow on my once-lanky 5-foot-10 frame.

4   Then I got lucky. I went to college, joined the Navy Reserves, and got involved with a health magazine. I learned how to manage my diet. But most of the teenagers who live, as I once did, on a fast-food diet won't turn their lives around: They've crossed under the golden arches to a likely fate of lifetime obesity. And the problem isn't just theirs—it's all of ours. Before 1994, diabetes in children was generally caused by a genetic disorder—only about 5 percent of childhood cases were obesity-related, or Type 2, diabetes. Today, according to the National Institutes of Health, Type 2 diabetes accounts for at least 30 percent of all new childhood cases of diabetes in this country.

5   Not surprisingly, money spent to treat diabetes has skyrocketed, too. The Centers for Disease Control and Prevention estimate that diabetes accounted for $2.6 billion in health care costs in 1969. Today's number is an unbelievable $100 billion a year.

6   Shouldn't we know better than to eat two meals a day in fast-food restaurants? That's one argument. But where, exactly, are consumers—particularly teenagers—supposed to find alternatives? Drive down any thoroughfare in America, and I guarantee you'll see one of our country's more than 13,000 McDonald's restaurants. Now, drive back up the block and try to find someplace to buy a grapefruit.

7   Complicating the lack of alternatives is the lack of information about what, exactly, we're consuming. There are no calorie information charts on fast-food packaging the way there are on grocery items. Advertisements don't carry warning labels the way tobacco ads do. Prepared foods aren't covered under Food and Drug Administration labeling laws. Some fast-food

purveyors will provide calorie information on request, but even that can be hard to understand.

8   For example, one company's Web site lists its chicken salad as containing 150 calories; the almonds and noodles that come with it (an additional 190 calories) are listed separately. Add a serving of the 280-calorie dressing, and you've got a healthy lunch alternative that comes in at 620 calories. But that's not all. Read the small print on the back of the dressing packet and you'll realize it actually contains 2.5 servings. If you pour what you've been served, you're suddenly up around 1,040 calories, which is half of the government's recommended daily calorie intake. And that doesn't take into account that 450-calorie super-size Coke.

9   Make fun if you will of these kids launching lawsuits against the fast-food industry, but don't be surprised if you're the next plaintiff. As with the tobacco industry, it may be only a matter of time before state governments begin to see a direct line between the $1 billion that McDonald's and Burger King spend each year on advertising and their own swelling health-care costs.

10   And I'd say the industry is vulnerable. Fast-food companies are marketing to children a product with proven health hazards and no warning labels. They would do well to protect themselves, and their customers, by providing the nutritional information people need to make informed choices about their products. Without such warnings, we'll see more sick, obese children and more angry, litigious parents. I say, let the deep-fried chips fall where they may.

Letters to the editor in response to "Don't Blame the Eater"

Fast Food Responsibility

David Zinczenko hits the nail on the head when he asks the rhetorical question, "Whatever happened to personal responsibility?" But then he misses his own point when he goes on to say that McDonald's and the other fast-food chains deserve to be sued because obese children don't have access to healthy alternatives and don't have calorie charts and warning labels to let them know how bad fast food is for them. Even children should understand what it means when they step on the scale and they, like Zinczenko, weigh 200 pounds at age 15.

Fast food is just like other hazards in life such as alcohol and cars. It's OK in moderation and it's dangerous when taken to extremes. And everybody, including kids, knows this even without a warning label to tell them, so let's put the responsibility back on the consumer and save the fast-food industry from frivolous lawsuits.

Pamela LaVerne
Elk Grove, California

It doesn't take a rocket scientist to understand the relationship between eating and activity. Eat a lot, do nothing, and get fat. Eat a lot, exercise a lot, and stay healthy. You don't need a warning label to tell you.

The lawsuits against McDonald's on behalf of two obese girls are just as ludicrous as the lawsuits against the tobacco industry. When people make bad choices, whether it's smoking two packs a day or eating a Whopper and fries, they should face their own consequences. Next thing you know, people will be suing GM because the car made them drive too fast and get into an accident or Caltrans because the highway let them go over the speed limit. They have no one to blame but themselves.

Americans have developed a victim mentality. They want to find someone to blame for everything that happens to them, and all the better if that someone has deep pockets. It's time they grow up and realize that they need to change their bad habits and take charge of their lives.

Mitch Jordan
Sacramento, California

I'd like to congratulate the two girls who are suing McDonald's. It's time the fast-food industry is called to answer for the deceptions that they have put over on our nation's kids. If you go into your local fast-food outlet, you'll see signs proclaiming super-size burgers and fries that cost only a little more than smaller sizes. You'll see kids' meals with toys designed to target children who are too little to understand nutritious eating. What you won't see is any nutrition information that's aimed at children. When did Ronald McDonald ever promote healthy eating?

Certainly, adults are responsible for making healthy choices, but children often have no choices. As Zinczenko says, latchkey kids often have to fend for themselves. At the same time they are easy targets for unscrupulous advertisers. So kudos to the kids' filing the lawsuits, and let's hope that McDonald's will see the error of its ways.

Carlyle Wong
Granite Bay, California

It's absolutely absurd that two young women can sue McDonald's for making them fat. And I even agree with Zinczenko that children may not be responsible for their own obesity when they eat too much junk food. But what Zinczenko is ignoring is parental responsibility. Where were the parents when their kids were eating all those burgers? How come parents these days aren't steering their kids to healthy food? Why aren't they teaching them that a steady diet of fat and sugar will make them fat and possibly diabetic? Why aren't they home-cooking them healthy food? Why aren't they sending them to school with fruit and vegetables in their lunch bags? Even parents who have to work can see to it that there's healthy food in the refrigerator for kids after school.

The real problem is not that McDonald's sells fattening food. The real problem is that parents don't want to take responsibility for their children. They sit them in front of the TV. They let them run wild on the streets. And they turn over the job of feeding them to a corporation that only cares about its profits. It's time that parents got back to their foremost duty, which is to give their children the time and care that they deserve.

Patricia Gonzalez
Davis, California

Page 48 is blank.

Fast Food: Who's to Blame?

Reading selections for this module:

Brownlee, Shannon. "It's Portion Distortion That Makes America Fat." *Sacramento Bee.* 5 Jan. 2003.

Barboza, David. "If You Pitch It, They Will Eat." *New York Times.* 3 Aug. 2003.

Weintraub, Daniel. "The Battle Against Fast Food Begins in the Home." *Sacramento Bee.* 17 Dec. 2002.

Zinczenko, David. "Don't Blame the Eater." *New York Times.* 23 Nov. 2002.

Ching, Roberta. Letters to the editor in response to "Don't Blame the Eater." 2003.

Reading Rhetorically

Prereading

Activity 1

Getting Ready to Read

Now that you have brainstormed words that you associate with french fries from a fast-food restaurant, write for 10 minutes on this topic:

Who's at fault for America's growing weight problem?

Activity 2

Surveying the Text

Before you read Brownlee's "Portion Distortion" and Barboza's "If You Pitch It," discuss the following questions.

1. What do the titles, "It's Portion Distortion That Makes America Fat" and "If You Pitch It, They Will Eat," tell you about the authors' positions on who is responsible for America's growing weight problem?

2. What do you think is the purpose of these articles?

3. "Portion Distortion" was published in *The Sacramento Bee,* and "If You Pitch It" was published in *The New York Times.* What similarities do you think the articles might have? What differences? Do you think they will be equally reliable?

4. What else can you tell about the articles just by looking at them?

When you read Weintraub, Zinczenko, and the letters to the editor, discuss the following questions.

**Activity 2
(Continued)**

1. On the basis of the title of his article, what do you think Weintraub's position will be? In what ways do you think his article will be like those of Brownlee and Barboza? In what ways do you think it will be different? What do you think his purpose is?

2. On the basis of the title of his article, what do you think Zinczenko's position will be? Which of the other authors do you think he might agree with?

3. What do you expect is the purpose of the letters to the editor written in response to Zinczenko? How will they be different from Zinczenko's article?

4. What else can you tell about the letters just by looking at them?

Activity 3

Making Predictions and Asking Questions

Discuss the following items about Brownlee's article, "Portion Distortion," and Barboza's article, "If You Pitch It."

1. Read the first three and the last paragraphs of Brownlee's article. What is the point of comparing burgers, fries, and cigarettes? What arguments do you think she will make?

2. Read the first three and the last paragraph of Barboza's article. According to Barboza, who is responsible for America's weight problem? What arguments do you think he is going to make?

3. Who is the intended audience for these articles? How do you know?

4. What information and ideas are the authors likely to draw on to convince you of their positions?

5. Reword the titles and subtitles and turn them into questions for you to answer after you have read the full articles.

Now discuss the following items about Weintraub's "The Battle Against Fast Food," Zinczenko's "Don't Blame the Eater," and the letters to the editor.

1. Read the first two and the last paragraphs of Weintraub's article. According to Weintraub, who is responsible for America's obesity problem? What arguments do you think he will make?

2. How do you think he will respond to the arguments raised by Brownlee and Barboza?

3. Read the first two and the last paragraphs of Zinczenko's article. Why does he bring up Jay Leno's monologue? According to Zinczenko, who is responsible for America's obesity problem? What arguments do you think he will make?

4. Zinczenko and Weintraub both argue in part from personal experience. How do their viewpoints differ?

5. Read the last paragraph of each of the letters to the editor. In each case, identify who the writer thinks is to blame. How do you know?

Activity 4

Introducing Key Vocabulary

Semantic Map

Your teacher will divide you into groups and assign a word to your group. Your teacher will give categories that relate to the word or ask you to create the categories. You will list specific examples for each category as a group.

Activity 5

Assessing Key Vocabulary

Vocabulary Self-Assessment Chart

Word	Definition	Know It Well	Have Heard of It	Don't Know It
Vocabulary from Brownlee's "Portion Distortion" and Barboza's "If You Pitch It"				
portion	*a serving of food*			
distortion				
manipulation				
revenue				
induce				
promotional				
marketing				
class-action				
proliferation				
Vocabulary from Weintraub's "The Battle Against Fast Food"				
epidemic				
step up to the plate				
face up to the fact				

Word	Definition	Know It Well	Have Heard of It	Don't Know It
Vocabulary from Weintraub's "The Battle Against Fast Food"				
crunched data				
implement				
prevalence				
incentives				
sloth				
opiate				
purveyors				
Vocabulary from Zinczenko's "Don't Blame the Eater" and the letters to the editor				
latchkey kid				
prepared food				
alternatives				
launching				
vulnerable				
litigious				
liability				
entitled				
defendant				
plaintiff				
clogging				
credibility				

Reading

<table>
<tr><td>Activity 6</td><td>

First Reading

Read each article as your teacher assigns it. As you read, think about the predictions you made. You may notice words you worked with in the previous activities. As you look at the words, think about personal connections you can make with them and with the other words. Group them together if they relate.

</td></tr>
<tr><td>Activity 7</td><td>

Rereading the Text

Your teacher will divide the class into two groups. If you are in Group A, you are assigned Brownlee's "Portion Distortion." If you are in Group B, you are assigned Barboza's "If You Pitch It."

Group A

Now that you know what "Portion Distortion" is about, answer the following questions:

1. Think back to your original predictions. Which were right? Which did you have to modify as you read "Portion Distortion"?

2. What is the main idea of "Portion Distortion"? According to Brownlee, who is to blame for America's obesity problem? Underline or highlight the sentence that most clearly indicates who is to blame.

3. What does Brownlee think is the solution to the problem?

Group B

Now that you know what "If You Pitch It" is about, answer the following questions:

1. Think back to your original predictions. Which were right? Which did you have to modify as you read "If You Pitch It"?

2. What is the main idea of "If You Pitch It"? Underline or highlight the sentence that most clearly indicates the main idea.

3. What does Barboza think is the solution to the problem?

</td></tr>
<tr><td>Activity 8</td><td>

Annotating the Text

Group A

Reread Brownlee's "Portion Distortion," and annotate it as you go along. Underline, highlight, draw arrows, and write comments in the left-hand margin about the main ideas, questions or objections, and connections between the ideas. Write your reactions to what Brownlee says in the right-hand margin.

Compare your annotations with those of a classmate in Group A. Then, if you choose, revise your annotations.

</td></tr>
</table>

STUDENT VERSION

Activity 8 (Continued)

Group B

Reread Barboza's "If You Pitch It" and annotate it as you go along. Underline, highlight, draw arrows, and write comments in the left-hand margin about the main ideas, questions or objections, and connections between the ideas. Write your reactions to what Barboza says in the right-hand margin.

Compare your annotations with those of a classmate in Group B. Then, if you choose, revise your annotations.

Activity 9

Looking Closely at Language

Answer the following questions:

1. According to Zinczenko's "Don't Blame the Eater," why are kids suing McDonald's?
2. According to Zinczenko, what are the choices for American kids to get an affordable meal? Use the word "option" in your answer.
3. What causes 30 percent of the new cases of childhood diabetes in America?
4. Give an example of an alternative to fast food. How easy is it for kids to purchase that alternative?
5. Do people who buy fast food know how many calories they are eating? Use the word "consume" or "consumer" in your answer.
6. What do you think of kids who file lawsuits against the fast-food industry?
7. Do you agree with Zinczenko that the fast-food industry is vulnerable?
8. Do you make informed choices when you buy fast food?

Activity 10

Considering the Structure of the Text

Reread Zinczenko's "Don't Blame the Eater," and then do the following:

- Draw a line across the page where the introduction ends. Is it after the first paragraph, or are there more introductory paragraphs? How do you know?
- Draw a line across the page where the conclusion begins. Is it the last paragraph, or are there several concluding paragraphs? How do you know?
- Discuss in groups or as a class why the lines were drawn where they were. In this activity, think and reasoning about organizational structure is more important than agreeing on where the lines should be drawn.
- Further divide the body of the text into sections by topics (what each section is about).

| Activity 10 (Continued) | • Write a short description of what each section is about, what it says about that topic, and why the writer put it there (the rhetorical function of the section). |

Now answer the following questions:

- How does each section affect the reader? What is the writer trying to accomplish?
- What does each section say? What is the content?
- Which section is the most developed?
- Which section is the least developed? Does it need more development?
- Which section is the most persuasive? The least persuasive?
- On the basis of your chart of the text, what do you think is the main argument? Is that argument explicit or implicit?

Make a map of the ideas in the article by doing the following:

- Draw a circle in the center of the page and label it with the text's main idea.
- Record the text's supporting ideas on branches that connect to the central idea.
- Ask yourself how the ideas are related to one another.

Compare your map with a partner's. Make any changes needed to make your map reflect the ideas of the article more accurately.

Activity 11

Revisiting Key Vocabulary

Discuss the denotations (literal meaning) and connotations (the feelings or ideas a word suggests) of these words from Barboza's "If You Pitch It":

- blitzkrieg
- perverts (verb)
- assault
- threatening
- lock out

What does the use of these words imply about the author's view of fast-food marketing?

If you are in Group A, work with a Group A member to identify "loaded" words in Brownlee's "Portion Distortion."

If you are in Group B, work with a Group B member to identify other "loaded" words in Barboza's "If You Pitch It."

Now share with the class the words you have found.

Activity 12

Refining Key Vocabulary

Getting Ready to Write

This exercise is designed to help you become aware of not only the word meanings but of word forms as well.

1. Some critics of the fast-food industry _____ that it intentionally tries to make us eat too much.

2. Increasing _____ sizes while keeping costs down induces customers to eat more.

3. Parents are _____ for making sure their children eat nutritious food and get enough exercise.

4. The lack of physical education in the schools is contributing to the epidemic of childhood _____.

5. It's the fault of parents who let their children eat _____ food.

6. We shouldn't _____ junk food until we encourage more personal responsibility for one's own health.

7. _____ for fast food should carry warning labels such as those for tobacco and alcohol.

8. Fast-food restaurants need to _____ nutrition information to consumers.

Postreading

Activity 13

Summarizing and Responding

Group A

Write a summary of Brownlee's "Portion Distortion," following the guidelines in the Peer Response to Summary form. Then write your response to Brownlee's views.

Now exchange your summary/response with a partner from Group B. Use the Peer Response form to evaluate your partner's summary/response to "If You Pitch It."

Group B

Write a summary of Barboza's "If You Pitch It," following the guidelines in the Peer Response to Summary form. Then write your response to Barboza's views.

Now exchange your summary/response with a partner from Group A. Use the Peer Response form to evaluate your partner's summary/response to "Portion Distortion."

Peer Response to Summary

1. **Does the writer include the author's name in the first sentence of the summary?**　　　　　Yes _____

   Writer: Include the author's name.　　　　　No _____

2. **Does the writer include the title of the essay in the first sentence of the summary?**　　　　　Yes _____

   Writer: Include the title of the essay.　　　　　No _____

   Is the title in quotation marks?　　　　　Yes _____

   Writer: Punctuate the title using quotation marks.　　　　　No _____

3. **Does the first sentence clearly state the main idea of the article?**　　　　　Yes _____

   Writer: State the main idea in the first sentence. Make sure it is clear and accurate.　　　　　No _____

   You can improve your first sentence by _____

   _____

   _____

4. **Does the writer include all of the important ideas or supporting points from the essay?**　　　　　Yes _____

   Writer: You left out an important point (specify which):　　　　　No _____

   _____

   _____

   _____

5. **Does the writer use his/her own words?**　　　　　Yes _____

   Writer: You used the author's words instead of your own.
   (Indicate where—give paragraph or line number.)　　　　　No _____

6. **Does the writer keep his/her own opinions *out* of the summary?**　　　　　Yes _____

   Writer: You mentioned your opinion in the summary.
   (Indicate where—give paragraph or line number.)　　　　　No _____

   Remember to save your opinion for your response!

   (From *LS 15 Course Materials*, California State University, Sacramento; copyright 2003)

Activity 14

Thinking Critically

Think about the following questions, and then write your answers.

Questions about Logic (Logos)

1. Which article is the most convincing?
2. What are the major claims presented in that article?
3. Are there claims in the article that are weak or unsupported? What are they?
4. What other counterarguments could the author consider?
5. Has the author left out an argument on purpose?

Questions about the Writer (Ethos)

1. What is the author's background?
2. Is this author knowledgeable? Smart? Successful?
3. What does the author's style and language tell you about him or her?
4. Do you trust this author? Why or why not?
5. Do you think this author is deceptive? Why or why not?
6. Do you think this author is serious? Why or why not?

Questions about Emotions (Pathos)

1. How does the article affect you? Which parts?
2. Do you think the author is trying to manipulate your emotions? How?
3. Do your emotions conflict with your logical interpretation of the arguments?
4. Does the author use humor? How does this affect your acceptance of his or her ideas?

Writing Rhetorically

Prewriting

Activity 15

Reading the Assignment

On-Demand Writing Assignment

You will have 45 minutes to plan and write an essay on the topic below. Before you begin writing, read the passage carefully and plan what you will say. Explain Weintraub's argument and discuss the extent to which you agree or disagree with his analysis. Support your position by providing reasons and examples from your own experience, observations, or reading. Your essay should be as well-organized and carefully written as you can make it.

As Americans add pounds, critics are increasingly blaming the fast-food industry. Teenagers have filed lawsuits blaming McDonald's for their health problems, and a public health group in California has asked the governor to declare child-hood obesity a state of emergency. But parents—not the fast-food companies, not the government—are in the best position to fight the epidemic of overweight children. Parents are responsible for teaching kids healthy eating and exercise habits. Parents are to blame if they let kids eat unhealthy foods and sit in front of the television or computer for hours at a time. We have laws against parents leaving a loaded weapon where children can find and use it to hurt them-selves or others. It's time to get parents to take the same responsibility to protect their children from unhealthy foods and lack of exercise.

Adapted from Daniel Weintraub's
"The Battle Against Fast Food Begins in the Home"
The Sacramento Bee, December 17, 2002

Explain Weintraub's argument and discuss the extent to which you agree or disagree with his analysis. Support your position, providing reasons and examples from your own experience, observations, or reading.

Take the following steps for this exercise:

- Read the assignment carefully.
- Decide which issue you are going to discuss.
- Discuss the purpose of the assignment. What will you try to accomplish in your essay?

Getting Ready to Write

As you think about what you will write, answer the following questions about the passage included in the writing assignment.

1. What are the author's major claims?
2. Which claim is the strongest? The weakest? Has he or she left any out?
3. How credible is the author on this topic?
4. How does the argument affect you emotionally?
5. Has the author tried to manipulate your emotions? How?

Formulating a Working Thesis

Writing down a tentative thesis at this point is a good habit to develop in your writing process. Your thesis should be a complete sentence and can be revised several times. But a focused thesis statement will keep your writing on track.

Record your responses to the following questions in preparation for writing your tentative thesis statement:

Activity 17 (Continued)

- What specific question will your essay answer? What is your response to this question? (This is your tentative thesis.)
- What support have you found for your thesis?
- What evidence have you found for this support? For example, you can use facts, statistics, quotes from authorities, personal experience, anecdotes, stories, scenarios, and examples.
- How much background information do your readers need to understand your topic and thesis?
- If readers were to disagree with your thesis or the validity of your support, what would they say? How would you address their concerns (what would you say to them)?

Now draft a possible thesis for your essay.

Writing

Activity 18

Composing a Draft

When you write an argument essay, choose an approach to the subject that matters to you. If you have strong feelings, you will find it much easier to gather evidence and convince your readers of your point of view. Keep in mind, however, that your readers might feel just as strongly about the opposite side of the issue. The following guidelines will help you write a good argument essay.

1. **State your opinion on the topic in your thesis statement.** To write a thesis statement for an argument essay, you must take a stand for or against an action or an idea. In other words, your thesis statement should be debatable—a statement that can be argued or challenged and will not be met with agreement by everyone who reads it. Your thesis statement should introduce your subject and state your opinion about that subject.

   Daniel Weintraub's thesis is the third line of the passage: "But parents—not the fast food companies, not the government—are in the best position to fight the epidemic of overweight children." This is Weintraub's position, and it is a debatable thesis. Some other statements about fast food and the epidemic of overweight children would not be debatable and therefore would not be effective theses.

   Not debatable: The number of obese children has more than doubled since 1980.

   Not debatable: Many people blame the fast-food industry for making them fat.

   The first example is a statistic (a fact based on research). It is not an opinion and cannot be used as a thesis. The second example is a statement about other people's opinions, but it is not the writer's opinion.

2. Take your audience into consideration as you write your essay.
When you write your essay, assume that your audience is well-informed generally but may not have the specific knowledge that you have gained by reading and discussion as you moved through the Fast Food unit. You need to provide your readers with information and your sources for that information whether you are citing statistics or paraphrasing someone else's argument. In a true timed-writing situation, you will not have access to sources, but you can still refer to information you learned in a class, read in an article, or found on a Web site. Just be sure to mention where you found it (not a formal reference but an acknowledgment that it comes from another source).

You may also want to let your readers know who you are. Think about the information that Zinczenko provided about his development from "a typical mid-1980s latchkey kid" to a writer for a health magazine. That information helped us to decide how credible his opinions were. In the same way, you can let your readers know, for example, that you are a high school student so that when you talk about the easy access you have to junk food at school, they know you are in a good position to know this.

You also need to assume that some of your readers will disagree with you (remember, your thesis is going to be debatable). If you acknowledge some possible alternative positions and explain why they are not as strong as your own, that will strengthen your argument. For example, Weintraub acknowledges that some people blame fast-food companies and other people blame the government for America's weight problem. He gets those arguments on the table before he goes on to his own argument that parents are the ones who bear the greatest blame.

3. Choose evidence that supports your thesis statement. Evidence is probably the most important factor in writing an argument essay. Without solid evidence, your essay is nothing more than opinion; with it, your essay can be powerful and persuasive. If you supply convincing evidence, your readers will not only understand your position but may agree with it.

Evidence can consist of facts, statistics, statements from authorities, and examples or personal stories. Examples and personal stories can be based on your own observations, experiences, and reading, but your opinions are not evidence. Other strategies, such as comparison/contrast, definition, and cause/effect, can be particularly useful in building an argument. Use any combination of evidence and writing strategies that supports your thesis statement.

In the readings for the Fast Food assignment, you can find several different types of evidence. Here are some examples:

Facts

As early as 1972, McDonald's introduced its large-size fries (Brownlee, paragraph 13).

An existing law requires an average of at least 20 minutes per day of physical education (Weintraub, paragraph 9).

Statistics

Since 1980, the number of obese children has more than doubled to 16 percent (Barboza, paragraph 9).

About 20 percent of the nation's schools now offer brand-name fast food (Barboza, paragraph 21).

Diabetes accounts for $100 billion a year in health-care costs today (Zinczenko, paragraph 5).

Statements from Authorities

Statement by Lisa Young, a nutritionist at New York University (Brownlee, paragraph 21).

Quote by Susan Linn, a Harvard psychologist who studies children's marketing (Barboza, paragraph 5).

Statistics from the Centers for Disease Control and Prevention (Barboza, paragraph 9).

Examples and Personal Stories

Zinczenko's personal story (Zinczenko, paragraphs 2–4)

4. **Anticipate opposing points of view.** In addition to stating and supporting your position, anticipating and responding to opposing views are important. Presenting only your side of the argument leaves half the story untold—the opposition's half. If you acknowledge that there are opposing arguments and answer them, your argument is stronger.

In paragraph 13 of "The Battle Against Fast Food Begins at Home," Weintraub acknowledges the argument that busy parents, especially single parents, don't have the time to cook healthy meals or the energy to restrict TV and video games. He counters the argument in the next paragraph where he describes the strategies used in his own home. By acknowledging the argument (more fully developed in Zinczenko's opinion piece), he increases his own credibility.

5. **Find some common ground.** Pointing out common ground between you and your opponent is also an effective strategy. Common ground refers to points of agreement between two opposing positions. For example, one person might be in favor of gun control and another strongly opposed. But they might find common ground—agreement—in the need to keep guns out of teenagers' hands. Locating some common ground is possible in almost every situation. When you state in your essay that you agree with your opponent on certain points, your reader sees you as a fair person.

Weintraub advocates making individuals responsible for their children's health rather than having government intervene, but he suggests a middle ground between individual responsibility and government intervention. He advocates having health agencies do "more to encourage these kinds of simple policies in the home" (paragraph 16).

6. **Maintain a reasonable tone.** Just as you probably wouldn't win an argument by shouting or making mean or nasty comments, don't expect your readers to respond well to such tactics. Keep the "voice" of your essay calm and sensible. Your readers will be much more open to what you have to say if they think you are a reasonable person.

Weintraub maintains a reasonable tone throughout his article. He believes that parents are endangering their children's health and makes the analogy to leaving a loaded gun where children can use it, but he doesn't say parents are stupid or lazy. Instead, he suggests that they are uninformed, and he acknowledges the difficulties they face in raising healthy children. We are more ready to accept his conclusion that more education is needed because he makes a reasonable argument rather than a strident appeal.

7. **Organize your essay so that it presents your position as effectively as possible.** By the end of your essay, you want your audience to agree with you. So you want to organize your essay in such a way that your readers can easily follow it. The number of your paragraphs will vary depending on the nature of your assignment, but the following outline shows the order in which the features of an argument essay are most effective:

Introduction
Background information
Introduction of subject
Statement of your opinion

Body Paragraphs
Common ground
Lots of evidence (both logical and emotional)
Opposing point of view
Response to opposing point of view

Conclusion
Restatement of your position
Call for action or agreement

The arrangement of your evidence in an argument essay depends to a great extent on your readers' opinions. Most arguments will be organized from general to particular, from particular to general, or from one extreme to another. When you know that your readers already agree with you, arranging your details from general to particular or from most to least important is usually most effective. With this order, you are building on your readers' agreement and loyalty as you explain your thinking on the subject.

If you suspect that your audience does not agree with you, reverse the organization of your evidence and arrange it from particular to general or from least to most important. In this way, you can take your readers step by step through your reasoning in an attempt to get them to agree with you.

Weintraub's essay follows the general outline just presented. Here is a skeleton outline of his essay.

Introduction

Background about the recommendations of the California Center for Public Health Advocacy's recommendations to reduce childhood obesity.

Weintraub's own position that parents, with some help, can and should teach their children healthy eating and exercise habits.

Body Paragraphs

The Center's report

- Data on childhood obesity
- Analysis of causes: fast food, portion sizes, junk food at school, advertising of junk food, and lack of PE
- Recommendations: required PE, nutritional standards for schools, working water fountains

Recommendations ineffective unless parents accept their roles:

- Loaded gun analogy
- Reasons parents resort to fast food and TV
- Strategies used in the Weintraub home: limit junk food at home; eat home-cooked meals, limit TV time; encourage organized sports and outdoor activities

Conclusion

Organizations such as the Center for Public Health Advocacy need to encourage parents to take an active role in monitoring their children's eating and exercise habits.

Organizing the Essay

The following items are traditional parts of all essays:

- An introduction (usually one or two paragraphs) that "hooks" the reader and provides a thesis statement or road map for the reader
- The body (as many paragraphs as necessary), which supports the thesis statement point by point
- A conclusion (usually only one paragraph) that summarizes the main points and explains the significance of the argument

The number of paragraphs in an essay depends on the nature and complexity of your argument.

**Activity 19
(Continued)**

Here are some additional hints for helping you organize your thoughts:

Introduction

- You might want to include the following in your introductory paragraphs:
    - A "hook" to get the reader's attention
    - Background information the audience may need
    - A thesis statement, along with some indication of how the essay will be developed ("forecasting"). *Note:* A thesis statement states the topic of the essay and the writer's position on that topic. You may choose to sharpen or narrow the thesis at this point.

Body

- Paragraphs that present support of the thesis statement with topic sentences supported by evidence. (See "Getting Ready to Write.")
- Paragraphs that include different points of view or address counter-arguments.
- Paragraphs or sentences where you address those points of view by doing the following:
    - Refuting them
    - Acknowledging them but showing how your argument is better
    - Granting them altogether but showing they are irrelevant
- Evidence that you have considered the values, beliefs, and assumptions of your audience as well as your own values, beliefs, and assumptions. Evidence that you have found some common ground that appeals to the various points of view of readers is also necessary.

Conclusion

- A final paragraph (or paragraphs) that includes a solid argument to support the thesis and indicates the significance of the argument—the "so what" factor

---

Activity 20

Developing the Content

Here are a few highlights about developing your essay:

- Most body paragraphs consist of a topic sentence (or an implied topic sentence) and concrete details to support that topic sentence.
- Body paragraphs give evidence in the form of examples, illustrations, statistics, and so on and analyze the meaning of the evidence.
- Each topic sentence is usually directly related to the thesis statement.
- No set number of paragraphs makes up an essay.
- The thesis dictates and focuses the content of an essay.

Revising and Editing

Activity 21

Revising the Draft

You now need to work with the organization and development of your draft to make sure that your essay is as effective as possible.

Peer Group Work

In groups of three or four, each of you should read his or her essay aloud to other members of the group. Then complete Part I of the Evaluation Form for each essay.

Paired Work

Work in pairs to decide how you want to revise the problems that group members identified.

Individual Work

Revise the draft based on the feedback you have received and the decisions you have made with your partners. Consider these additional questions for individual work:

- Have I responded to the assignment?
- What is my purpose for this essay?
- What should I keep? What is most effective?
- What should I add? Where do I need more details, examples, and other evidence to support my point?
- What could I get rid of? Did I use irrelevant details? Was I repetitive?
- What should I change? Are parts of my essay confusing or contra-dictory? Do I need to explain my ideas more fully?
- What should I rethink? Was my position clear? Did I provide enough analysis to convince my readers?
- How is my tone? Am I too overbearing or too firm? Do I need qualifiers?
- Have I addressed differing points of view?
- Does my conclusion show the significance of my essay?
- Have I used key vocabulary words correctly to represent the ideas from the article? Have I used words that refer to specific facts from the text?

Activity 22

Editing the Draft

You now need to work with the grammar and mechanics of your draft to make sure that your use of language is effective and conforms to the guidelines of standard written English.

Individual Work

Edit your draft based on the information you have received from your instructor or a tutor. Use the editing checklist provided by your teacher. The suggestions below will also help you edit your own work.

Activity 22 (Continued)	**Editing Guidelines for Individual Work**

Editing Guidelines for Individual Work

- If possible, set your essay aside for 24 hours before rereading to find errors.
- If possible, read your essay out loud so you can hear your errors.
- Focus on individual words and sentences rather than overall meaning. Take a sheet of paper and cover everything except the line you are reading. Then touch your pencil to each word as you read.
- With the help of your teacher, figure out your own pattern of errors—the most serious and frequent errors you make.
- Only look for one type of error at a time. Then go back and look for a second type, and if necessary, a third.
- Use the dictionary to check spelling and confirm that you've chosen the right word for the context.

Activity 23

Reflecting on the Writing

When you have completed your own essay, answer these six questions.

1. What was most difficult about this assignment?
2. What was easiest?
3. What did you learn about arguing by completing this assignment?
4. What do you think are the strengths of your argument? Place a wavy line by the parts of your essay that you feel are very good.
5. What are the weaknesses, if any, of your paper? Place an X by the parts of your essay you would like help with. Write any questions you have in the margin.
6. What did you learn from this assignment about your own writing process—about preparing to write, writing the first draft, revising, and editing?

Page 68 blank

Fast Food: Who's to Blame?

On-Demand Writing Assignment

You will have 45 minutes to plan and write an essay on the topic assigned below. Before you begin writing, read the passage carefully and plan what you will say. Your essay should be as well-organized and carefully written as you can make it.

As Americans add pounds, critics are increasingly blaming the fast-food industry. Teenagers have filed lawsuits blaming McDonald's for their health problems, and a public health group in California has asked the governor to declare childhood obesity a state of emergency. But parents—not the fast food companies, not the government—are in the best position to fight the epidemic of overweight children. Parents are responsible for teaching healthy eating and exercise habits. Parents are to blame if they let their kids eat unhealthy foods and sit in front of the television or computer for hours at a time. We have laws against parents leaving a loaded weapon where children can find and use it to hurt themselves or others. It's time to get parents to take the same responsibility to protect their children from unhealthy foods and lack of exercise.

Adapted from Daniel Weintraub's
"The Battle Against Fast Food Begins in the Home"
The Sacramento Bee, December 17, 2002

Explain Weintraub's argument and discuss the extent to which you agree or disagree with his analysis. Support your position, providing reasons and examples from your own experience, observations, or reading.

The sample student essays that follow reflect the EPT Scoring Guide's criteria.

Sample student essay with a score of 6:

Daniel Weintraub, in "The Battle Against Fast Food Begins in the Home," states that parents are responsible for the increasing epidemic of child obesity. Parents need to be responsible enough to teach their children healthy eating & exercise habits. In our world today, children sit around & play video games all day, if they are allowed to. Weintraub argues that parents need to "step up to the plate" and get children involved in some type of exercise. I agree that parents need to take more responsibility for child obesity, but schools, fast food companies & the government also need to take that same initiative.

Parents have a lot of influence on their children from the day that child is born. Children learn how to talk from their parents, how to respect their elders and they *should* learn healthy eating & exercising habits from their parents. There are many steps to take in showing a child what is healthy & unhealthy. A parent could make sure that a child receives a serving of fruits or vegetables at lunch & dinner, eliminate soda from the house and even eliminate all junk food from the house. From a young age, my parents taught me to have an apple for a snack instead of a cookie & that I should be getting 5 servings of fruits or vegetables a day. This lesson has influenced me even until today when my friends & I will go and eat a salad at lunch instead of pizza or chips. I have also eliminated all soda from my diet.

Parents need to show their children that exercise is not a bad thing. At a young age, parents need to show children that there are other things to do, like playing tag or playing at the park, than just watching t.v. Parents could introduce their children to different sports until the child finds one that he or she is interested in. My parents entered me in dance class & were lucky in finding that that was what I enjoyed. I have been dancing since I was three years old & I also played soccer for 8 years. It isn't very difficult to turn off a t.v. and send your children outside to play.

Parents are not solely responsible for child obesity; schools, fast food companies & the government also need to take action against child obesity. Schools today do not provide a great selection of healthy food. My student body is luck that we have an off-campus lunch but even then it is difficult to find healthy food. Fast food companies definitely need some blame. With advertising that appeals to children, it is no wonder that America is fat. Through whining for that toy that a child can get with a kid's meal, the parent is pressured to go to a fast food place.

Daniel Weintraub argues that parents are responsible for child obesity. I agree with Weintraub but schools & fast food companies also need to help in the fight against child obesity.

Commentary

This essay illustrates the EPT Scoring Guide's criteria for a score of 6. The superior response indicates that the writer is very well-prepared to handle college-level reading and writing.

- The writer clearly explains Weintraub's argument regarding childhood obesity in the first paragraph and takes a thoughtful position, contending that Weintraub is right to a degree but that "schools, fast food companies & the government also need to take that same initiative."
- The writer skillfully restates Weintraub's argument in the first paragraph and makes a further connection in the second paragraph by saying, "they *should* learn healthy eating & exercising habits from their parents." However, the emphasized "should" suggests that the writer questions whether this always happens. The conclusion again refers back to Weintraub.
- The essay demonstrates "quality and clarity of thought" with its careful analysis of both the strengths and weaknesses of Weintraub's somewhat overstated position.
- The essay reflects an effective use of topic statements and strong personal examples to both support Weintraub's argument that parents are responsible for childhood obesity with respect to eating and exercise habits and make the case that others are responsible as well.
- Sentence structure is varied and word choice is precise.
- The essay has few errors.

Sample student essay with a score of 5:

America is now known as the fattest country in America. Many of our country's people blame the fast food industry for over-advertising, selling unhealthy food, and selling oversized portions. However, others feel that America's obeisity is a matter of personal responsibility. In his article "The battle against fast food begins in the home," Daniel Weintraub explains that parents need to take responsibility for the eating habits of their kids, and I agree with his opinion in this matter.

As Americans, we are given the freedom of choice, however, before we become adults, it is our parents that have to teach us how to make the right decisions. This is Weintraub's point. If parents are not willing to teach their kids the dangers of eating too much fast food and not getting enough exercise, then those kids have no way to make the right choices. Kids learn best at an early age, therefore, teaching them good habits will allow them to make the correct decisions later.

I agree with Weintraub's opinion that parents are responsible. Obviously, fast food companies are going to market towards kids; they are more impressionable. Because of this, if parents would start teaching kids early on, they could use that impressionable quality to their advantage. The benefits of education are apparent in almost everything we do. For example, a better educated person can solve problems quickly and easily. The same goes for someone educated in terms of health habits. They can make the best choices because they have been taught to do so. Fast food companies provide a service. It is up to us, or our parents if we are not yet of age, to decide how much of that service we should use.

In conclusion, Daniel Weintraub is correct in his assesment of one of the causes of America's obeisity. The truth is that no child can grow up to be an intelligent human being without a proper education, wether it be in mathematics or eating habits. Fast food companies are always going to compete for customers and try to make money, but they cannot control our decisions. The only people that can make choices for us our ourselves, and we cannot make the right choices without proper education from our parents. We cannot blame others for our own problems. Only when parents and the population of American in general are educated and choose to live healthy lifestyles will the country's obeisity cease.

Commentary

This essay illustrates the EPT Scoring Guide's criteria for a score of 5. The clear competence of the essay indicates that this writer is quite ready to handle college-level reading and writing.

- The writer addresses the topic of childhood obesity clearly, summarizing and then agreeing with Weintraub's position. Further references to Weintraub in the body and conclusion maintain a clear focus on the argument.
- The essay presents a well-reasoned response, indicating that various factors contribute to childhood obesity but finally siding with Weintraub in placing the responsibility on parents: *"We cannot make the right choices without proper education from our parents."*
- The essay shows some depth of thought in making the case that adults are responsible for making their own sound choices while parents are responsible for the choices their children make. However, the writer simply dismisses the responsibility of the fast-food industry without analysis.
- The essay is fairly clearly organized around the ideas that parents are responsible for their children's choices and that the best way to counter fast-food advertising is through education; however, some repetition and a lack of strong examples weaken the writer's argument.
- The sentences are varied and word choices are generally precise and effective.
- The essay has only a few minor errors: failure to use a semicolon with "however," misspelling of "obesity," and the distracting repetition of "America" in the first line.

Sample student essay with a score of 4:

Obesity Can Be Stopped Within the Home

The article titled, "The battle against fast food begins in the home," is the author's Daniel Weintraub, point of view on the rising obesity problem in America. Mr. Weintraub wrote this particular piece with one intention; to educate the readers with his own views. Mr. Weintraub doesn't blame the Government, or advertising for American's weight problem. But, instead he feels that parents are the sole component. He not only blames parents for

5

their children's poor eating habits, but also for they lack of exercise, and physical activity. I strongly agree with Mr. Weintraub because of the dynamics and regimne of parent's lives today and parents wanting to blame everyone and thing but themselves.

I strongly agree with Mr. Weintraub because of the dynamics and regimne of parent's lives today. Mr. Weintraub makes the point in his article that, "Fast Food is fast.", and "It can also seem cheap." (Weintraub) This is just what parents who work all day want. They want to feed their children, not cook but feed, and relax after a hard days work. They may not mean to, but they are already to blame for their child's eating habits. However, taking the easy route, they have already put their children at risk. The dynamics of their daily regimne naturally allow them to feed their child "junk".

Not only do I believe that Mr. Weintraub is correct because of the dynamics and regimne of parent's lives today, but I also strongly Agree with Mr. Weintraub because of parents wanting to blame everyone and thing but themselves. First off, in an article written by Shannon Brownlee titled, "Its Portion distortion that makes America fat," a mother who was suing McDonalds stated, "1 always believed McDonalds food was healthy for my son." (Brownlee) This statement shows a parent who is willing to blame a company, whose sole purpose is making money, for her child's obesity. All the while parents eat, themselves, the exact same food as their child. They don't hold any responsibility that maybe their child will mimic these same habits. In the "Letters to the Editor" section a woman, Patricia Gonzalez, poses a good question; "Why aren't they (parents) home cooking them (children) healthy food?" (Letters to Editor) Instead of parents complaining about how companies made their kids fat, or how advertising hooked their kids, why don't they eliminate these factors and cook their children a meal they know is healthy?

I strongly agree with Mr. Weintraub because of the dynamics and regimne of parent's lives today and parents wanting to blame everyone and thing but themselves. Mr. Weintraub expressed the right point. As Americans, we need to take responsibility ourselves and not just blame other people. Parents could eliminate obesity before it became a problem in their child's life. That is why I strongly agree with Mr. Weintraub.

Commentary

4

This essay illustrates the EPT Scoring Guide's criteria for a score of 4. This adequate response to the topic suggests that the writer should be able to handle college-level reading and writing.

- The writer clearly addresses Weintraub's argument that parents are responsible for the epidemic of childhood obesity but fails to explain why the fast-food companies, "whose sole purpose is making money," do not share responsibility.
- The writer generally understands the passage and develops a sensible, if somewhat simplistic, response: "why don't they . . . cook their children a meal they know is healthy?"
- The essay has a clear organization around the issues of parents' lack of time—"dynamics and regimne of parent's lives"—and parents' desire to

shift blame to others. However, well-chosen examples would strengthen the support for this argument.

- The essay demonstrates adequate use of syntax and language; however, word choice is sometimes imprecise. For example, "The article . . . is the point of view . . ." and "hold any responsibility." "Dynamics" and "regimne" are used both imprecisely and repetitively.
- The writer has general control of grammar and usage; however, errors in punctuation and capitalization are frequent and distracting.

Sample student essay with a score of 3:

Who is to blame the parents, fast food companies, the government or yourself? People now a days are so quick to sue fast food companies for making them fat but its all about self control. One should know his or her own body and watch what they eat. Fast food places are on almost every corner but doesn't mean their making you eat there.

In New York a teenager is sueing McDonald's for making her fat. He weighs in at 400 pounds. His mother says "I always believed McDonald's food was healthy for my son". How is this possible? Two patty cheeseburgers, deep fried potatoes, and a large cup of soda is clearly not healthy. This kid probably ate at McDonald's majority of the time but I doubt he ate there everyday for every meal so how is McDonald's fully to blaim. Whatever happen to exercising, if this teenager was getting the required exercise there is no way he could way in at 400 pounds.

Don't get me wrong I'm not just on the fast food companies' side. Yes McDonald's super-sizing most of their meals is a little extreme. Having good deals like dollar nugget Tuesdays is also a big temptation. Fast food companies could cut down on the location of there restuarants. Being that its so convinent that it's close to your house, cheap and fast is another way that makes Americans so addicted.

In conclusion, Both Americans and Fast Food Companies can change for the better. Americans start taking some responsibility for what you put into your own body. Fast Food Companies think of how many lives are at risk because of what your feeding them and cut back on expanding your franchises.

3

Commentary

This essay illustrates the EPT Scoring Guide's criteria for a score of 3. Although the essay indicates a developing competence on the part of the writer, it is flawed in significant ways that suggest the writer needs additional practice before being able to succeed in college-level reading and writing.

- The writer does not arrive at a thesis until the conclusion, which states, "In conclusion, Both Americans and Fast Food Companies can change for the better." Even if this thesis had been presented in the introduction, however, it would need to be made more specific.
- The writer does not summarize or explain Weintraub's argument and fails to respond to the argument that parents are primarily responsible for their children's eating and exercise habits.

- The writer does not use Weintraub's argument about the role of parents to develop the response; as a result, the essay is not focused on Weintraub's argument but instead focuses entirely on the responsibility of the individual and the fast-food industry.
- The essay demonstrates simplistic thinking. It ignores the socioeconomic and developmental issues that can impede children and parents from making wise decisions about what they eat. It also ignores the imperative for businesses to make money when it suggests that McDonald's "could cut down on the location of there restaurants."
- A skeletal organization is present, with the two body paragraphs each addressing a single idea that is summarized in the conclusion.
- The paragraphs are underdeveloped; they need additional specifics and analysis. In addition, the role of parental responsibility needs to be explored. The paragraphs need effective topic sentences relating back to a controlling idea or thesis.
- The writer's language is highly informal, relying on a series of rhetorical questions and colloquial comments ("Who is to blame . . .?" "How is this possible?" "Whatever happen to exercising?" "Don't get me wrong.") in place of analysis.
- The writer uses vague or incorrect pronoun reference ("one should know . . . and watch what they eat"; "but doesn't mean their making you eat there"), and sentence structure is weak ("Being that its so convinent . . . is another way that makes Americans so addicted."). The main errors, however, are in the mechanics, with numerous errors in punctuation, spelling, and capitalization.

Sample student essay with a score of 2:

Bigger isnt always better

Last year a Bronx teenager who weighted in at a wooping 400 pounds sat in a confrence room while their mother tried to file a suit againt McDonald's for make her kid fat. When ask why she replyed "I always believed McDonald's food was healthy for my son." More and more american's are trying to blame fast food for the reason they are fat, but is it what they eat or how much. Shannon Brownlee asked this question and this is what she found.

Portion sizes has been creeping up ward science 1972. That when McDolands introduced it's large size fries. (which now was smaller than a medium today.) And now they make more money then ever, they do it by consumer manipulation. Example 7-Eleven can sell the 64-ounce Double Gulp for only 37 cents more the 16-ounce 89 cent regular Gulp. "You'd feel ripped off if you bought the smaller size." And thats just the way I feel when I go to fast food why not get the bigger size your pay just as much as a regular. After reading Shannon Brownlee's article I understand and agree that people arn't getting fat from the food but from how much they eat. So maybe all those mom's should stop getting mad that their kid are getting fat and be mad at their kid for eating so much and throwing away money on food that 70% of the time they don't finish!

2

Commentary

This essay illustrates the EPT Scoring Guide's criteria for a score of 2. The serious flaws here indicate that this writer will need considerable additional practice before being able to succeed in college-level reading and writing.

- The writer does not summarize or respond to Weintraub's argument, instead lifting portions from another article by Shannon Brownlee about fast food.
- The writer does not use the passage at all.

Sample student essay with a score of 1:

Many people blame the fast food industry for making them obese. But it's not their fault it is the fault of the parents. It is theirs for not teaching the person how to eat right. It is the parents responsibility to teach their children o eat right and to excise at lest once a day.

Americans have taken the blame of obesity and put it one that fast food industry. Many parents have filled lawsuits against McDonalds for their health problems.

1

Commentary

This essay illustrates the EPT Scoring Guide's criteria for a score of 1. The fundamental deficiencies of this essay clearly indicate that the writer needs much additional practice to be ready to succeed at college-level reading and writing.

- The essay's length—six sentences—is insufficient to respond to the question.
- The writer misunderstands the passage and fails to refer to it.
- The essay is repetitive. The first and fifth sentences repeat each other, as do the second, third, and fourth sentences.
- The writer culls the idea of parental responsibility from the passage but offers no support, reasons, or examples as the prompt instructs.
- The essay appears to be incomplete. It ends with a (misstated) statement of fact from the passage that either belongs in the summary portion of the essay or should be omitted in lieu of the writer's own opinions and support—the better option.
- The writer lacks basic control of syntax and vocabulary.
- The writer has serious and persistent errors in grammar, usage, and mechanics that severely interfere with meaning. Pronoun confusion ("It is theirs . . . "), preposition misuse ("blame of obesity"), and punctuation errors are profound.

Going for the Look

Module 2

Going for the Look

Teacher Version

Reading Rhetorically

Prereading 1
   Introducing Key Concepts 1
   Getting Ready to Read............................. 1
   Surveying the Text 2
   Making Predictions and Asking Questions........... 2
   Introducing Key Vocabulary 3

Reading 5
   First Reading 5
   Looking Closely at Language 6
   Rereading the Text 7
   Considering the Structure of the Text 8
   Analyzing Stylistic Choices 12

Postreading 15
   Summarizing and Responding 15
   Thinking Critically 17
   Revisiting Key Vocabulary 19

Connecting Reading to Writing

Writing to Learn and Using the Words
   of Others 21

Writing Rhetorically

Prewriting 21
   Reading the Assignment 21
   Getting Ready to Write........................... 22
   Formulating a Working Thesis 24

Writing 25
   Composing a Draft................................ 25
   Organizing the Essay 29
   Developing the Content 30

Revising and Editing.................................... 30
   Revising the Draft............................... 30
   Editing the Draft 31
   Reflecting on the Writing........................ 32

Evaluating and Responding 33
   Grading Holistically............................. 33
   Responding to Student Writing 33
   Using Portfolios 34

Rubric.. 35

Reading Selection

"Going for the Look, but Risking Discrimination" 37

Student Version

Activity 1: Introducing Key Concepts 41
Activity 2: Getting Ready to Read 41
Activity 3: Surveying the Text 41
Activity 4: Making Predictions and Asking Questions 41
Activity 5: Introducing Key Vocabulary............. 42
Activity 6: First Reading......................... 42
Activity 7: Looking Closely at Language........... 42
Activity 8: Rereading the Text.................... 43
Activity 9: Considering the Structure of the Text 43
Activity 10: Analyzing Stylistic Choices.......... 48
Activity 11. Summarizing and Responding........... 50
Activity 12: Thinking Critically 51
Activity 13: Revisiting Key Vocabulary............ 52
Activity 14: Reading the Assignment.............. 53
Activity 15: Getting Ready to Write 53
Activity 16: Formulating a Working Thesis........ 54
Activity 17: Composing a Draft 54
Activity 18: Organizing the Essay............... 58
Activity 19: Developing the Content............. 59
Activity 20: Revising the Draft 59
Activity 21: Editing the Draft................. 60
Activity 22: Reflecting on the Writing.......... 61

Sample Student Essays

On-Demand Writing Assignment and Scored
   Student Essays 63

Going for the Look, but Risking Discrimination

by Steven Greenhouse
The New York Times, July 13, 2003

1   A funny thing happens when Elizabeth Nill, a sophomore at Northwestern University, goes shopping at Abercrombie & Fitch.

2   At no fewer than three Abercrombie stores, she says, managers have approached her and offered her a job as a clerk.

3   "Every time this happens, my little sister says, 'Not again,'" said Ms. Nill, who is 5-foot-6 and has long blond hair. She looks striking. She looks hip. She looks, in fact, as if she belongs in an Abercrombie & Fitch catalog.

4   Is this a coincidence? A fluke? No, says Antonio Serrano, a former assistant Abercrombie store manager in Scranton, Pa. It's policy.

5   "If someone came in with a pretty face, we were told to approach them and ask them if they wanted a job," Mr. Serrano said. "They thought if we had the best-looking college kids working in our store, everyone will want to shop there."

6   Abercrombie's aggressive approach to building a pretty and handsome sales force, an effort that company officials proudly acknowledge, is a leading example of what many industry experts and sociologists describe as a steadily growing trend in American retailing. From Abercrombie to the cosmetics giant L'Oreal, from the sleek W hotel chain to the Gap, businesses are openly seeking workers who are sexy, sleek or simply good-looking.

7   Hiring for looks is old news in some industries, as cocktail waitresses, strippers and previous generations of flight attendants know all too well. But many companies have taken that approach to sophisticated new heights in recent years, hiring workers to project an image.

8   In doing so, some of those companies have been skirting the edges of antidiscrimination laws and provoking a wave of private and government lawsuits. Hiring attractive people is not necessarily illegal, but discriminating on the basis of age, sex or ethnicity is. That is where things can get confusing and contentious.

9   "If you're hiring by looks, then you can run into problems of race discrimination, national origin discrimination, gender discrimination, age discrimination and even disability discrimination," said Olophius Perry, director of the Los Angeles office of the Equal Employment Opportunity Commission, which has accused several companies of practicing race and age discrimination, by favoring good-looking young white people in their hiring.

10   Some chains, most notably the Gap and Benetton, pride themselves on hiring attractive people from many backgrounds and races. Abercrombie's "classic American" look, pervasive in its store and catalogs and on its Web site, is blond, blue-eyed and preppy. Abercrombie finds such workers and

models by concentrating its hiring on certain colleges, fraternities and sororities.

11   The company says it does not discriminate. But in a lawsuit filed last month in Federal District Court in San Francisco, some Hispanic, Asian and black job applicants maintained otherwise. Several plaintiffs said in interviews that when they applied for jobs, store managers steered them to the stockroom, not to the sales floor.

12   In interviews, managers like Mr. Serrano described a recruiting approach used by Abercrombie, which has become one of the most popular retailers among the nation's youth.

13   "We were supposed to approach someone in the mall who we think will look attractive in our store," said Mr. Serrano, who said he quit when told he would be promoted only if he accepted a transfer. "If that person said, 'I never worked in retailing before,' we said: 'Who cares? We'll hire you.' But if someone came in who had lots of retail experience and not a pretty face, we were told not to hire them at all."

14   Tom Lennox, Abercrombie's communications director, emphatically denied job bias but acknowledged the company likes hiring sales assistants, known as brand representatives, who "look great."

15   "Brand representatives are ambassadors to the brand," Mr. Lennox said. "We want to hire brand representatives that will represent the Abercrombie & Fitch brand with natural classic American style, look great while exhibiting individuality, project the brand and themselves with energy and enthusiasm, and make the store a warm, inviting place that provides a social experience for the customer."

16   Retailers defend that approach to hiring as necessary and smart, and industry experts see the point.

17   "In today's competitive retail environment, the methods have changed for capturing the consumers' awareness of your brand," said Marshal Cohen, a senior industry analyst with the NPD Group, a market research firm. "Being able to find a brand enhancer, or what I call a walking billboard, is critical. It's really important to create an environment that's enticing to the community, particularly with the younger, fashionable market. A guy wants to go hang out in a store where he can see good-looking gals."

18   While hiring by looks has a long history, some sociologists and retail consultants agree that the emphasis has increased—not at WalMart and other mass marketers, but at upscale businesses.

19   The federal government has accused some of the businesses of going too far. The hotel entrepreneur Ian Scharger agreed to a $1.08 million settlement three years ago after the Equal Employment Opportunity Commission accused his Mondrian Hotel in West Hollywood of racial discrimination for firing nine valets and bellhops, eight of them nonwhite. Documents filed in court showed that Mr. Schrager had written memos saying that he wanted a trendier group of workers and that the fired employees were "too ethnic."

20   Last month the commission reached a $5,000 settlement with 36th Street Food and Drink, a restaurant in St. Joseph, Mo., after accusing it of age discrimination against a 47-year-old waitress. The waitress, Michele Cornell, had worked at the restaurant for 23 years, but when it reopened after renovations, it refused to rehire her because, the commission said, she no longer fit the young, trendy look it had adopted.

21   "The problem with all this image stuff is it just reeks of marketing for this white-bread, Northern European, thin, wealthy, fashion-model look," said Donna Harper, supervisory attorney in the commission's St. Louis office. "We all can't be Anglo, athletic and young."

22   Ms. Harper said an employer who insisted on hiring only athletic-looking people could be viewed as discriminating against a person in a wheelchair. Employers who insisted on hiring only strapping, tall people might be found guilty of discriminating against Mexican-Americans or Asian-Americans, who tend to be shorter, she added.

23   Stephen J. Roppolo, a New Orleans lawyer who represents many hotels and restaurants, said: "Hiring someone who is attractive isn't illegal per se. But people's views on what's attractive may be influenced by their race, their religion, their age. If I think Caucasian people are more attractive than African-American people, then I may inadvertently discriminate in some impermissible way. I tell employers that their main focus needs to be hiring somebody who can get the job done. When they want to hire to project a certain image, that's where things can get screwy."

24   Image seemed very much in evidence the other evening at the Abercrombie & Fitch store in Water Tower Place, one of Chicago's most upscale malls. Working there was a 6-foot-2 sales clerk with muscles rippling under his Abercrombie T-shirt and a young long-haired blond clerk, her navel showing, who could have been a fashion model.

25   "If you see an attractive person working in the store wearing Abercrombie clothes, it makes you want to wear it, too," said Matthew Sheehey, a high school senior from Orland Park, a Chicago suburb.

26   Elysa Yanowitz says that when she was a West Coast sales manager for L'Oreal, she felt intense pressure to hire attractive saleswomen, even if they were incompetent. In fact, she says, company officials sought to force her out after she ignored an order to fire a woman a top manager described as not "hot" enough.

27   "It was pretty well understood that they had to have magazine-look quality," she said of the sales force. "Everyone is supposed to look like a 110-pound model."

28   L'Oreal officials did not respond to a request for comment.

29   Melissa Milkie, a sociology professor at the University of Maryland who has written about perceptions of beauty, said: "Good-looking people are treated better by others. Maybe companies have noticed that hiring them impacts their bottom line. Whether that's morally proper is a different question."

Page 40 blank

Going for the Look

Reading selection for this module:
Greenhouse, Steven. "Going for the Look, but Risking Discrimination." *New York Times.* 13 July 2003.

Reading Rhetorically

Prereading

Activity 1	**Introducing Key Concepts**
	Your teacher will give you several magazine ads for clothing stores. Working with your group, list as many words as you can that describe "the look" of the model or models in each ad.
Activity 2	**Getting Ready to Read**
	Quickwrite: Should companies be able to hire only people who project the company image?
Activity 3	**Surveying the Text**
	Discuss the following questions with your class:
	1. What does the title of Greenhouse's article, "Going for the Look, but Risking Discrimination," tell you about the topic of this article?
	2. The article was published in *The New York Times.* What do you expect from an article published by this newspaper? Will it be interesting? Will you be able to believe what the author says?
	3. What can you tell about the article by looking at its length and the length of its paragraphs?
Activity 4	**Making Predictions and Asking Questions**
	1. Read the first five paragraphs. What are they about? Now read the last paragraph. Melissa Milkie states, "Whether that's morally proper is a different question." What is it that she is wondering about?

| Activity 4 (Continued) | 2. What do you think this article is going to be about?
3. What do you think is the purpose of this article?
4. Who do you think is the intended audience for this piece? What other audiences might be interested in this topic?
5. Will the article take a position on the topic of hiring people to project a certain image? Why do you think so?
6. Turn the title into a question (or questions) to answer after you have read the text. |

| Activity 5 | **Introducing Key Vocabulary**

A semantic map (or web) will help you organize the terms your teacher will give you for this activity.

Directions:

1. Write the topic in the center of the map.
2. Create categories based on the topic.
3. List words that fall under the categories. |

Reading

| Activity 6 | **First Reading**

You have read the first five paragraphs and the conclusion. Now read the rest of the article silently. As you read, think about the predictions you have made, and then answer the following questions.

1. Of your original predictions, which were right? Which did you have to modify as you reread "Going for the Look"?
2. Find and underline the most significant sentence in the article. Why is it the most important sentence?
3. What is the main idea of "Going for the Look"? Write it in the box at the end of the article. |

| Activity 7 | **Looking Closely at Language**

Vocabulary Self-Assessment Chart

This vocabulary self-assessment chart will help you think about whether a word is familiar and to what degree. It will also help draw your attention to particular words that are important to understand the article. Use concise definitions to fill out the chart. |

Word	Definition	Know It Well	Have Heard of It	Don't Know It
coincidence				
aggressive				

**Activity 7
(Continued)**

Word	Definition	Know It Well	Have Heard of It	Don't Know It
discriminating				
pervasive				
emphatically				
upscale				
reeks of				
inadvertently				
impermissible				
incompetent				
impacts				

Activity 8

Rereading the Text

Now that you know what Greenhouse's "Going for the Look" is about, go back and reread it.

Using a highlighter or pencil, mark the following parts of the text:

1. Where the introduction ends
2. Where Greenhouse identifies the issue or problem he is writing about
3. The examples Greenhouse gives
4. The argument of retailers
5. The advice of the lawyer
6. The customer's viewpoint
7. The conclusion

In the right-hand margin, write your reactions to what Greenhouse and the people he quotes are saying.

Now exchange your copy of "Going for the Look" with your partner. Read your partner's annotations and reactions, and then talk about what you chose to mark and how you reacted to the text. Did you and your partner agree on what the main idea is?

Activity 9

Considering the Structure of the Text

Fill in the spaces after each section with the content and/or purpose of the preceding paragraphs.

Going for the Look, but Risking Discrimination

by Steven Greenhouse
The New York Times, July 13, 2003

1   A funny thing happens when Elizabeth Nill, a sophomore at Northwestern University, goes shopping at Abercrombie & Fitch.

Activity 9 (Continued)

2   At no fewer than three Abercrombie stores, she says, managers have approached her and offered her a job as a clerk.

3   "Every time this happens, my little sister says, 'Not again,'" said Ms. Nill, who is 5-foot-6 and has long blond hair. She looks striking. She looks hip. She looks, in fact, as if she belongs in an Abercrombie & Fitch catalog.

4   Is this a coincidence? A fluke? No, says Antonio Serrano, a former assistant Abercrombie store manager in Scranton, Pa. It's policy.

Content and Purpose:

---

5   "If someone came in with a pretty face, we were told to approach them and ask them if they wanted a job," Mr. Serrano said. "They thought if we had the best-looking college kids working in our store, everyone will want to shop there."

6   Abercrombie's aggressive approach to building a pretty and handsome sales force, an effort that company officials proudly acknowledge, is a leading example of what many industry experts and sociologists describe as a steadily growing trend in American retailing. From Abercrombie to the cosmetics giant L'Oreal, from the sleek W hotel chain to the Gap, businesses are openly seeking workers who are sexy, sleek or simply good-looking.

7   Hiring for looks is old news in some industries, as cocktail waitresses, strippers and previous generations of flight attendants know all too well. But many companies have taken that approach to sophisticated new heights in recent years, hiring workers to project an image.

8   In doing so, some of those companies have been skirting the edges of antidiscrimination laws and provoking a wave of private and government lawsuits. Hiring attractive people is not necessarily illegal, but discriminating on the basis of age, sex or ethnicity is. That is where things can get confusing and contentious.

9   "If you're hiring by looks, then you can run into problems of race discrimination, national origin discrimination, gender discrimination, age discrimination and even disability discrimination," said Olophius Perry, director of the Los Angeles office of the Equal Employment Opportunity Commission, which has accused several companies of practicing race and age discrimination by favoring good-looking young white people in their hiring.

44 | GOING FOR THE LOOK   CSU EXPOSITORY READING AND WRITING COURSE | SEMESTER ONE

Activity 9
(Continued)

Content and Purpose:

10   Some chains, most notably the Gap and Benetton, pride them-selves on hiring attractive people from many backgrounds and races. Abercrombie's "classic American" look, pervasive in its store and catalogs and on its Web site, is blond, blue-eyed and preppy. Abercrombie finds such workers and models by concen-trating its hiring on certain colleges, fraternities and sororities.

11   The company says it does not discriminate. But in a lawsuit filed last month in Federal District Court in San Francisco, some Hispanic, Asian and black job applicants maintained otherwise. Several plaintiffs said in interviews that when they applied for jobs, store managers steered them to the stockroom, not to the sales floor.

12   In interviews, managers like Mr. Serrano described a recruiting approach used by Abercrombie, which has become one of the most popular retailers among the nation's youth.

13   "We were supposed to approach someone in the mall who we think will look attractive in our store," said Mr. Serrano, who said he quit when told he would be promoted only if he accepted a transfer. "If that person said, 'I never worked in retailing before,' we said: 'Who cares? We'll hire you.' But if someone came in who had lots of retail experience and not a pretty face, we were told not to hire them at all."

14   Tom Lennox, Abercrombie's communications director, emphati-cally denied job bias but acknowledged the company likes hir-ing sales assistants, known as brand representatives, who "look great."

15   "Brand representatives are ambassadors to the brand," Mr. Lennox said. "We want to hire brand representatives that will represent the Abercrombie & Fitch brand with natural classic American style, look great while exhibiting individuality, project the brand and themselves with energy and enthusiasm, and make the store a warm, inviting place that provides a social experience for the customer."

STUDENT VERSION

Content and Purpose:

16   Retailers defend that approach to hiring as necessary and smart, and industry experts see the point.

17   "In today's competitive retail environment, the methods have changed for capturing the consumers' awareness of your brand," said Marshal Cohen, a senior industry analyst with the NPD Group, a market research firm. "Being able to find a brand enhancer, or what I call a walking billboard, is critical. It's really important to create an environment that's enticing to the community, particularly with the younger, fashionable market. A guy wants to go hang out in a store where he can see good-looking gals."

Purpose:

18   While hiring by looks has a long history, some sociologists and retail consultants agree that the emphasis has increased—not at WalMart and other mass marketers, but at upscale businesses.

19   The federal government has accused some of the businesses of going too far. The hotel entrepreneur Ian Scharger agreed to a $1.08 million settlement three years ago after the Equal Employment Opportunity Commission accused his Mondrian Hotel in West Hollywood of racial discrimination for firing nine valets and bellhops, eight of them nonwhite. Documents filed in court showed that Mr. Schrager had written memos saying that he wanted a trendier group of workers and that the fired employees were "too ethnic."

20   Last month the commission reached a $5,000 settlement with 36th Street Food and Drink, a restaurant in St. Joseph, Mo., after accusing it of age discrimination against a 47-year-old waitress. The waitress, Michele Cornell, had worked at the restaurant for 23 years, but when it reopened after renovations, it refused to rehire her because, the commission said, she no longer fit the young, trendy look it had adopted.

21   "The problem with all this image stuff is it just reeks of marketing for this white-bread, Northern European, thin, wealthy, fashion-model look," said Donna Harper, supervisory attorney in the commission's St. Louis office. "We all can't be Anglo, athletic and young."

22   Ms. Harper said an employer who insisted on hiring only athletic-looking people could be viewed as discriminating against a person in a wheelchair. Employers who insisted on hiring only strapping, tall people might be found guilty of discriminating against Mexican-Americans or Asian-Americans, who tend to be shorter, she added.

23   Stephen J. Roppolo, a New Orleans lawyer who represents many hotels and restaurants, said: "Hiring someone who is attractive isn't illegal per se. But people's views on what's attractive may be influenced by their race, their religion, their age. If I think Caucasian people are more attractive than African-American people, then I may inadvertently discriminate in some impermissible way. I tell employers that their main focus needs to be hiring somebody who can get the job done. When they want to hire to project a certain image, that's where things can get screwy."

Purpose:

24   Image seemed very much in evidence the other evening at the Abercrombie & Fitch store in Water Tower Place, one of Chicago's most upscale malls. Working there was a 6-foot-2 sales clerk with muscles rippling under his Abercrombie T-shirt and a young long-haired blond clerk, her navel showing, who could have been a fashion model.

25   "If you see an attractive person working in the store wearing Abercrombie clothes, it makes you want to wear it, too," said Matthew Sheehey, a high school senior from Orland Park, a Chicago suburb.

Purpose:

26   Elysa Yanowitz says that when she was a West Coast sales manager for L'Oreal, she felt intense pressure to hire attractive saleswomen, even if they were incompetent. In fact, she says, company officials sought to force her out after she ignored an order to fire a woman a top manager described as not "hot" enough.

27   "It was pretty well understood that they had to have magazine-look quality," she said of the sales force. "Everyone is supposed to look like a 110-pound model."

28   L'Oreal officials did not respond to a request for comment.

Purpose:

29   Melissa Milkie, a sociology professor at the University of Maryland who has written about perceptions of beauty, said: "Good-looking people are treated better by others. Maybe companies have noticed that hiring them impacts their bottom line. Whether that's morally proper is a different question."

Purpose:

Analyzing Stylistic Choices

Words

Greenhouse's "Going for the Look" is about American retailing, in which advertising jargon often substitutes for ordinary language. What do the following phrases from paragraphs 15 and 17 *really* mean? Why do marketing experts use jargon?

- Brand representative
- Ambassadors to the brand
- Natural classic American style
- Social experience for the customer
- Brand enhancer

- Walking billboard
- Enticing to the community

Sentences

- Greenhouse writes about Elizabeth Nill, "She looks striking. She looks hip. She looks, in fact, like she belongs in an Abercrombie & Fitch catalog" (paragraph 3). Why does he repeat "She looks . . . "? Why does he says the third time, "She looks, in fact, as if she belongs in an Abercrombie & Fitch catalog"?
- In paragraph 19, why is "too ethnic" in quotation marks? How is this use of quotation marks different from their use with "classic American" in paragraph 10?

Paragraphs

- Look at paragraph 16. Why do you think it has only one sentence?
- How would you combine the short, journalistic paragraphs into longer ones that would each contain one main idea? Draw lines to show which paragraphs you would combine.

Essay

- Greenhouse quotes several different people. Using the tone you think they would use, read aloud what they say. What kind of person do you think each one is? How much do you think you can trust what they say? Why?

  1. **Mr. Serrano, a former Abercrombie & Fitch employee:**

     "We were supposed to approach someone in the mall who we think will look attractive in our store. If that person said, 'I never worked in retailing before,' we said: 'Who cares? We'll hire you.' But if someone came in who had lots of retail experience and not a pretty face, we were told not to hire them at all."

  2. **Tom Lennox, Abercrombie's communications director:**

     "Brand representatives are ambassadors to the brand. We want to hire brand representatives that will represent the Abercrombie & Fitch brand with natural classic American style, look great while exhibiting individuality, project the brand and themselves with energy and enthusiasm, and make the store a warm, inviting place that provides a social experience for the customer."

  3. **Marshal Cohen, a senior industry analyst with the NPD Group, a market research firm**

     "In today's competitive retail environment, the methods have changed for capturing the consumers' awareness of your brand. Being able to find a brand enhancer, or what I call a walking billboard, is critical. It's really important to create an environment that's enticing to the community, particularly with the younger, fashionable market. A guy wants to go hang out in a store where he can see good-looking gals."

4. Donna Harper, supervisory attorney in the Equal Employment Opportunity Commission's office in St. Louis

"The problem with all this image stuff is it just reeks of marketing for this white-bread, Northern European, thin, wealthy, fashion-model look. We all can't be Anglo, athletic and young."

- How formal or informal is "Going for the Look"? How would the text be different if it were intended for a group of retailers? What if it were intended for employment counselors who help people apply for jobs?

Postreading

Activity 11

Summarizing and Responding

Write a summary of the article. When you finish, exchange your summary with a partner. Use the Peer Response to Summary Form to evaluate your partner's summary/response.

Peer Response to Summary

1. Does the writer include the author's name in the first sentence of the summary?

Yes _____

Writer: Include the author's name.

No _____

2. Does the writer include the title of the essay in the first sentence of the summary?

Yes _____

Writer: Include the title of the essay.

No _____

Is the title in quotation marks?

Yes _____

Writer: Punctuate the title using quotation marks.

No _____

3. Does the first sentence clearly state the main idea of the article?

Yes _____

Writer: State the main idea in the first sentence. Make sure it is clear and accurate.

No _____

You can improve your first sentence by _____

_____

_____

4. Does the writer include all of the important ideas or supporting points from the essay?

Yes _____

Writer: You left out an important point (specify which):

No _____

_____

_____

_____

5. Does the writer use his/her own words?   Yes _____

Writer: You used the author's words instead of your own.
(Indicate where—give paragraph or line number.)   No _____

**6. Does the writer keep his/her own opinions *out*
of the summary?**   Yes _____

Writer: You mentioned your opinion in the summary.
(Indicate where—give paragraph or line number.)   No _____

Remember to save your opinion for your response!

(From *LS 15 Course Materials*, California State University, Sacramento; copyright 2003)

Thinking Critically

Work with your group to answer the assigned questions. Select a reporter to write down your group's answers. If you finish early, go on to the other questions. Then share your answers with the class.

Group 1

1. Why did Greenhouse tell the story of Elizabeth Nill's experience at Abercrombie & Fitch? What is your reaction to the story?
2. In the conclusion, Greenhouse quotes a sociology professor, Melissa Milkie, who says, "Maybe companies have noticed that hiring [good-looking people] impacts their bottom line" (paragraph 29). What does this mean? Is it a good justification?
3. Who do you think makes the best argument either for or against hiring for "the look"? Why?

Group 2

1. Have you observed stores or restaurants that seem to have hired their employees to project a certain image? How do you feel about this practice?
2. Do you think that Greenhouse represents both sides of the argument objectively or does he appeal to the reader's emotions? Give examples of either the way he is objective or the way he slants the arguments.
3. Stephen J. Roppolo, a New Orleans lawyer, says if employers hire on the basis of people's looks, they "may inadvertently discriminate in an impermissible way" (paragraph 23). Is he implying that the employers are discriminating because they are greedy and want to make a bigger profit? Why or why not?

Group 3

1. Greenhouse says, "That is where things can get confusing and contentious" (paragraph 8). What does "contentious" mean? What is this paragraph saying about the trend toward hiring people on the basis of looks?

2. What do you think of the argument that "a guy wants to go hang out in a store where he can see good-looking gals" (paragraph 17)? Do you think that statement is a fair way of making the retailers' argument?

3. Greenhouse says, "In doing so [hiring for looks], some of those companies have been skirting the edges of antidiscrimination laws and provoking a wave of private and government lawsuits" (paragraph 8). Do you think you would be justified in suing a company like Abercrombie's if they turned you down for a job and you thought it was because you weren't "blond, blue-eyed and preppy"? Why or why not?

Activity 13

Revisiting Key Vocabulary

Now that you have read and reread the article and have thought about the arguments it contains about hiring people according to their looks, it is time to look again at vocabulary. This time you are going to look at words you may want to use when you write about the issue. Fill in the blanks in the following sentences with the word that best fits the meaning from the list of words provided by your teacher.

1. Retailers want _____to recognize their brand so they will buy products from their store.

2. Stores that hire only attractive employees run the risk of _____ against other qualified applicants.

3. Abercrombie & Fitch offered Elizabeth Nill a job because they thought she _____ the right image.

4. It does not make sense for a store to hire someone who is _____simply because that person is good-looking.

5. Retailers contend that hiring on the basis of looks is not _____, but discriminating on the basis of age, sex, or ethnicity is.

6. Some job _____ claimed they were not given sales jobs because of the color of their skin.

7. Retailers _____ aggressively for their customers' business.

8. The hiring of workers who project a certain _____ can be part of a retailer's marketing strategy.

Writing Rhetorically

Prewriting

Activity 14	### Reading the Assignment

Reading the assignment carefully to make sure you address all aspects of the prompt is important.

On-Demand Writing Assignment

You will have 45 minutes to plan and write an essay on the topic assigned below. Before you begin writing, read the passage carefully and plan what you will say. Explain Cohen's argument and discuss the extent to which you agree or disagree with his analysis. Support your position, providing reasons and examples from your own experience, observations, or reading. Your essay should be as well-organized and carefully written as you can make it.

"Retailers defend the approach to hiring based on image as necessary and smart, and industry experts see the point. 'In today's competitive retail environment, the methods have changed for capturing the consumer's awareness of your brand,' said Marshal Cohen, a senior industry analyst with the NPD Group, a market research firm. 'Being able to find a brand enhancer, or what I call a walking billboard, is critical. It's really important to create an environment that's enticing to the community, particularly with the younger, fashionable market. A guy wants to go hang out in a store where he can see good-looking gals.'"

Explain Cohen's argument and discuss the extent to which you agree or disagree with his analysis. Support your position, providing reasons and examples from your own experience, observations, or reading.

Take the following steps for this exercise:

- Read the assignment carefully.
- Decide which issue you are going to discuss.
- Discuss the purpose of the assignment. What will you try to accomplish in your essay?

Activity 15	### Getting Ready to Write

1. What are the author's major claims?
2. What are the strongest claims? What are the weakest?
3. Have arguments been left out?
4. What can we infer about the author?
5. How does he appeal to our emotions?

Activity 16

Formulating a Working Thesis

Writing down a tentative thesis at this point is a good habit to develop in your writing process. Your thesis should be a complete sentence and can be revised several times. But a focused thesis statement will keep your writing on track.

Record your responses to the following questions in preparation for writing your tentative thesis statement.

- What specific question will your essay answer? What is your response to this question? (This is your tentative thesis.)
- What support have you found for your thesis?
- What evidence have you found for this support? For example, use facts, statistics, statements from authorities, personal experiences, anecdotes, stories, scenarios, and examples.
- How much background information do your readers need to understand your topic and thesis?
- If readers were to disagree with your thesis or the validity of your support, what would they say? How would you address their concerns (what would you say to them)?

Now draft a possible thesis for your essay.

Writing

Activity 17

Composing a Draft

When you write an argument essay, choose an approach to the subject that matters to you. If you have strong feelings, you will find it much easier to gather evidence and convince your readers of your point of view. Keep in mind, however, that your readers might feel just as strongly about the opposite side of the issue. The following guidelines will help you write a good argument essay.

1. **State your opinion on the topic in your thesis statement.** To write a thesis statement for an argument essay, you must take a stand for or against an action or an idea. In other words, your thesis statement should be debatable—a statement that can be argued or challenged and will not be met with agreement by everyone who reads it. Your thesis statement should introduce your subject and state your opinion about that subject.

Greenhouse's thesis is not explicit (he doesn't say it directly), but you can infer that his thesis is that retailers need to hire for appearance in order to attract consumers and increase profits. This is Cohen's position, and it is a debatable thesis. Some other statements about hiring for appearance would not be debatable and therefore would not be effective theses:

Not debatable: Today's retailers operate in a competitive environment.

Not debatable: Retailers want to create a shopping environment that attracts consumers.

Both examples are simply statements of fact that most people would agree are true. They would not be effective theses because no one would argue with them.

2. **Take your audience into consideration as you write your essay.** When you write your essay, assume that your audience is well-informed generally but may not have the specific knowledge that you have gained by reading "Going for the Look" and the discussions you had about it. You need to provide your readers with information and your source for that information whether you are citing statistics or paraphrasing someone else's argument. In a true timed-writing situation, you will not have access to sources other than short passages, but you can still refer to information you learned in a class, read in an article, or found on a Web site. Just be sure to mention where you found it (not a formal reference but an acknowledgment that it comes from another source).

You may also want to let your readers know who you are. Think about how you formed judgments about the various "authorities" that are quoted in "Going for the Look." You can let your readers know, for example, that you are a high school student and that you have had friends who may have been offered jobs at stores because of their "look." Your readers will understand that you are in a good position to make this observation.

You also need to assume that some of your readers will disagree with you (remember, your thesis is going to be debatable). Acknowledge some possible alternative positions and explain why they are not as strong as your own to help respond to potential objections. For example, Stephen Roppolo acknowledges that hiring someone who is attractive is not illegal. He gets that argument on the table before he goes on to his own argument that the "main focus needs to be hiring someone who can get the job done." Cohen, on the other hand, doesn't even acknowledge that arguments can be made against hiring based on image.

3. **Choose evidence that supports your thesis statement.** Evidence is probably the most important factor in writing an argument essay. Without solid evidence, your essay is nothing more than opinion; with it, your essay can be powerful and persuasive. If you supply convincing evidence, your readers will not only understand your position but perhaps agree with it.

Evidence can consist of facts, statistics, statements from authorities, and examples or personal stories. Examples and personal stories can be based on your own observations, experiences, and reading, but your opinions are not evidence. Other strategies, such as comparison/contrast, definition, and cause/effect, can be particularly useful in building an argument. Use any combination of evidence and writing strategies that supports your thesis statement.

In "Going for the Look," most of the evidence is from authorities who have varying degrees of credibility and personal stories. Here are some examples:

Statements from Authorities

- Statement by Olophius Perry, director of the Los Angeles office of the Equal Employment Opportunity Commission about the danger of discrimination from hiring on the basis of looks (paragraph 9).
- Claims from interviews used as evidence in the lawsuit against Abercrombie & Fitch (paragraphs 11–13).
- Quotation from Stephen J. Roppolo, a New Orleans lawyer who represents hotel and restaurants (paragraph 23).
- Quotation from Melissa Milkie, a sociology professor who has written about perceptions of beauty (paragraph 29).

Examples and Personal Stories

- Elizabeth Nill's personal story (paragraphs 1–5).

4. **Anticipate opposing points of view.** In addition to stating and supporting your position, anticipating and responding to opposing views are important. Presenting only your side of the argument leaves half the story untold—the opposition's half. If you acknowledge that there are opposing arguments and answer them, your reader will be more convinced of your argument.

Greenhouse presents the retailers' point of view that hiring based on appearance is "necessary and smart" by citing an expert, Marshal Cohen.

5. **Find some common ground.** Pointing out common ground between you and your opponent is also an effective strategy. Common ground refers to points of agreement between two opposing positions. For example, one person might be in favor of gun control and another strongly opposed. But they might find common ground—agreement—in the need to keep guns out of teenagers' hands. Locating some common ground is possible in almost every situation. When you state in your essay that you agree with your opponent on certain points, your reader sees you as a fair person.

In "Going for the Look," Roppolo attempts to find common ground. Instead of telling his business clients that what they are doing is illegal and immoral, Roppolo tells them that they "may inadvertently discriminate in some impermissible way" if they hire based on attractiveness. He implies that if they currently discriminate, it is by accident, not because they are bad or greedy. That makes it easier for them to then accept his advice to not discriminate when hiring.

6. **Maintain a reasonable tone.** Just as you probably wouldn't win an argument by shouting or making mean or nasty comments, don't expect your readers to respond well to such tactics. Keep the "voice" of your essay calm and sensible. Readers will be much more open to what you have to say if they think you are a reasonable person.

   Roppolo uses a reasonable tone. Donna Harper, the lawyer in St. Louis, uses a more strident tone: "The problem with all this image stuff is it just reeks of marketing for this white-bread, Northern European, thin, wealthy, fashion-model look." A retailer might be justifiably offended by her tone and therefore much less likely to take advice from her. However, she isn't trying to persuade store owners; she's trying to persuade a jury to convict store owners, so her tone is intentional.

7. **Organize your essay so that it presents your position as effectively as possible.** By the end of your essay, you want your audience to agree with you. So you need to organize your essay in such a way that your readers can easily follow it. The number of your paragraphs may vary (depending on the nature of your assignment), but the following outline shows the order in which the features of an argument essay are most effective:

   Introduction
   - Background information
   - Introduction of subject
   - Statement of your opinion

   Body Paragraphs
   - Common ground
   - Lots of evidence (logical and emotional)
   - Opposing point of view
   - Response to opposing point of view

   Conclusion
   - Restatement of your position
   - Call for action or agreement

   The arrangement of your evidence in an argument essay depends to a great extent on your readers' opinions. Most arguments will be organized from general to particular, from particular to general, or from one extreme to another. When you know that your readers already agree with you, arranging your details from general to particular or from most to least important is usually most effective. With this order, you are building on your readers' agreement and loyalty as you explain your thinking on the subject.

   If you suspect that your audience does not agree with you, reverse the organization of your evidence and arrange it from particular to general or from least to most important. In this way, you can take

STUDENT VERSION

your readers step by step through your reasoning in an attempt to get them to agree with you.

Greenhouse's article follows the general outline just presented. Here is a skeleton outline of his essay:

Introduction

- Personal story of Elizabeth Nill
- Abercrombie & Fitch as an example of the trend toward hiring for looks

Body Paragraphs

- Discussion of the trend toward hiring workers to project an image and the legal issues it raises
- The Abercrombie & Fitch lawsuit
- The retailers' point of view that hiring for looks is necessary and smart
- Discrimination issues
- Additional examples of hiring for appearance in retail

Conclusion

- Quotation from expert focusing on the apparent conflict between a sound business strategy versus the morality of hiring based on looks

Activity 18

Organizing the Essay

The following items are traditional parts of all essays:

- An introduction (usually one or two paragraphs) that "hooks" the reader and provides a thesis statement or road map for the reader
- The body (as many paragraphs as necessary), which supports the thesis statement point by point
- A conclusion (usually only one paragraph) that summarizes the main points and explains the significance of the argument

The number of paragraphs in an essay depends on the nature and complexity of your argument.

Here are some additional hints to help you organize your thoughts.

Introduction

- You might want to include the following in your introductory paragraph or paragraphs:
  - A "hook" to get the reader's attention
  - Background information the audience may need
  - A thesis statement, along with some indication of how the essay will be developed ("forecasting"). *Note:* A thesis statement states the topic of the essay and the writer's position on that topic. You may choose to sharpen or narrow the thesis at this point.

Activity 18 (Continued)	**Body** • Paragraphs that present support of the thesis statement, usually in topic sentences supported with evidence. (See "Getting Ready to Write.") • Paragraphs that include different points of view or address counter-arguments • Paragraphs or sentences where the writer addresses those points of view by doing the following: – Refuting them – Acknowledging them but showing how the writer's argument is better – Granting them altogether but showing they are irrelevant • Evidence that you have considered the values, beliefs, and assumptions of your audience; your own values, beliefs, and assumptions; and whether you have found some common ground that appeals to the various points of view **Conclusion** • A final paragraph (or paragraphs) that includes a solid argument to support the thesis and indicates the significance of the argument—the "so what" factor
Activity 19	**Developing the Content** Here are a few highlights on essay development: • Most body paragraphs consist of a topic sentence (or an implied topic sentence) and concrete details to support that topic sentence. • Body paragraphs give evidence in the form of examples, illustrations, statistics, and so on and analyze the meaning of the evidence. • Each topic sentence is usually directly related to the thesis statement. • No set number of paragraphs makes up an essay. • The thesis dictates and focuses the content of an essay.

Revising and Editing

Activity 20	**Revising the Draft** You now need to work with the organization and development of your draft to make sure that your essay is as effective as possible. **Peer Group Work** In groups of three or four, each student should read his or her essay aloud to other members of the group. Then, for each essay, complete Part I of the Evaluation Form your teacher will supply.

Activity 20 (Continued)

Paired Work

Work in pairs to decide how you want to revise the problems that group members identified.

Individual Work

Revise the draft based on the feedback you have received and the decisions you have made with your partners. Consider these additional questions for individual work:

- Have I responded to the assignment?
- What is my purpose for this essay?
- What should I keep? What is most effective?
- Where do I need more details, examples, and other evidence to support my point?
- What could I get rid of? Did I use irrelevant details? Was I repetitive?
- What should I change? Are parts of my essay confusing or contra-dictory? Do I need to explain my ideas more fully?
- What should I rethink? Was my position clear? Did I provide enough analysis to convince my readers?
- How is my tone? Am I too overbearing or too firm? Do I need qualifiers?
- Have I addressed differing points of view?
- Does my conclusion show the significance of my essay?
- Have I used key vocabulary words correctly to represent the ideas from the article? Have I used words that refer to specific facts from the text?

Activity 21

Editing the Draft

You now need to work with the grammar and mechanics of your draft to make sure that your use of language is effective and conforms to the guidelines of standard written English.

Individual Work

Edit your draft based on the information you have received from your instructor or a tutor. Use the editing checklist provided by your teacher. The suggestions below will also help you edit your own work.

Editing Guidelines for Individual Work

- If possible, set your essay aside for 24 hours before rereading to find errors.
- If possible, read your essay out loud so you can hear your errors and rough spots.
- At this point, focus on individual words and sentences rather than overall meaning. Take a sheet of paper and cover everything except the line you are reading. Then touch your pencil to each word as you read.
- With the help of your teacher, figure out your own pattern of errors— the most serious and frequent errors you make.

- Look for only one type of error at a time. Then go back and look for a second type, and if necessary, a third.
- Use the dictionary to check spelling and confirm that you've chosen the right word for the context.

Activity 22

Reflecting on the Writing

When you have completed your own essay, answer these six questions:

1. What was most difficult about this assignment?
2. What was easiest?
3. What did you learn about arguing by completing this assignment?
4. What do you think are the strengths of your argument? Place a wavy line by the parts of your essay that you feel are very good.
5. What are the weaknesses, if any, of your paper? Place an X by the parts of your essay you would like help with. Write any questions you have in the margin.
6. What did you learn from this assignment about your own writing process—about preparing to write, about writing the first draft, about revising, and about editing?

Page 62 is blank

Sample Student Essays

Going for the Look

On-Demand Writing Assignment

You will have 45 minutes to plan and write an essay on the topic assigned below. Before you begin writing, read the passage carefully and plan what you will say. Explain Cohen's argument and discuss the extent to which you agree or disagree with his analysis. Support your position, providing reasons and examples from your own experience, observations, or reading. Your essay should be as well-organized and carefully written as you can make it.

> "Retailers defend the approach to hiring based on image as necessary and smart, and industry experts see the point. 'In today's competitive retail environment, the methods have changed for capturing the consumer's awareness of your brand,' said Marshal Cohen, a senior industry analyst with the NPD Group, a market research firm. 'Being able to find a brand enhancer, or what I call a walking billboard, is critical. It's really important to create an environment that's enticing to the community, particularly with the younger, fashionable market. A guy wants to go hang out in a store where he can see good-looking gals.'"

Explain Cohen's argument and discuss the extent to which you agree or disagree with his analysis. Support your position, providing reasons and examples from your own experience, observations, or reading.

The sample student essays that follow reflect the EPT Scoring Guide's criteria.

Sample student essay with a score of 6:

Portable Posters

In today's society, marketing is being taken to new heights. Not only do companies spend a majority of their money on advertising, they also use their employees as portable posters. If employees are supposed to be "walking billboards," then most people would agree that not everyone will be eligible for that particular position. Discrimination is defined as showing favor unjustly. What some corporations are doing today is clearly unjust. People cannot control their appearance completely. Therefore, I must agree with Steven Greenhouse, the author of "Going for the Look, but Risking Discrimination." Mr. Greenhouse has clearly shown in his article that only hiring certain people that "look great," is definitely discrimination and should not occur. That is why I disagree with Mr. Cohen's analysis. It is a known fact that one cannot sell everything by appearance alone.

Mr. Cohen is a senior industry analyst with the NPD Group, a market research firm. He said, "Retailers defend the approach to hiring based on image as necessary and smart, and the industry experts see the point." I thought that people were supposed to be hired based on their ability. In fact, Stephen J. Roppolo, a New Orleans lawyer who represents many hotels and restaurants, said "I tell employers that their main focus needs to be hiring somebody who can get the job done." Hiring for looks must be fairly risky from a legal standpoint because even lawyers that represent the businesses are saying that they should hire based on merit so that they do not get into trouble with the law.

I have seen some first hand examples of questionable hiring practices. Many of the restaurants near my home are excellent examples of hiring based on appearance. At the restaurants, I have noticed that the servers are usually Caucasian and that the bus-boys and chefs tend to be Mexican-Americans. I have also noticed that the Chinese restaurants in my area only have Asian-Americans as waiters and waitresses. I thought that America was on the way to becoming a place full of equal opportunity. Apparently, we are taking a step back, instead of moving forward.

Is hiring based on how attractive people are illegal? No, there is not a specific law saying that businesses cannot. Just because it is not illegal does not mean that it should be done. I feel that Mr. Cohen's analysis is not correct. If a company had an extremely innovative and sought after product due to its wide range of uses and quality, the company would not need to stoop to such discriminatory hiring practices. The product would simply sell itself. After all, every company would love to get by without spending one dime on advertising. Imagine a world where everyone was hired based on merit. Productivity would increase everywhere because people would be doing what they are best at instead of just standing around and "looking great."

6

Commentary

This essay illustrates the EPT Scoring Guide's criteria for a score of 6. The superior response indicates that the writer is very well-prepared to handle college-level reading and writing.

- The writer understands and focuses clearly on the topic raised by the quotation in the thesis, " . . . only hiring certain people that 'look great,' is definitely discrimination and should not occur."
- The summary of Cohen's argument is clear and accurate, and the paraphrasing is effective.

- The writer analyzes the issue of hiring for looks thoughtfully and has developed an insightful response focused on the legal implications of the practice.
- The essay is coherently organized and developed with a body paragraph of analysis and a paragraph citing the example of hiring on the basis of appearance in ethnic restaurants, which extends the response beyond that which is provided in the reading passage. The conclusion makes a strong case for hiring on the basis of merit.
- The writer demonstrates a strong command of language and syntactic variety, alternating fluent, longer sentences with short sentences to make a point.
- The essay is virtually error-free and reflects the writer's command of the conventions of incorporating the words and ideas of others into the writer's response to an argument.

Sample student essay with a score of 5:

Discrimination Vs Wealth

One of the biggest problems causing separation in today's society is discrimination based on looks. Our morality is constantly decreasing due to greed and selfishness. At one point in time we focused on the well being of every human being no matter their race, color or gender; looks meant nothing while love and friendships meant everything. On the contrary to Marshal Cohen's statement that a "brand enhancer" or a "walking bill board" is critical, hiring people based on looks is not morally correct, and morality should be held above money and reputation.

Hiring by looks can cause numerous amounts of issues, both at the governmental level and the emotional level. As Olophius Perry stated in the article, Going for the Look but Risking Discrimination, "If you're hiring by looks, then you can run into problems of race discrimination, national origin discrimination, gender discrimination, age discrimination, and even disability discrimination."(Greenhouse 1). Our country specifically was founded on equality and equal opportunity for all. When businesses start hiring based on looks and/or gender, our country's morals begin to slip slowly through Uncle Sam's fingers. Discrimination of any sort may also cause a person great emotional damage. Perhaps a hard working, well-kept, person was turned away from a job because of his or her un-attractive face, that person could be so hurt that they commit suicide; while one person gets richer because of this life changing decision they made, another person's sanity is lost. This type of discrimination is not worth the pain and suffering of one human being in return for fame and money.

Young men and women are used as sex symbols in today's twisted society. Many companies will hire young attractive women based on their beauty with the intention of giving men something to look at as well as giving them an incentive to come into their store. As Marshal Cohen replied, "A guy wants to go hang out in a store where he can see good looking gals" (Greenhouse 3) shows that companies hire these girls only to bring in more profits by using them as an object, rather than a person, that men can drool over. What kind of messages are we sending to our future generations? Is it that girls must learn that they will not receive respect and that they need to weigh 110 pounds with big lips in order to be successful in life? Pressures are enormously overwhelming on today's young adults to look "perfect" in society's eyes. The pressures build up and eventually lead to up to unhealthy alternatives to being skinny, becoming "built", or having the exact look being sought. While our society may look better if we allow companies to hire by looks, it is also increasingly becoming unhealthy.

In conclusion, hiring based on looks solely to raise profits is ethically and morally wrong. This idea will eventually bring our morality to an end. Health rates will drop and human sanity will continue to be taken away. In order to save our society and its morals, we should ban discrimination, or as some would call it hiring based on looks.

Commentary

This essay illustrates the EPT Scoring Guide's criteria for a score of 5. The clear competence of the essay indicates that this writer is quite ready to handle college-level reading and writing.

- The writer understands the topic and accurately summarizes Cohen's position, using his phrases "brand enhancer" and "walking bill board." The essay's thesis is clear, but the writer could have sharpened it by refraining from presenting it as a three-part divided thesis.
- The essay reflects the writer's understanding of some of the complexity of the issue. The analysis of the impact of the practice of "hiring for the look" on young adults' self-image is thoughtful and adds depth, but the assertion that it causes insanity and suicides is unsubstantiated.
- The essay is well-organized and coherent, with the writer focusing on the legal implications of hiring on the basis of looks in the first body paragraph and the individual implications in the second. Each paragraph is thoroughly developed, and the conclusion presents a strong recommendation.
- The essay displays some syntactic variety and facility, with occasional lapses in word choice and sentence construction.
- The essay has scattered errors in grammar, usage, and mechanics (e.g., "numerous amounts of issues," "using them as an object, rather than a person, that men can drool over").

Sample student essay with a score of 4:

Beauty = Money

Marshall Cohen's argument is basically that beautiful women sell, and I strongly agree. It's true that guys want to hang out in places where there are beautiful women. It's also true that these women represent an image and that if that image is pleasing to the eye then other women will want to emulate it.

5

Being a guy, I know the power women have over us as a gender; especially the good looking ones. The fact is that businesses know this and exploit it. Last year alone I must have spent a good 300 dollars because a cute girl would ask me to donate to the charity, or that I looked good in a pair of pants she wanted me to buy. Also, it's how most guys decide on things. Take for instance if there were two restaurants that served similar food. We would almost always end up going to the one with the good looking waitresses. Guys are suckers for cute girls and will spend great amounts of time and money just to the around them. However, men aren't nearly as bad as women.

When the average girl sees a super model or Britney Spears wearing Abercrombie and Fitch they think the key to being beautiful and popular is to match their wardrobes. They feel that if they dress like their idols they'll be more important in the public eye. I have a friend that buys every outfit she sees Mandy Moore wear on television. It's already cost her over a thousand dollars, but she doesn't mind just as long as people make her feel important.

In the end using beautiful people to advertise your product translates to one thing: money. The equation is simple, the better the girl looks the more money you make, and as long as the public sees beauty as only skin deep this will always be true.

4

Commentary

This essay illustrates the EPT Scoring Guide's criteria for a score of 4. This adequate response to the topic suggests that the writer should be able to handle college-level reading and writing.

- The writer demonstrates a generally accurate but somewhat simplistic understanding of the passage, summarizing it as "beautiful women sell." The writer accepts this argument on the basis of his own experience and develops his response accordingly.
- The essay maintains a clear focus on the point. It is organized around the assertion that both men and women are attracted to businesses that "hire for the look." However, it never acknowledges the legal or moral counterarguments to this position.
- The personal examples support the writer's position and are developed in some detail, but the essay would have been strengthened by more analysis of the issues.
- The language is fluent and often colloquial ("Guys are suckers for cute girls"), in keeping with the writer's personal approach to the topic. However, some sentences are not formed correctly (e.g., " . . . because a cute girl would ask me to donate to the charity, or that I looked good. . . ."; "Take for instance if there were two restaurants that served similar food.")
- The essay generally demonstrates control of grammar, usage, and mechanics.

Going For the Look

There are three types of people in the world when it comes to style. There are the fashionable, who care what they look like and what other people think. There are the unfashionable, who think they are fashionable but do not run with the trend. Then there are the people in between. They could care less what others think.

To try to get people to buy their products, a producer will look at all three types of people and chose the one that best fits the product. So the Gap would choose someone who looks good in their product. There are certain clothes that fit certain bodies certain ways. People do not want to see a fat, ugly person in tight pants and a short shirt.

A place like Hot Topic wants to draw in a punk rocker crowed so they will hire people that look as if they are punk rockers. These people will have many piercings and tattoos that are visible to the public. Only certain people do not think that that stuff is not attractive and Hot Topic wants to bring them into the store.

Thrift stores and hand me down stores would hire the last type of person. People who shop at those stores do not care what they look like or cannot afford to shop anywhere else. These people cannot choose what the person selling their clothes looks like.

In conclusion, there are three types of people in the fashion industry. Some are shoe-ins for certain jobs just from what they look like. Others cannot get those jobs if they tried. Cohen's statement is correct. Now a day people hire for looks not skill.

3

Commentary

This essay illustrates the EPT Scoring Guide's criteria for a score of 3. Although the essay suggests a developing competence, it is flawed in significant ways that suggest the writer's need for additional practice before being ready to succeed in college-level reading and writing.

- The writer does not explain Cohen's argument, instead writing an essay about style.
- The thesis, "There are three types of people in the world when it comes to style," does not focus on the issue of "hiring for the look." The writer addresses the issue in the body of the essay by saying that Gap and Hot Topic hire people who look good in the company's clothes, while thrift stores have no choice in who they hire; however, the writer directly addresses Cohen's argument only in the final sentences.
- The body paragraphs are series of assertions that lack effective transitions.
- Most of the sentences lack variety (e.g., the series of "There are . . ." sentences in the introduction), and word choice is imprecise ("that stuff").
- The essay has an accumulation of errors, especially in spelling and punctuation.

Going for the Look

Cohen's argument expresses his oppions and his only the may not matter in the sites of other people. I don't agree or disagree with his argument. I hold this position because of three reasons, for starters is the retailers choice who he or she wants to hire not his. And for there businesses to expand and to grow then they must hire whoever appeals to the consumer. Last his argument may or may not be true and tell complete truth, so I'm not going to base my facts or opions on him because sometimes you should keep them to your self.

As I Said before it is the retailers choice who they want to hire and if you must ensist on talking bad about these people then you must have problems with yourself maybe your jellous, just because your not in the positon to hire whoever you want doesn't mean the people that do make those choices wheather they are right or wrong.

The retailers must hire the right personel to appeal to the consumer if that means only hireing whites, just blacks or purple, green, yellow it does not matter because that is what they have to do to sell there product.

My third and final reason is that I don't really want to agree or disagree baed on the facts that he is giving me are more better things to worry about then I some stores have racial issues that is there business not yours.

To conclude Cohen argument expresses his own oppions that might be better kept to himself.

2

Commentary

This essay illustrates the EPT Scoring Guide's criteria for a score of 2. The serious flaws here indicate that this writer will need considerable additional practice before being ready to succeed in college-level reading and writing.

- The writer demonstrates a basic understanding of the passage but is unable to respond meaningfully to the topic, instead resorting to a personal attack on Cohen.
- The writer fails to respond to Cohen's argument with a focused thesis. The sentence "I don't agree or disagree with this argument" suggests a failure to understand the need to take a position and provide evidence to support it.
- Although the writer attempts three body paragraphs, they are severely underdeveloped.
- The writer lacks basic control of syntax and vocabulary.
- The writer has serious and persistent errors in grammar, usage, and mechanics that severely interfere with meaning. In particular, the sentence boundary errors and serious spelling errors obscure the meaning.

Their many methods of hiring people. Many markets know hire just because of the image of a person. In my opinion I agree and disagree to a certain point. Their could be certain stores that have people who have expirence, no experience, and just for the look.

When you have a pearson who has experience you could expeted from them to accomplished their job. They would always be on time or even earlier. You would not hear bad comments about that person Their very reasponsable and would not complain about geting their job done

Commentary

1

This essay illustrates the EPT Scoring Guide's criteria for a score of 1. The fundamental deficiencies of this essay clearly indicate that the writer needs much additional practice to be ready to succeed at college-level reading and writing.

- The writer indicates only a slight understanding of the passage and fails to refer to Cohen's argument.
- The essay seems to be about qualifications for jobs, with one qualification being "the look." However, the relationship of the thesis to the topic is not clear. The sentence, "In my opinion I agree and disagree to a certain point" suggests a serious lack of focus.
- The essay appears to be incomplete, with the second and third body paragraphs and the conclusion implied by the thesis but unwritten.
- The writer lacks basic control of syntax and vocabulary.
- The writer has serious and persistent errors in mechanics that severely interfere with meaning. Spelling and verb form errors are pervasive.

The Rhetoric of the Op-Ed Page:
Ethos, Pathos, and Logos

Module 3

The Rhetoric of the Op-Ed Page: Ethos, Pathos, and Logos

Teacher Version

Reading Rhetorically

Prereading 2
   Introducing Key Concepts 2
   Getting Ready to Read 2
   Surveying the Text 4
   Making Predictions and Asking Questions 5
   Introducing Key Vocabulary 6

Reading 8
   First Reading 8
   Looking Closely at Language 9
   Rereading the Text 10
   Analyzing Stylistic Choices 11
   Considering the Structure of the Text 13

Postreading 17
   Summarizing and Responding 17
   Thinking Critically 17

Connecting Reading to Writing

Writing to Learn 19
Using the Words of Others 19

Writing Rhetorically

Prewriting 21
   Reading the Assignment 21
   Getting Ready to Write 22

Writing 24
   Composing a Draft 24

Revising and Editing 24
   Revising the Draft 24
   Editing the Draft 25

Evaluating and Responding 27
   Responding to Student Writing 27
   Alternative On-Demand Writing Assignment 28

Reading Selections

"Three Ways to Persuade" 29
"A Change of Heart About Animals" 33
Letters to the editor in response to "A Change of Heart
   About Animals" 36

Student Version

Activity 1: Getting Ready to Read 37
Activity 2: Surveying the Text 38
Activity 3: Making Predictions and Asking Questions 38
Activity 4: Introducing Key Vocabulary 39
Activity 5: First Reading 40
Activity 6: Looking Closely at Language 40
Activity 7: Rereading the Text 40
Activity 8: Analyzing Stylistic Choices 41
Activity 9: Considering the Structure of the Text 42
Activity 10. Summarizing and Responding 42
Activity 11: Thinking Critically 43
Activity 12: Using the Words of Others 44
Activity 13: Reading the Assignment 46
Activity 14: Getting Ready to Write 46
Activity 15: Composing a Draft 47
Activity 16: Revising the Draft 48
Activity 17: Editing the Draft 49

Evaluation Form 51

Sample Student Letters to the Editor

Writing Assignment and Scored Student Letters
   to the Editor 53

Three Ways to Persuade

by John R. Edlund

1 Over 2,000 years ago the Greek philosopher Aristotle argued that there were three basic ways to persuade an audience that you were right: *ethos, logos,* and *pathos.*

Ethos: The Writer's Character or Image

2 The Greek word *ethos* is related to our word "ethics" or "ethical," but a more accurate modern translation might be "image." Aristotle uses ethos to refer to the speaker's character as it appears to the audience. Aristotle says that if we believe that a speaker has good sense, good moral character, and goodwill, we are inclined to believe what that speaker says to us. Today we might add that a speaker should also appear to have the appropriate expertise or authority to speak knowledgeably about the subject matter. *Ethos* is an important factor in advertising, both for commercial products and in politics. For example, when an actor in a pain reliever commercial puts on a doctor's white coat, the advertisers are hoping that wearing this coat will give the actor the authority to talk persuasively about medicines. Of course, in this case the actor's *ethos* is a deceptive illusion.

3 In our society, sports heroes, popular actors and actresses, and rock stars are often seen as authorities on matters completely unrelated to their talents. This is an instance of the power of image. Can you think of some examples?

4 A writer's *ethos* is created largely by word choice and style. Student writers often have a problem with *ethos* because they are asked to write research papers, reports, and other types of texts as if they have authority to speak persuasively, when in fact they are newcomers to the subject matter and the discourse community. Sometimes students try to create an academic image for themselves by using a thesaurus to find difficult and unusual words to sprinkle throughout their texts. Unfortunately, this sort of effort usually fails, because it is difficult to use a word correctly that you have not heard or read in context many times.

5 Sometimes a writer or speaker will use what is called an *ad hominem* argument, an argument "against the man." In this strategy, the writer attacks the character or personality of the speaker instead of attacking the substance of his or her position. This kind of argument is usually considered to be a logical fallacy, but it can be very effective and is quite common in politics.

Questions for Discussion

1. What kind of image do you want to project to your audience?
2. What can you do to help project this image?
3. What words or ideas do you want to avoid in order to not harm your image?
4. What effect do misspelled words and grammatical errors have on your image?

Logos: Logical Arguments

6   In our society, logic and rationality are highly valued, and this type of persuasive strategy is usually privileged over appeals to the character of the speaker or to the emotions of the audience. However, formal logic and scientific reasoning are usually not appropriate for general audiences, so we must rely on a more rhetorical type of reasoning.

7   For Aristotle, formal arguments are based on what he calls "syllogisms." This is reasoning that takes the following form:

All men are mortal.
Socrates is a man.
Therefore, Socrates is mortal.

8   However, Aristotle notes that in ordinary speaking and writing we often use what he calls a rhetorical syllogism or an "enthymeme." This is an argument in which some of the premises remain unstated or are simply assumed. For example, no one in ordinary life would think that Socrates could be immortal. We would simply *assume* that Socrates could be killed or that he would die of natural causes after a normal lifespan. Not all assumptions are as trivial as this one, however.

9   For example, when bubonic plague swept through Europe and parts of Asia in the fourteenth century, killing as much as three-quarters of the population in less than 20 years, it was not known how the disease was spread. At one point, people thought that the plague was spread by cats. If you *assume* that cats spread the disease, the obvious solution to the problem is to eliminate the cats, and so people began killing cats on sight. However, we now know that plague is spread by fleas, which live on rats. Because cats kill rats, killing off the cat population led to an increase in the rat population, a corresponding increase in plague-carrying fleas, and thus an increase in cases of plague in humans. Killing off the cats was a logical solution to the problem of plague, but it was based on a faulty assumption.

10   Rhetorical arguments are often based on probabilities rather than certain truth. The people of medieval Europe really had no way to determine what the real cause of the plague was, but they felt that they had to do something about it, and the cat hypothesis seemed probable to them. Unfortunately, this is true of many of the problems we face even today; we can not know with absolute certainty what the real solution is, yet we must act anyway.

11   Persuasion, to a large extent, involves convincing people to accept our assumptions as probably true. Similarly, exposing questionable assumptions in someone else's argument is an effective means for preparing the audience to accept the writer's own contrary position.

Questions for Discussion

1. Imagine some arguments that start from faulty assumptions, such as "If pigs could fly," or "If money grew on trees." What would be some of the logical consequences?

2. Do logical arguments provide better support for a position than arguments that are based on authority or character? In other words, would you support a policy just because a celebrity or an important expert supported it?
3. Can you think of a time when you used a logical argument to persuade someone of something? What was it?

Pathos: **The Emotions of the Audience**

12   Most of us think that we make our decisions based on rational thought. However, Aristotle points out that emotions such as anger, pity, and fear (and their opposites) powerfully influence our rational judgments. Due to this fact, much of our political discourse and much of the advertising we experience is directed toward moving our emotions.

13   Anger is a very powerful motivating force. Aristotle points out that if we want to make an audience angry we need to know three things: (1) the state of mind of angry people; (2) who the people are that this audience usually gets angry at; and (3) on what grounds this audience gets angry at those people. The recent breakup of Yugoslavia into separate countries provides many examples of the power of this kind of rhetoric. Yugoslavia was created after the Second World War out of several smaller states, including Croatia, Serbia, Bosnia-Herzegovena, and Slovenia. Within each state there were ethnic and religious minorities with long histories of conflict. While Yugoslavia was under the control of the Soviet Union, these conflicts were kept in check by military force. With the collapse of the Soviet Union, new political structures were necessary, and political opportunities arose for the ambitious. The leaders of various factions, understanding Aristotle's three points very well, began to mobilize their followers to war by reminding them of their historical grievances against other groups. Serbian leaders published photographs of atrocities allegedly committed by Croatians during WWII, reviving a conflict from 50 years earlier. Individuals were inspired through this angry rhetoric to attack, rape, and kill, simply because of their ethnicity or religion, neighbors that had lived near them all their lives.

14   Many political decisions have an emotional motivation. For example, when a gunman with an assault rifle shot up a schoolyard full of children, people were suddenly interested in banning such weapons. In this case several emotions are involved, but perhaps the strongest one is pity for the small children and their families. The logical arguments for banning or not banning assault rifles had not changed at all, but people were emotionally engaged with the issue after this event and wanted to do something.

15   Many advertisements for consumer goods aim to make us insecure about our attractiveness or social acceptability, and then offer a remedy for this feeling in the form of a product. This is a common strategy for selling mouthwash, toothpaste, chewing gum, clothing, and even automobiles.

16   Appeals to the emotions and passions are very effective rhetorical techniques, and very common in our society. You may find it necessary to use them yourself.

Questions for Discussion

1. Can you think of an advertisement for a product or a political campaign that uses your emotions to persuade you to believe something? Describe it, and analyze how it works.
2. Do you think it is unfair or deceptive to try to use emotions to persuade people?
3. Have you ever made a decision based on your feelings that you regretted later?

A Change of Heart About Animals

by Jeremy Rifkin

They are more like us than we imagined, scientists are finding.

Los Angeles Times, September 1, 2003

1   Though much of big science has centered on breakthroughs in biotechnology, nanotechnology, and more esoteric questions like the age of our universe, a quieter story has been unfolding behind the scenes in laboratories around the world—one whose effect on human perception and our understanding of life is likely to be profound.

2   What these researchers are finding is that many of our fellow creatures are more like us than we had ever imagined. They feel pain, suffer and experience stress, affection, excitement, and even love—and these findings are changing how we view animals.

3   Strangely enough, some of the research sponsors are fast-food purveyors, such as McDonald's, Burger King, and KFC. Pressured by animal-rights activists and by growing public support for the humane treatment of animals, these companies have financed research into, among other things, the emotional, mental, and behavioral states of our fellow creatures.

4   Studies on pigs' social behavior funded by McDonald's at Purdue University, for example, have found that they crave affection and are easily depressed if isolated or denied playtime with each other. The lack of mental and physical stimuli can result in deterioration of health.

5   The European Union has taken such studies to heart and outlawed the use of isolating pig stalls by 2012. In Germany, the government is encouraging pig farmers to give each pig 20 seconds of human contact each day and to provide them with toys to prevent them from fighting.

6   Other funding sources have fueled the growing field of study into animal emotions and abilities.

7   Researchers were stunned recently by findings (published in the journal *Science*) on the conceptual abilities of New Caledonian crows. In controlled experiments, scientists at Oxford University reported that two birds named Betty and Abel were given a choice between using two tools, one a straight wire, the other a hooked wire, to snag a piece of meat from inside a tube. Both chose the hooked wire. Abel, the more dominant male, then stole Betty's hook, leaving her with only a straight wire. Betty then used her beak to wedge the straight wire in a crack and bent it with her beak to produce a hook. She then snagged the food from inside the tube. Researchers repeated the experiment, and she fashioned a hook out of the wire nine of out of 10 times.

8   Equally impressive is Koko, the 300-pound gorilla at the Gorilla Foundation in Northern California, who was taught sign language and has mastered more than 1,000 signs and understands several thousand English words. On human IQ tests, she scores between 70 and 95.

9   Tool-making and the development of sophisticated language skills are just two of the many attributes we thought were exclusive to our species. Self-awareness is another.

10   Some philosophers and animal behaviorists have long argued that other animals are not capable of self-awareness because they lack a sense of individualism. Not so, according to new studies. At the Washington National Zoo, orangutans given mirrors explore parts of their bodies they can't otherwise see, showing a sense of self. An orangutan named Chantek who lives at the Atlanta Zoo used a mirror to groom his teeth and adjust his sunglasses.

11   Of course, when it comes to the ultimate test of what distinguishes humans from the other creatures, scientists have long believed that mourning for the dead represents the real divide. It's commonly believed that other animals have no sense of their mortality and are unable to comprehend the concept of their own death. Not necessarily so. Animals, it appears, experience grief. Elephants will often stand next to their dead kin for days, occasionally touching their bodies with their trunks.

12   We also know that animals play, especially when young. Recent studies in the brain chemistry of rats show that when they play, their brains release large amounts of dopamine, a neurochemical associated with pleasure and excitement in human beings.

13   Noting the striking similarities in brain anatomy and chemistry of humans and other animals, Stephen M. Siviy, a behavioral scientist at Gettysburg College in Pennsylvania, asks a question increasingly on the minds of other researchers. "If you believe in evolution by natural selection, how can you believe that feelings suddenly appeared, out of the blue, with human beings?"

14   Until very recently, scientists were still advancing the idea that most creatures behaved by sheer instinct and that what appeared to be learned behavior was merely genetically wired activity. Now we know that geese have to teach their goslings their migration routes. In fact, we are finding that learning is passed on from parent to offspring far more often than not and that most animals engage in all kinds of learned experience brought on by continued experimentation.

15   So what does all of this portend for the way we treat our fellow creatures? And for the thousands of animals subjected each year to painful laboratory experiments? Or the millions of domestic animals raised under the most inhumane conditions and destined for slaughter and human consumption? Should we discourage the sale and purchase of fur coats? What about fox hunting in the English countryside, bull fighting in Spain? Should wild lions be caged in zoos?

16   Such questions are being raised. Harvard and 25 other U.S. law schools have introduced law courses on animal rights, and an increasing number

of animal-rights lawsuits are being filed. Germany recently became the first nation to guarantee animal rights in its constitution.

17   The human journey is, at its core, about the extension of empathy to broader and more inclusive domains. At first, the empathy extended only to kin and tribe. Eventually it was extended to people of like-minded values. In the nineteenth century, the first animal humane societies were established. The current studies open up a new phase, allowing us to expand and deepen our empathy to include the broader community of creatures with whom we share the Earth.

Jeremy Rifkin, author of *The Biotech Century,* is the president of the Foundation on Economic Trends in Washington, D.C.

Letters to the editor in response to "A Change of Heart About Animals"

Re "A Change of Heart About Animals," Commentary, Sept. 1: Jeremy Rifkin argues that science has shown that the differences between animals and humans are less than we think and that we should extend more "empathy" to animals. I disagree. In nature, animals naturally kill and eat each other. If the hawk does not care about the feelings of the rabbit that it eats, why should humans be any different? Is Rifkin saying that nature is wrong

Rifkin goes so far as to say that pigs need social contact and should be provided with toys. There are many real human children in the world who do not have these things. Are animals more important than human children? Should our society spend scarce resources on toys for pigs?

Anyone who has owned a pet knows that animals can feel pain, happiness, anger, and other simple emotions. Most people have heard a parrot or a mynah bird talk, but this is just imitation and mimicry. We don't need science to tell us that animals can do these things. However, does a parrot understand what it is saying? Can an animal write a poem, or even a grocery list?

Rifkin is simply an animal-rights activist hiding behind a handful of scientific studies. He wants to ignore human suffering and focus on animal discomfort. He wants animals to have more rights than humans. Let's not be fooled.

Bob Stevens

Many thanks to Jeremy Rifkin for showing us that science supports what we pet owners and animal-rights activists have known in our hearts all along: animals have feelings and abilities not very different from humans. I found the stories about Koko, the gorilla who is fluent in sign language, and Betty and Abel, the tool-making crows, intriguing and heartwarming. When will more people begin to realize that we share this world with many creatures deserving of our care and respect?

However, Rifkin should take his argument farther. Animals have a right to live without being confined, exploited, tormented, or eaten. That means no animal experimentation, no fur or leather clothing, and a vegan or vegetarian lifestyle. Meat eating and animal abuse lead to spiritual disturbance and physical disease. Let's free ourselves from the evils of the past and live in harmony with our fellow creatures!

Lois Frazier

The Rhetoric of the Op-Ed Page: Ethos, Logos, and Pathos

Reading selections for this module:

Edlund, John R. "Three Ways to Persuade."

Rifkin, Jeremy. "A Change of Heart About Animals." *Los Angeles Times.* 1 Sept. 2003: B15.

Edlund, John R. Letters to the editor in response to "A Change of Heart About Animals." 2003.

In this assignment sequence, you will learn how to use Aristotle's concepts of ethos, logos, and pathos to analyze editorials and opinion pieces. You will read an opinion piece about scientific studies of animal behavior and learn how to write a letter to the editor of a newspaper.

Reading Rhetorically

Prereading

Activity 1

Getting Ready to Read

This activity focuses on ways to persuade. Your teacher will give you an opportunity to define the term "persuade." Then read "Three Ways to Persuade" by John R. Edlund. When you finish the article, engage in the option assigned by your teacher.

Option 1: Think of something you tried to persuade a parent, teacher, or friend to do or believe. It might have been to buy or pay for something, to change a due date or a grade, to change a rule or decision, to go somewhere, or some other issue. What kinds of arguments did you use? Did you use logic? Did you use evidence to support your request? Did you try to present your own character in a way that would make your case more believable? Did you try to engage the emotions of your audience? Write a short description of your efforts to persuade your audience in this case.

Option 2: In a small group, discuss the strategies your friends use when they are trying to borrow a car, go to a concert, buy new clothes, or achieve some other desired result. Pick a situation and write a short skit showing those persuasive strategies in action.

Activity 1 (Continued)

Each skit should employ logical, emotional, and ethical persuasion. Rehearse and perform your skit for the class.

After you have completed the option assigned, discuss the following questions:

1. Do people use Aristotle's concepts of ethos, logos, and pathos every day, without thinking about it?
2. Do these concepts apply to politics and advertising as well as person-to-person persuasion?
3. Are there other means of persuasion that Aristotle did not discuss?

Activity 2

Surveying the Text

Look at the article "A Change of Heart About Animals" by Jeremy Rifkin. Think about the following questions:

1. Where and when was this article published?
2. Who wrote the article? Do you know anything about this writer? (Hint: Look at the end of the article.) How could you find out more?
3. What is the subtitle of the article? What does that tell you about what the article might say?
4. The article was published on the editorial page. What does that mean?

Activity 3

Making Predictions and Asking Questions

As you look at the text of "A Change of Heart About Animals," answer and then discuss the following questions:

1. What does it mean to have "a change of heart"?
2. What are some common ideas or feelings people have about animals?
3. What kinds of things might cause someone to change his or her ideas or feelings about animals?
4. What are some groups of people who have strong feelings about how animals are treated? What do you know about them? What do they usually believe?
5. What is a vegetarian or a vegan? Do you know anyone who is a vegetarian? What does he or she think about eating animals?
6. What do you know about the author? Do you think he might be a vegetarian?
7. The first paragraph mentions breakthroughs in biotechnology and nanotechnology. Do you think this article is about those things? Why or why not?
8. This article appeared in a newspaper. What does that mean about the audience? Is this an article for scientists?

Activity 3
(Continued)

9. What do you think is the purpose of this article? Does the writer want readers to change their minds about something?
10. Will the article be negative or positive in relation to the topic? Why?
11. What argument about the topic might it present? What makes you think so?
12. Turn the title into a question (or questions) to answer after you have read the text.

Activity 4

Introducing Key Vocabulary

When you read "A Change of Heart About Animals," you will need to know the following terms to understand the text:

humane and inhumane

cognitive

genetically wired

empathy

Think about words that you know that sound similar to these and may be related. For example, "humane" is related to "human," and "empathy" is related to the Greek word *pathos* in "Three Ways to Persuade."

Create a word tree based on the root of a word from the text or one listed above. Here is an example of a word tree for "cognitive."

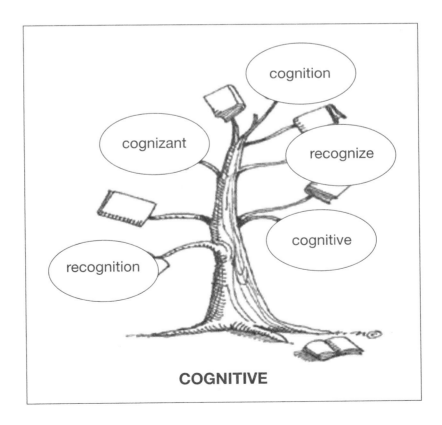

COGNITIVE

Reading

Activity 5

First Reading

Now you are ready to read Jeremy Rifkin's "A Change of Heart About Animals." For the first time through, you should read to understand the text. Read as if you trust Rifkin, and focus on what he is trying to say. Try to see whether the predictions you have made about the text are true. Is the article about what you thought it would be about? Does Rifkin say what you thought he would say? When you have finished reading, answer the following questions:

1. Which predictions turned out to be true?
2. What surprised you?
3. What does Rifkin want readers to believe?
4. What are some of the things people believe humans can do that animals cannot? How does Rifkin challenge those beliefs?
5. What authorities does Rifkin use to support his case?
6. What action does Rifkin want readers to take?
7. How does Rifkin organize his essay? Is it an effective organization?

Activity 6

Looking Closely at Language

Create a visual representation of "your" word, study its origin or history, and be prepared to share it (and its synonyms and antonyms) with the class. You might choose to construct a tree, chart, or table from Activity 4.

Activity 7

Rereading the Text

You should question the text in your second reading, "reading against the grain" and playing the disbelieving (or doubting) game. As you read, look for claims and assertions made by Rifkin. Does he back them up? Do you agree with them?

As you read, do the following:

- Underline (with a double underline) or highlight in one color the thesis and major claims or assertions made in the article.
- Underline (with a single underline) or highlight in a second color the evidence in support of the claims and assertions.
- Write your comments and questions in the margins.

After reading the article again, answer the following questions:

1. What is the thesis of Rifkin's article?
2. Are there any claims made by Rifkin that you disagree with? What are they?
3. Are there any claims that lack support?

Activity 8

Analyzing Stylistic Choices

Loaded Words: Language that Puts a Slant on Reality

Part A

Reread Rifkin's article, looking for "loaded" words—words Rifkin uses to evoke a positive or negative emotional response from the reader. List at least five words and explain whether each has a positive or negative connotation. What neutral word might Rifkin have used instead that has the same meaning but not the same emotional impact?

Rifkin's Word	Positive/Negative Connotation	Neutral Word/ General Denotation

Part B

Answer the following questions about the Rifkin article:

1. How would you describe the style of this article? Is it formal? Informal? Academic? Scientific? Conversational?
2. What is the effect of giving the names of most of the animals involved in the experiments, but not the names of the scientists?
3. Throughout most of the article, Rifkin refers to "researchers" and "scientists." In paragraph 13, however, he directly quotes Stephen M. Siviy, whom he refers to as "a behavioral scientist at Gettysburg College in Pennsylvania." What is the effect of this sudden specificity?
4. What is the effect of all the rhetorical questions in paragraph 15, followed by "such questions are being raised" in the next paragraph?

Activity 9

Considering the Structure of the Text

Now that you have read and discussed the content of the Rifkin essay, you are ready to begin analyzing the organizational structure. First, divide the text into sections:

- Draw a line across the page where the introduction ends. Is the line after the first paragraph, or are there more introductory paragraphs?
- Divide the body of the essay into sections on the basis of the topics addressed.
- Draw a line where the conclusion begins. Is it the last paragraph, or does it begin before that?

You are now ready to begin a process called "descriptive outlining":

- Write brief statements describing the rhetorical function and content of each paragraph or section.
  - What does each section do for the reader? What is the writer trying to accomplish?
  - What does each section say? What is the content?
- After making the descriptive outline, ask questions about the article's organizational structure:
  - Which section is the most developed?
  - Which section is the least developed? Does it need more development?
  - Which section is the most persuasive? The least?

From your work charting the text, what do you think is the essay's main argument? Is it explicit or is it implicit?

Postreading

Activity 10

Summarizing and Responding

Use the marginal comments you made in the "Considering the Structure of the Text" activity to write a concise summary of the Rifkin article.

Activity 11

Thinking Critically

At this point, the concepts of ethos, logos, and pathos come back into play. From the analysis you have done so far, you should be well-prepared to analyze the logic and support of the arguments, the character and intentions of the author, and the emotional effects on the reader of the language used and the details provided.

Questions about Logic (Logos)

1. Locate major claims and assertions you have identified in your previous analysis and ask yourself: Do I agree with Rifkin's claim that . . . ?
2. Look at support for major claims and ask yourself: Is there any claim that appears to be weak or unsupported? Which one, and why?
3. Can you think of counterarguments that the author does not deal with?
4. Do you think Rifkin has left something out on purpose? Why or why not?

Questions about the Writer (Ethos)

1. Who is Rifkin? If you have not done so already, do an Internet search to find out something about him. What is his profession? What does he usually write about? Does everybody agree with him? Do the facts you find about his life, his credentials, and his interests make him more credible to you? Less credible?
2. Pick one of the studies Rifkin mentions and try to find out more. Is Rifkin's description of the study accurate?
3. Does Rifkin have the right background to speak with authority on this subject?
4. What does the author's style and language tell you about him?
5. Do you trust this author? Do you think this author is deceptive? Why or why not?

Questions about Emotions (Pathos)

1. Rifkin says that Germany is encouraging farmers to give pigs human contact and toys. Does this fact have an emotional impact on the reader? If so, what triggers it? What are some other passages that have an emotional effect?
2. Rifkin calls his essay "A Change of Heart About Animals." Does this imply that the scientific discoveries he summarizes here should change how we *feel* about animals?
3. Does this piece affect you emotionally? Which parts?
4. Do you think Rifkin is trying to manipulate your emotions? How?
5. Do your emotions conflict with your logical interpretation of the arguments? In what ways?

Connecting Reading to Writing

Using the Words of Others

One of the most important features of academic writing is the use of the words and ideas from written sources to support the writer's own points. There are essentially three ways to incorporate words and ideas from sources:

- **Direct quotation.** Jeremy Rifkin says, "Studies on pigs' social behavior funded by McDonald's at Purdue University, for example, have found that they crave affection and are easily depressed if isolated or denied playtime with each other" (15).
- **Paraphrase.** In "A Change of Heart About Animals," Jeremy Rifkin notes that McDonald's has funded studies on pigs that show that they need affection and playtime with one another (15).
- **Summary.** In "A Change of Heart About Animals," Jeremy Rifkin cites study after study to show that animals and humans are more alike than we think. He shows that animals feel, reason, make and use tools, learn and use language, and mourn their dead. One study even shows that pigs need affection and playtime with one another, and enjoy playing with toys (15).

Documentation. You will also need to learn to take notes with full citation information. For print material, you will need to record, at a minimum, the author, title, city of publication, publisher, date of publication, and page number. The two most common documentation formats used are Modern Language Association (MLA), which is used mainly by English departments, and the American Psychological Association format (APA).

MLA Format

Books. Here is the Works Cited format for a typical book in MLA style:

Bean, John C., Virginia A. Chappell, and Alice M. Gilliam. *Reading Rhetorically: A Reader for Writers.* New York: Longman, 2002.

Newspapers. Here is the bibliographic information for the article quoted above, in MLA format. The fact that it was published in a newspaper changes the format and the information given somewhat:

Rifkin, Jeremy. "A Change of Heart About Animals." Editorial. *Los Angeles Times.* 1 Sept. 2003: B15.

Web Sites. To document a Web site, you will need to give the name of the author (if known), the title of the site (or a description, such as "Homepage," if no title is available), the date of publication or update (if known), the name of the organization that sponsors the site, the date of access, and the Web address (URL) in angle brackets. For example:

University Writing Center. 26 June 2003. University Writing Center, California Polytechnic State University, Pomona. 26 May 2004 <http://www.csupomona.edu/uwc/>.

The author for the above site is unknown, so no author name is given. This entry would appear in the Works Cited section alphabetized by "university."

In-Text Documentation. The MLA style also requires in-text documentation for every direct quotation, indirect quotation, paraphrase, or summary. Many students are confused about this, believing that documentation is necessary only for direct quotations. If the author is given in the text, the page number should be given in parentheses at the end of the sentence containing the material. For example, here is a paraphrase of material from the Rifkin article (because the author is not named in the text, his last name goes in parentheses):

It is well-established that animals can learn to use sign language. A long-term study at the Gorilla Foundation in Northern California shows that Koko, a 300-pound gorilla, can use more than 1,000 signs to communicate with her keepers and can understand several thousand English words. She also scores between 70 and 95 on human IQ tests (Rifkin 15).

An academic paper is most often a dialogue between the writer and his or her sources. When you learn to quote, paraphrase, summarize, and document sources correctly, you are well on your way to college-level writing.

This short discussion presents only the basic concepts of MLA documentation. You will also need access to the *MLA Handbook,* which covers the system in detail.

Practice with Sources. Choose three passages from the Rifkin article you might be able to use in an essay. You may want to choose passages you strongly agree or disagree with.

- First, write each passage down as a correctly punctuated and cited direct quotation.
- Second, paraphrase the material in your own words and provide the correct citation.
- Third, respond to the idea expressed in the passage by agreeing or disagreeing with it and explaining why, again with the correct citation.

Writing Rhetorically

Prewriting

Activity 13

Reading the Assignment

A common way to respond to an editorial is to write a letter to the editor. Now that you have worked extensively with this text, you are ready to write a well-informed response to Rifkin's ideas.

Writing Assignment

After thinking about your reading, discussion, and analysis of Rifkin's article and the letters in response to it, what do you personally think about Rifkin's point? Do you think it is true, as Rifkin says, that "many of our fellow creatures are more like us than we had ever imagined"? Do you think we need to change the way we treat the animals around us? Or do you think Rifkin is wrong? Write a letter expressing your viewpoint to the editor of the newspaper.

If you like, you may start out with "Dear Editor:"

Activity 14

Getting Ready to Write

Before you write your own letter in response to Rifkin, look at the two sample letters to the editor written in response to "A Change of Heart About Animals." Then discuss the following questions:

1. Bob Stevens disagrees with Rifkin and makes several points. Does Stevens refute Rifkin's arguments?
2. In his first paragraph, Stevens argues that because a predator (such as a hawk) does not feel empathy for its prey, humans do not need to feel empathy for the animals they eat and that such feelings would be unnatural. Do you agree?
3. Stevens notes that some animals can mimic human speech but argues that they do not understand what they are saying. What would Rifkin say to this?
4. Stevens implies that it would be a waste of resources to give toys to pigs, especially when some human children do not have them. Do we respond logically or emotionally to this argument? Is this argument fair to Rifkin?
5. Is it true, as Stevens argues, that Rifkin wants animals to have more rights than humans?
6. Lois Frazier says that pet owners know that animals have feelings and abilities not too different from humans. Do some pet owners treat their pets like people? Is this a good thing? Why or why not?

**Activity 14
(Continued)**

7. Frazier argues that Rifkin needs to take his argument further and promote a vegetarian lifestyle with no animal products. Is this a reasonable conclusion to draw from Rifkin's arguments? Do you agree with him?

Some things to note before writing your letter to the editor are as follows:

- A good letter to the editor is focused and concise. It should make your point, but no words should be wasted. It is sometimes best to write a longer draft, and then cut out everything that is not essential.
- Newspaper editors often cut letters to fit the available space or to make a letter more focused. If your letter is published unedited, you are very lucky.
- Some letters respond to the thesis of the editorial, either in support or disagreement, and provide further arguments or further evidence. Other letters focus on one point made by the original author and support it, question it, or refute it.
- These days, most letters are e-mailed to the newspaper. To get a letter published in a major newspaper, you must write it quickly and send it within a day or two of the publication date of the editorial to which you are responding.
- If the newspaper wants to publish your letter, you will normally receive a call or an e-mail to get permission and to verify that you really are who you say you are.
- Newspapers are interested in a wide range of viewpoints from diverse citizens. If your letter is a good expression of a particular viewpoint, brings up new information or arguments, or has some particularly good phrases, it has a good chance of being published.

Writing

Activity 15

Composing a Draft

Writing the first draft of your letter to the editor is a chance for you to organize your thoughts and get your ideas down on paper. Use any notes you made as you read and discussed the Rifkin article. Consider the suggestions about writing letters to the editor from Activity 14, and write your first draft.

Revising and Editing

Activity 16

Revising the Draft

The most natural way to improve a letter to the editor is to share it with others before you send it. Working with partners or in groups, share your drafts and give each other feedback. Listen to what others say—even those who disagree with you.

Peer Group Work

Break into groups of three or four. Each student will read his or her letter aloud to the other members of the group. Then complete Part I of the Revising Checklist (page 51) of the Evaluation Form for each member's letter.

Paired Work

Now work in pairs to decide how you want to revise the problems that group members have identified.

Individual Work

Revise the draft on the basis of the feedback you have received and the decisions you have made with your partner. Consider these additional questions for your individual work:

- Have I responded to the assignment?
- What is my purpose for this essay?
- What should I keep? What is the most effective?
- What should I add? Where do I need more details, examples, and other evidence to support my point?
- What could I omit? Do I use irrelevant details? Am I repetitive?
- What should I change? Are parts of my essay confusing or contradictory? Do I need to explain my ideas more fully?
- What should I rethink? Is my position clear? Do I provide enough analysis to convince my readers?
- How is my tone? Am I too overbearing or too firm? Do I need qualifiers?
- Have I addressed differing points of view?
- Does my conclusion show the significance of my essay?

Activity 17

Editing the Draft

Once you are satisfied with the tone and content of your letter, you should proofread it for spelling, grammar, and punctuation errors. The following guidelines will help you edit your draft.

Editing Guidelines for Individual Work

- If possible, set your essay aside for 24 hours before rereading it to find errors.
- Read your essay aloud to so you can hear errors and rough spots.
- At this point, focus on individual words and sentences rather than on overall meaning. Take a sheet of paper and cover everything except the line you are reading. Then touch your pencil to each word as you read.
- With the help of your teacher, figure out your own pattern of errors—the most serious and frequent errors you make.
- Look for only one type of error at a time. Then go back and look for a second type and, if necessary, a third.
- Use the dictionary to check spelling and to confirm that you have chosen the right word for the context.

The scoring guide on the next page may be used to evaluate your final product.

Scoring Guide for Letters to the Editor

Categories

- Focus
- Word choice, including the use of text from the article
- Argument and support, including the use of logical, emotional, and/or ethical appeals
- Grammar and mechanics

Scoring

Score of 4—Superior

- The letter is tightly focused on the issue or issues raised in the editorial, article, or opinion piece to which it responds.
- The letter uses words effectively and efficiently and quotes key words and phrases from the article.
- The letter makes a clear point or points and provides convincing support for those points, including logical, emotional, and/or ethical appeals.
- There are no grammatical or mechanical errors.

Score of 3—Good

- The letter focuses on an issue or issues raised in the editorial, article, or opinion piece to which it responds.
- The letter uses words accurately and effectively.
- The letter makes a clear point or points and provides support for those points.
- Grammatical or mechanical errors, if present, are minor.

Score of 2—Fair

- The letter discusses an issue or issues raised in the editorial, article, or opinion piece to which it responds but may be unclear or vague as to its focus.
- The letter is sometimes repetitive or vague in language.
- The letter does not make a clear point or does not provide support for its points.
- Grammatical or mechanical errors inhibit communication.

Score of 1—Poor

- The letter fails to clearly address an issue raised in the article.
- The letter is vague, repetitive, or confusing.
- The letter fails to make a clear point.
- Grammatical and mechanical errors confuse and distract the reader.

Evaluation Form

Based on the CSU English Placement Test (EPT)

Part I: Revising Checklist—Mark the appropriate categories.

	Superior	Strong	Adequate	Marginal	Weak	Very Weak	Comments
Response to the topic	Addresses the topic clearly and responds effectively to all aspects of the task.	Addresses the topic clearly but may respond to some aspects of the task more effectively than others.	Addresses the topic but may slight some aspects of the task.	Distorts or neglects aspects of the task.	Indicates confusion about the topic or neglects important aspects of the task.	Suggests an inability to comprehend the question or to respond meaningfully to the topic.	
Understanding and use of the assigned reading	Demonstrates a thorough critical understanding of the assigned reading in developing an insightful response.	Demonstrates a sound critical understanding of the assigned reading in developing a well-reasoned response.	Demonstrates a generally accurate understanding of the assigned reading in developing a sensible response.	Demonstrates some understanding of the assigned reading but may misconstrue parts of it or make limited use of it in developing a weak response.	Demonstrates very poor understanding of the main points of the assigned reading. Does not use the reading appropriately in developing a response or may not use the reading at all.	Demonstrates little or no ability to understand the assigned reading or to use it in developing a response.	
Quality and clarity of thought	Explores the issues thoughtfully and in depth.	Shows some depth and complexity of thought.	May treat the topic simplistically or repetitively.	Lacks focus or demonstrates confused or simplistic thinking.	Lacks focus and coherence and often fails to communicate ideas.	Is unfocused, illogical, or incoherent.	
Organization, development, and support	Is coherently organized and developed, with ideas supported by apt reasons and well-chosen examples.	Is well-organized and developed, with ideas supported by appropriate reasons and examples.	Is adequately organized and developed, generally supporting ideas with reasons and examples.	Is poorly organized and developed, presenting generalizations without adequate support or details without generalizations.	Has very weak organization and development, providing simplistic generalizations without support.	Is disorganized and undeveloped, providing little or no relevant support.	
Syntax and command of language	Has an effective, fluent style marked by syntactic variety and a clear command of language.	Displays some syntactic variety and facility in the use of language.	Demonstrates adequate use of syntax and language.	Has limited control of syntax and vocabulary.	Has inadequate control of syntax and vocabulary.	Lacks basic control of syntax and vocabulary.	
Grammar, usage, and mechanics (See list on next page for details)	Is generally free from errors in grammar, usage, and mechanics.	May have a few errors in grammar, usage, and mechanics.	May have some errors but generally demonstrates control of grammar, usage, and mechanics.	Has an accumulation of errors in grammar, usage, and mechanics that sometimes interfere with meaning.	Is marred by numerous errors in grammar, usage, and mechanics that frequently interfere with meaning.	Has serious and persistent errors in grammar, usage, and mechanics that severely interfere with meaning.	

STUDENT VERSION

Part II: Editing Checklist

Problem	Questions	Comments
Sentence boundaries	Are there fragments, comma splices, or fused sentences?	
Word choice	Are word choices appropriate in meaning, connotation, and tone?	
Subject-verb agreement	Do main verbs agree with the subject in person and number?	
Verb tense	Is the tense appropriate to the topic and style? Does the writing shift back and forth from present to past inappropriately?	
Word forms	Are any parts of verb phrases missing or incorrect? Are verb endings correct? Do other words have correct endings and forms?	
Noun plurals	Do regular plurals end in "s"? Are irregular plurals correct? Are there problems with count and non-count nouns?	
Articles	Are articles (a, an, and the) used correctly? (Note: Proper nouns generally don't have an article, with exceptions such as "the United States" and "the Soviet Union," which are more like descriptions than names.)	
Spelling	Are words spelled correctly?	
Punctuation	Are periods, commas, and question marks used correctly? Are quotations punctuated correctly? Are capital letters used appropriately?	
Pronoun reference	Does every pronoun have a clear referent? (Note: Pronouns without referents or with multiple possible referents create a vague, confusing style.)	
Other problems	Are there other important problems?	

The Rhetoric of the Op-Ed Page: Ethos, Logos, and Pathos

Writing Assignment

After thinking about your reading, discussion, and analysis of Rifkin's article and the letters in response to it, what do you personally think about Rifkin's point? Do you think it is true, as Rifkin says, that "many of our fellow creatures are more like us than we had ever imagined"? Do you think we need to change the way we treat the animals around us? Or do you think Rifkin is wrong? Write a letter expressing your viewpoint to the editor of the newspaper.

The sample letters in this section were scored using the scoring guide accompanying the assignment. (This scoring guide includes four score points, not six.)

Sample student letter to the editor with a score of 4 (Superior):

Dear Editor:

Jeremy Rifkin claimed in his September 5th letter declaring that animals were capable of every emotion a human being was, and demanding that all people extend a sense of equality and empathy to animals equal to that they would give another human being. This is obviously absurd and, if you really take a step back and look at the process behind the idea, ironic.

This stems from the fact that one of the topics that differentiate human beings from animals is their ability to feel at all good or bad regarding the fates of creatures outside their species. If humanity is expected to step above animals in terms of not killing those creatures that would reasonably be food for us were we still merely hunter-gatherers, then does it not follow that we have stepped above our animal instinct to kill, eat, mate, and escape our predators? Rifkin tries to convince us that animals experience understand the concept of mortality by using observations of elephants, who "often stand next to their dead kin for days." (9) If understanding mortality can be recognized by proximity to a corpse, then must vultures be the most conscious of all animals to that impending fate of death? If humanity is the most capable and versatile of the animals, so as to even consider such thoughts as this, shouldn't we be preserved? If we test a cure for a disease that will save thousands or even millions of human beings on a lab rat or an animal bred specifically by humans to serve a like purpose, is it not reasonable? As Rifkin commented, a lab rat's brain, when they play, "release[s] large amounts of dopamine."(9) Does the ability to experience pleasurable feelings keep its predator from eating it, or it from eating its predator, if it gets the chance?

The only reason people call for people to take a more "natural" view of life is because they are mistaking eating salads and clearing away pollution for the less appealing idea of killing whatever animal you can find that is smaller than you when you feel hungry. While it is very much like humankind to feel for other creatures around us, we should not be confused as to which of human or animal requires our attention or empathy more.

4

Commentary

- The writer maintains a tight focus throughout the letter, accurately and succinctly summarizing the issue at hand before offering a strong and argumentative point that is based on the prompt.
- The writer quotes from Rifkin's article, choosing material appropriately and incorporating it smoothly, effectively, and correctly (including the use of brackets where appropriate).
- The writer makes a variety of appeals. The letter appeals to logos, for example, by exploiting a nuance of Rifkin's argument that animals both play and mourn; in response, the letter points out that "one of the topics that differentiate human beings from animals is their ability to feel at all good or bad regarding the fates of creatures outside their species."
- The writer uses a series of rhetorical questions as appeals to logic, emotion, and ethics.
- The grammar, usage, and syntax in the letter are sophisticated, including the use of the subjunctive voice ("were we still hunter-gatherers"). Minor issues with items such as pronouns and demonstratives do not interfere with meaning and would, for many readers, pass undetected.

Sample student letter to the editor with a score of 3 (Good):

Dear Editor:

Jeremy Rifkin makes some very good points about how complex animals' thinking is and how they might feel emotions similar to humans. However, putting animals on the same level as humans distracts from the beneficial roles animals can play in research. Many of the drugs we use today were developed by using animals and the drugs' safety for humans was tested on animals. Although modern technology has allowed us to evaluate drugs and medical techniques more without animals, nevertheless some testing and experimentation using animals is unavoidable. I wonder how anyone would feel if their child were sick and a medicine that might help could not be developed because no experiments on animals were allowed?

Rifkin ends his article by saying that our new understanding of animals should encourage us to have empathy for them. Certainly his article suggests that we should not treat animals inhumanely. For example we no longer need to hunt animals for their fur to keep us warm. Animals used for food or for science should be treated as humanely as possible. However, we do need to keep a perspective and realize that the humane use of animals for science can help us improve the lives of many sick people.

3

Commentary

- The writer maintains a steady focus on the issue, offering a brief and mostly accurate summary of Rifkin's article.
- The writer uses a strategy of dividing the letter into two main ideas, each of which argues against one of the points from Rifkin's article (one paragraph about animals' similarities to humans and the other about the need for humans to empathize with animals).
- The essay does not quote Rifkin directly but illustrates and paraphrases his ideas accurately.
- The writer uses concrete examples (a sick child, the treatment of lab and food animals) to support the letter's points. The letter includes a small amount of repeated material but otherwise offers good support for clear points.
- Although the use of language is less sophisticated than that in the "4" essay, errors of grammar and mechanics are minor and do not obscure meaning. The writer includes a few mistakes in punctuation, conjunction ("Although modern technology has allowed us to evaluate drugs and medical techniques without animals, nevertheless some testing . . ."), and pronoun reference, all of which could be easily repaired.

Sample student letter to the editor with a score of 2 (Fair):

Dear Editor:

RE: "A Change of Heart about Animals" by Jeremy Rifkin. This article talks about how animals are so much like us. This article did not reach to me as some of my fellow classmates. Rifkin tried to have his audience sympathize and feel bad for the animals. Animals do not have the mentality to think as high as a level as us. Animals may feel pain, may feel depress and lonely but do they feel guilt, ambition, or pride? Rifkin talks about that we should spend time with pigs for a small time of the day with them when I know fathers that don't even talk to their children or they even mistreat them. "We should give toys to the pigs Rifkin says." I rather save a starving kid or family before I give a pig a toy. To be blunt and honest I really don't care how my breakfast lived or even if it lived a happy life. That will not change the fact that it's going to end up on my plate next to my eggs. There are some animals that are somewhat intelligent. The gorilla coco shows that it has some intelligence. It takes mental thought to remember over a thousand signs and speech patterns but she is still an animal. I see it as a ridiculous thought of having animals included in our constitution. Animals were created to eaten and not given a second thought. I do not believe in animal cruelty but I am a realist and humans are the dominant animals are not that's how it should be.

Commentary

- The writer responds to the issue of similarities between animals and humans but lumps a variety of similarities and differences together in a single paragraph.
- The writer regularly uses vague language, as in the statement, "This article did not reach to me as some of my fellow classmates." In addition, the letter repeats points about intelligence without offering additional support or analysis.
- The writer's points often are unclear, as in the statement, "I see it as a ridiculous thought of having animals included in our constitution," which appears mysteriously toward the end of the letter.
- The letter's logic is flawed. For example, the writer points out that Koko has "some intelligence" but "she is still an animal," an issue that is not under debate.
- Errors of grammar and mechanics interfere with communication ("Animals do not have the mentality to think as high as a level as us"). The writer misspells vocabulary from Rifkin's article, struggles with verb forms, confuses pronoun reference, and fails to include necessary punctuation.

Sample student letter to the editor with a score of 1 (Poor):

Dear Editor:

Jeremy Rifkin is true on his article, "A Change of Heart about Animals." Especially when he mentioned, "many of our fellow creatures are more like us than we had ever imagined." They have many similarities to humans for example: the way they feel, suffer, experience stress and affection like love. So why shouldn't we treat animals like humans? For this reason we should have more consideration with animals. To treat them with respect. Why should we kill them when they don't harm us or deserve it?

Let us not take away the right animals have to enjoy life.

Commentary

- The letter focuses on the issue raised by Rifkin, but only through summary. The writer agrees with Rifkin but offers no argument of his or her own.
- The letter contains insufficient text beyond the summary to make an argument.
- The letter fails to make a clear point. It merely asks the question, "Why should we kill them when they don't harm us or deserve it?" that it purports to answer.
- Errors of grammar and mechanics confuse and distract the reader. The writer struggles with sentence fragments, syntax ("Rifkin is true on his article"), and punctuation.

The Value of Life

Module 4

The Value of Life

Teacher Version

Reading Rhetorically

Prereading 2
   Getting Ready to Read.................................. 2
   Introducing Key Concepts 2

Text 1—Hamlet's Soliloquy

   Surveying the Text 4
   Making Predictions and Asking Questions.............. 4
   Introducing Key Vocabulary 5
Reading 7
   First Reading 7
   Rereading the Text and Looking Closely
      at Language.. 7
Postreading 8
   Thinking Critically 8
   Charting Multiple Texts............................... 9

Text 2—*It's Not About the Bike*

Prereading 11
   Surveying the Text 11
   Making Predictions and Asking Questions.............. 12
   Introducing Key Vocabulary 12
Reading 13
   First Reading 13
   Rereading the Text and Looking Closely
      at Language.. 13
Postreading 14
   Thinking Critically 14
   Charting Multiple Texts............................... 16

Text 3—"What Is a Life Worth?"

Prereading 16
   Surveying the Text 16
   Making Predictions and Asking Questions.............. 17
   Introducing Key Vocabulary 17
Reading 18
   First Reading 18
   Rereading the Text 19
Postreading 20
   Thinking Critically 20
   Charting Multiple Texts............................... 21

Text 4—"Human Life Value Calculator"

Prereading 21
   Surveying the Text 21
   Making Predictions and Asking Questions.............. 22
   Introducing Key Vocabulary 23
Reading 23
   First Reading 23
   Rereading the Text 24
Postreading 25
   Thinking Critically 25
   Charting Multiple Texts............................... 26

Connecting Reading to Writing

Writing to Learn 26
Using the Words of Others............................ 27

Writing Rhetorically

Prewriting 28
   Reading the Assignment 28
   Getting Ready to Write............................... 29
   Formulating a Working Thesis 30
Writing 31
   Composing a Draft 31
   Organizing the Essay 31
   Developing the Content 31
Revising and Editing.................................... 32
   Revising the Draft...................................... 32
   Editing the Draft 33
   Reflecting on the Writing........................... 34
Evaluating and Responding 34
   Responding to Student Writing 34

Rubric... 35

Charting Multiple Texts 36

Reading Selections

Hamlet's Soliloquy 37
Excerpt from *It's Not About the Bike: My Journey
   Back to Life* 39
"What Is a Life Worth?" 42
"The Human Life Value Calculator" 49

Student Version

Activity 1: Getting Ready to Read 53
Activity 2: Introducing Key Concepts 53

Text 1—Hamlet's Soliloquy

Activity 3: Surveying the Text 54
Activity 4: Making Predictions and Asking Questions 54
Activity 5: Introducing Key Vocabulary 55
Activity 6: First Reading 56
Activity 7: Rereading the Text and Looking Closely
    at Language 56
Activity 8: Thinking Critically 57
Activity 9: Charting Multiple Texts 57

Text 2—*It's Not About the Bike*

Activity 10: Surveying the Text 59
Activity 11: Making Predictions and Asking Questions ...59
Activity 12: Introducing Key Vocabulary 59
Activity 13: First Reading 60
Activity 14: Rereading the Text and Looking Closely
    at Language 60
Activity 15: Thinking Critically 61
Activity 16: Charting Multiple Texts 61

Text 3—"What Is a Life Worth?"

Activity 17: Surveying the Text 62
Activity 18: Making Predictions and Asking Questions ...62
Activity 19: Introducing Key Vocabulary 62
Activity 20: First Reading 63
Activity 21: Rereading the Text 63
Activity 22: Thinking Critically 64
Activity 23: Charting Multiple Texts 65

Text 4—"Human Life Value Calculator"

Activity 24: Surveying the Text 65
Activity 25: Making Predictions and Asking Questions ...65
Activity 26: Introducing Key Vocabulary 66
Activity 27: First Reading 66
Activity 28: Rereading the Text...................66
Activity 29: Thinking Critically 67
Activity 30: Charting Multiple Texts 67

Activity 31. Writing to Learn....................67
Activity 32. Using the Words of Others 67
Activity 33. Reading the Assignment 68
Activity 34. Getting Ready to Write 69
Activity 35. Formulating a Working Thesis........69
Activity 36. Composing a Draft 70
Activity 37. Organizing the Essay 70
Activity 38. Developing the Content 71
Activity 39. Revising the Draft 71
Activity 40. Editing the Draft...................72
Activity 41. Reflecting on the Writing 72

Charting Multiple Texts 73

Sample Student Essays

Writing Assignment and Scored Student Essays.......75

Hamlet's Soliloquy

(from Shakespeare's *Hamlet, Prince of Denmark,* Act III, Section 1)

HAMLET:

To be, or not to be—that is the question:		
Whether 'tis* nobler in the mind to suffer	*it is	
The slings and arrows of outrageous fortune		
Or to take arms against a sea of troubles		
And by opposing end them. To die, to sleep—		5
No more—and by a sleep to say we end		
The heartache, and the thousand natural shocks		
That flesh is heir to. 'Tis a consummation*	*resolution	
Devoutly to be wished. To die, to sleep—		
To sleep—perchance to dream: ay, there's the rub,*	*problem	10
For in that sleep of death what dreams may come		
When we have shuffled off this mortal coil,*	*life	
Must give us pause. There's the respect		
That makes calamity* of so long life.	*tragedy	
For who would bear the whips and scorns of time,		15
Th' oppressor's wrong, the proud man's contumely,*	*contempt	
The pangs of despised love, the law's delay,		
The insolence of office, and the spurns		
That patient merit of th' unworthy takes,		
When he himself might his quietus* make	*death	20
With a bare bodkin*? Who would fardels† bear,	*dagger †burdens	

To grunt and sweat under a weary life,

But that the dread of something after death,

The undiscovered country, from whose bourn*   *border

No traveler returns, puzzles the will,   25

And makes us rather bear those ills we have

Than fly to others that we know not of?

Thus conscience does make cowards of us all,

And thus the native hue* of resolution   *natural
color

Is sicklied o'er with the pale cast of thought,   30

And enterprise of great pitch and moment

With this regard their currents turn awry

And lose the name of action.

Excerpt from

It's Not About the Bike: My Journey Back to Life

by Lance Armstrong with Sally Jenkins

1   I want to die at a hundred years old with an American flag on my back and the star of Texas on my helmet, after screaming down an Alpine descent on a bicycle at 75 miles per hour. I want to cross one last finish line as my stud wife and my 10 children applaud, and then I want to lie down in a field of those famous French sunflowers and gracefully expire, the perfect contradiction to my once-anticipated poignant early demise.

2   A slow death is not for me. I don't do anything slow, not even breathe. I do everything at a fast cadence: eat fast, sleep fast. It makes me crazy when my wife, Kristin, drives our car, because she brakes at all the yellow caution lights, while I squirm impatiently in the passenger seat.

3   "Come on, don't be a skirt," I tell her.

4   "Lance," she says, "marry a man."

5   I've spent my life racing my bike, from the back roads of Austin, Texas, to the Champs-Elysées, and I always figured if I died an untimely death, it would be because some rancher in his Dodge 4x4 ran me headfirst into a ditch. Believe me, it could happen. Cyclists fight an ongoing war with guys in big trucks, and so many vehicles have hit me, so many times, in so many countries, I've lost count. I've learned how to take out my own stitches: all you need is a pair of fingernail clippers and a strong stomach.

6   If you saw my body underneath my racing jersey, you'd know what I'm talking about. I've got marbled scars on both arms and discolored marks up and down my legs, which I keep clean-shaven. Maybe that's why trucks are always trying to run me over; they see my sissy-boy calves and decide not to brake. But cyclists have to shave, because when the gravel gets into your skin, it's easier to clean and bandage if you have no hair.

7   One minute you're pedaling along a highway, and the next minute, boom, you're face-down in the dirt. A blast of hot air hits you, you taste the acrid, oily exhaust in the roof of your mouth, and all you can do is wave a fist at the disappearing taillights.

8   Cancer was like that. It was like being run off the road by a truck, and I've got the scars to prove it. There's a puckered wound in my upper chest just above my heart, which is where the catheter was implanted. A surgical line runs from the right side of my groin into my upper thigh, where they cut out my testicle. But the real prizes are two deep half-moons in my scalp, as if I was kicked twice in the head by a horse. Those are the leftovers from brain surgery.

9   When I was 25, I got testicular cancer and nearly died. I was given less than a 40 percent chance of surviving, and frankly, some of my doctors were just being kind when they gave me those odds. Death is not exactly cocktail-party conversation, I know, and neither is cancer, or brain surgery, or matters below the waist. But I'm not here to make polite conversation. I want to tell the truth. I'm sure you'd like to hear about how Lance Armstrong became a Great American and an Inspiration To Us All, how he won the Tour de France, the 2,290-mile road race that's considered the single most grueling sporting event on the face of the earth. You want to hear about faith and mystery, and my miraculous comeback, and how I joined towering figures like Greg LeMond and Miguel Indurain in the record book. You want to hear about my lyrical climb through the Alps and my heroic conquering of the Pyrenees, and how it felt. But the Tour was the least of the story.

10   Some of it is not easy to tell or comfortable to hear. I'm asking you now, at the outset, to put aside your ideas about heroes and miracles, because I'm not storybook material. This is not Disneyland, or Hollywood. I'll give you an example: I've read that I flew up the hills and mountains of France. But you don't fly up a hill. You struggle slowly and painfully up a hill, and maybe, if you work very hard, you get to the top ahead of everybody else.

11   Cancer is like that, too. Good, strong people get cancer, and they do all the right things to beat it, and they still die. That is the essential truth that you learn. People die. And after you learn it, all other matters seem irrelevant. They just seem small.

12   I don't know why I'm still alive. I can only guess. I have a tough constitution, and my profession taught me how to compete against long odds and big obstacles. I like to train hard and I like to race hard. That helped, it was a good start, but it certainly wasn't the determining factor. I can't help feeling that my survival was more a matter of blind luck.

13   When I was 16, I was invited to undergo testing at a place in Dallas called the Cooper Clinic, a prestigious research lab and birthplace of the aerobic exercise revolution. A doctor there measured my VO$_2$ max, which is a gauge of how much oxygen you can take in and use, and he says that my numbers are still the highest they've ever come across. Also, I produced less lactic acid than most people. Lactic acid is the chemical your body generates when it's winded and fatigued—it's what makes your lungs burn and your legs ache.

14   Basically, I can endure more physical stress than most people can, and I don't get as tired while I'm doing it. So I figure maybe that helped me live. I was lucky—I was born with an above-average capacity for breathing. But even so, I was in a desperate, sick fog much of the time.

15   My illness was humbling and starkly revealing, and it forced me to survey my life with an unforgiving eye. There are some shameful episodes in it: instances of meanness, unfinished tasks, weakness, and regrets. I had to ask myself, "If I live, who is it that I intend to be?" I found that I had a lot of growing to do as a man.

16   I won't kid you. There are two Lance Armstrongs, pre-cancer, and post. Everybody's favorite question is "How did cancer change you?" The real question is how didn't it change me? I left my house on October 2, 1996, as one person and came home another. I was a world-class athlete with a mansion on a riverbank, keys to a Porsche, and a self-made fortune in the bank. I was one of the top riders in the world and my career was moving along a perfect arc of success. I returned a different person, literally. In a way, the old me did die, and I was given a second life. Even my body is different, because during the chemotherapy I lost all the muscle I had ever built up, and when I recovered, it didn't come back in the same way.

17   The truth is that cancer was the best thing that ever happened to me. I don't know why I got the illness, but it did wonders for me, and I wouldn't want to walk away from it. Why would I want to change, even for a day, the most important and shaping event in my life?

18   People die. That truth is so disheartening that at times I can't bear to articulate it. Why should we go on, you might ask? Why don't we all just stop and lie down where we are? But there is another truth, too. People live. It's an equal and opposing truth. People live, and in the most remarkable ways. When I was sick, I saw more beauty and triumph and truth in a single day than I ever did in a bike race—but they were human moments, not miraculous ones. I met a guy in a fraying sweatsuit who turned out to be a brilliant surgeon. I became friends with a harassed and overscheduled nurse named LaTrice, who gave me such care that it could only be the result of the deepest sympathetic affinity. I saw children with no eyelashes or eyebrows, their hair burned away by chemo, who fought with the hearts of Indurains.

19   I still don't completely understand it.

20   All I can do is tell you what happened.

What Is a Life Worth?

**To compensate families of the victims of Sept. 11, the government
has invented a way to measure blood and loss in cash.
A look at the wrenching calculus.**

by Amanda Ripley

With reporting by Nadia Mustafa and Julie Rawe/New York
and Karen Tumulty/Washington

Time, **February 11, 2002**

1   A train barreled over Joseph Hewins' body on a wintry evening in 1845
in the Massachusetts Berkshires. Hewins had spent the workday shoveling
snow off the tracks, only to be killed on his trip back to town when a
switchman got distracted. Hewins left behind a wife and three children, who
were poor even before his death. His widow sued but lost at every level. Had
the train merely chopped off Hewins' leg, the railroad would have paid. But
in the perverse logic of that time, when a man died, he took his legal claims
with him. And so the thinking went for most of the century, until something
unheard of began to happen. The courts started to put a dollar value on a
life—after death.

2   The concept of assigning a price tag to a life has always made people
intensely squeamish. After all, isn't it degrading to presume that money can
make a family whole again? And what of the disparities? Is a poor man's
life worth less than a rich man's? Over the past 100 years, U.S. courts have
crafted their answers to these questions. Forensic economists testify on the
value of a life every day. They can even tell you the average valuation of an
injured knee (about $200,000). But until now, the public at large has not had
to reckon with the process and its imperfections. Until the terrorist attacks of
Sept. 11 created a small city's worth of grieving families and the government
established an unprecedented fund to compensate them, the mathematics of
loss was a little-known science. Now the process is on garish display, and it is
tempting to avert the eyes.

3   On the morning of Jan. 18 [2002], about 70 family members file into the
rows of crimson seats at the Norwalk, Conn., city hall auditorium. They
listen quietly to special master Kenneth Feinberg, whom the government
has entrusted with dispersing its money to those most affected by the
Sept. 11 tragedy. His first job is to persuade them to join the federal Victim
Compensation Fund, the country's largest experiment in paying mass victims
and their families without placing blame. The effort is being closely watched
for the precedents it will set.

4   Much has been made of the enormous charity funds raised after the
attacks. Donations to those groups do funnel thousands of dollars to the
victims' families—in particular, the families of firefighters and police officers.

But overall, the nearly $2 billion in charity money is chump change compared with the cash that will flow out of government coffers. There is no limit to the federal fund, but the tab is likely to be triple the size of the charity pot. And while charity funds are doled out to a vast pool of people, including businesses hurt by the attacks, the government money will go exclusively to the injured and to families of the deceased.

5   Feinberg, in a black-and-white polka dot tie, speaks in short, punchy sentences and a loud voice. He has already given the speech 32 times up and down the East Coast. The main thrust: The government, for the first time ever, has agreed to write large checks to victims' families without any litigation. The checks will arrive within four months after a claim is filed—no legal fees, no agonizing 10-year lawsuit. But every award will be based on a cold calculus, much the way courts handle wrongful-death claims.

6   That means different sums for different families. In a TIME/CNN poll taken last month, 86 percent said all families should receive the same amount. But that's not how it's going to work.

7   The calculus has several steps, Feinberg explains. First, the government will estimate how much a victim would have earned over his or her lifetime had the planes never crashed. That means a broker's family will qualify for a vastly higher award than a window washer's family. To estimate this amount, each family was handed an easy-to-read chart on the way into the meeting: Find your loved one's age and income and follow your finger to the magic number. Note that the lifetime earnings have been boosted by a flat $250,000 for "pain and suffering"—noneconomic losses, they are called. Tack on an extra $50,000 in pain and suffering for a spouse and for each child. The charts, while functional, are brutal, crystallizing how readily the legal system commodifies life.

8   Then—and this is crucial—don't get too excited. That first number may be quite high—in the millions for many. But you must, according to the rules of the fund, subtract all the money you are getting from other sources except charities. A court settlement would not be diminished this way, but this is not a court, Feinberg repeatedly points out. Deduct life insurance, pension, Social Security death benefits, and workers' compensation. Now you have the total award the government is offering you for your loss.

9   The deductions have the effect of equalizing the differences in the awards. Critics have called this Feinberg's "Robin Hood strategy." For many people in the room, the number is now at or close to zero. Feinberg says he will make sure no one gets zero. "Leave it to me," he says. But nowhere will that be written into the rules when they are finalized in mid-February. Likewise, many fiancés and gay partners will be at the mercy of Feinberg's discretion in seeking awards. Before finding out exactly what they will get—and the rules are complex—families will have to agree never to sue anyone for the attacks. "Normally, that would be a difficult call," says Feinberg. "Not here. The right to sue in this case is simply not a reasonable alternative."

10   That's because Congress has capped the liability of the airlines, the airport owners, the aircraft manufacturers, the towers' landlord, and the city of New York. In the name of the economy, the government severely restricted the victims' rights to sue—whether they join the fund or not. It is this lack of a viable option, even if they would not take it, that galls many families.

11   Congress created the fund as a safety net for the victims' families, to ensure that they maintain something resembling their current standard of living—whether they get assistance from private insurance or government money. The families see it as so much more. For the traumatized, the charts are like a Rorschach test. Some view the money as a halfhearted apology for the breakdown in security and intelligence that made the attacks possible. Others can't help seeing the award as a callous measure of their loved one's value. Many regard it as a substitute for the millions they think they may have got in court, had the liability not been capped. When the total comes out to be underwhelming, these families take it personally. There's a fundamental clash between the way they interpret the purpose of the fund and the way the government sees it.

12   After Feinberg speaks, he stands back and braces himself for an artillery of angry rhetorical questions. Gerry Sweeney, whose brother died in Tower 2, Floor 105, points at Feinberg and explains why $250,000 is not enough for pain and suffering in the case of her now fatherless nephew. "Have you ever seen a twelve-year-old have a nervous breakdown?" she asks. Another woman concocts an analogy to illustrate for Feinberg what it was like to talk to loved ones as they came to accept their imminent, violent deaths and to watch the towers collapse on live TV. "If your wife was brutally raped and murdered and you had to watch and listen to it happen, what would you think the right amount would be?" Finally, Maureen Halvorson, who lost her husband and her brother, speaks up from the front row in a quiet, bewildered voice. "I just can't accept the fact that the Federal Government is saying my husband and my brother are worth nothing." Feinberg is silent.

13   The more than 3,000 victims of the Sept. 11 attacks are frozen in snapshots, wide-smiling men and women in crisp suits and uniforms who liked to build birdhouses on weekends and play practical jokes. In the literature of grief, they have become hardworking innocents, heroes, and saints. But those they left behind are decidedly human. Some compete with others for most bereaved status; others demand an apology even when no one is listening. Some are popping pills, and others cannot leave the house. Most days, they are inconsolable. And as the rest of the country begins to ease back into normalcy, these families stand, indignant, in the way.

14   Already, some Americans have lost patience with them. "My tax money should not be given to someone with a $750,000 mortgage to pay who needs a set of fresh, matching towels in her bathroom every season," one person wrote anonymously to the Department of Justice's Web page on victim compensation. "I'm shocked and appalled and very disappointed," wrote a Florida resident, "that some individuals are living in such a rare and well-gilded ivory tower that they feel $250,000 is not sufficient compensation. Most of us, the working people of America, make $20,000 to $40,000 per year. Where do these wealthy, spoiled, greedy folks in New York get off, pretending that what happened to them was so uniquely horrible? I'm over it. Yeah, it was unique. Yeah, it was horrible. Yeah, I sent money to help. And after reading about them suing for more money, I begin to regret it."

15   It's true that some families' behavior has been less than dignified. The divorced parents of a woman killed in the Pentagon, who are eligible for money because their daughter left no dependents, have filed competing claims. Lawyers are now involved. Says her father: "I guarantee she loved her daddy as much as she loved her mom. I feel that I'm entitled to something."

16   And it's also a fact that these families will get more money from charities and the government combined than anyone has so far received after the Oklahoma City bombing or the 1998 bombing of the Nairobi embassy. For that matter, if these victims had been killed in a drive-by shooting, they probably would not have received more than a few thousand dollars from state victim-compensation funds.

17   That fact is not lost on the public, particularly people whose relatives have died in everyday tragedies. At the *Wichita Eagle* in Kansas, editorial-page director Phil Brownlee has received calls and letters from locals disgusted by the families' complaints, and he agrees. "It's just frustrating that the goodwill demonstrated by the government seems to be deteriorating," he says. "Now you've got families who are upset with what most Americans deem to be generous contributions. It's the loss of the spirit of Sept. 11, the souring of that sense of solidarity."

18   But it may not be fair to compare Sept. 11 with a street crime or even Oklahoma City. After all, these recent attacks involved an orchestrated, simultaneous security breach on four airplanes, carried out by 19 men who had been living and training on our soil. A better comparison might be past international terrorist attacks and plane crashes. Those that have been resolved—and that's a major distinction—do show higher payouts than the average amount likely to come out of the Sept. 11 federal fund.

19   In 25 major aviation accidents between 1970 and 1984, the average compensation for victims who went to trial was $1 million in current dollars, according to a Rand Corp. analysis. Average compensation for cases settled without a lawsuit was $415,000. The biggest aviation payout in history followed the crash of Pan Am Flight 103 over Lockerbie, Scotland, in 1988. Settlements ranged all over the spectrum, with a couple dozen exceeding $10 million, according to Manhattan attorney Lee Kreindler, who acted as lead counsel. Dividing the total $500 million payout over the 270 victims yields an average award of $1.85 million. However, the families had to hand about a third of their awards to their lawyers, and they waited seven to eight years to see any money. And the families of the six people killed in the 1993 World Trade Center bombing are still waiting for their day in civil court.

20   In the end, most families will probably choose the fund over litigation. The Lockerbie millions are simply not a realistic possibility. It is always extremely difficult to sue the government. And the liability for the Sept. 11 attacks was capped by Congress at about $1.5 billion per plane. So while the families of those killed in the Pennsylvania and Pentagon crashes may have enough to go around, there are far too many victims in New York. "The court model works perfectly when you don't have $50 billion in damages or 3,000 deaths," says Leo Boyle, a Boston lawyer and president of the Association of Trial Lawyers of America, which supports the fund option and has lined up more than 2,000 attorneys to offer free help navigating its rules. Even without the caps, Boyle insists, victims could not have extracted more money by putting United and American Airlines through bankruptcy. So far, only a handful of suits have been filed.

21   In any event, there was no talking Congress out of the liability caps when it drafted the airline-bailout package 10 days after the attacks. The airlines could not fly without insurance, and their coverage was far short of what it would take to pay the damages. Federal Reserve Chairman Alan Greenspan privately told congressional leaders that getting the planes up again was the single biggest "multiplier" that could revive the economy on every level. So the Democrats, who usually balk at limiting the ability to sue, accepted the idea of an airline bailout—as long as it came with a mechanism to compensate victims. Oklahoma Senator Don Nickles, the No. 2 Republican in the Senate and a longtime proponent of tort reform, pushed hard to limit how much the victims' families could claim, but he did not prevail.

22   But once the interim rules were drawn up by Feinberg's office—in conjunction with the Department of Justice and the Office of Management and Budget—there were some surprises. In particular, the figures for pain and suffering astonished some who had backed the fund. "The numbers are low by any measure," says Boyle. Feinberg says he chose the $250,000 figure because that's how much beneficiaries receive from the Federal Government when firefighters and police die on the job. The additional $50,000 for the spouse and each child is, he admits, "just some rough approximation of what I thought was fair." He calls the fund "rough justice."

23   The American Tort Reform Association, backed mostly by Republicans, has been lobbying since 1986 to limit noneconomic damages in some suits to $250,000. John Ashcroft, head of the Justice Department, pushed for such a cap on punitive damages when he was a senator. But Feinberg, a Democrat, insists he was not pressured by the administration to keep the numbers low.

24   No matter how many times tearful widows accuse him of protecting the airlines, Feinberg does not blush. A lawyer with decades of experience in the messy art of compromise (Feinberg was special master for the $180 million distributed to veterans exposed to Agent Orange), he is accustomed to rage. "On Tuesday I get whacked for this or that in New Jersey. The next day it's New York. It goes with the job." But he rejects the theory that greed is a factor. "People have had a loved one wrenched from them suddenly, without warning, and we are only five months beyond that disaster. It was nearly yesterday. And they are desperately seeking, from what I've seen, to place as much of a value on that lost loved one as they can. So here is where they seek to amplify the value of that memory. They do it by saying we want more, as a validation of the loss. That's not greed. That's human nature."

25   Susan and Harvey Blomberg of Fairfield County, Conn., have been to three meetings on the victim-compensation fund, even though, as parents of a victim who has left a wife and kids behind, they are not in line for compensation. The rules give preference to the victim's spouse and children. But the Blombergs come to these meetings to be part of something, to be counted. And they linger after everyone else has left. "My daughter-in-law was upset when we went to the meetings," Susan says. "She said, 'It's not really about you. It's about the widows and children.' And I said, 'I want more information.' You can't compare grief, because nobody can get inside you. But I feel like an orphan. When they did this formula, why didn't they consider the parents? My daughter-in-law was married for five years. We had Jonathan for 33 years."

26   "It's a horrible thing that this is where our energies need to be pulled," says Cheri Sparacio, 37, the widow of Thomas Sparacio, a currency trader at Euro Brokers who died in Tower 2. In their modest house in Staten Island, littered with the toys of her twin two-year-olds, she explains why she sees the estimated $138,000 she would get from the fund as a cheap bribe. "The government is not taking any responsibility for what it's done. This was just one screw-up after another." She is also worried about her financial stability; in less than a month, she will have their third child. Thomas was the primary wage earner, although Cheri worked as a part-time school psychologist until Sept. 11. She doesn't see how she can go back to work with an infant and two toddlers unless she hires full-time help. "Please, come step into my shoes for a minute," she says, her eyes flat and unblinking. "I am not looking to go to Tahiti."

27   But uptown in the apartment where Samuel Fields once lived, the fund acts like a quiet equalizer, a way for the government to guarantee that victims with less insurance emerge with basic support. Fields was a security guard for six years in Tower 1. He made $22,000 a year and lived with his family in a housing project in Harlem. On Sept. 11, he helped people evacuate the building and then went back inside to help some more. Fields never came home. Next month his widow Angela will give birth to their fifth child. Because Fields made a small salary, his family's preliminary award is less than Sparacio's. But his family's deductions are also smaller. In the end, Angela's estimated $444,010 award will probably be three times the size of Cheri's.

28   In valuing different lives differently—the first part of the equation—the fund follows common legal practice. Courts always grant money on the basis of a person's earning power in life. That's because the courts are not attempting to

replace "souls," says Philip Bobbitt, a law professor at the University of Texas who has written about the allocation of scarce resources in times of tragedy. "We're not trying to make you psychologically whole. Where we can calculate the loss is in economic loss." The Feinberg plan differs from legal norms in deducting the value of life insurance and pensions. Also, it allows no flexibility in determining noneconomic damages. In court, pain and suffering would be weighed individually.

29   Money aside, a lawsuit can be an investigative device like no other, forcing answers about what led to a death. Some Sept. 11 families say they might file suit for that reason alone, even if they never get a dime. And for other families, there is enormous value in no lawsuits at all. David Gordenstein lost his wife, Lisa Fenn Gordenstein, on American Flight 11. "Am I sad? I've had my heart torn out," he says. But he would rather devote his life to raising his two young daughters than pursuing a lawsuit. He will probably file a claim with the federal fund, which he acknowledges is not perfect. "I am proud of what my country tried to do. I think the intention is noble."

30   The night before Lisa died, she slipped a clipping under the door of David's home office, something she often did. It was a saying from theologian Charles Swindoll that read, "Attitude, to me, is more important than facts. It is more important than the past, than education, than money, than circumstances, than failures, than successes, than what other people think or say or do . . . . It will make or break a company, a church, a home." David read it at her memorial. And while he jokes that it's kind of clichéd—"typical Lisa"—he says he thinks its message might help carry his family through this.

Human Life Value Calculator

LIFE

About Us | Contact Us | Press Room | Home   Search

Life Insurance

Life Insurance   Health Insurance   Disability Insurance   Long-Term Care Insurance   Small Business Planning   Find an Agent

Who needs it?

What are the different types?

How much do I need?

  Human life value calculator

  Insurance needs calculator

What to know when buying?

Where do I buy it?

Life events

Printable consumer guide

Glossary

meetLIFEstories

How much do I need?

Human life value calculator

The human life value calculator has been designed to help you assess your financial value to those you love by estimating the future financial contributions you will make to your family ... or, more starkly, the financial loss that your family would incur if you were to die today. For the purposes of this calculator, a human life only has economic value in its relation to other lives, specifically a spouse or dependent children. Therefore, if you have neither, the calculator will not generate a result.

Please note, this calculator will provide only a rough sense of your human life value, which can be a factor in determining the amount of insurance you should have in your financial portfolio. Typically, the amount of life insurance someone needs is less than his or her human life value due to the availability of other sources of income (e.g., existing life insurance coverage, Social Security benefits, etc.). For an analysis of your life insurance needs, please visit the Life Insurance Needs Calculator or contact a professional agent or advisor in your area.

This calculator projects typical lifetime income for someone with the characteristics you provide in the input section, less taxes and expenditures devoted to your own consumption, plus any fringe benefits your family receives from your employer, such as health insurance, and the services you provide around the house. The resulting estimate is an approximate measure of your net financial contribution to your family - your human life value.

This human life value calculator should not be viewed as a comprehensive assessment. For example, you will notice that it does not account for the specific occupation and education of you or your spouse. Also, to simplify your responses, only general information is sought regarding your non-wage income, which impacts both your consumption and your income taxes. Furthermore, the dollar value of your fringe benefits is assumed to be equal to the average for someone of your income and family situation. Nevertheless, we believe that, given the limited information the calculator is using, it is the best estimate available. Click here for more information on the assumptions used to generate these estimates.

Enter only numbers or letters, no commas or dollar signs.

1. Your age at nearest birthday:
20

2. Sex:
Female ▾

3. Your planned retirement age (e.g., 65):
65

4. Major occupation category: 6 ▾
   1. Executive, Administrative, and Managerial
      (e.g., Chief Executives, Managers, Accountants, Marketers, Buyers)
   2. Professional Specialty
      (e.g., Engineers, Scientists, Teachers, Lawyers, Doctors, Nurses, Artists)
   3. Technicians, Computer Programmers, and Related Support
      (e.g., Electrical, Mechanical and Health Technicians)

4. Sales
   -(e.g., Real Estate, Insurance, Retail and Personal Services)

5. Administrative Support, Including Clerical Support

6. Service and Public Safety
   -(e.g., Food, Health and Cleaning Services, Police, Firefighters, and Security)

7. Farming, Forestry, Fishing

8. Craft, Repair, Skilled Laborers
   -(e.g., Mechanics, Construction Workers, Textile and Food Production, Inspectors)

9. Operators, Fabricators, Laborers
   -(e.g., Machine Operators, Motor Vehicle Operators, Assembler, Rail Transportaion)

5. Your annual wage earnings before taxes:

```
18000
```

6. Does your employer provide fringe benefits?

```
Yes ▼
```

7. Do you have a spouse?

```
No ▼
```

   If yes, then:
   Age of spouse:

   ```
   ```

   Is spouse employed?

   ```
   No ▼
   ```

   Spouse's planned retirement age (e.g., 65):

   ```
   ```

   Spouse's annual wage earnings before taxes:

   ```
   ```

8. Annual non-wage earnings (e.g. investment or rental income)

```
0
```

9. Ages of children under 23:

   Analysis   Clear Form

Return to calculator input

Back to Top

LIFE AND HEALTH INSURANCE FOUNDATION FOR EDUCATION   2175 K STREET, NW, SUITE 250   WASHINGTON, DC 20037-1809   202-464-5000

Your estimated human life value - the value today of your future contributions to your household - $661,219 or about 37 times your current annual income. If you were to die today, this amount is roughly what your family would need to maintain the same standard of living they will enjoy over the course of your anticipated working life. The graphs below provide a step-by-step overview of how your approximate human life value has been estimated.

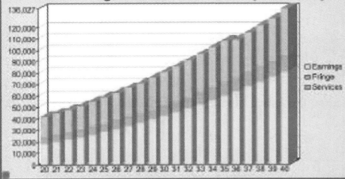

Services	$ 379,412
Fringe	114,762
Earnings	547,498
Total	$ 1,041,672

This graph shows projections of your annual earnings, fringe benefits and household services for each future year. These projections were based on the information you provided, along with data from the U.S. Census, the professional economics literature, the U.S. Chamber of Commerce and various research universities.

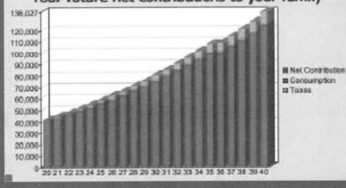

Services	$ 379,412
Fringe	114,762
Earnings	547,498
Total	$ 1,041,672
Taxes	- 63,233
Consumption	- 317,220
Net Contribution	$ 661,219

This graph shows projections of your consumption and income taxes. They were derived using information from the United States Bureau of Labor Statistics and the Internal Revenue Service. When your consumption and taxes are subtracted from the sum total of your earnings, fringe benefits and services, the result is the net financial contribution you are likely to make to your family in each and every year. This net contribution is also shown in the graph.

Present Value of Your Human Life Value = $661,219

This final graph isolates the net contributions illustrated in the graph above. They comprise your human life value. The dollar value listed above is the amount of money that would need to be invested today - in a risk-free investment - to replace this human life value in the event of your death. Said another way, it is the amount necessary today to provide the same standard of living to your family that you would have provided had you lived.

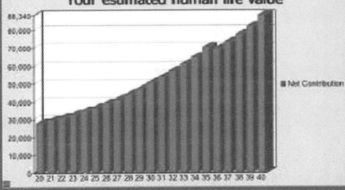

READING SELECTIONS

Page 52 blank

The Value of Life

Reading selections for this module:

Shakespeare, William. *Hamlet.* Act III, Sc. 1: Hamlet's "To be, or not to be" soliloquy.

Armstrong, Lance, with Sally Jenkins. Excerpt from *It's Not About the Bike: My Journey Back to Life.* New York: Putnam, 2000. 1–5.

Ripley, Amanda. "What Is a Life Worth?" *Time* 11 Feb. 2002.

The Life and Health Insurance Foundation for Education. LIFE. "The Human Life Value Calculator" <http://www.lifeline.org/build/human_life_value_calculator/index.php?pt=lfhlvc&m=1>.

> The assignment sequence you're about to begin will ask you to read several different texts, each of which addresses the issue of how life is valued. As you will see, the texts provide very different ways of thinking about how we can, do, and should value life.

Reading Rhetorically

Prereading

Activity 1	**Getting Ready to Read** Before you read what others say about the value of life, take a few minutes to respond in writing to the following quickwrite prompt: What does being alive mean to you? How do you assign value to life? What makes life challenging? What makes it worth living? Describe a few examples that help to show your thinking about how people should value life.
Activity 2	**Introducing Key Concepts** This activity will help you build your understanding of the many meanings suggested by the concept of "life." Use the model below to explore the ways in which society defines "life" in various contexts.

Activity 2
(Continued)

Concept: *Life*

Example sentence:

Synonyms: Contexts:

Examples: Non-examples:

Text 1—Hamlet's Soliloquy

Activity 3

Surveying the Text

The first text you will read is the famous "To be, or not to be" speech from Shakespeare's play *Hamlet, Prince of Denmark,* which was published in 1604 under the title *The Tragicall Historie of Hamlet, Prince of Denmarke*. That speech is a soliloquy, a convention used by playwrights to allow the audience to hear the thoughts of a character. Take a few moments to look over the text, and then answer the following questions:

- What prior experiences have you had reading plays?
- What did you notice about the page format and annotations?
- What did you notice about the text structure?

Activity 4

Making Predictions and Asking Questions

When approaching a new text, you should always try to draw on your prior experiences to help you predict what the text might be about. The following questions will help you to do so:

- What is a tragedy? What themes and outcomes would you expect to find in a tragedy?
- What do you know about the language in plays written by Shakespeare? What have you done in the past to help yourself read Shakespeare effectively?
- The soliloquy here begins with a famous quotation: "To be, or not to be—that is the question." What do you think is "the question" Hamlet is asking? How do you think he might answer it?

Activity 5

Introducing Key Vocabulary

Shakespeare's texts are often difficult because he uses words that are no longer in frequent use, even though they were common when he wrote his plays. Several words in the soliloquy fit into this category. You will see in the text that some words are marked with an asterisk (*); a definition or synonym is provided to the right of the line for those words.

Polar Opposites

An important rhetorical device Shakespeare uses in Hamlet's soliloquy is antithesis, or a balance of opposites. Hamlet explores a series of oppositional relationships in his speech, beginning with the question of "to be, or not to be." For this vocabulary activity, you will explore some of these antithetical relationships by brainstorming antonyms for the terms listed below.

Term	Antonym
1. oppression	
2. action	
3. endurance	
4. mystery	
5. life	

Word Families

List as many words as possible that are related to the following five concepts from Hamlet's soliloquy: action, thought, suffering, mortality, and fear. You may include synonyms directly from the text along with any other words you believe are related to the concept. Word families are not simply lists of synonyms; they may include any sets of words that frequently appear together. For example, "brackish" and "water" are part of the same word family.

Example:

Resolution: end (line 5), consummation (line 8), will (line 25), decision, outcome, and result

1. action:

2. thought:

3. suffering:

4. mortality:

5. fear:

Reading

Activity 6

First Reading

Read the soliloquy from *Hamlet.* Although it is quite short, it packs much meaning into its 33 lines. You may need to read it more than once before you feel you have a good grasp on the ideas it contains.

Background

At this point in the play, Hamlet feels that he is in a crisis. His father died a few months earlier under mysterious circumstances. Hamlet discovers that his father was secretly murdered—by Hamlet's uncle, Claudius. Making things even worse, Claudius then marries Hamlet's mother. Hamlet does not know what to do about this knowledge. He wonders whether he can trust anyone or if perhaps he is going crazy.

As you first read the text, focus on what you see as the "big picture" Hamlet describes. Based on this first reading, would you say that Hamlet is an optimist or a pessimist? What are your reasons for thinking so?

Activity 7

Rereading the Text and Looking Closely at Language

Strategic Marking of the Text

Because this series of texts focuses on the way people value life, you will now need to take a second look at the soliloquy. This time, read the text with a yellow highlighter or colored pencil (or devise some other way of marking the text in a unique and easily recognizable way), marking the places in the text where Hamlet describes what it means to be alive.

> **Example:** In lines two and three, Hamlet describes life as "the slings and arrows of outrageous fortune," so you could highlight that phrase as an example of what Hamlet thinks it means "to be."

Characterizing the Text

Take a look at the parts of the soliloquy you have highlighted and compare them with a classmate's markings. Find a few examples that you both have marked and mark the examples with a "+" or "–" to indicate whether the examples show a positive (+) outlook on life or a negative (–) one. For the example above—"the slings and arrows of outrageous fortune"—you would mark a "–" because it compares being alive to being under attack. After you have marked several such examples, reflect on the question asked earlier: At this moment, does it seem as if Hamlet is an optimist or a pessimist?

Paraphrasing the Text

Continuing to work with your partner, choose three of your samples and paraphrase them. "Paraphrasing" means putting the ideas of another writer into your own words. Again using the "slings and arrows of outrageous fortune" example, a paraphrase might sound something like this: "Hamlet compares being alive to having fate shoot arrows at him." As you paraphrase, pay attention to the style used by Shakespeare to convey his ideas. What is the difference between having Hamlet say that life is like "the slings and arrows of outrageous fortune" and having him just say, "Life isn't very pleasant"? What are the effects of Shakespeare's stylistic choices as a writer?

Postreading

Activity 8

Thinking Critically

We identified the genre earlier as a drama, but more specifically, this is a soliloquy. As noted earlier, a soliloquy is a dramatic convention that allows a character to speak aloud his or her thoughts. From your reading of the soliloquy, answer the following questions:

- Does the soliloquy form seem to favor the expression of emotion (pathos) or logic (logos)? Explain why you think so.
- Does Hamlet's soliloquy use emotion (pathos) to create a specific effect on the reader? If so, describe how emotion is used.
- Does Hamlet's soliloquy use logic (logos) to create a specific effect on the reader? If so, describe how the logic is used.
- When Hamlet speaks his soliloquy, he is in crisis. How do his circumstances position Hamlet to speak with authority (ethos) about the value of life? Does Hamlet seem to be speaking about his life in particular or about the quality of life in general?
- As careful readers, we are of course aware that it is not really Hamlet speaking, but a character created by Shakespeare. Does Shakespeare seem like someone whose opinions and attitudes are worth considering? Why?

Activity 9

Charting Multiple Texts

Take a look at the chart constructed for this assignment. It is a "graphic organizer"—a fancy name for something that helps you keep track of various pieces of information and the relationships among those pieces. Because the chart is rather small and you will be doing a lot of writing on it, you might want to get a larger piece of paper and create your own chart. The chart will prove useful in the writing assignment you will complete at the end of this module.

Directions: As you look down the side of the chart, you will see that it asks you for information about the different texts you will be reading in this assignment:

- Title
- Author
- Genre

The title and author are self-explanatory. "Genre" means "type," so you are asked to describe the type of writing. For this first text, you would put "Drama" or "Play" as the genre.

Across the top of the chart are the ideas you will be tracking as you read the texts in this module. They are presented in the form of questions:

- What is the text's big issue?
  - This asks you to identify the "main idea" of the text.

- What claim does the text make?
  - This asks you to identify the writer's perspective on the main idea.

- What are examples or quotes from the text?
  - This is where you would put examples given by the writer to help the reader understand his or her claim. The quotes and para- phrases you worked on earlier will fit well here. Be sure to include page or line numbers (or both) to identify where you found the quote or idea.

- What do you think about the text's claim?
  - In this box, you will explain your response to the text's claim, including to what extent (if any) you agree with it.

- What are your examples?
  - Give a few examples from your own experiences that help explain your response to the text's claim.

- How does this text connect to other texts?
  - If you see a similarity to another text, make note of it here. Connections can be made even among texts that have very different claims.

Take a few moments to fill in the chart for Hamlet's soliloquy. The final box on making connections may be left blank for the moment.

Text 2—*It's Not About the Bike*

Prereading

Activity 10

Surveying the Text

The second text is an excerpt from *It's Not About the Bike: My Journey Back to Life* by Lance Armstrong with Sally Jenkins. The excerpt you will read is from the book's opening chapter. Prior to reading, try to answer the questions below. They are designed to help you activate your schema, which is a technical term that means you generate some prior knowledge so you will be ready to read and comprehend more actively.

- What do you know about Lance Armstrong? If you do not know anything about him, try doing a quick Internet search and see what comes up.
- What is the significance of the fact that the book was written by Armstrong *with* Sally Jenkins?
- What kind of text—what genre—do you think this book is?

Activity 11

Making Predictions and Asking Questions

The following questions will help you make specific predictions about the content of Armstrong's text:

- What topics do you think Armstrong might talk about that are related to the issue of how society values life?
- Do you think Armstrong's claim about the value of life will agree with Hamlet's or not?

Activity 12

Introducing Key Vocabulary

Although the excerpt from Armstrong's autobiography is generally an easy, straightforward text to read, there are a few vocabulary words you might want to review prior to reading. When you run into those words during your reading of the text, note the context of each word and write a "best guess" synonym for it. Your teacher may want you to compare your work with your classmates.

- expire
- poignant
- demise
- cadence
- marbled
- acrid
- puckered
- catheter

| Activity 12 (Continued) | • constitution |
| | • articulate |

Which sets or pairs of words are related to each other? Which words refer to death? Which words refer to the body? Do you think you might encounter additional word families in this excerpt? Which ones?

Reading

| Activity 13 | **First Reading** |

Read the text by Armstrong. As you read, pay attention to the way Armstrong talks about the value of life. As you did with Hamlet, try to determine whether Armstrong appears to be generally pessimistic or optimistic in this passage. In addition, answer this question: Does Armstrong also present an argument about the value of death?

| Activity 14 | **Rereading the Text and Looking Closely at Language** |

Strategic Marking of the Text

First Highlighting: As you did with the Shakespeare text, you will mark Armstrong's text. This time, use an orange-colored highlighter or colored pencil (or devise some other method of marking the text differently than you marked the soliloquy). Highlight the sentences, phrases, or words Armstrong uses to describe what he thinks it means to be alive.

Characterizing the Text

Once you have highlighted Armstrong's text, compare what you have selected to highlight with the choices a classmate has made. Then, working with your partner, mark some of the commonly highlighted parts with a "+" or "–" sign to indicate whether each quote shows a generally positive or negative outlook on life. Discussing the results with your partner, decide how you would answer this question about Armstrong's outlook on life: Is he an optimist or a pessimist?

Strategic Marking of the Text

Second Highlighting: Go through the text once more, this time with a yellow highlighter. Imagine that you are reading Armstrong's text from Hamlet's perspective. Highlight any passages that Hamlet would find particularly interesting or compelling. Some of these may be the same words you have already highlighted, while others will be new.

Connecting the Texts—The Mock Interview

Armstrong and Hamlet, in their respective texts, provide quite different perspectives on the meaning and value of life. Working with your partner, envision a scenario in which Hamlet somehow would have the opportunity to interview Armstrong and vice versa. One of you should write out a series of at least five questions that Hamlet would ask Armstrong, while the other writes five questions for Armstrong to ask Hamlet.

Activity 14 (Continued)	When the questions are finished, take on the personas of these two and conduct the interviews. Be sure to give answers that are in keeping with the points of view provided in the two texts. After conducting the mock interviews, discuss the relative viewpoints of the characters. How well would they get along with one another? How would each respond to the arguments made by the other?

Here are some sample interview questions:

- How do you feel you have been treated by other people?
- Are you afraid of death?
- Are there any benefits to suffering?
- How do you approach challenges?

Postreading

Activity 15	### Thinking Critically

Armstrong's text is an autobiography. As with the soliloquy we examined earlier, the form of this writing has an effect on how it is read and understood. The questions below will help you assess Armstrong's text.

- An autobiography is a form of nonfiction—a text that tells the "truth." Do you think Armstrong is being truthful in his account of his life? Explain your reasoning.
- Armstrong's autobiography is written "with" Sally Jenkins. What role do you think Jenkins played in the writing of the text? How does her participation in the creation of the text influence your interpretation of Armstrong's story? In other words, how does the combination of Armstrong and Jenkins as authors affect the "ethos" of the text?
- Do you think Armstrong's story has an impact on the reader because of its use of logic (logos) or emotion (pathos) or both?
- Unlike Hamlet, Armstrong is not in the midst of his crisis when he writes his story; instead, he writes about his experiences in hindsight. Does that have an impact on Armstrong's ability to make his ideas and story compelling to the reader? Explain your reasoning.

Activity 16	### Charting Multiple Texts

Make an entry in your chart for the Armstrong text. Fill it out as you did with the soliloquy. When you reach the entry for "How does this text connect to other texts?", briefly describe the ways in which Armstrong responds to or challenges the assertions Shakespeare makes in his soliloquy for Hamlet.

Text 3—"What Is a Life Worth?"

Prereading

Activity 17	### Surveying the Text

The article "What Is a Life Worth?" comes from the February 12, 2002, issue of *Time* magazine. Take a look at its form and length. How much time do you think it will take to read this piece? Have you read anything from *Time* magazine? What do you know about that publication? What kinds of articles are commonly included in it? What types of people do you think compose the magazine's primary readership?

Activity 18	### Making Predictions and Asking Questions

This article includes the following subtitle: "To compensate families of the victims of Sept. 11, the government has invented a way to measure blood and loss in cash. A look at the wrenching calculus."

- What predictions can you make about the article's content from this subtitle?
- What connections do you think you might see between this article and the previous two texts you have read?
- The first two texts took first-person perspectives on the subject. Do you anticipate that this article will continue in that vein, or will it be different? Why do you think so?

Activity 19	### Introducing Key Vocabulary

Below, you will find three groupings of vocabulary words taken from "What Is a Life Worth?" The first group consists of words related to the legal and financial aspects of the article. The second list contains terms that convey information with particular emotional connotations. The final set of words is made up of terms that are used to describe the workings of the governmental plan to compensate 9/11 family victims. Working alone or with a partner, look over each list of words and provide a brief definition for the words you do not know well. Pay particular attention to the ways in which the words connect to one another (e.g., people *litigate*, or sue, because they want somebody to *compensate* them for a loss).

Financial and legal terms

- compensate
- litigation
- commodify
- valuation
- discretion

Activity 19 (Continued)	• liability
	• beneficiary
	• tort
	• allocation
	• disparity

Emotion-laden words

- squeamish
- garish
- gall
- traumatize
- callous
- inconsolable
- indignant
- balk
- deteriorate

Descriptive terms

- rhetorical
- Rorschach test
- artillery
- analogy
- solidarity
- orchestrated
- concoct
- mechanism

Reading

Activity 20

First Reading

As you read "What Is a Life Worth?" for the first time, look for the main issues and the various stances people take in response to those issues. Be sure to also look for connections to the idea of valuing life and to what was previously said about valuing life by Shakespeare and Armstrong.

How is "life" defined in this text? For example, does "life" refer to a human body, a soul, human experience, existence, or quality of life? Does this definition include a person's personal life and professional or working life?

Activity 21

Rereading the Text

Strategic Marking of the Text

Choose two highlighter or pencil colors and revisit the text of the article on 9/11. The two colors will be used to mark two different aspects of the article. With the first color, highlight the words, phrases, and sentences from the article that describe valuing life in *legal* and *financial* terms. With the second color, highlight the words, phrases, and sentences that describe valuing life in *human* and *emotional* terms.

Summarizing the Text

Using the sections you highlighted in the previous step, write a summary of the article's descriptions of how life is valued and people's responses to that valuing of life. Your summary should include only the most important ideas and must be limited to six sentences. If your teacher allows, you may want to work on this summary with a partner.

Connecting the Texts

With a partner, read the summary you wrote in the previous step. One of you should read the summary from the perspective of Hamlet; the other should take on the persona of Armstrong. Discuss with your partner how each would probably react to the way that "What Is a Life Worth?" describes the value of life.

- Would Hamlet agree with any of the ideas presented in the article? If so, which ones?
- Would Armstrong agree with any of the ideas in the article? If so, which ones?
- Would Armstrong and Hamlet be in agreement at all in the way they might interpret this article's ideas? If so, how?

Postreading

Activity 22

Thinking Critically

The previous two texts (the soliloquy and the autobiographical excerpt) both provide very personal approaches to the idea of valuing life. The current text, though, is an article from a respected national news magazine. The following questions will help you work through some of the implications of the text's structure and features on the interpretation and understanding of the text:

- Most news articles such as "What Is a Life Worth?" try to take an objective, unbiased approach. Would you agree that this text is unbiased, or do you think it favors one perspective? Explain your answer.
- What kinds of evidence does Ripley, the author of the article, use to get across the key ideas and issues associated with the compensation of 9/11 victims and their families? Are any specific types of evidence more compelling to you as a reader? Less compelling?
- How accurate do you think the information in the article is? In other words, do you think *Time* magazine and Ripley are to be trusted? Why or why not?
- Does the article use logic, emotion, or both to make an impact on the reader? If so, describe how. Compare that use to the way logic and emotion are used by Shakespeare, Armstrong, or both.

Activity 23	**Charting Multiple Texts**
	Make a third entry on your chart for "What Is a Life Worth?" Feel free to use the highlighting, summarizing, connections, and critical thinking work you did previously as a way to fill out the chart.

Text 4—"Human Life Value Calculator"

Prereading

Activity 24	**Surveying the Text**
	This text comes from an Internet resource called the "Life and Health Insurance Foundation for Education." Viewing the actual Web site is certainly preferable to looking at the printed text; the Web site's human life value calculator is available for examination at http://www.life-line.org/life_how_human.html.

- If your classroom has computer access, visit the Web site. Click around and look at the types of information available on the site as well as information about the organization that publishes the site. What appears to be the purpose of the site? How is the site organized?
- If you do not have Internet access, simply scan the text and take inventory of its attributes. What type of text does it appear to be? What are the features of the text, including the presence of such things as headings and graphs?
- This text comes from an Internet site whose domain name ends in ".org" instead of the more common ".com." Do you know what this ending to the site's address signifies?

Activity 25	**Making Predictions and Asking Questions**
	This text is quite different from the previous three texts. It is not personal or narrative, as the first two texts were, nor is it an informative text designed for a general audience. Instead, as you probably noticed when surveying the text, it is an interactive site, asking the reader to provide data to input and generating specific information based on the particular data provided by the user. The Web-based pages are called the "Human Life Value Calculator." Answer the following questions on the basis of what you know so far before you begin to read:

- What do you think might be the purpose of a text like this?
- Who might use this text?
- Since this text claims to calculate human life value, do you anticipate that this will have the most connections to Hamlet's soliloquy, Armstrong's autobiography, or Ripley's *Time* article? Why?

STUDENT VERSION

Activity 26

Introducing Key Vocabulary

The vocabulary terms listed below come from the Web site text. Many of these terms are similar to those in the list of legal and financial terms from "What Is a Life Worth?" In the same way that finding connections among ideas in different texts helps us to better understand those ideas, finding connections among vocabulary words helps us to better understand those words. As you find definitions for the terms below, try to include a similar term from the previous vocabulary lists.

- assess
- incur
- expenditure
- consumption
- fringe benefits
- contribution

Reading

Activity 27

First Reading

Read through the text, noting the way that a life's value is determined by the Human Life Value Calculator. Pay particular attention to the data input, which reflects a twenty-year-old single mother working in a service industry. If you have access to the Web site itself, you can choose a variety of data inputs to see how the results vary. Try providing different age, gender, occupation, and income information, and then examine the effect on the results. As you make sense of the calculator and its workings, make note of any connections you see to the previous texts we have read.

Activity 28

Rereading the Text

Strategic Marking of the Text

This activity is a variation on the kind of highlighting you did with the *Time* magazine article. Once again, you will be using two colors to mark the text for two different aspects. This time, however, you will be using the highlighter colors to indicate your own responses to the ideas within the text. With one color, highlight the parts of the text with which you find yourself in agreement. Use the other color to highlight the parts of the text that you either disagree with or that raise questions for you.

Responding to the Text

Look over the highlighting you did in the previous step. Write a brief response—no more than eight sentences—to the Human Life Value Calculator Web site. The response should describe what the Web site asserts about human life's value and your reactions to those assertions. Remember, your response doesn't have to be in complete agreement or disagreement with the text; you might agree with some aspects and disagree with others.

Postreading

Activity 29	**Thinking Critically**

- The Web site text you have been studying differs structurally (that is, in the way it is put together) from the prior texts. Make a list of several of the differences between this text and the others.
- Unlike the other texts, the Human Life Value Calculator has no single identified author. Does the lack of a named author affect your level of belief in the text's ideas and purpose? How can you find out more about the text and whose interests it represents?
- Did this text produce in you an emotional response of any sort? If so, briefly describe it.
- Consider the charts that the calculator produces. How well do you understand the meaning of these charts? How do the three charts differ? Does the use of all of the numbers within the charts seem to make a logical argument about the value of life?

Activity 30	**Charting Multiple Texts**

As you did with the previous texts, fill out a chart entry for the Web site. To facilitate this task, you may refer, as needed, to the highlighting you have done, your responses, and the questions (above) you just answered.

Connecting Reading and Writing

Activity 31	**Writing to Learn**

Many of the activities you have completed so far have involved writing. These kinds of informal writing assignments are part of a process called "writing to learn." You have been using writing, in essence, as a way for you to understand and interpret the texts you have been reading. Such informal writing is also a useful tool for helping you get ready to do more formal writing, as with the writing assignment you'll find below. To help you construct a claim for your essay as you work on this assignment, be sure to revisit the informal writing you have done. The chart, in particular, will help you to synthesize information for your paper.

Activity 32	**Using the Words of Others**

When you write anything in response to a text you have read, you will have to describe for your reader what the original text says. This can be done through direct quotations (saying precisely what the original author said), paraphrasing (providing a specific idea from the text,

Activity 32 (Continued)	but putting it in your own words), and summarizing (providing the primary ideas from the text in a generalized form). The activities you have already completed have asked you to find quotations, provide paraphrases, and write summaries, so you should be well prepared for using the words of Shakespeare, Armstrong, Ripley, and the makers of the human life value calculator within your formal essay.

When you use any method for representing the ideas from another text in your own writing, you must provide a citation. Your teacher will probably already have described for you the type of citation you need to use for this class, so be sure to follow those instructions carefully. Remember, even when you are summarizing and paraphrasing, you still must attribute the ideas to the original writer.

Writing Rhetorically

Prewriting

Activity 33

Reading the Assignment

As you read the assignment below, make note of the type of writing you are required to complete, the sources you may need to describe and discuss in your writing, and the audience for your writing.

> **Writing Assignment**
>
> So far in this assignment sequence, we have heard a number of different voices giving insights into the value of life. Hamlet's soliloquy offers an emotional, metaphor-laden glimpse into the thinking of a young man contemplating suicide. Lance Armstrong's autobiography uses storytelling from a first-person perspective to get across how the famed cyclist thinks about life. Amanda Ripley's article from *Time* magazine provides insight into the problems involved in translating the concept of valuing life from abstract terms into actual dollars and cents. The Human Life Value Calculator establishes specific criteria for assigning monetary value to a person's life.
>
> You might not fully agree or disagree with any of the texts' essential claims about the value of life. This makes your voice an important contribution to this discussion about how we should value human life. Where do your ideas fit into the terrain mapped by the other texts we have read? Is it right to assign dollar values to a person's life? Do suffering and illness impact how we should value life? Assume that the audience for your piece consists of intelligent citizens interested in this issue—the same types of people, for instance, who would read *Time* magazine.

As you write your essay, think about the different ways the authors we have read make their points about valuing life. Depending on the points you are trying to make, you might want to use some metaphors for life, as Hamlet does, or tell some stories the way Armstrong does. You may choose to include some words from people you interview, as Ripley does in her article, or you might even choose to establish some criteria for how human life should be calculated in monetary terms. As you construct your essay, make conscious choices about the ways you can represent your ideas to your reader.

How should our society assign value to human life?

Be sure to refer to and cite the readings. You may also use examples from your personal experience or observations.

Analyzing the Assignment

A "Do/What Chart" is a strategy you can use to clarify directions. To create a "Do/What Chart," draw a T-graph in your notes, labeling one side "Do" and the other side "What." Then list verbs from the prompt in the "Do" column and the objects of those verbs in the "What" column.

Do	What

Activity 34

Getting Ready to Write

Revisit the chart you made while reading the texts. Pay particular attention to the column that asks about your opinion of each text's claims. This will help you to determine where your ideas fit within the "conversation" about valuing life that takes place in the texts we read. Try writing sentences that fill in these blanks as a way of determining your own position.

• "I agree most with the ideas in _____ because _____."
• "I agree least with the ideas in _____ because _____."

Activity 35

Formulating a Working Thesis

Your essay's thesis is the primary claim that you will be making about valuing life. There are several attributes of claims that form the basis of successful essays. A good claim is:

• **Clear.** Your reader should easily understand your essay's claim.
• **Compelling.** The claim should be interesting to your reader and should make the reader want to read your entire paper.

Activity 35 (Continued)

- **Complex.** A claim that is too simple will not engage your reader and won't contribute significantly to the "conversation" about the topic.
- **Contestable.** Any claim that no one would disagree with is unlikely to be of interest to your reader.

Try writing a few claims for your essay. It might be helpful to think of your claim as a response to a specific question whose answer matters to the essay's audience. For instance, your claim should try to answer the question, "How should people value life in contemporary American society?" Your claim could take the form of a sentence that combines both an **assertion**—a statement of your opinion—and a **rationale**—a generalized reason in support of the assertion. Here are a couple of examples of claims that take this form:

- Schools should put more money into academics than into athletics because the primary goal of a school is to educate students, not to train athletes.
- The *Star Wars* films remain popular because they show the classic tale of an individual's triumph over oppression.

Put your claim into this assertion-rationale form, and you will be ready to begin drafting your essay.

Writing

Activity 36

Composing a Draft

Every writer's process for crafting a paper's first draft is unique. Some prefer to write an entire paper at a single sitting; others carefully plan the paper with outlines or maps prior to writing. The importance of a paper's first draft is that it provides an opportunity for you to shape your ideas into a coherent, written form.

Activity 37

Organizing the Essay

There are as many ways of organizing an essay as there are writers. Even so, essays will always have a beginning, middle, and end.

- The beginning—which may be one or more paragraphs long—sets up the essay's central question and claim.
- The middle of the essay provides ideas and evidence for the claim you are making. The evidence you provide may come in a number of forms, including quotations from the texts we have read and examples from your own life and experience. The chart you have completed may be helpful in this regard.
- The end is where you reach conclusions about the question and argue that your claim is the most reasonable way of answering the question.

Activity 38	Developing the Content

Read the following guidelines about developing support for your essay and discuss them with your classmates.

- Body paragraphs give evidence in the form of examples, illustrations, statistics, and so forth and analyze the meaning of the evidence.
- Each body paragraph is usually directly related to the question that the claim is attempting to answer.
- No set number of paragraphs make up an essay.

Revising and Editing

Activity 39	Revising the Draft

Revising your essay means looking at it again. Revision is often difficult because as writers, we know what we are trying to say; our essays, therefore, make sense to us. In order to revise effectively, we have to be able to look at our writing from a new perspective. Having classmates or others read our work provides new viewpoints that can lead us to revise effectively. Remember that the point is not for the readers to "fix" your essay; the readers' job is simply to give you feedback about how they read and made sense of your essay. As the writer, you are in charge of responding to what your readers tell you about the essay and doing the work necessary to make it more reader-friendly and effective.

Your teacher may provide you with some activities for revising your essay. Some suggestions for ways to look at your essay that will provide you with feedback are listed below:

- Put your draft aside for a few days, and then reread it. This allows you to develop some "critical distance" from the essay and usually makes it easier to see places that may need some revision.
- Ask a classmate to read the essay with a few highlighters or colored pencils. They can use red to signify places where you used powerful words, green for ideas that need to "grow" a little more, and so forth.
- Have a couple of classmates read your essay out loud together while you overhear their conversation about the essay. As they stop and discuss various parts of the paper, pay attention to what they say. Their reactions may give you very good insights into how to revise your paper.

Activity 40

Editing the Draft

Editing is often confused with revising, but editing has more to do with making your essay "clean"—that is, free of errors—while revising is about making your ideas come through as clearly as possible. Of course, editing may happen all through the process of writing, but the editing stage of writing comes when your essay is nearly in its finished form. Editing your paper is like giving a car a nice tune-up and polish before a car show; it lets the paper really shine. Here are some ideas for editing your paper:

- Read your paper aloud. This will help you identify places where a sentence doesn't sound quite right or spots where you might need to adjust punctuation or word choice.
- Ask a classmate or parent to read the paper and make suggestions about sentence construction, punctuation, verb tenses, and spelling.
- Run the essay through the computer's spelling and grammar check. Make sure to look carefully at the suggestions made by the computer and ask someone you trust—a teacher, classmate, or parent—if you have doubts. Computers often suggest the wrong word for misspellings (if you misspell "definitely" by writing "definately," for example, the computer will probably suggest that the correct spelling is "defiantly"), so pay close attention.

Activity 41

Reflecting on the Writing

After your essay is finished, reflect on the processes you went through to write the paper. Answer the following questions:

- How helpful did you find the highlighting, charting, and question-answering activities?
- How much was your writing affected by having kept notes in the charts?
- How helpful were the prewriting and revising activities?
- What did you learn from reading and writing in this assignment module?
- Which strategies will you use again when you are asked to read and write assignments like this one in the future?

Charting Multiple Texts

Text Information	What is the text's big issue?	What claim does the text make?	What are the examples/quotes from the text?	What do you think about the text's claim?	What are your examples?	How does this text connect to other texts?
Title: Author: Genre:						
Title: Author: Genre:						
Title: Author: Genre:						
Title: Author: Genre:						

Page 74 blank

The Value of Life

Writing Assignment

So far in this assignment sequence, we have heard a number of different voices giving insights into the value of life. Hamlet's soliloquy offers an emotional, metaphor-laden glimpse into the thinking of a young man contemplating suicide. Lance Armstrong's autobiography uses storytelling from a first-person perspective to get across how the famed cyclist thinks about life. Amanda Ripley's article from *Time* magazine provides insight into the problems involved in translating the concept of valuing life from abstract terms into actual dollars and cents. The Human Life Value Calculator establishes specific criteria for assigning monetary value to a person's life.

You might not fully agree or disagree with any of the texts' essential claims about the value of life. This makes your voice an important contribution to this discussion about how we should value human life. Where do your ideas fit into the terrain mapped by the other texts we have read? Is it right to assign dollar values to a person's life? Do suffering and illness impact how we should value life? Assume that the audience for your piece consists of intelligent citizens interested in this issue—the same types of people, for instance, who would read *Time* magazine.

As you write your essay, think about the different ways the authors we have read make their points about valuing life. Depending on the points you are trying to make, you might want to use some metaphors for life, as Hamlet does, or tell some stories the way Armstrong does. You may choose to include some words from people you interview, as Ripley does in her article, or you might even choose to establish some criteria for how human life should be calculated in monetary terms. As you construct your essay, make conscious choices about the ways you can represent your ideas to your reader.

How should our society assign value to human life?

Be sure to refer to and cite the readings. You may also use examples from your personal experience or observations.

The sample student essays that follow reflect the EPT Scoring Guide's criteria.

Sample student essay with a score of 6:

The Value of Life

Should people put the value of life into monetary value or should life be kept solely as an emotional quantity? People and societies throughout the ages have been trying to answer the problem of putting the value of life into terms of dollar bills. The ancient Egyptians buried their dead with all of their worldly belongings. They believed a person's monetary worth on Earth was over, and they should take all of that earthly worth with them to the afterlife. Modern day Americans are different from the Egyptians. Today people believe that the families of the dead should be compensated for "their" loss.

It is true that life is a precious commodity much like a diamond. But unlike a diamond, life has no set monetary value. But today's government is trying to change that. After the tragedies of September 11, 2002, the federal government started a federal fund to help the victims and families of victims of the attacks. This fund would give priority to people who were injured in the attacks, then to the spouse, and then to the parents. Sounds great doesn't it? Your husband dies and now you just lost your income, and the government is going to pay you for your loss. Well don't jump on the bandwagon so fast now. This might sound great now, but once you are knee deep in the program, it won't be so fun. To figure out how much money a person will receive from this fund is determined by a multi-step process. First they figure out how much an individual would have earned had there been no attacks. This would mean that a banker's family would earn far more than the family of a janitor in the buildings. Is it true that a banker is worth more to society than a janitor? Is a lawyer more important than a desk clerk? Then the fund adds $250,000 as a base cover, and then another $50,000 for a spouse and each child (Ripley 12). This would imply that a married man who has 6 kids in more important than a married man with no children at all. Is it more important in society to "make babies" than it is to just live your life? What about people who haven't yet had a chance to start a family because their lives were cut so short? Now all that money sounds like a blessing, doesn't it?

Well now that you have your foundation money, now you have to subtract the money you get from life insurance, pension, Social Security death benefits, and worker's compensation. After these "little" subtractions, you now have the total that you are going to receive from the government's fund. Now you are going to be hit with new questions after all this, for example is a rich man with high life insurance, high pension, and no children worth less than a poor man with no life insurance, no job, and ten children (Ripley 13)? The answer to all these questions is no. The lives of all people should be valued at the same price, if you are to set a price at all. A rich man should be the same as a poor man; a woman with no children should have the same life value as a woman with seven kids. The point is that if the government is going to put a monetary value of a human life, than it should be the same for everyone. "We hold these truths to self-evidence: that all men are created equal" (King Jr.).

There are many arguments against putting a money value on human life and two of the most impressive come from Alephonsion Deng and Lance Armstrong. Alephonsion Deng is one of the Sudanese Lost Boys. "We crossed a thousand miles of war ravaged country without the hope of sanctuary. Bullets replaced food, medicine, shelter and my loving parents. I lived on wild vegetable, ate mud from Mother Earth, and drank urine from my own body" (Deng 16). He had to walk across an entire country from refugee camp to refugee camp, always with the thought of death behind him. He didn't have the luxury of being able to go down to the grocery store when he ran out of food. He had to scavenge for what ever he could get his hands on. If Mr. Deng was asked about the government's 9/11 victims fund, which is set to put a monetary value on life, he would probably be outraged. After what he had been through he would probably say that it is impossible to turn something as valuable as life into terms of money.

Lance Armstrong survived a long battle with cancer, and after this battle came out with a new outlook on life. "When I was 25, I got testicular cancer and nearly died. I was given less than a 40 percent chance of surviving, and frankly, some of my doctors were just being kind when they gave me those odds" (Armstrong 1). Before having the ordeal with cancer his out look on life was just live it fast, everything was fast for him. After surviving the unbeatable he came out with a brand new outlook on his value of life. He now preached that life can end very quickly and that everyone should live their lives to the fullest terms possible. If someone asked Lance Armstrong about the government trying to put life into terms of dollars, bills, he would have a heart attack. Much like Mr. Deng, he would think that life is precious and the government should not demean it by trying to bring money into the same picture frame as life.

Should life be put into monetary values? The answer is no. Life is way too precious of a commodity to put into terms of money. People who have been on the brink of death would all say that you cannot put a value on the natural high that is known as life. To go back to an earlier metaphor, life truly is like the most precious and valuable of gems. They are similar in rareness and beauty, but are different in the fact that gems have a set money value, but life is a lot more stupendous than any gem on Earth. That is why life doesn't have a monetary value and never should.

Work Cited

Armstrong, Lance, and Sally Jenkins. It's Not About the Bike: My Journey Back to life. New York: Penguin Putnam, 2001.

Deng, Alephonsion. "I have Had to Learn to Live With Peace." Newsweek 31 October 2005: 16.

King, Jr., Martin Luther. "I Have A Dream". Mephis Educational Computer Connectivity Alliance. 11/21/05. http://www.mecca.org/~crights/dream.html.

Ripley, Amanda. "What is Life Worth?" Time December 2002: 12-13.

Shakespeare, William. Hamlet. New York: Simon and Schuster, 1992.

Unknown, Human Life Value Calculator. Life and Insurance Foundation for Education. November 14, 2005 http://www.life-line.org/life_human.html.

Commentary

This essay illustrates the EPT Scoring Guide's criteria for a score of 6. The superior response indicates that the writer is very well prepared to handle college-level reading and writing. Because this prompt asks for an edited (that is, revised and polished) essay, student papers should reflect the appropriate degree of organization, content, and editing.

- The writer addresses the entire topic and responds fully to all aspects of the prompt.
- The writer demonstrates a thorough critical understanding of the readings by incorporating them into the argument and by quoting them extensively, accurately, and, generally, in correct MLA format; occasional "dropped in" quotations indicate that the writer has not yet fully mastered this process.
- The writer uses rhetorical questions to undercut the assumptions made by sources with whose opinions the writer disagrees; rhetorical questions are occasionally overused, but the writer attempts to mitigate them with details from the reading.
- The writer has a smooth and easy writer's voice, addressing the reader directly and confidently.
- The essay uses a sophisticated inductive strategy, marshaling evidence first and saving the conclusions for later.
- The essay remains focused throughout.
- The essay makes use of source material beyond the readings; it also ties different types of support material together nicely.
- The writer avoids a formulaic essay approach and brings the reader "full circle" at the end by returning to the opening idea (the gem).
- Errors are rare and do not detract from meaning.

Sample student essay with a score of 5:

The Value of Life

People often question how we should measure the value of life. Can life be calculated into dollars and cents? Should ones value be determined by their life's accomplishments? Or does the value of one's life depend solely upon how much that individual embraces and loves their existence? In my personal experience I have found the latter to be true. Life is given value and meaning by one enjoying and accepting it.

Someone once said "You should not fear death, but fear the unlived life". This means that one should not fear the end of a journey, but enjoy the trip. To me this is absolutely true. Why should we spend our time fearing the inevitable? We are given only a few short years to experience the world, friendships, loves, and losses. Even the bad experiences teach us to appreciate the good ones. This doesn't mean we should all go out and be terrible people just so we will appreciate our good experiences, but rather that we should learn from our mistakes. Lance Armstrong's view of life is similar to this; he says that sometimes life is fun, and great, and other times it is horrible, but whether good or bad our experiences make us stronger people. It is these experiences which give our lives meaning.

Meaning and value however, are completely different issues. So how can the value of one's entire life and worth be translated into monetary values? The people at most life insurance companies will tell you it is a simple mathematical process based on age, physical health, and income. Subtract $1000 for every year over 40, subtract for any diseases, or illnesses, add 50 times their yearly income and voila! You'll have the value of anyone's life calculated in an instant! Unfortunately, this process cannot be applied to memories and experiences. You can't subtract points for every bad experience, lost love, and abandoned friendship and even the bad memories are carried around with us forever. Amanda Ripley's article, from TIME magazine, outlines, some of the problems with calculating the monetary value of life. Many people view the amount of money they receive as a measure of their loved one's value, which creates problems for the people who have to award the money. Calculating the value of life in dollar worth can be a complicated issue involving tough emotional and moral dilemmas.

Value is something which each individual assigns to their life depending on how much meaning it has to them self and others. A life is not a self contained object; it is a network which is shared with others. All people have value not just to themselves but to others as well. If you died tomorrow you entire network of friends and family would surely mourn for you. All of the people whose lives you have touched would mourn for you. In Hamlet's soliloquy, he neglected to consider what effect his life had on his family and friends. Everyone whether they realize it or not, has some kind of effect on the people around them. Hamlet thought of his own life as worthless and thought everyone else did too.

Life's value cannot be determined by dollar value, popularity or even by one's accomplishments. If one doesn't value life them self then they will be unhappy therefore making people around them unhappy. People must depend on themselves to make their lives valuable and meaningful. Ultimately it is people's own ability and willingness to value life which gives them worth.

Bibliography

Armstrong, Lance, and Sally Jenkins. It'ss Not About the Bike: My Journey Back to life. New York: Penguin Putnam, 2001.

Ripley, Amanda. "What is Life Worth?" Time December 2002: 12-13.

Shakespeare, William. Hamlet. New York: Simon and Schuster, 1992.

Unknown, Human Life Value Calculator. Life and Insurance Foundation for Education. November 14, 2005 http://www.life-line.org/life_human.html.

Commentary

This essay illustrates the EPT Scoring Guide's criteria for a score of 5. The clear competence of the essay indicates that this writer is quite ready to handle college-level reading and writing. Because this prompt asks for an edited (that is, revised and polished) essay, student papers should reflect the appropriate degree of organization, content, and editing.

- The essay thoroughly addresses the prompt and raises the pertinent question of the difference between value and money.
- The writer remains focused throughout the essay, offers a clear thesis about enjoyment and acceptance, and pursues that thesis throughout the supporting paragraphs.
- The writer uses transitions to guide the reader, such as the sentence that ends the second paragraph, "It is these experiences which give our lives meaning," which transitions to the opening sentence of the third paragraph, "Meaning and value however, are completely different issues."
- Occasional shifts in diction (for example, "one" in first paragraph, to "we" in the second, to "you" in third) are distracting; the essay mainly uses a conversational tone that works very well for this writer.
- The writer makes a lovely case in the fourth paragraph for life as a "network" rather than a "self-contained object."
- The essay's second half begins to repeat itself, particularly in the final two paragraphs, although the writer attempts to mitigate this repetition by using the Hamlet example.
- Errors in grammar, usage, and mechanics are minor; the writer could use some practice with commas.

Sample student essay with a score of 4:

The Value of Life

The value of life. What is it exactly? We will never know the true definition of the value of life because there are so many different perspectives in this world and everyone will think their perspective is right.

According to the Human Life Calculator, our value is based on the amount of money we will make in our lives and nothing more. It depends on the money we make, how many children we have, and how much we spend on ourselves each month. Some people find it fair to actually compare the value of life to the dollar amount they are worth. They might even look into it so much that people choose their partner according to their monetary values and not the emotional attachment. There are many people like that these days that only worry about money and what society thinks of them instead of wanted to be truly happy.

I don't agree with the Human Life Value Calculator what so ever. No person's life should be estimated on their monetary worth. It should go deeper then that. It all depends on how they want to live there life and if they think they live it to the fullest. If they live it to only become rich and die rich then so be it that is their own personal value. But to assume that every person values their life that way is completely and utterly wrong

When it comes to Hamlet, he wonders if there is even a value to life. "To be, or not to be—that is the question:" that is his main issue throughout the entire play. He pretty much loses everything that means anything to him in his life so he can't help but wonder if there is even a point anymore. Anything he truly valued, such as his father and Ophelia, was taken from him. He has nothing to value so why should he question the value of life?

Life has many hardships no matter who you are, even if you are Hamlet.

It still has a value to it. It teaches you to value you what you have because you never know when or they may not be there.

Lance Armstrong is a whole different story. He looks at life in such a positive perspective now unlike before. Unlike many people, he was given a second chance to live his life. He values every single thing because he never knows when it will be his time to go. He was luck the first time but no one know if he will be next time, if there is a next time. He learned the hard way not to take life for granted but to take advantage of it and live everyday as though it were your last.

Not everyone is as lucky as Lance Armstrong. He now realizes how valuable his life and everyone in it is but that's because he was given a second chance. There are so many people out there who wish they would have realized how valuable everything was before it was too late because they didn't get that second chance. We may not realize it until it happens but when we or a loved one goes through suffering or illness it truly impacts how we value life. It makes us face the reality that not everyday is guaranteed and people will not stay with us forever no matter how much we wish they would.

I think, as a society, we should value life not by how much money we have or how much we are worth but by how much we enjoy life and everyone in it. It shouldn't take the death of a loved one for us to realize everyday is valuable. We should wake up everyday realizing it's a new day and be thankful for it. I'm not saying to wake up and say "today might be my last" but realize it, embrace it. Take nothing fro granted and live everyday to its fullest. If you love someone then tell them. If you want to start a business then do what it take to start one. Do whatever you have to so that when you leave this world you are happy with who you are and what you accomplished. Don't expect to have no regrets or make no mistakes because those are what helped to form you to the person you become over time. I admit I am far fro perfect but that is what makes me and I am happy with myself. I love my life and everyone in it who helps to form it. I wouldn't take anything back or do anything over because if I did I wouldn't be the intelligent, free spirited, young woman I am today. I value my life to the fullest and it will never be based on money or praying to be given a second change because I didn't live it right the first time.

Works Cited

Armstrong, Lance and Sally Jenkins. It's Not About The Bike: My Journey Back To Life.New York: Berkley Trade, 1991.

Human Life Value Calculator

Shakespeare, William. Hamlet. Ed. Alan Durband. London: Hutchinson and Co., 1986.

4

Commentary

This essay illustrates the EPT Scoring Guide's criteria for a score of 4; however, it is a strong 4. This adequate response to the topic suggests that the writer should be able to handle college-level reading and writing. Because this prompt asks for an edited (that is, revised and polished) essay, student papers should reflect the appropriate degree of organization, content, and editing.

- The essay is a classic "befuddling" 4 paper; it wobbles between a 5 paper and a 3 paper, never really settling in either camp.
- The writer opens with a rhetorical question and then moves quickly to a clear, if simplistic, thesis.
- The writer attempts to integrate the readings by including supporting detail, although the essay offers only a single direct quotation.
- The works cited list provides a quasi-MLA format for sources.
- The logic in the third paragraph fails to persuade; the writer opens by showing Hamlet questioning life's value and then closes with the question, "He has nothing to value so why should he question the value of life?"
- The essay is somewhat repetitive, restating the idea of personal satisfaction as the best gauge of life's value.
- The essay lacks transitions in general, although the opening sentence of the penultimate paragraph, "Not everyone is as lucky as Lance Armstrong," is an exception.
- The writer opens each paragraph with a statement that focuses on the reading; however, the second half of each paragraph, which features the writer's own experience and opinions, generally becomes repetitive, rambles, or offers a cliched conclusion.
- The writer struggles with usage (than/then, there/their, everyday/every day), mechanics (especially punctuation), and grammar, although such instances do not greatly detract from meaning; the shifts in person in paragraph six, however, are quite distracting.

Sample student essay with a score of 3:

Extreme Life

What is life? I don't know, but I know it is full of obstacles. Sometimes they are small, sometimes they aren't. I don't think there is a point to it, but who knows? Another thing I know, everybody dies at the end, so why won't people live it to the maxim instead of just sitting on their bums and doing nothing, Being alive to me is to experience new adventures and to have fun.

Life is worth living for as long as you can. As Lance Armstrong said, "I want to die at a hundred years old with an American Flag on my back on the star of Texas on my helmet." It is very fun living out to your maximum, doing extreme sports like bungi jumping. I think that life should be extreme. It is also nice to come back home to someone who loves you and cares about you. I love food; I think it's another great thing to spend time with friends, especially when you can dig in and pig out. Its nice to have friends that are there for you when you have problems, and you know that they will help you out. Life is just a great things, but it doesn't always feel like it.

"To be or not to be" is Hamlet's famous quote. I bet every single person on earth has come to this decision. Besides the great things in life, you come across difficulties. For example losing the loved one. I think that hurts the most. Another thing is when you don't feel loved or accepted. That's when people come out of their limit and start doing bad stuff like drugs. When it gets really out of hand, they try to commit suicide. I believe that anybody who tried it or attempts suicide it are failures in life. As Lance Armstrong said, "Why don't we all just stop and lie down where we are?" what is we just do it? It's just an easy way out of life, escaping all the obstacles and pain. There is a lot of it. You friend can stab you in the back, your family member can die, there are just too many to name. You should just love life enough to struggle through the painful times.

"Why would I want to change, even for a day, the most important and shaping event in my life?" Lance Armstrong's words. Express how I feel. I would not give me life up for anything. I have made many of bad mistakes that I should not have done, but those mistakes make me the person I am today. I wouldn't want to look or be any different than I am right now. I love my life, and I hope everyone else does too because it's the only one we've got. You will have to start loving it or that only one wont be a good one.

3

Commentary

This essay illustrates the EPT Scoring Guide's criteria for a score of 3. Although the essay suggests developing competence, it is flawed in significant ways that suggest the writer needs additional practice before being able to succeed in college-level reading and writing. Because this prompt asks for an edited (that is, revised and polished) essay, student papers should reflect the appropriate degree of organization, content, and editing.

- The essay responds to the prompt at the opening, although it moves away from the prompt later.
- The writer attempts to define life itself rather than discuss the value of life.
- The writer offers a thesis about adventures and fun but does little to offer support for that thesis.
- The essay's paragraphs, although short, are overworked in that they contain several ideas competing for space; the essay does not attempt to separate paragraphs into discrete ideas.
- The paragraph about eating and hanging out with friends struggles with logic, perhaps because the writer is still trying to connect the evidence to the thesis; by the third paragraph, the writer seems willing to move away from the thesis completely.
- The opening of the third paragraph ("'To be or not to be' is Hamlet's famous quote. I bet every single person on earth has come to this decision") makes neither logical nor rhetorical sense.
- The writer attempts to quote texts directly but lacks the skill to incorporate quoted material properly.
- The writer shows a limited syntactic repertoire; the first paragraph, for example, contains four rhetorical questions out of six "sentences."
- Errors of grammar, usage, and mechanics accumulate to detract from meaning; there are several missing apostrophes and fragments (see the second sentence of the final paragraph, for example).

Value of Life

This is a question that runs through everybody's mind. What would somebody pay for a life? What would you do if your life ended tomorrow? Would you tell someone that you cared about the most that you loved them? What would you do for your final hours? How do you think the people aboard the 9/11 plane attack felt as soon as they knew that they weren't going to see their families anymore? These questions are all very goods questions but the most important one is "Have you been living the life that you wanted to live"?

Humans always follow others ways of posture and ways of thinking. People picking up laughs, looks, even the way they think about other people. Think of it this way...if someone put a gun to year head and they said, "Give me three reasons why I should not pull this trigger"? What would you say? It might sound like a harsh, blunt question but if you think about it.... where you living your life to the fullest?

Posers always get on everybody's nerves. They are going to look back on their lives and think what they did was really stupid. Their values of life are following somebody's else's footstep, following others stories, what they like, don't like because they can't think for themselves. They rely on other people to make their decisions for them.

The final thought is the toughest thought of all. Things all bundled up inside your head. The only thing to realize is that people don't make you who you are. You make the decisions that will lead your life, the rest of your life. What would your family get if you died? "Tack on an extra $50,000 in pain and suffering for a spouse and for each child." That's what you would get. Now think to yourself, are you living your life to the fullest, what you think is good?

Ripley, Amanda. "What is a life worth?" <u>Time</u>: 11 Feb. 2002.

2

Commentary

This essay illustrates the EPT Scoring Guide's criteria for a score of 2. The serious flaws here indicate that this writer will need considerable additional practice before being able to succeed in college-level reading and writing. Because this prompt asks for an edited (that is, revised and polished) essay, student papers should reflect the appropriate degree of organization, content, and editing.

- The essay opens with a statement about questions, followed by six rhetorical questions in a row.
- The writer seriously overuses the questioning strategy, with three additional questions in the second paragraph and two in the fourth (concluding) paragraph; the essay itself finishes with a question.
- The essay neglects the prompt; it discusses "values" rather than the value of life.
- The final paragraph attempts to approach the prompt by quoting Ripley (although the writer does not attribute the quoted material), but the quotation is ineffectively dropped into the concluding text.

- The essay does not demonstrate any discernible organizational strategy.
- Some sentences make no sense at all, such as "People picking up laughs, looks, even the way they think about other people."
- Errors in grammar, usage, and mechanics are present but not all that profound; lack of logic and content is the issue with this essay.

Sample student essay with a score of 1:

The Value of Life

People put a money aspect on people for example, when people have money then we need them, we don't even care about anyone unless they have money. When disaters like sunamis happen, people want to find there family but dont understand the water infected and no one no's what's happening to any one any where.

Katrina for example. They (the army) use colors were dead are, yellow were sick are, green x marking the spot were people who are worth saving were. We help people every where in the world but no our own people, to save them, even the army was there making every one get out of there house if they wanted to or not, they might get shot if not. People have always come here to make a new lives and this is what happens? Its way messed up. Is this how to value people?

Shakespeare new how bad life can be. "To be or not to be" said Hamlet who thought not. We have to find out a way to help and over come what might happen next so every one is not so discouraged because money is not the answer or stocks or bonds or jewelers but only love.

1

Commentary

This essay illustrates the EPT Scoring Guide's criteria for a score of 1. The fundamental deficiencies here indicate that this writer will need a great deal of additional practice before being able to succeed in college-level reading and writing. Because this prompt asks for an edited (that is, revised and polished) essay, student papers should reflect the appropriate degree of organization, content, and editing.

- The writer offers no apparent thesis in response to the prompt.
- The essay seems to address the issue of over-emphasis on money when human worth is calculated, but the language of the essay is too incoherent to read between the lines.
- Each paragraph may have a single idea, but those ideas are nearly impossible to tease out.
- The writer struggles with the basic skills of English prose. Errors are significant, pervasive, and profound as they obscure meaning.

Page 86 blank

Racial Profiling

Module 5

Racial Profiling

Teacher Version

Reading Rhetorically

Prereading 1
  Getting Ready to Read.. 1
  Surveying the Text 2
  Making Predictions and Asking Questions............... 2
  Introducing Key Concepts.................................... 4
  Introducing Key Vocabulary 5

Reading 6
  First Reading 6
  Looking Closely at Language 6
  Rereading the Text 7
  Analyzing Stylistic Choices 8
  Considering the Structure of the Text 8

Postreading 9
  Summarizing and Responding 9
  Thinking Critically 10

Connecting Reading to Writing

Writing to Learn 13
Using the Words of Others..................................... 13

Writing Rhetorically

Prewriting 15
  Reading the Assignment 15
  Getting Ready to Write.. 16
  Formulating a Working Thesis 17

Writing 17
  Composing a Draft... 17
  Organizing the Essay 21
  Developing the Content 22

Revising and Editing... 23
  Revising the Draft.. 23
  Editing the Draft 24
  Reflecting on the Writing..................................... 25

Evaluating and Responding 26
  Grading Holistically... 26
  Responding to Student Writing 26
  Using Portfolios.. 27

Reading Selection

"Hounding the Innocent" 29

Student Version

Activity 1: Getting Ready to Read 31
Activity 2: Surveying the Text 31
Activity 3: Making Predictions and Asking Questions 32
Activity 4: Introducing Key Concepts 32
Activity 5: Introducing Key Vocabulary......................... 33
Activity 6: First Reading... 34
Activity 7: Looking Closely at Language......................... 34
Activity 8: Rereading the Text...................................... 34
Activity 9: Analyzing Stylistic Choices........................... 35
Activity 10: Considering the Structure of the Text........... 35
Activity 11. Summarizing and Responding...................... 35
Activity 12: Thinking Critically 36
Activity 13: Using the Words of Others.......................... 38
Activity 14: Reading the Assignment.............................. 39
Activity 15: Getting Ready to Write 40
Activity 16: Formulating a Working Thesis...................... 40
Activity 17: Composing a Draft 40
Activity 18: Organizing the Essay 44
Activity 19: Developing the Content............................... 45
Activity 20: Revising the Draft 47
Activity 21: Editing the Draft....................................... 47
Activity 22: Reflecting on the Writing............................ 48

Prewriting Strategies... 49

Evaluation Form 50

Sample Student Essays

Writing Assignment and Scored Student Essays.............. 53

Hounding the Innocent

by Bob Herbert
The New York Times, June 13, 1999

1   An anti-loitering law that allowed the Chicago police to arrest more than 42,000 people from 1992 to 1995 was declared unconstitutional in June of 1999 by the Supreme Court.

2   [Supreme Court Justice] Antonin Scalia howled in dissent, which should tell you something. The law was an abomination, just like the practice in New York of stopping and frisking black and Hispanic people by the tens of thousands for no good reason and just like the practice of pulling over and harassing perfectly innocent black and Hispanic motorists on streets and highways in many parts of the country.

The Faces of Ethnic Profiling

3   Ethnic profiling by law-enforcement authorities in the United States comes in many forms, and all of them are disgusting.

4   In the summer of 1998, sadistic members of the State Police in Oklahoma spent more than two hours humiliating Rossano Gerald, a thirty-seven-year-old Army sergeant, and his twelve-year-old son, Greg.

5   Sergeant Gerald was pulled over and interrogated. He was ordered out of his car and handcuffed. The troopers asked if he had any guns. They asked permission to search the car, and when he refused they searched it anyway. They separated Greg from his father and locked him in a police vehicle. They interrogated him. They brought drug-sniffing dogs to the scene. They dismantled parts of the car. When they finally tired of the madness, they told Sergeant Gerald he was free to go. No arrest was made. Greg, of course, was petrified. When the ordeal ended, he wept uncontrollably.

6   Why did this happen? Greg and Sergeant Gerald were guilty of America's original sin. They were born black.

Profiling Targets the Innocent

7   In New York, profiling was not only perpetuated but elevated to astonishing new heights during the regime of [New York City Mayor] Rudolph Giuliani. Here, the targets are mostly pedestrians, not motorists. Young black and Hispanic males (and in some cases females) are stopped, frisked, and harassed in breathtaking numbers.

8   By the police department's own count, more than 45,000 people were stopped and frisked by members of the Street Crimes Unit in 1997 and 1998. But the total number of arrests made by the unit over those two years was less than 10,000. And it is widely believed that the number of people

stopped during that period was far higher than the 45,000 reported by the cops. The true number likely was in the hundreds of thousands.

9   Ira Glasser, executive director of the American Civil Liberties Union [ACLU], noted that two things characterize the New York City stops: "Virtually everybody is innocent, and virtually everybody is not white."

10   Mayor Giuliani, like most public officials, will not acknowledge that his police officers are targeting people by race. "The stops are driven by the descriptions of the person who committed the crime," Mr. Giuliani said.

11   Spare me. The vast majority of these stops are in no way connected to the commission of a specific crime, and the mayor knows it. They are arbitrary and unconscionable intrusions on the rights of New Yorkers who are supposed to be protected, not humiliated, by the police.

Profiling Is Extensive

12   Most Americans have no idea of the extent of the race-based profiling that is carried out by law-enforcement officials and the demoralizing effect it has on its victims. The ACLU, in a report called "Driving While Black: Racial Profiling on Our Nation's Highways," said, "No [people] of color [are] safe from this treatment anywhere, regardless of their obedience to the law, their age, the type of car they drive, or their station in life."

13   The Chicago law that resulted in more than 42,000 arrests over three years was aimed at curbing gang activity. It was clearly unconstitutional. It made it a crime for anyone in the presence of suspected gang members to "remain in any one place with no apparent purpose" after being told by the police to move on.

14   Why should one's purpose for being in a public place have to be apparent? As a reporter for *The New York Times,* I might be in the presence of a suspected gang member. What business is that of the police? And how could that possibly be a legitimate basis for an arrest?

15   The suit challenging the law was brought by the Chicago office of the ACLU. A spokesman for the group noted that the "vast majority" of the people arrested under the law were African-American or Hispanic. What a surprise.

Racial Profiling

Reading selection for this module:
Herbert, Bob. "Hounding the Innocent." *The New York Times.* 13 June 1999.

Reading Rhetorically

Prereading

Activity 1	**Getting Ready to Read**

The following argument, "Hounding the Innocent" by Bob Herbert, was first published in *The New York Times* on June 13, 1999. It tries to persuade its readers that law-enforcement agents should not take action on the basis of race alone. It uses a combination of logic and emotion to achieve its purpose. Have you ever been stopped by the police because of your appearance? If you have, what was your reaction? If you haven't, what do you think your reaction would be? Why do you think you would react this way?

Quickwrite: What do you know about this topic? What do you think about it? Write for five minutes. Then discuss your response with a partner.

Activity 2	**Surveying the Text**

Surveying your reading material (no matter what its length) will give you an overview of what it is about and how it is put together. To learn how to survey an essay, answer the following questions.

1. Who is the author of this essay?
2. When and where was this essay published?
3. What organizational signposts do you notice in this essay?
4. What do you think each of these sections will talk about?

| Activity 3 | **Making Predictions and Asking Questions** |

Making predictions about your reading will help you read actively rather than passively. Active reading promotes learning. Your answers to the following questions will guide you through the process.

1. What do you think this essay is going to be about?
2. What do you think is the purpose of this essay?
3. Who do you think is the intended audience for this piece? What brings you to this conclusion?
4. What do you think the writer wants the reader to do or believe?
5. On the basis of the title and other features of the selection, what information or ideas might this essay present?
6. Will the article be negative or positive in relation to the topic? How did you come to this conclusion?
7. What argument about the topic might the article present? What makes you think so?
8. Turn the title into a question (or questions) for you to answer after you have read the essay.

| Activity 4 | **Introducing Key Concepts** |

Understanding key concepts in a reading selection is essential to good comprehension. Below are some important words from Herbert's essay. Write down your thoughts on these terms. Then complete the vocabulary-building activity that follows.

race
prejudice
ethnic
anti-Semitism
discrimination
preconceived notions
profiling
stereotyping

Activity 4
(Continued)

Vocabulary Building

Complete a "cubing" activity for four of the words listed above. For this exercise, fill in all the squares below for each of the words you choose:

Describe it: What are its colors, shapes, sizes, smells, tastes, sounds?	**Compare it:** What is it similar to?
Associate it: What does it make you think of?	**Analyze it:** How is it made?
Apply it: What can you do with it? How can it be used?	**Argue for it or against it:**

Activity 5

Introducing Key Vocabulary

The following vocabulary words are important to your understanding of this essay, so the definitions are provided for you:

profiling (from the subtitle): making judgments about someone on the basis of appearance

abomination (paragraph 2): an object that is intensely disliked

dismantled (paragraph 5): taken apart

perpetuated (paragraph 7): continued

unconscionable (paragraph 11): not reasonable

Use two of these words to define two words on the previous list (from "Introducing Key Concepts").

STUDENT VERSION

Reading

Activity 6 | **First Reading**

We all process reading material differently. No one way is better than another. To demonstrate the variety of approaches to this essay, read it aloud, and talk about your responses to the following questions:

1. Which of your predictions turned out to be true?
2. What surprised you?
3. Are you persuaded by the text?

Activity 7 | **Looking Closely at Language**

To continue to build on your understanding of the key words in this essay, discuss the following questions with your class:

1. What is racial profiling?
2. Why does Herbert use the word "Faces" in the subtitle of the first section of the essay?
3. What connotations does "anti-loitering" have for you?

Activity 8 | **Rereading the Text**

As you read the essay again, do the following tasks:

• Record the essay's thesis.

• State the thesis as a question.

• Highlight the details throughout the essay that directly answer the question you have written.

• On your copy of the essay, label the following points in the left-hand margin:

    The introduction
    The issue or problem the author is writing about
    Examples given by the author
    The author's main arguments
    The conclusion

• In the right-hand margin, write your reactions to what the author is saying.

Activity 9	**Analyzing Stylistic Choices**

Answer the following questions about the author's use of words and sentences to help you understand how the text works.

Words

1. What does the term "racial profiling" bring to mind for you? Which words or synonyms are repeated?
2. Why do you think they are repeated?
3. Paragraph 5 of this essay has several strong words that draw on readers' emotions. Circle the words that are the most highly charged and be prepared to explain your choices. Why did you choose certain words over others in the paragraph?

Sentences

1. Is the author's sentence structure mostly varied or not? What effect does the variety or lack of variety have on the essay?
2. Are the sentences readable? Explain your answer.

Activity 10	**Considering the Structure of the Text**

Learning more about the structure of the text will give you a better understanding of the writer's approach to its content. Your work on this activity will help you understand the text's structure.

Making Discoveries

1. What is the main method of organization in this essay?
2. Working in pairs, create a picture outline showing how this essay is structured. Talk with your partner until you have negotiated a graphic outline that represents how the essay is laid out.

Analyzing Your Findings

1. As a whole class, discuss how the text is organized.
2. Working in pairs or small groups, determine the major parts of the text and their purposes.

Postreading

Activity 11	**Summarizing and Responding**

The act of summarizing makes us put someone else's ideas into our own words as it improves our understanding of those ideas. In groups of three or four, summarize the essay's main points in no more than five sentences. Then generate five questions that might serve as the basis of a class discussion. Use at least five vocabulary words from this module in your summary.

Thinking Critically

The following questions and activities will help you gain a deeper understanding of the Herbert essay. Answer the following questions as thoroughly as you can. Then complete the quickwrite and the PAPA Square.

Questions about Logic (Logos)

1. What are two major assertions the author makes in this essay?
2. Highlight the support the author provides for these assertions.
3. Can you think of counterarguments the author does not deal with?
4. Do you think the author has left something out on purpose? Why?

Questions about Emotions (Pathos)

1. Does this piece affect you emotionally? Which parts?
2. Do you think the author is trying to manipulate the reader's emotions? How?
3. Do your emotions conflict with your logical interpretation of the arguments?
4. Does the author use humor? How does that affect your acceptance of the author's ideas?

Questions about the Writer (Ethos)

1. Does this author have the right background to speak with authority on this subject?
2. Is this author knowledgeable? Smart? Successful?
3. What does the author's style and language tell you about him?
4. Do you trust this author? Why or why not?
5. Do you think this author is deceptive? Why or why not?
6. Do you think this author is serious?

Quickwrite (five minutes)

Choose one of the following topics and write about it for five minutes:

1. What does the writer want us to believe?
2. What is your response to one of the author's main ideas?

What did you learn from this exercise? Write for five more minutes.

Activity 12 (Continued)

PAPA Square

A PAPA Square helps you analyze the rhetorical strategies in your reading and in your own writing. To apply this exercise to your reading, answer the questions around the outside of the box in reference to the essay. In the center, identify the stylistic devices and logical, emotional, and ethical appeals the writer uses to persuade his or her audience.

Now fill in the PAPA Square for the Herbert essay.

Purpose
(What is the writer's purpose?)

Audience
(Who is the audience?)

Argument
(What is the thesis or argument?)

Rhetorical Methods and Strategies

Logical Appeals

Pathetic Appeals

Ethical Appeals

Stylistic Devices

Persona
(What is the author's persona or public image?)

Connecting Reading to Writing

Activity 13

Using the Words of Others

One of the most important features of academic writing is the use of words and ideas from written sources to support your own points. Essentially, there are three ways to incorporate words and ideas from sources into your own writing:

1. **Direct quotation.** Bob Herbert says, "Most Americans have no idea of the extent of the race-based profiling that is carried out by law enforcement officials and the demoralizing effect it has on its victims" (17).

2. **Paraphrase.** In "Hounding the Innocent," Bob Herbert notes that racial profiling is more extensive than we realize and is demoralizing to its victims (17).

3. **Summary.** In "Hounding the Innocent," Bob Herbert cites statistics and stories from different parts of the country to prove that racial profiling is extensive and unjust. According to the author, "ethnic profiling" is practiced in a variety of ways throughout the United States, and no people of color, either walking or driving, are safe from its effects (17).

Documentation. You will also need to learn to take notes with full citation information. For print material, you need to record at least the author's name, title of the publication, city of publication, publisher, publication date, and page number.

The two most common documentation formats are the Modern Language Association (MLA) format, which is used mainly by English departments, and the American Psychological Association (APA) format.

MLA Format

Books. Here is the citation in MLA format for a typical book:

Bean, John C., Virginia A. Chappell, and Alice M. Gilliam. *Reading Rhetorically: A Reader for Writers.* New York: Longman, 2002.

Newspapers. Here is the bibliographic information for the Herbert article in MLA format. The fact that it was published in a newspaper changes the format and the information slightly:

Herbert, Bob. "Hounding the Innocent." *The New York Times.* 13 June 1999, Sec. 4: 17.

Web Sites. You might also want to incorporate material from Web sites into your writing. To document a Web site, you need to give the author's name (if known), the title of the site (or a description, such as "Home-page," if no title is available), the date of publication or most recent update (if known), the name of the organization that sponsors the site, the date of access, and the Web address (URL) in angle brackets; for example,

Activity 13 (Continued)

University Writing Center. 26 June 2003. University Writing Center, California Polytechnic State University, Pomona. 26 May 2004 <http://www.csupomona.edu/uwc>.

Because the name of the author is unknown for the above site, it is left out. This entry would appear in the Works Cited section, alphabetized as "University."

In-Text Documentation. The MLA style also requires in-text documentation for every direct quotation, indirect quotation, paraphrase, or summary. If the author's name is given in the text, the page number is furnished in parentheses at the end of the sentence containing the material. If not, both the name and page number must be furnished. For example, because the author is not named in the following excerpt from the Herbert article, his last name is placed in parentheses, along with the page number, at the end of the quotation:

> "In New York, profiling was not only perpetuated but elevated to astonishing new heights during the regime of [New York City Mayor] Giuliani. Here, the targets are mostly pedestrians, not motorists. Young black and Hispanic males (and in some cases females) are stopped, frisked, and harassed in breathtaking numbers" (Herbert 17).

Practice with Sources. Choose three passages from the Herbert text that you might be able to use in an essay. First, write down each passage as a correctly punctuated direct quotation. Second, paraphrase the material in your own words. Finally, respond to the idea expressed in the passage by agreeing or disagreeing with it and explaining why. Now you are ready to use this material in an essay.

Writing Rhetorically

Prewriting

Activity 14

Reading the Assignment

Reading the assignment carefully to make sure you address all aspects of the prompt is important.

Writing Assignment

Write an essay that presents your opinion on a controversial issue of your choice. Begin with a debatable thesis statement. Then follow the guidelines for writing an argument essay. As you write your essay, be sure you support your opinions with reasons. If something in the media (such as a newspaper article, ad, or speech) inspired this assignment, attach a copy to your paper before you turn it in.

Activity 14 (Continued)	Take the following steps for this exercise:

- Read the assignment carefully.
- Decide which issue you are going to discuss.
- Discuss the purpose of the assignment. What will you try to accomplish in your essay?

Activity 15	

Getting Ready to Write

The following exercises will help you move from reading to writing.

Choose a controversial issue on your campus or in the news that is important to you. Use one or more of the techniques from the list of Prewriting Strategies on page 49 to generate ideas on the issue. Then consult your campus or local newspaper for ideas if you'd like. What is the exact issue? Why is it important? Why do people care about it? How do you think the issue should be resolved?

Activity 16	

Formulating a Working Thesis

Writing down a tentative thesis at this point is a good habit to develop in your writing process. Your thesis must be a complete sentence and can be revised several times. A *focused* thesis statement will keep your writing on track.

Record your responses to the following questions in preparation for writing your tentative thesis statement:

1. What specific question will your essay answer? What is your response to this question? (This is your tentative thesis.)
2. What support have you found for your thesis?
3. What evidence have you found for this support (facts, statistics, statements from authorities, personal stories, examples)?
4. How much background information do your readers need to understand your topic and thesis?
5. If readers were to disagree with your thesis or the validity of your support, what would they say? How would you address their concerns (what would you say to them)?

Now draft a possible thesis for your essay.

Writing

Activity 17	

Composing a Draft

When you write an argument essay, choose a subject that matters to you. If you have strong feelings, you will find it much easier to gather evidence and convince your readers of your point of view. Keep in mind, however, that your readers might feel just as strongly about the opposite side of the issue. The following guidelines will help you write a good argument essay.

1. **State your opinion on the topic in your thesis statement.** To write a thesis statement for an argument essay, you will need to take a stand for or against an action or an idea. In other words, your thesis statement must be debatable—a statement that can be argued or challenged and that will not be met with agreement by everyone who reads it. Your thesis statement introduces your subject and states your opinion about that subject.

   Bob Herbert's thesis is in his third paragraph: "Ethnic profiling by law-enforcement authorities in the United States comes in many forms, and all of them are disgusting." This is a debatable thesis. Some other statements on the topic of ethnic profiling would not be good thesis statements:

   > **Not debatable:** Ethnic profiling by law-enforcement authorities in the United States often involves African Americans and Hispanics.

   > **Not debatable:** Some law-enforcement agencies have strict rules regarding ethnic profiling.

   Herbert sets up his essay with some facts about anti-loitering laws and a reference to the practice in New York of stopping and frisking blacks and Hispanics. This background information leads up to his thesis statement.

2. **Find out as much as you can about your audience before you write.** Knowing your readers' background and feelings on your topic will help you choose the best supporting evidence and examples. Suppose that you want to convince people in two different age groups to quit smoking. You might tell the group of teenagers that cigarettes make their breath rancid, their teeth yellow, and their clothes smelly. But with a group of adults, you might discuss the horrifying statistics on lung and heart disease associated with long-term smoking.

   Herbert's essay was first published in *The New York Times,* which addresses a fairly educated audience. The original readers probably thought much like he does on this issue. So he chose his support as if he were talking to people who agree with him.

3. **Choose evidence that supports your thesis statement.** Evidence is probably the most important factor in writing an argument essay. Without solid evidence, your essay is nothing more than opinion; with it, your essay can be powerful and persuasive. If you supply convincing evidence, your readers will not only understand your position but perhaps agree with it.

   Evidence can consist of facts, statistics, statements from authorities, and examples or personal stories. Examples and personal stories can be based on your own observations, experiences, and reading, but your opinions are not evidence. Other strategies, such as comparison/contrast, definition, and cause/effect, can be particularly useful in building an argument. Use any combination of evidence and writing strategies that supports your thesis statement.

In his essay, Herbert uses several different types of evidence. Here are some examples:

Facts

- An anti-loitering law was declared unconstitutional in June 1999 (paragraph 1).
- Sergeant Rossano Gerald was stopped by the Oklahoma police in the summer of 1998 (paragraph 4).

Statistics

- Chicago police arrested over 42,000 people from 1992 to 1995 for loitering (paragraph 1).
- In New York, more than 45,000 people were stopped and frisked by the Street Crimes Unit in 1997 and 1998 (paragraph 8).
- Only 10,000 arrests were made in New York in 1997 and 1998 (paragraph 8).

Statements from Authorities

- Quote by Ira Glasser, ACLU director (paragraph 9)
- Quote by Mayor Giuliani (paragraph 10)
- ACLU report (paragraph 12)

Examples and Personal Stories

- Story about Sergeant Gerald and his son (paragraphs 4–6)

4. **Anticipate opposing points of view.** In addition to stating and supporting your position, anticipating and responding to opposing views are important. Presenting only your side of the argument leaves half the story untold—the opposition's half. If you acknowledge that there are opposing arguments and answer them, you will be more convincing.

   In paragraph 10, Herbert acknowledges as opposition a statement made by Mayor Giuliani. Giuliani flatly denies the claims against his police force: "The stops are driven by the descriptions of the person who committed the crime." By acknowledging this statement, Herbert raises his credibility. He then goes on to counter Giuliani's claim in the next paragraph.

5. **Find some common ground.** Pointing out common ground between you and your opponent is also an effective strategy. "Common ground" refers to points of agreement between two opposing positions. For example, one person might be in favor of gun control and another strongly opposed. But they might find common ground—agreement—in the need to keep guns out of teenagers' hands. Locating some common ground is possible in almost every

situation. When you state in your essay that you agree with your opponent on certain points, your reader sees you as a fair person.

Herbert assumes that most of his readers know that ethnic profiling by law-enforcement agencies is going on around the country. His job, then, is to prove the extent and unfairness of it.

6. **Maintain a reasonable tone.** Just as you probably wouldn't win an argument by shouting or making mean or nasty comments, don't expect your readers to respond well to such tactics. Keep the "voice" of your essay calm and sensible. Your readers will be much more open to what you have to say if they think you are a reasonable person.

Herbert maintains a reasonable tone throughout his essay. He is occasionally lighthearted and sometimes sarcastic: "Spare me" (paragraph 11) and "What a surprise" (paragraph 15). But even when he quotes some unbelievable statistics, as he does in paragraphs 1 and 8, he keeps his voice under control and, therefore, earns the respect of his readers.

7. **Organize your essay in such a way that it presents your position as effectively as possible.** You want your audience to agree with you by the end of your essay, so you need to organize it in such a way that your readers can easily follow it. The number of paragraphs will vary depending on the nature of your assignment, but the following outline shows the order in which the features of an argument essay are most effective:

Introduction
Background information
Introduction of the subject
Statement of your opinion

Body Paragraphs
Common ground
Lots of evidence (logical and emotional)
Opposing points of view
Response to the opposing points of view

Conclusion
Restatement of your position
Call for action or agreement

The arrangement of your evidence in an argument essay depends to a great extent on your readers' opinions. Most arguments will be organized from general to particular, from particular to general, or from one extreme to another. When you know that your readers already agree with you, arranging your details from general to particular or from most to least important is usually the most effective approach. Using this order, you build on your readers' agreement and loyalty as you explain your thinking on the subject.

STUDENT VERSION

Activity 17 (Continued)

If you suspect that your audience does not agree with you, reverse the organization of your evidence and arrange it from particular to general or from least to most important. In this way, you take your readers step by step through your reasoning in an attempt to get them to agree with you.

Herbert's essay follows the general outline just presented. Here is a skeleton outline of his essay:

Introduction

Background statistics and facts about anti-loitering laws and stopping and frisking

Body Paragraphs

The Faces of Ethnic Profiling

Subject introduced: racial profiling
Statement of opinion: racial profiling is disgusting
Evidence—example: Sergeant Gerald's story

Profiling Targets the Innocent

Evidence—fact: blacks and Hispanics stopped in New York
Evidence—statistics: more than 45,000 people stopped; fewer than 10,000 arrested
Evidence—statements from authorities: Ira Glasser, ACLU director
Opposing point of view: Mayor Giuliani
Response to opposition: Herbert's opinion

Conclusion: Profiling Is Extensive

Restatement of the problem: extent of race-based profiling
Evidence—statements from authorities: quotation from ACLU report
Evidence—statistics: more than 42,000 arrests in Chicago in three years
Herbert's opinion
Evidence—fact: ACLU lawsuit
Herbert's final comment

Activity 18

Organizing the Essay

The following items are traditional parts of all essays:

- The introduction (usually one or two paragraphs), which "hooks" the reader and provides a thesis statement or road map for the reader
- The body (as many paragraphs as necessary), which supports the thesis statement point by point
- The conclusion (usually only one paragraph), which summarizes the main points and explains the significance of the argument

The number of paragraphs in an essay depends on the nature and complexity of your argument.

| Activity 18 (Continued) | Here are some additional hints to help you organize your thoughts: |

Introduction

- You might want to include the following in your introductory paragraph:
  - A "hook" to get the reader's attention
  - Background information the audience may need
  - A thesis statement along with some indication of how the essay will be developed ("forecasting"). *Note:* The thesis statement states the topic of the essay and the writer's position on that topic. You may choose to sharpen or narrow your thesis at this point.

Body

- Paragraphs that present support for the thesis statement, usually in topic sentences supported with evidence. (Refer to "Getting Ready to Write.")
- Paragraphs that include different points of view or address counter-arguments
- Paragraphs or sentences in which you address those points of view by doing the following:
  - Refuting them
  - Acknowledging them but showing your argument is better
  - Granting them altogether but showing they are irrelevant
- Evidence that you have considered the values, beliefs, and assumptions of the audience; your own values, beliefs, and assumptions; and some common ground that appeals to the various points of view

Conclusion

- A final paragraph (or paragraphs) that includes a solid argument to support the thesis and indicates the significance of the argument—the "so what?" factor

Draw horizontal lines through your essay to distinguish these three parts, and label them in the margin.

Activity 19

Developing the Content

Read the following highlights about developing your essay. Then discuss them with your classmates, and complete the PAPA Square on your own writing.

- Most body paragraphs consist of a topic sentence (or an implied topic sentence) and concrete details that support that topic sentence.
- Body paragraphs give evidence in the form of examples, illustrations, statistics, etc., and analyze the meaning of the evidence.
- Each topic sentence is usually directly related to the thesis statement.
- No set number of paragraphs makes up an essay.
- The thesis dictates and focuses the content of an essay.

PAPA Square

A PAPA Square helps you analyze the rhetorical strategies in your reading and in your own writing. You have already applied this exercise to your reading. To apply this exercise to your writing, answer the questions around the outside of the box in reference to your own essay. In the center, identify the stylistic devices and logical, emotional, and ethical appeals you use to persuade your audience.

Now fill in the PAPA Square for your essay.

Purpose
(What is your purpose?)

Audience
(Who is your
audience?)

Argument
(What is your thesis
or argument?)

Rhetorical Methods and Strategies

Logical Appeals

Pathetic Appeals

Ethical Appeals

Stylistic Devices

Persona
(What is your persona or public image?)

Revising and Editing

Activity 20

Revising the Draft

You now need to review the organization and development of your draft to make sure your essay is as effective as possible.

Peer Group Work

Working in groups of three or four, read your essay aloud to the other members of the group. Then use Part I of the Evaluation Form (on page 50) as a revising checklist for each essay.

Paired Work

Work in pairs to decide how you will revise the problems that group members identified.

Individual Work

Revise the draft based on the feedback you have received and the decisions you have made with your partners. Consider these questions as revision guidelines for your individual work:

1. Have I responded to the assignment?
2. What is my purpose for this essay?
3. What should I keep? Which parts are the most effective?
4. What should I add? Where do I need more details, examples, and other evidence to support my point?
5. What could I delete? Do I use irrelevant details? Am I repetitive?
6. What should I change? Are parts of my essay confusing or contradictory? Do I need to explain my ideas more fully?
7. What should I rethink? Is my position clear? Have I provided enough analysis to convince my readers?
8. How is my tone? Am I too overbearing or too firm? Do I need qualifiers?
9. Have I addressed differing points of view?
10. Does my conclusion show the significance of my essay?
11. Have I used key vocabulary words correctly to represent the ideas from the article? Have I used words that refer to specific facts from the text?

Activity 21

Editing the Draft

Edit your draft on the basis of the information you have received from your instructor or from a tutor. Use Part II of the Evaluation Form on page 51 as an editing checklist. The following editing guidelines will also help you to edit your own work:

1. If possible, set your essay aside for 24 hours before rereading it to find errors.
2. If possible, read your essay aloud so you can hear errors and rough spots.

Activity 21 (Continued)

3. Focus on individual words and sentences rather than on the overall meaning. Take a sheet of paper and cover everything except the line you are reading. Then touch your pencil to each word as you read.
4. With the help of your teacher, figure out your own pattern of errors—the most serious and frequent errors you make.
5. Look for only one type of error at a time. Then go back and look for a second type and, if necessary, a third.
6. Use the dictionary to check spelling and confirm that you have chosen the right word for the context.

Activity 22

Reflecting on the Writing

Reflecting on your writing is an essential part of improving on your next assignment. When you have completed your essay, answer these six questions, and submit your thoughts with your final draft.

1. What was most difficult about this assignment?
2. What was easiest?
3. By completing this assignment, what did you learn about arguing?
4. What do you think are the strengths of your argument? Place a wavy line by the parts of your essay that you feel are very good.
5. What are the weaknesses, if any, of your paper? Place an X by the parts of your essay you would like help with. Write any questions you have in the margin.
6. What have you learned from this assignment about your own writing process—about preparing to write, about writing the first draft, about revising, and about editing?

Prewriting Strategies

Brainstorming: Based on free association, this is the act of making a list of related words and phrases.

Clustering/webbing: This is the process of "mapping" any ideas that come to mind on a specific topic. This strategy involves writing a key word or phrase in the center of the page, drawing a circle around it, then writing down and circling any related ideas that come to mind and drawing lines to the words that prompted the new words.

Discussing: This is the act of talking with another person about your subject matter and grappling aggressively with your ideas in the process.

Freewriting: Based on free association, this is the strategy of writing for a brief period of time about anything that comes to your mind.

Outlining: This is the listing of the main ideas and details related to your subject in the order in which you will probably address them.

Questioning: This is the process of asking questions that will generate new ideas and topics. This process is often based on the five Ws and one H: Who? What? Why? Where? When? and How?

Scanning: This is the process of scanning and spot reading to generate specific ideas and form opinions.

Evaluation Form

Based on the CSU English Placement Test (EPT)

Part I: Revising Checklist—Mark the appropriate categories.

	Superior	Strong	Adequate	Marginal	Weak	Very Weak	Comments
Response to the topic	Addresses the topic clearly and responds effectively to all aspects of the task.	Addresses the topic clearly but may respond to some aspects of the task more effectively than others.	Addresses the topic but may slight some aspects of the task.	Distorts or neglects aspects of the task.	Indicates confusion about the topic or neglects important aspects of the task.	Suggests an inability to comprehend the question or to respond meaningfully to the topic.	
Understanding and use of the assigned reading	Demonstrates a thorough critical understanding of the assigned reading in developing an insightful response.	Demonstrates a sound critical understanding of the assigned reading in developing a well-reasoned response.	Demonstrates a generally accurate understanding of the assigned reading in developing a sensible response.	Demonstrates some understanding of the assigned reading but may misconstrue parts of it or make limited use of it in developing a weak response.	Demonstrates very poor understanding of the main points of the assigned reading. Does not use the reading appropriately in developing a response or may not use the reading at all.	Demonstrates little or no ability to understand the assigned reading or to use it in developing a response.	
Quality and clarity of thought	Explores the issues thoughtfully and in depth.	Shows some depth and complexity of thought.	May treat the topic simplistically or repetitively.	Lacks focus or demonstrates confused or simplistic thinking.	Lacks focus and coherence and often fails to communicate ideas.	Is unfocused, illogical, or incoherent.	
Organization, development, and support	Is coherently organized and developed, with ideas supported by apt reasons and well-chosen examples.	Is well-organized and developed, with ideas supported by appropriate reasons and examples.	Is adequately organized and developed, generally supporting ideas with reasons and examples.	Is poorly organized and developed, presenting generalizations without adequate support or details without generalizations.	Has very weak organization and development, providing simplistic generalizations without support.	Is disorganized and undeveloped, providing little or no relevant support.	
Syntax and command of language	Has an effective, fluent style marked by syntactic variety and a clear command of language.	Displays some syntactic variety and facility in the use of language.	Demonstrates adequate use of syntax and language.	Has limited control of syntax and vocabulary.	Has inadequate control of syntax and vocabulary.	Lacks basic control of syntax and vocabulary.	
Grammar, usage, and mechanics (See list on next page for details)	Is generally free from errors in grammar, usage, and mechanics.	May have a few errors in grammar, usage, and mechanics.	May have some errors but generally demonstrates control of grammar, usage, and mechanics.	Has an accumulation of errors in grammar, usage, and mechanics that sometimes interfere with meaning.	Is marred by numerous errors in grammar, usage, and mechanics that frequently interfere with meaning.	Has serious and persistent errors in grammar, usage, and mechanics that severely interfere with meaning.	

Part II: Editing Checklist

Problem	Questions	Comments
Sentence boundaries	Are there fragments, comma splices, or fused sentences?	
Word choice	Are word choices appropriate in meaning, connotation, and tone?	
Subject-verb agreement	Do main verbs agree with the subject in person and number?	
Verb tense	Is the tense appropriate to the topic and style? Does the writing shift back and forth from present to past inappropriately?	
Word forms	Are any parts of verb phrases missing or incorrect? Are verb endings correct? Do other words have correct endings and forms?	
Noun plurals	Do regular plurals end in "s"? Are irregular plurals correct? Are there problems with count and non-count nouns?	
Articles	Are articles (*a, an,* and *the*) used correctly? (*Note:* Proper nouns generally don't have an article, with exceptions such as "the United States" and "the Soviet Union," which are more like descriptions than names.)	
Spelling	Are words spelled correctly?	
Punctuation	Are periods, commas, and question marks used correctly? Are quotations punctuated correctly? Are capital letters used appropriately?	
Pronoun reference	Does every pronoun have a clear referent? (*Note:* Pronouns without referents or with multiple possible referents create a vague, confusing style.)	
Other problems	Are there other important problems?	

Page 52 is blank.

Sample Student Essays

Racial Profiling

Writing Assignment

Write an essay that presents your opinion on a controversial issue of your choice. Begin with a debatable thesis statement. Then follow the guidelines for writing an argument essay. As you write your essay, be sure you support your opinions with reasons. If something in the media (such as a newspaper article, ad, or speech) inspired this assignment, attach a copy to your paper before you turn it in.

The sample student essays that follow reflect the EPT Scoring Guide's criteria.

Sample student essay with a score of 6:

To the Police, Leave My Friend Alone

Although I have never been racially profiled, one of my good friends has. She was driving her aunt's car on vacation last summer on the east coast when the cops pulled her over, and wrote her a speeding ticket. They told her she had to come back, and go to court during the school year or she could pay them right now. In cash. My friend paid the bill. By the way, my friend is Black.

In the article, "Hounding the Innocent," Bob Herbert says that "Most Americans have no idea of the extent of the race-based profiling that is carried out by law-enforcement officials and the demoralizing effect it has on its victims." Herbert is only half right. Most White Americans "have no idea," about how much profiling goes on, but most non-White Americans know how common it is, because they are the victims. Racial profiling is definitely a bigger problem then most of us realize.

Herbert gives examples of racial profiling in diverse places like New York, and Chicago, and places you wouldn't think profiling would happen, like Oklahoma. For example, he tells a terrible story of Rossano Gerald and his son Greg, who were pulled over and interrogated by police. The police separated the father from his son, they searched the car, and they even used drug-sniffing dogs. By the time they were finished, the little boy, "wept uncontrollably." This kind of event is ridiculous. When I was a little kid, my Mom and Dad told me that if I was ever in trouble, I should look for a policeman to help me. After talking with my friend and reading Herbert, I am not sure if the police are there to help at all.

Some people might say that racial profiling is good, because it can help law enforcement officials arrest terrorists and other criminals. I agree, an old lady probably will not be carrying a bomb at the airport, but I would rather search too many people then not enough. Second, people might also say like Mayor Giuliani does, "The stops are driven by the descriptions of the person who committed the crime." Herbert responds by saying that most stops are not connected to any one crime but are, "arbitrary and unconscionable intrusions." I find myself forced to agree.

What should we do about racial profiling? If non-White Americans are already aware of the problem, which it seems to me they are, then the next step is to make White Americans more aware. This is a place where the media can help, since they have everyone's attention, like Bob Herbert does. Also, people who see the police racially profiling someone should do something, for example, taking pictures with their cell phones so that every one else can see what is happening. Finally, police agencies and lawmakers must make racial fairness a priority. We are a Nation of many races, and we will never have harmony if law-abiding people like my friend driving down the road are afraid of the police who are suppose to protect them. We want happy citizens, not demoralized victims.

6

Commentary

This essay illustrates the EPT Scoring Guide's criteria for a score of 6. The superior response indicates that this writer is very well-prepared to handle college-level reading and writing.

- The writer approaches the topic clearly and directly, without resorting to pre-essay "throat-clearing" strategies, by citing a specific example from a friend's experience.
- The essay offers a strong, early thesis, supporting that thesis without using a formulaic approach and taking a stand that acknowledges points of both agreement and disagreement with Herbert.
- The writer obviously understands the Herbert passage and uses it extensively within the essay, quoting both directly and indirectly from the article and using one of Herbert's points to make a final appeal.
- The writer avoids excessive mimicking of Herbert's pattern of organization.
- The writer moves beyond the Herbert article to make a personal argument based on the article without relying excessively on Herbert's material.
- The writer occasionally has trouble moving beyond personal experience as a lens through which to view the topic but makes the effort to consider other viewpoints (members of the non-majority culture, persons who might disagree with the writer's position).

- The logic wavers a bit in the fourth paragraph, but the writer is able to recover and continue with the argument.
- The essay moves beyond summary of and agreement with Herbert to posing a possible solution.
- The writer uses transitions, both within ("for example," "also") and between paragraphs ("Some people might say . . .") to guide the reader through the essay.
- The writer uses a variety of syntactic structures.
- Errors in grammar (subjunctive mood), usage (than/then), and mechanics (commas, capitalization) are reasonably rare and do not interfere with meaning. The single sentence fragment in the opening paragraph appears to be intentional.

Sample student essay with a score of 5:

Racial profiling has many negative impacts. Those impacts include the discomfort and humiliation of many minority citizens, the lack of unity in the American people, and the possibility of a real criminal getting away because he is not a minority thus becoming a threat to society. Racial profiling is all of America's fears surfacing; America needs to overcome these fears in order to stop racial profiling.

There are many cases, though not all cases, where police use their authority to shame members of minority groups. Statistics show that if a black man in a nice care and a white man in a nice car drive by a police officer speeding at the same time, the police officer is more likely to pull over the black man. This is just a scenario, but it happens every day. This can be shameful and humiliating, to be judged by the color of skin or an accent. Its not fair, its not equal, and its not just. Police officers are supposed to be protecting and serving everyone, not just white people.

When people are judged daily because of skin color and nationality there will be a lack of unity. How can people unite if they can not look past the surface? They can not. Racial profiling is a great divider among the people in America. There is a saying, "United we stand, but divided we fall", If America can not look past its differences, and this problem worsens, then America, the land of the great, will fall.

When police officers choose who to search or harass by skin color, accent, or nationality, they may be letting real criminals get away, while searching innocent people. While not all people from minority groups are innocent, neither are all white people. Searching a man simply because he is black takes time away from catching a real criminal, maybe a white man, who may then become a danger to society.

Racial profiling is something that may never stop in America. It is wrong and unjust, but many will forever be ignorant to the problem and its possible solutions. Still, it is something worth fighting for, for the many who suffer because of the problem and for this country in general.

Commentary

This essay illustrates the EPT Scoring Guide's criteria for a score of 5. The clear competence of the essay indicates that this writer is quite ready to handle college-level reading and writing.

- The essay responds to the topic clearly and effectively.
- The writer offers a thesis that moves beyond the Herbert reading to postulate a cause for racial profiling.
- The essay's approach is somewhat formulaic (the three reasons are provided in the first paragraph and then repeated and developed, one at a time, in the subsequent paragraphs).
- The body paragraphs are obviously guided by the writer's own thesis instead of by mere repetition of Herbert's thesis.
- The writer uses a variety of syntax, effectively mixing an assortment of sentence styles, and includes a rhetorical question to help support the argument.
- The writer uses appropriate examples and reasons, including personal opinion ("they may be letting real criminals get away," "How can people unite if they can not look past the surface?").
- Errors such as missing apostrophes ("its not equal") and pronoun vagueness (the "it is something worth fighting for" in the final paragraph seems to refer to racial profiling) are minor and do not interfere with meaning.

Sample student essay with a score of 4:

Racial Profiling is Crude

Racial profiling has become a huge problem since 9/11. Bob Herbert in his essay believes that all forms of racial profiling are disgusting. Ethnic profiling against innocent people should not be tolerated at any time because it is discrimination against those who are of a different race.

Racial profiling is unjust because innocent people can get arrested just because they look a certain way. "In the summer of 1998, sadistic members of the State Police in Oklahoma spent more than two hours humiliating Rossano Gerald, a 37-year-old Army sergeant, and his 12-year-old son, Greg" (Herbert 3). The police believe that judging someone by the way they look will solve their problem in the search on terrorist, however, it is also putting other people's lives in jeopardy. The State Police of Oklahoma did not have a legit reason to pull him over therefore they let him go after they searched his whole car and cuffed him. That is not okay in any way, shape or form and it should not be allowed.

The consistence of profiling continues to take over lives of those that are "colored." "No people of color are safe form this treatment anywhere, regardless of their obedience to the law, their age, the type of car they drive, or their station in life" (Herbert 4). Are the police saying that if they are driving while it is black outside that only white people can be out? That is the most ridiculous thing anyone could ever say. It is unjust and not fair. Racial profiling is intended for a good reason, which is to find suspected terrorist, however it is unconstitutional to pick on someone just because they are "colored."

Ethnic profiling should never be tolerated regardless of the purpose. It is not fair and nobody deserves to be picked on just because they are a different color. Herbert in his essay believes the same.

4

Commentary

This essay illustrates the EPT Scoring Guide's criteria for a score of 4. This adequate response to the topic suggests that the writer should be able to handle college-level reading and writing.

- The essay stays on topic.
- Shifts in diction between formal and informal ("did not have a legit reason") are distracting.
- The essay is somewhat repetitive, repeating the main point over and over instead of providing explanation or analysis.
- The writer's sentence structure is similarly repetitive, although the writer does occasionally attempt a more complex sentence (see the final sentence of the third paragraph).
- The essay includes two direct quotations from Herbert; however, these quotations are simply dropped into the writer's text rather than being integrated smoothly.
- The writer attempts to look at the opposing viewpoint ("Racial profiling is intended for a good reason") but struggles in language while trying to answer that viewpoint.
- Errors in punctuation (commas are a particular problem), pronoun agreement, usage ("can not"), and pronoun reference are common but do not generally interfere with meaning (the rhetorical question in the third paragraph is an exception here).

Sample student essay with a score of 3:

Racial Profiling

Everyone has different opinions on Racial Profiling, some people say there are benefits or others have negative impacts on racial profiling. There really are not any benefits on racial profiling, because racial profiling is completely wrong no matter what. How can it be right to see a black or Hispanic person in a car and pull them over because they think they are doing something illegally and then finding out nothing was wrong, they were innocent? It is so sad to see that happen to someone innocent.

Racial Profiling is taught not inherited, nobody is ever born to hate, but everyone learns racism from parents, friends, family, or adults. Hate can not be stopped, nobody can change anyone else, but it does not make sense that people want to teach their kids racism.

Harassing perfectly innocent black and Hispanic motorists on streets and highways is just completely dumb. "No people of color are safe from this treatment anywhere, regardless of their obedience to the law, their age, type of car they drive, or their station is life" (Herbert 4). Supposedly most of the stops that are being done to black and Hispanic people are driven by the descriptions of the person who committed the crime. But, seriously the majority of the stops are in no way connected to the commission of a specific crime, and everyone knows it. More than half of the Americans have no idea of the extent of the race-based profiling that is carried out by law-enforcement officials.

Commentary

This essay illustrates the EPT Scoring Guide's criteria for a score of 3. Although the essay suggests the writer's developing competence, it is flawed in significant ways that indicate the writer needs additional practice before being able to succeed in college-level reading and writing.

- The essay offers a thesis in response to the prompt but buries the thesis in the middle of the first paragraph.
- The essay's body paragraphs do not support the writer's thesis; each paragraph has its own unique direction.
- The essay's body paragraphs attempt to use specific details, but the second paragraph, which relies on the writer's experience, provides a general statement without reasons or examples in support.
- The writer offers a single direct quotation from Herbert but drops it into the text rather than incorporating it.
- The essay ends abruptly and without coming to any conclusions.
- Misused idioms ("benefits on racial profiling"), missing commas, comma splices, nonstandard capitalization ("Racial Profiling"), and awkward syntax (see the penultimate sentence of the first paragraph) are quite common, and their accumulation obscures the writer's meaning.

Sample student essay with a score of 2:

Racial profiling is a despicable act. Its has been always as a negative affliction to the society. Bob Herbert tries to persuade its readers that law enforcement agents should not take no action base on race alone. Multiples of law enforcement agents in the United States are humiliating people due to the color of their skin. This is racial profiling an is simply unjust. This has to be stop no matter what in the United States. Is embarrassing what people are living through in the U.S, which holds mostly the best constitution in the nation.

In the summer of 1 998 state police in Oklahoma spent more than two hours humiliating Rossano Gerald, a 37-year-old Army sergeant, and his 12-year-old son, Greg. Gerald was interrogated and was search without permission. Agents also separated Rossano from Greg, which he was put in the patrol car. Patrol agents made damage to Rosanno's car by searching for illegal stuff he didn't carried at all. Two hours have passed and no arrest was made and the patrol agents told Rossano and Greg that they were free to go.

Many Americans are not being well informed with racial profiling. Bob Herbert in his article is explaining everything at its best. With facts and opinions he has achieve the eyes every reader. His stories are a strong reaction of life in the U.S. Herbert also state the fact, which the vast majority of these stops are in no way connected to the commission of a specific crime. Herbert's article also proves laws and courts that had happen, due to racial profiling.

Racial profiling has to be stop in every way there is, is humiliating to see and is strongly unjust. Many people cannot believe how many patrolmen have done these acts in all the states of the nation. Is hard to learn the truth, but people live in racist world that might never end. Herbert's article is a perfect text of writing for people to read in order to receive information that is hard to believe that it happens in the United States.

2

Commentary

This essay illustrates the EPT Scoring Guide's criteria for a score of 2. The serious flaws here indicate that this writer will need considerable additional practice before being able to succeed in college-level reading and writing.

- The writer attempts a thesis based on the prompt, but the essay begins to deteriorate immediately after the first sentence.
- The essay has significant errors of logic (see the final sentence of the first paragraph).
- The essay is repetitive; the third paragraph, for example, simply restates the writer's agreement with Herbert multiple times.
- Errors of grammar, usage, and mechanics are pervasive, profound, and often make the essay incoherent. This essay suffers from unclear pronoun reference and missing inflections ("This has to be stop" covers both of these issues), shifts of verb tense within sentences (see the final sentence of the second paragraph), faulty sentence structure ("he has achieve the eyes every reader"), and missing articles and demonstratives ("Is hard to learn the truth, but people live in racist world"), among other concerns.

Sample student essay with a score of 1:

Persuasive Essay

This article by Bob Herbet is discussing the faces of ethnic profiling, profiling targets innocent, and profiling is extensive. I agree with Bob Herbet.

"Greg and Sergeant Gerald were guilty of America's original sin. They were born black," as discussed by Herbet. Sargeant Gerald was pulled over and interrogated at gunpoint while his son wept uncontrollably. Why do Police do acts like this now a day? The reasons is Gerald and Greg were born black. I strongly agree with Bob Herbert, all racial profiling are very disgusting, the State Police should no way do such act.

"Mayor Giuliani, like most public officials, will not acknowledge that his police officer are targeting people by race," wrote Ira Glasser from the ACLU. New York Police admitted arresting more than 45,000 people, a huge amount but true number was far higher, says Glasser. Although stops are done by the description of the crimnal. People has opinion that now a days public officials would want to target people by race instead of crimnal acts.

I also agree with Herbet that profiling have demoralizing effect on it's victims. "Why should one's purpose for being in a public place have to be apparent." As said before profiling, is very disgusting. It shows many face, all of them are aimed at perfectly innocent. Bob Hebert is right, hounding innocent citizens is not job of the Police.

1

Commentary

This essay illustrates the EPT Scoring Guide's criteria for a score of 1. The fundamental deficiencies of this essay clearly indicate that the writer needs much additional practice to be ready to succeed at college-level reading and writing.

- The essay summarizes the article rather than making an argument.
- The writer quotes Herbert but also uses material directly from the article without using quotation marks or otherwise attributing the material; the most "correct" sentences in the essay, even if not in quotation marks, come more or less verbatim from Herbert.
- The writer attempts a debatable thesis statement but rather than offering an argument, the essay merely restates Herbert's article, then agrees with the article without adding specific support.
- The essay suffers from significant logic issues (see the last two sentences of the third paragraph).
- Quoted material, either attributed or not, provides the bulk of the essay's content.
- The essay is highly repetitive, both in its reuse of the Herbert material and its own internal reasoning.
- The writer even has difficulty correctly transcribing material directly from the essay ("Bob Hebert," "his police officer are") and incorrectly attributes material.
- The writer struggles with verb use ("profiling have demoralizing effect"), confusion of singular and plural forms ("all racial profiling are very disgusting"), article use ("but true number was far higher"), spelling ("crimnal," "admmitted"), fragments, and usage; these issues are distracting and interfere with meaning.

Juvenile Justice

Many Kids Called Unfit for Adult Trial:
Those Under 15 Often Blind to the Long-Term Results of Their Choices, a Study Says

by Greg Krikorian
The Sacramento Bee, March 3, 2003

1   Thousands of juveniles tried as adults in the United States may be incompetent to stand trial because they are emotionally or intellectually unable to contribute to their own defense, according to a juvenile-justice study to be released today.

2   The study, directed by a University of Massachusetts professor, found that one-third of the eleven- to thirteen-year-olds studied and 20 percent of those fourteen or fifteen years old had levels of reasoning and awareness comparable to those of mentally ill adults judged not competent to stand trial.

3   And in examining 1,400 males and females in four jurisdictions, researchers concluded that age and intelligence—not gender, ethnicity, socioeconomic factors or even prior run-ins with the law—were the most significant factors in determining a youth's ability to understand the judicial process.

4   "It is a violation of constitutional rights to be a defendant in a criminal proceeding when you are not competent to defend yourself," said Laurence Steinberg, a Temple University psychology professor and director of the John D. and Catherine T. MacArthur Foundation research network that co-funded the study.

5   "In all likelihood, a large number of juveniles being tried as adults are not competent to stand trial," Steinberg said.

6   While the study did not address whether any youths were wrongly convicted, Steinberg said, its findings did suggest that "thousands" of juveniles went to adult trial when they should not have because their ability to understand the proceedings was "seriously impaired."

7   For the study, researchers tested eleven- to twenty-four-year-olds in Los Angeles, Philadelphia, north Florida and northern and eastern Virginia—with half of those studied in juvenile detention and the other half living in the community. The research showed that the performance in reasoning and understanding for youths ages sixteen and seventeen did not differ from those at least eighteen years of age.

8   But the study found that when compared with young adults, children ages eleven to thirteen were more than three times as likely to be found "seriously impaired" in understanding the judicial process and aiding their own defense. Similarly, it found those fourteen or fifteen years old were twice as likely to be "seriously impaired" in such awareness and reasoning.

9   "For example," the study says, "younger individuals were less likely to recognize the risks inherent in different choices and less likely to think about

the long-term consequences of their choices"—including confessions as opposed to remaining silent during police questioning.

10   Study director Thomas Grisso, a clinical psychologist and psychiatry professor at the University of Massachusetts medical school, said the issues of age and maturity manifested themselves in ways well beyond the obvious. Even when young teens understand their immediate circumstances and the judicial proceedings, Grisso said, the research found "there are still questions about their ability to make decisions and grasp the long-range" consequences.

11   Government statistics, researchers said, show that 200,000 juveniles each year are tried as adults.

12   The report follows a decade of state efforts to make it easier to try children as adults. Between 1992 and 1999, every state except Nebraska passed laws making it easier to for juveniles to be tried as adults, according to the National Center for Juvenile Justice, a private, nonprofit research group. Even though Nebraska passed no new laws on the subject during that seven-year period, it is among the 14 states, and the District of Columbia, that allow prosecutors to file charges against juveniles in criminal court.

13   Twenty-three states have no minimum age. Two, Kansas and Vermont, can try ten-year-old children as adults.

14   Given the study's conclusion that large numbers of juveniles may be incompetent or barely competent to stand trial, Grisso and Steinberg said they hope lawmakers nationwide will examine the fairness of the juvenile-justice system.

15   However, Kent Scheidegger, legal director of the conservative Criminal Justice Legal Foundation, said the vast majority of teenagers, even young ones, know enough to be tried in adult court. "The notion that teenagers are not capable of understanding what is going on I find not credible in the case of mentally normal teenagers," he said.

Supreme Court to Rule on Executing Young Killers

by Adam Liptak
The New York Times, January 3, 2005

1   In August, six months after the United States Supreme Court agreed to consider the constitutionality of the juvenile death penalty, Robert Acuna, a high school student from Baytown, Tex., was put on trial for his life. The jury convicted Mr. Acuna of killing two elderly neighbors, James and Joyce Carroll, when he was seventeen, shooting them "execution style," as prosecutors described it, and stealing their car. At sentencing, when jurors weighed his crime against factors counseling leniency, Mr. Acuna's youth should have counted in his favor.

2   Instead, his brooding and volatile adolescent demeanor may have hurt more than helped, and the Houston jury sentenced him to die. "They probably thought that he wasn't showing remorse," said Mr. Acuna's mother, Barbara. Renee Magee, who prosecuted Mr. Acuna, now eighteen, agreed that his behavior at the trial had alienated the jury. "He was very nonchalant," Ms. Magee said. "He laughed at inappropriate things. He still didn't quite get the magnitude of everything he did."

3   Mr. Acuna is the latest person to enter death row for a crime committed before age eighteen. He may also be the last. If the Supreme Court prohibits the execution of sixteen- and seventeen-year-olds in a case it accepted a year ago, involving a Missouri man, the lives of Mr. Acuna and 71 other juvenile offenders on death row will be spared.

4   A central issue before the court, which is expected to rule in the next few months, is whether the plummeting number of such death sentences—there were two last year—lends weight to the argument that putting youths on death row amounts to cruel and unusual punishment. Supporters of the juvenile death penalty argue that the small number proves instead that the system works and that juries are making discerning choices on whom to sentence to death, taking due account of the defendants' youth and reserving the ultimate punishment for the worst of the worst.

5   But a look at the cases of some of the juvenile offenders now on death row raises questions about how reliable and consistent juries have been in making those decisions. Age can shape every aspect of a capital case. Crimes committed by teenagers are often particularly brutal, attracting great publicity and fierce prosecutions. Adolescents are more likely to confess, and are not adept at navigating the justice system.

6   Jurors' reactions to teenagers' demeanor and appearance can be quite varied. The defendants they see have aged an average of two years between the crime and the trial. And jurors may not necessarily accept expert testimony concerning recent research showing that the adolescent brain is not fully developed.

7   The Supreme Court in 1988 banned the execution of those under six-teen at the time of their crimes. During arguments in October on whether to move that categorical line to eighteen, Justice Antonin Scalia said the drop in juvenile death sentences was proof that juries could be trusted to sort through and weigh evidence about defendants' youth and culpability. "It doesn't surprise me that the death penalty for sixteen- to eighteen-year-olds is rarely imposed," Justice Scalia said. "I would expect it would be. But it's a question of whether you leave it to the jury to evaluate the person's youth and take that into account or whether you adopt a hard rule."

8   Juries in capital cases involving juvenile offenders certainly place great weight on the defendants' youth. The defendants seldom testify, but jurors inspect them closely and draw conclusions from how they look and handle themselves. And the very same factors may cut both ways. Adolescent recklessness may suggest diminished responsibility to some and a terrible danger to others.

9   The youth of Christopher Simmons, the defendant whose case is now before the Supreme Court, was such a double-edged sword. Mr. Simmons was seventeen in 1993, when he and a friend robbed, bound and gagged Shirley Crook, forty-six, and pushed her into a river, where she drowned. During Mr. Simmons's sentencing hearing, a Missouri prosecutor scoffed at the notion that Mr. Simmons's age should count as a mitigating factor in his favor. "Seventeen years old," the prosecutor, George McElroy, said. "Isn't that scary? Doesn't that scare you? Mitigating? Quite the contrary, I submit. Quite the contrary."

10   Mr. Acuna had a tough-looking buzz cut at the time of the killings, said Tim Carroll, the son of the couple Mr. Acuna killed. At the trial, he looked different. "He appeared as though someone had tried to make him look eight years old all over again," Mr. Carroll said. "His hair was all combed down, almost in little bangs."

Kids Are Kids—Until They Commit Crimes

by Marjie Lundstrom
The Sacramento Bee, March 1, 2001

1   A week from now, a judge in Florida will decide how old Lionel Tate really is.

2   Never mind that he is indisputably twelve at the time of "the incident." Is he a boy? Or a man?

3   It is a vexing question these days for the under-eighteen crowd, the group we routinely write off as "only kids." It's why they can't smoke, or drink, or go to R movies without our OK. It's why they don't vote. It's why they have curfews. It's why we fret over their Internet access and fuss about driving privileges.

4   Hey, they're only kids.

5   That is, until they foul up. Until they commit crimes. And the bigger the crime, the more eager we are to call them adults.

6   It's a glaring inconsistency that's getting more glaring by the hour as children as young as twelve and thirteen are being charged as adults in America's courts.

7   A California appeals court recently stuck its nose into the quandary of when to charge young offenders as adults, returning that power to judges, not prosecutors.

8   Meanwhile, in Texas, a lawmaker has had it. You want to throw the adult book at kids? Fine, says Democratic state Rep. Ron Wilson of Houston.

9   Lower the voting age to fourteen.

10   And really, in light of things, how wacky is that? Today we are witness to criminal defendants—facing life sentences without parole—who cannot shave, still play with fire trucks and love to act out scenes from television or video games.

11   On March 9, Lionel Tate—who was twelve when he savagely beat to death a six-year-old girl—will likely learn if he must spend life in prison after his lawyer unsuccessfully tried to put pro wrestling on trial. Now fourteen and convicted as an adult of first-degree murder, Tate supposedly was imitating his World Wrestling Federation heroes when he pummeled his playmate, less than a third his size.

12   Last month in Sacramento, a fifteen-year-old Yuba City youth who report-edly claimed he was mimicking a TV program about little girls who rob a bank was given a 26-years-to-life prison term. Tried as an adult, Thomas A. Preciado was fourteen when he stabbed to death a minimart clerk.

13   In April, Court TV will air live daily coverage of the trial of Nathaniel Bra-zill, now fourteen, charged as an adult with first-degree murder. Brazill was thirteen and already in trouble for throwing water balloons when he returned to his Lake Worth, Fla., middle school and shot to death an English teacher, who would not let him say good-bye to two girls on the final day of classes.

14   This is not to say that the boys' crimes were not heinous, or that they should go unpunished. No one's talking about coddling here. But the zeal to corral wildly troubled, ever-younger kids and ram them through the adult system belies everything the juvenile justice system is all about: that kids are different. Their reasoning is not fully developed.

15   They are not adults.

16   "We've created this image that teenagers are something to be feared," said Dan Macallair of the Center on Juvenile and Criminal Justice in San Francisco.

17   This warped vision of America's youth was given an unfortunate boost with the recent arrest of two seemingly "good kids" in the brutal slayings of two Dartmouth College professors. Before they were even arrested, prosecutors had charged the teenagers, sixteen and seventeen, as adults.

18   Trouble is, statistics don't bear out the hysteria. While politicians and prosecutors press for hard-line stands against youthful offenders—nearly every state has moved to make it easier to charge kids as adults—juvenile crime is way down.

19   The nation's juvenile arrest rate for murder fell 68 percent from 1993 to 1999, hitting its lowest level since 1966, according to the Justice Department. The juvenile arrest rate for violent crime overall fell 36 percent from 1994 to 1999.

20   Macallair believes the excitable media have perpetuated and fueled the youth-violence scare of the 1980s. In fact, California voters were so persuaded by tough-on-crime rhetoric they passed Proposition 21 last March, shifting the power from judges to prosecutors in deciding which juveniles to charge as adults in certain crimes.

21   Sensibly, the 4th District Court of Appeals in San Diego disagreed, finding that the provision violated the separation-of-powers principle. The San Diego district attorney has vowed to appeal.

22   But the fact remains, politics and demagoguery do not make good public policy. Research suggests that adolescents squeezed through the adult system are more likely to come out as violent career criminals than similar kids handled on the juvenile side.

23   More lives, lost.

24   So what, then, to do about Lionel Tate—a kid who apparently still doesn't understand that "pile-driving" fellow inmates is not a good thing?

25   In another week, he will find out who tucks him in at night. And where.

Startling Finds on Teenage Brains

by Paul Thompson
The Sacramento Bee, Friday, May 25, 2001

1   Emotions ran high at the trial of Nathaniel Brazill in West Palm Beach, Fla., two weeks ago. Friends of slain teacher Barry Grunow called for the death penalty, while a growing crowd of demonstrators outside the courthouse wielded hastily written placards reading, "A child is not a man." Jurors returned with their verdict May 16: Fourteen-year-old Brazill, charged in last May's shooting of middle-school teacher Grunow, was found guilty of second-degree murder.

2   A Florida grand jury had previously ruled that Brazill, who frequently looked dazed during the trial, would be tried as an adult, and if he had been convicted of first-degree murder he would have faced life in prison without parole. But Brazill's immaturity was evident throughout this incident—from the act itself of Brazill's shooting a teacher he considered one of his favorites, to his subsequent inability to give a reason for doing so, to the various quizzical looks that came across his face as the verdicts were read.

3   In terms of cognitive development, as research on the human brain has shown, Brazill—and any other young teen—is far from adulthood.

4   Over the last several years, as school shootings have seemed to occur with disturbing frequency, startling discoveries have emerged about the teenage brain. The White House held a televised conference on adolescent development in May of last year, and a flurry of papers on the teen brain has appeared in top science journals. Reporters and teen advocates ask: Do the studies help explain the impulsive, erratic behavior of teens? The biggest surprise in recent teen-brain research is the finding that a massive loss of brain tissue occurs in the teen years.

5   Specifically, my own research group at the University of California, Los Angeles, and our colleagues at the National Institutes of Health have developed technology to map the patterns of brain growth in individual children and teenagers. With repeated brain scans of kids from three to twenty, we pieced together "movies" showing how brains grow and change.

6   Some changes make perfect sense: Language systems grow furiously until age twelve and then stop, coinciding with the time when children learn foreign languages fastest. Mathematical brain systems grow little until puberty, corresponding with the observation that kids have difficulty with abstract concepts before then. Basically, the brain is like a puzzle, and growth is fastest in the exact parts the kids need to learn skills at different times. So far, all well and good.

7   But what really caught our eye was a massive loss of brain tissue that occurs in the teenage years. The loss was like a wildfire, and you could see it in every teenager. Gray matter, which brain researchers believe supports

all our thinking and emotions, is purged at a rate of 1 percent to 2 percent a year during this period. Stranger still, brain cells and connections are only being lost in the areas controlling impulses, risk-taking, and self-control. These frontal lobes, which inhibit our violent passions, rash actions, and regulate our emotions, are vastly immature throughout the teenage years.

8   The implications are tantalizing. Brazill was only thirteen when he committed his crime. He said he made a "stupid mistake," but prosecutors argued that by bringing a gun to school he planned the crime.

9   Does "planning" mean the same thing for a thirteen-year-old, with his diminished capacity for controlling erratic behavior, as it means for an adult? The verdict, in this case, seems to line up with the research. The jurors, by returning a verdict of second-degree murder instead of first, indicated that they believe Brazill's actions, while not accidental, were not fully thought-out, either.

10 Linking this maelstrom of normal brain change with legal or moral accountability is tough: Even though normal teens are experiencing a wildfire of tissue loss in their brains, that does not remove their accountability. What is clear from the research is that the parts of the frontal lobes that inhibit reckless actions restructure themselves with startling speed in the teen years. Given this delicate—and drastic—reshaping of the brain, teens need all the help they can get to steer their development onto the right path.

11 While research on brain-tissue loss can help us to understand teens better, it cannot be used to excuse their violent or homicidal behavior. But it can be used as evidence that teenagers are not yet adults, and the legal system shouldn't treat them as such.

Paul Thompson is an assistant professor of neurology at the University of California, Los Angeles, School of Medicine.

Juvenile Justice

Reading selections for this module:

Krikorian, Greg. "Many Kids Called Unfit for Adult Trial." *Sacramento Bee* 3 Mar. 2003.
Liptak, Adam. "Supreme Court to Rule on Executing Young Killers." *New York Times* 3 Jan. 2005.
Lundstrom, Marjie. "Kids Are Kids—Until they Commit Crimes." *Sacramento Bee* 1 Mar. 2001.
Thompson, Paul. "Startling Finds on Teenage Brains." *Sacramento Bee* 25 May 2001.

Reading Rhetorically

Prereading

Activity 1

Getting Ready to Read

Quickwrite: If you committed a crime, do you think it would be fair for you to be punished the same way as an adult who committed the same crime?

Activity 2

Introducing Key Concepts

What characteristics make a person an adult, a juvenile, or a child? Who is a juvenile? What qualities are different for a juvenile compared with an adult or a child? Brainstorm a list of qualities that characterize a juvenile but not an adult or a child.

Definitions of some legal terms for killing someone are provided below. Study them and explain the differences in your own words. After you have studied the terms and their definitions, read the scenarios and complete the empty box in the table, "Matching Activity," by filling in the legal term for the crime described.

Definitions of Legal Terms

Homicide is the killing of one person by another, either intentionally or unintentionally. Homicide includes accidents and murder.

Murder is killing someone with malice of forethought. It could be done while committing another crime. Murder is always illegal.

First-degree murder is killing a person with malice of forethought; the killing was planned. It was done deliberately.

Second-degree murder is a killing done during a crime deemed dangerous to a human life. The crime was most likely not committed with the intention of killing.

Voluntary manslaughter is killing someone intentionally but without malice of forethought. For example, if the killing was a crime of passion (killing a spouse or lover because of jealousy), the intention was to kill. However, there was no malice of forethought because it was not planned.

Involuntary manslaughter is killing someone unlawfully but without malice of forethought. It was committed without intent to kill and without a conscious disregard for human life.

Matching Activity

Actual situation	Crime or conviction	Punishment or sentencing
A troubled seventeen-year-old girl has slowly poisoned her parents each night at dinner. After three months she came home to find them dead on the kitchen floor. The coroner's report indicated that cyanide poisoning caused their deaths.		Sentenced to life in prison without parole
Three sixteen-year-olds were hanging out at the park drinking whiskey. One boy started shoving his friend. Soon the shoving escalated into punching. One boy tripped, and his head hit a sharp-edged rock. The boy died before help arrived.		Sentenced to three years in prison after being tried as an adult
Suspicious that his girlfriend was cheating, a sixteen-year-old boy went to her house and found her in bed with his brother. Impulsively, he grabbed the nearest lamp and hit his brother on the head. His brother died two days later.		Sentenced to six years in prison
A thirteen-year-old boy broke into an auto parts business to steal hubcaps. The seventeen-year-old security guard picked up his boss's gun and fired two warning shots at the thief. The second shot hit the thirteen-year-old and killed him on the spot.		Sentenced to 15 years to life

Reading Selections
Supreme Court to Rule on Executing Young Killers
Kids Are Kids—Until they Commit Crimes

Activity 3

Surveying the Text

Surveying the text gives you an overview of what the articles are about and how they are put together. This activity will help you create a framework so that you can make predictions and form questions to guide your reading. Discuss the following questions with your class:

- What do the titles of the two articles "Supreme Court to Rule on Executing Young Killers" and "Kids Are Kids" tell you the articles will be about?
- "Kids Are Kids" was published in *The Sacramento Bee.* "Supreme Court to Rule" was published in *The New York Times.* What can you predict about the articles based on their lengths and the lengths of their paragraphs? How do you think the articles will be the same? How do you think they will be different?
- What issue do you think these articles are going to discuss? What positions do you think Liptak and Lundstrom will take?

Activity 4

Making Predictions and Asking Questions

Listen as your teacher reads the first three paragraphs of "Supreme Court to Rule on Executing Young Killers" and then discuss the following questions:

- What do you think "Supreme Court to Rule on Executing Young Killers" is going to be about?
- What do you think is the purpose of this text?
- Who do you think is the intended audience for this piece? How do you know this?
- Based on the title and what you have heard so far, what information and ideas might this article present?

Now read the first six paragraphs of "Kids Are Kids" silently.

- What is Lundstrom's opinion on the topic of juvenile crime?
- Turn the title into a question to answer as you read the essay.

Activity 5

Introducing Key Vocabulary

Create semantic maps for the words "juvenile crime" and "justice." Begin by brainstorming a list of words that relate to "juvenile crime"; sort these words into categories, and label each one using the graphic below. Do the same for "justice."

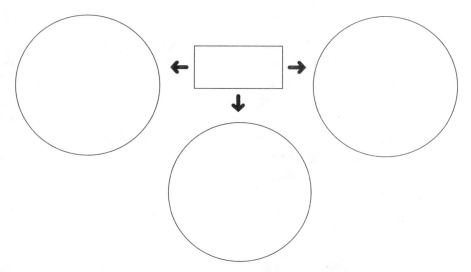

The words in the self-assessment chart are from the texts you will read. Predict word meanings and state how well you know the word.

Vocabulary Self-Assessment Chart

Word	Definition	Know It Well	Have Heard of It	Don't Know It
Vocabulary from Liptak's "Supreme Court to Rule on Executing Young Killers"				
constitutionality				
prosecutors				
demeanor				
remorse				
alienated				
nonchalant				
plummeting				
culpability				
mitigating				
Vocabulary from Lundstrom's "Kids Are Kids"				
inconsistency				
quandary				
heinous				
coddling				
perpetuating				

Reading

Activity 6

First Reading

The first reading of an essay is intended to help you understand the text and confirm your predictions. This step is sometimes called reading "with the grain" or "playing the believing game." As you read, think about the following questions:

• Which of your predictions turned out to be true?
• What surprised you?

As you read "Supreme Court to Rule" and "Kids Are Kids," you will find that the two articles discuss five recent cases in which teenagers were tried as adults for violent crimes. Fill out the following graphic organizer based on those cases:

Recent Cases of Juvenile Crime

Defendant	Age	Crime	Sentence

Now highlight places in the text in each article where arguments are made for and against punishing juveniles like adults.

Activity 7

Looking Closely at Language

The following questions are based on the article by Liptak, "Supreme Court to Rule on Executing Young Killers," and the one by Lundstrom, "Kids Are Kids." Answer them orally and in writing:

1. Do you think that sentencing juvenile killers to the death penalty is a "cruel and unusual" punishment? Use "constitutional" or "unconstitutional" in your answer.
2. Should juveniles be punished less harshly than adults? Use "leniently" in your answer.
3. Describe the demeanor of a teenager you know. Do you think that such a demeanor would cause a jury to be lenient?

Activity 7 (Continued)

4. Do you think execution should be banned for some age groups of juveniles? Which age groups?
5. What factors do you think juries should take into account when they sentence juveniles?
6. Do you agree with Lundstrom that it is inconsistent to deny privileges like voting and drinking to teenagers but then to sentence them as adults? Why?
7. Do you think juveniles should be tried as adults if they commit especially bad crimes? Use the word "heinous" in your answer.
8. Do you agree with Lundstrom that the media perpetuates the stereotype of violent youths?

Reading Selections
Many Kids Called Unfit for Adult Trial
Startling Finds on Teenage Brains

Prereading and First Reading

Your teacher will ask you to read two new articles, "Many Kids Called Unfit for Adult Trial" and "Startling Finds on Teenage Brains," using many of the same strategies you did for the first two articles.

Activity 8

Rereading the Text

In the initial reading, you read "with the grain," playing the "believing game." In the second reading, you should read "against the grain," playing the "doubting game." As you reread "Many Kids Called Unfit for Adult Trial" and "Startling Finds on Teenage Brains," make marginal notations.

1. Label the following in the left-hand margin:

   • The introduction
   • The issue or problem the author is writing about
   • The author's main arguments
   • The author's examples
   • The author's conclusion

2. In the right-hand margin, write your reactions to what the author is saying. You can ask questions, express surprise, disagree, elaborate, and note any moments of confusion.

3. As a class, discuss the annotation you and your classmates made on the first article. Now repeat this process for the second article. When you finish, exchange your copy with a partner. Read your partner's annotations, and then talk about what you chose to mark and how you reacted to the text. Did you agree on what the main idea was?

Activity 9

Analyzing Stylistic Choices

The choices writers make when they choose words and construct sentences create certain effects for their readers. "Startling Finds on Teenage Brains" is about scientific research conducted at UCLA and the National Institutes of Health, but Thompson does not use dry, scientific language. Discuss why Thompson chose the following words to describe teenage behavior and what happens to teenage brains.

Words

Paragraph 7
Massive
Wildfire
Purged
Violent passions
Rash actions
Vastly immature

Paragraph 9
Erratic behavior

Paragraph 10
Maelstrom
Reckless actions
Startling
Delicate
Drastic

Sentences

Thompson's sentences are fairly long and complex, but the last sentence in paragraph 6 is "So far, all well and good." Why is this sentence so short?

Activity 10

Considering the Structure of the Text

Create a descriptive outline of "Startling Finds on Teenage Brains" by describing the content and purpose of each section. The first section has been done as an example.

Startling Finds on Teenage Brains
by Paul Thompson
The Sacramento Bee, Friday, 25 May 2001

1   Emotions ran high at the trial of Nathaniel Brazill in West Palm Beach, Fla., two weeks ago. Friends of slain teacher Barry Grunow called for the death penalty, while a growing crowd of demonstrators outside the courthouse wielded hastily written placards reading, "A child is not a man." Jurors returned with their verdict May 16: Fourteen-year-old Brazill, charged in last

May's shooting of middle-school teacher Grunow, was found guilty of second-degree murder.

2   A Florida grand jury had previously ruled that Brazill, who frequently looked dazed during the trial, would be tried as an adult, and if he had been convicted of first-degree murder he would have faced life in prison without parole. But Brazill's immaturity was evident throughout this incident—from the act itself of Brazill's shooting a teacher he considered one of his favorites, to his subsequent inability to give a reason for doing so, to the various quizzical looks that came across his face as the verdicts were read.

3   In terms of cognitive development, as research on the human brain has shown, Brazill—and any other young teen—is far from adulthood.

Content and Purpose: *Nathaniel Brazill, a fourteen-year-old, was tried as an adult and found guilty of second-degree murder in the killing of his teacher. But research on the brain has shown that young teens are not adults in terms of development. The purpose is to raise the question of whether teenagers should be tried as adults.*

---

4   Over the last several years, as school shootings have seemed to occur with disturbing frequency, startling discoveries have emerged about the teenage brain. The White House held a televised conference on adolescent development in May of last year, and a flurry of papers on the teen brain has appeared in top science journals. Reporters and teen advocates ask: Do the studies help explain the impulsive, erratic behavior of teens? The biggest surprise in recent teen-brain research is the finding that a massive loss of brain tissue occurs in the teen years.

Content and Purpose:

---

5   Specifically, my own research group at the University of California, Los Angeles, and our colleagues at the National Institutes of Health have developed technology to map the patterns of brain growth in individual children and teenagers. With repeated brain scans of kids from 3 to 20, we pieced together "movies" showing how brains grow and change.

6   Some changes make perfect sense: Language systems grow furiously until age twelve and then stop, coinciding with the time when children learn foreign languages fastest. Mathematical brain systems grow little until puberty, corresponding with the observation that kids have difficulty with abstract concepts before then. Basically, the brain is like a puzzle, and growth is fastest in the exact parts the kids need to learn skills at different times. So far, all well and good.

7   But what really caught our eye was a massive loss of brain tissue that occurs in the teenage years. The loss was like a wildfire, and you could see it in every teenager. Gray matter, which brain researchers believe supports all our thinking and emotions, is purged at a rate of 1 percent to 2 percent a year during this period. Stranger still, brain cells and connections are only being lost in the areas controlling impulses, risk-taking, and self-control. These frontal lobes, which inhibit our violent passions, rash actions, and regulate our emotions, are vastly immature throughout the teenage years.

Content and Purpose:

8   The implications are tantalizing. Brazill was only thirteen when he committed his crime. He said he made a "stupid mistake," but prosecutors argued that by bringing a gun to school he planned the crime.

9   Does "planning" mean the same thing for a thirteen-year-old, with his diminished capacity for controlling erratic behavior, as it means for an adult? The verdict, in this case, seems to line up with the research. The jurors, by returning a verdict of second-degree murder instead of first, indicated that they believe Brazill's actions, while not accidental, were not fully thought-out, either.

Content and Purpose:

Activity 10 (Continued)	10 Linking this maelstrom of normal brain change with legal or moral accountability is tough: Even though normal teens are experiencing a wildfire of tissue loss in their brains, that does not remove their accountability. What is clear from the research is that the parts of the frontal lobes that inhibit reckless actions restructure themselves with startling speed in the teen years. Given this delicate—and drastic—reshaping of the brain, teens need all the help they can get to steer their development onto the right path.

11   While research on brain-tissue loss can help us to understand teens better, it cannot be used to excuse their violent or homicidal behavior. But it can be used as evidence that teenagers are not yet adults, and the legal system shouldn't treat them as such.

Paul Thompson is an assistant professor of neurology at the University of California, Los Angeles, School of Medicine.

Postreading

Activity 11

Summarizing and Responding

Write a summary of "Many Kids Called Unfit for Adult Trial" by Greg Krikorian.

Activity 12

Web Work

Do a Web search for Proposition 21, the California proposition that gave prosecutors the power to decide whether juveniles should be charged as adults for certain crimes. Read the arguments for and against the proposition, and then consider the questions in the next activity about Krikorian and Thompson's articles so you can see a range of possible arguments.

Activity 13

Thinking Critically

In your group, answer the following questions about the traditional rhetorical appeals that Greg Krikorian makes in "Many Kids Called Unfit for Adult Trial." Write down your group's answers so you can share them with your classmates.

Group 1

Questions about Logic (Logos)

1. What are Krikorian's major claims and assertions? Do you agree with his claims?
2. Are any of his claims weak or unsupported? Which claims, and why?

3. Can you think of counterarguments that Krikorian does not consider?
4. Do you think Krikorian left something out on purpose? Why?

Questions about the Writer (Ethos)

1. Krikorian is reporting on a study by Thomas Grisso. What is Grisso's background? Do you think he is trustworthy?
2. Krikorian also quotes Laurence Steinberg. Who is he? Is he a reliable person to interpret what the study means?
3. Krikorian is a staff writer for the *Los Angeles Times* who frequently writes about legal issues. Does he seem trustworthy to write about this topic? Why or why not?
4. Can you tell what Krikorian's point of view is, or can you tell only the point of view of the author of the study?

Questions about Emotions (Pathos)

1. Does "Many Kids" affect you emotionally? Which parts?
2. Do you think Krikorian is trying to manipulate your emotions? In what ways? At what point?
3. Do your emotions conflict with the logical interpretation of the arguments?

Group 2

Questions about Logic (Logos)

1. What are Thompson's major claims and assertions? Do you agree with his claims?
2. Are any of his claims weak or unsupported? Which claims, and why?
3. Can you think of counterarguments that Thompson does not consider?

Questions about the Writer (Ethos)

1. What is Thompson's background? Do you think he is trustworthy?
2. Does Thompson seem deceptive? Why or why not?
3. Can you tell what Thompson's point of view is?

Questions about Emotions (Pathos)

1. Does "Startling Finds" affect you emotionally? Which parts?
2. Do you think Thompson is trying to manipulate your emotions? In what ways? At what point?
3. Do your emotions conflict with the logical interpretation of the arguments?

Connecting Reading to Writing

Using the Words of Others

One of the most important features of academic writing is the use of the words and ideas from written sources to support your own points. Essentially, there are three ways to incorporate words and ideas from sources into your own writing:

1. **Direct quotation.** Paul Thompson says, "The biggest surprise in recent teen-brain research is the finding that a massive loss of brain tissue occurs in the teen years."
2. **Paraphrase.** In "Startling Finds on Teenage Brains," Paul Thompson notes that teenagers actually lose brain tissue, a finding that may explain their impulsive behavior.
3. **Summary.** In "Startling Finds on Teenage Brains," Paul Thompson summarizes recent research that shows teenagers actually lose brain tissue, a finding that may explain their impulsive and violent behavior. Such changes in the brain do not mean that teens are not responsible for their violent behavior, but Thompson believes they should not be treated as adults in the criminal justice system.

Documentation. You will also need to learn to take notes with full citation information. For print material you need to record at least the author's name, title of the publication, city of publication, publisher, date, and page number.

The two most common documentation formats are the Modern Language Association (MLA) format, used mainly by English departments, and the American Psychological Association format.

MLA Format

Books. Here is a citation in MLA format for a typical book:

> Bean, John C., Virginia A. Chappell, and Alice M. Gilliam. *Reading Rhetorically: A Reader for Writers.* New York: Longman, 2002.

Newspapers. Here is the bibliographic information for the Thompson article in MLA format. The fact that it was published in a newspaper changes the format and the information slightly:

> Thompson, Paul. "Startling Finds on Teenage Brains." *Sacramento Bee* 24 May 2001.

Web Sites. You might also want to incorporate material from Web sites. To document a Web site, you need to record the author's name (if known), the title of the site (or a description like "Homepage," if no title is available), the date of publication or most recent update (if known), the name of the organization that sponsors the site, the date of access, and the Web address (URL) in angle brackets. For example:

**Activity 14
(Continued)**

Primary Election 2000 Voter Guide. California Secretary of State. 31 December 2004. <http://primary2000.sos.ca.gov/VoterGuide/Propositions/21.htm>.

Because the name of the author is unknown for the above site, it is left out. This entry would appear in the Works Cited section, alphabetized as Primary Election.

In-Text Documentation. The MLA style also requires in-text documentation for every direct quotation, indirect quotation, paraphrase, or summary. If the author's name is given in the text, the page number should be furnished in parentheses at the end of the sentence containing the material. An example of paraphrased material from Thompson's article on teenage brain research follows. Because the author is not named in the text, the last name goes in the parentheses; since the article is short, no page numbers are needed:

> "Although the rise in teenage crime is alarming, it should not cause states to toughen their laws so that even young teens are treated like adults in the criminal justice system. Recent research on teenage brains shows that the areas of the brain that control decision-making undergo a loss of brain tissue which supports the argument that teenagers are different from adults and should be treated more leniently" (Thompson).

Practice with Sources. Choose three passages from the text you are reading that you might be able to use in an essay. First, write down each passage as a correctly punctuated direct quotation. Second, paraphrase the material in your own words. Finally, respond to the idea expressed in the passage by agreeing or disagreeing with it and explaining why. Now you are ready to use this material in an essay.

Writing Rhetorically

Prewriting

Activity 15

Reading the Assignment

Reading the assignment carefully to ensure you address all aspects of the prompt is critical.

> **Writing Assignment**
>
> Should teenagers accused of violent crimes be tried and sentenced as adults? Why or why not?
>
> Be sure to refer to and cite the readings and your Web-based research. You may also use examples from your personal experience or observations.

Activity 15 (Continued)	Take the following steps for this exercise:
	• Read the assignment carefully.
	• Decide which issue you are going to discuss.
	• Discuss the purpose of the assignment. What will you try to accomplish in your essay?

| Activity 16 | **Getting Ready to Write** |

The following exercise will help you move from reading to writing.

Consult newspapers and other documents on the Internet to find out the current status of the issue of trying and sentencing juveniles. What aspects of the issue are currently in the news? Why is it still important? Why do people care about it? Based on the articles you read as part of this assignment and on your own research, how do you think the issue should be resolved?

| Activity 17 | **Formulating a Working Thesis** |

Writing down a tentative thesis at this point is a good habit to develop in your writing process. Your thesis should be a complete sentence and can be revised several times. A focused thesis statement will keep your writing on track.

Record your responses to the following questions in preparation for writing a tentative thesis statement:

1. What specific question will your essay address? What is your response to this question? (This is your tentative thesis.)
2. What support have you found for your thesis?
3. What evidence have you found for this support? (Examples are facts, statistics, authorities, personal experience, anecdotes, stories, and scenarios.)
4. How much background information do your readers need to understand your topic and thesis?
5. If readers were to disagree with your thesis or the validity of your support, what might they say? How would you address their concerns (what would you say to them)?

Now draft a possible thesis for your essay.

Writing

Composing a Draft

When you write an argument essay, approach the subject in a way that matters to you. If you have strong feelings, you will find it much easier to gather evidence and convince your readers of your point of view. Keep in mind, however, that your readers might feel just as strongly about the opposite side of the issue. The following guidelines will help you write a good argument essay:

1. **State your opinion on the topic in the thesis statement.** To write a thesis statement for an argument essay, you must take a stand for or against an action or an idea. In other words, your thesis statement should be debatable—a statement that can be argued or challenged and that will not be met with agreement by everyone who reads it. Your thesis statement should introduce your subject and state your opinion about that subject.

As an example, Paul Thompson's thesis is partially stated and partially implied in the third paragraph:

"In terms of cognitive development, as research on the human brain has shown, Brazill—and any other young teen—is far from adulthood" (and therefore teens shouldn't be treated as adults in the justice system).

Is Your Thesis Debatable?

Not debatable. Teenagers in Florida can face life in prison if convicted of first-degree murder.

Not debatable. Studies explore the impulsive, erratic behavior of teens.

Although a writer's thesis usually comes in the first few paragraphs of an essay, Thompson is an example of a professional writer who does not state his thesis explicitly until the concluding paragraph. He does not reach his thesis until the final paragraph, where he concludes that (based on his research) teenage criminals should not be treated like adults. However, a reader can infer what Thompson's thesis will be from the quoted part of paragraph three ("In terms of cognitive development, as research on the human brain has shown, Brazill—and any other young teen—is far from adulthood"). The focus of the essay is consistent from the beginning even though the reader does not reach the thesis until the end.

2. **Find out as much as you can about your audience before you write.** Knowing your readers' background and feelings on your topic will help you choose the best supporting evidence and examples.

Thompson's essay was first published in *The Sacramento Bee*, which addresses a fairly educated California audience. However, most of the paper's readers are not doctors or researchers, so Thompson summarizes his research in an informal style and in terms that can be understood by any educated person. If he had been writing for a science journal, he would have used technical language and a more formal tone.

3. **Choose evidence that supports your thesis statement.** Evidence is probably the most important factor in writing an argument essay. Without solid evidence, your essay is nothing more than opinion; with it, your essay can be powerful and persuasive. If you supply convincing evidence, your readers will not only understand your position but may even agree with it.

Evidence can consist of facts, statistics, statements from authorities, and examples or personal stories. Examples and personal stories can be based on your own observations, experiences, and reading, but your opinions are not evidence. Other strategies, such as comparison/contrast, definition, and cause and effect, can be particularly useful in building an argument. Use any combination of evidence and writing strategies that supports your thesis statement.

In his essay, Thompson uses several different types of evidence. Here are some examples:

Facts

"Fourteen-year-old Brazill, charged in last May's shooting of middle-school teacher Grunow, was found guilty of second-degree murder" (paragraph 1).

"Mathematical brain systems grow little until puberty, corresponding with the observation that kids have difficulty with abstract concepts until then" (paragraph 6).

Statistics

"Gray matter, which brain researchers believe supports all our thinking and emotions, is purged at a rate of 1 percent to 2 percent a year during this period" (paragraph 7).

Reference to Authorities

"Specifically, my own research group at the University of California, Los Angeles, and our colleagues at the National Institutes of Health have developed technology to map the patterns of brain growth in individual children and teenagers" (paragraph 5).

Examples and Personal Stories

Story about Nathaniel Brazill (paragraphs 1 and 2)

4. **Anticipate opposing points of view.** In addition to stating and supporting your position, anticipating and responding to opposing views are important. Presenting only your side of the argument leaves half

the story untold—the opposition's half. If you acknowledge opposing arguments and answer them, your argument is strengthened.

In paragraph 10, Thompson admits that "linking this maelstrom of normal brain change with accountability is tough." This statement raises Thompson's credibility and then lets him counter the claim that normal teens, who also experience brain loss, do not commit murder. This leads to the more nuanced conclusion that teens should be held accountable but not be treated like adults.

5. **Maintain a reasonable tone.** Just as you probably wouldn't win an argument by shouting or making mean or nasty comments, don't expect your readers to respond well to such tactics. Keep the "voice" of your essay calm and sensible. Your readers will be much more open to what you have to say if they think you are a reasonable person.

Thompson maintains a reasonable tone throughout his essay. He doesn't attack the grand jury that ruled that Brazill should be tried as an adult or the people who believe that adolescents who commit heinous crimes should be treated like adults. Instead he presents scientific evidence to support the position that "a child is not a man" and emphasizes how enormous the brain changes are with his use of words like "massive," "wildfire," and "maelstrom." He implies that no reasonable person would argue that teenagers do not have "diminished capacity," but he never accuses his opponents of being unreasonable or scientifically uninformed.

6. **Organize your essay so that it presents your position as effectively as possible.** You want your audience to agree with you by the end of your essay, so you want to organize your essay in such a way that your readers can easily follow it. The number of paragraphs in your essay may vary depending on the nature of your assignment, but the following outline shows the order in which the features of an argument essay are most effective:

Introduction
Background information
Introduction of subject
Statement of writer's opinion

Body paragraphs
Common ground
Evidence that supports your argument (logical and emotional)
Opposing points of view
Response to opposing points of view

Conclusion
Restatement of your position
Call for action or agreement

The arrangement of evidence in an argument essay depends to a great extent on your readers' opinions. Most arguments will be organized from general to particular, from particular to general, or from one extreme to another. When you know that your readers already agree with you, arranging your details from general to particular or from most to least important is usually most effective. With this order, you are building on your readers' agreement and loyalty as you explain your thinking on the subject.

If you suspect that your audience does not agree with you, reverse the organization of your evidence and arrange it from particular to general or from least to most important. In this way, you take your readers step by step through your reasoning in an attempt to get them to agree with you.

Thompson's essay follows a slightly different pattern but is equally structured in order to convince his readers. Here is an outline of his article:

Introduction

> The story of Nathaniel Brazill
>
> Implied thesis: Brains of teenagers like Brazill are far from adulthood; therefore, teens shouldn't be treated like adults in the justice system.

Body paragraphs

Recent research on teenage brains

> Subject introduced: Research shows massive loss of brain tissue during teenage years.
>
> Summary of recent research
>
> Specific evidence from Thompson's research at UCLA

Implications of brain research

> Evidence: Jurors' verdict indicates they thought Brazill's crime was not fully thought-out.
>
> Discussion of link between brain changes and accountability
>
> Response to opposition: Teens should be accountable but not treated as adults.

Conclusion

> Brain research doesn't excuse teenage violence, but it confirms that the juvenile justice system should not treat teens like adults.

Activity 19

Organizing the Essay

The following items are traditional parts of all essays:

- The introduction (usually one or two paragraphs) that "hooks" the reader and provides a thesis statement or road map for the reader
- The body (as many paragraphs as necessary) that supports the thesis statement point by point
- The conclusion (usually only one paragraph) that summarizes the main points and explains the significance of the argument

The number of paragraphs in an essay depends on the nature and complexity of the argument.

Here are some additional hints to help you organize your thoughts:

Introduction

- You might include the following in your introductory paragraphs:
  - A "hook" to get the reader's attention
  - Background information the audience may need
  - A thesis statement, along with some indication of how the essay will be developed ("forecasting"). *Note:* A thesis statement states the topic of the essay and the writer's position on that topic. You may choose to sharpen or narrow your thesis at this point.

Body paragraphs

- Paragraphs that present support for the thesis statement, usually in topic sentences supported with evidence. (Refer to "Getting Ready to Write.")
- Paragraphs that include different points of view or address counter-arguments
- Paragraphs or sentences where you address those points of view by doing the following:
  - Refuting them
  - Acknowledging them but showing how your argument is better
  - Showing they are irrelevant
- Evidence that you have considered the values, beliefs, and assumptions of your audience; your own values, beliefs, and assumptions; and some common ground that appeals to the various points of view

Conclusion

- A final paragraph (or paragraphs) that includes a solid argument to support the thesis and indicates the significance of the argument—the "so what" factor

Draw horizontal lines through your essay to distinguish these three parts, and label them in the margin.

Developing the Content

Read the following highlights about developing your essay, and then discuss them with your classmates.

- Most body paragraphs consist of a topic sentence (or an implied topic sentence) and concrete details to support that topic sentence.
- Body paragraphs give evidence in the form of examples, illustrations, statistics, and so forth. They also analyze the meaning of the evidence.
- Each topic sentence is usually directly related to the thesis statement.
- No set number of paragraphs is required for an essay.
- The thesis dictates and focuses the content of an essay.

Revising the Draft

You now need to review the organization and development of your draft to make sure that your essay is as effective as possible.

Peer Group Work

Working in groups of three or four, each student will read his or her essay aloud to other members of the group. Then use Part I of the Evaluation Form as a revising checklist for each essay.

Paired Work

Work in pairs to decide how you will to revise the problems that group members identified.

Individual Work

Revise the draft based on the feedback you have received and the decisions you have made with your partners. Consider the following questions as revision guidelines for your individual work:

1. Have I responded to the assignment?
2. What is my purpose for this essay?
3. What should I keep? Which parts are most effective?
4. What should I add? Where do I need more details, examples, and other evidence to support my point?
5. What could I delete? Do I use irrelevant details? Am I repetitive?
6. What should I change? Are parts of my essay confusing or contradictory? Do I need to explain my ideas more fully?
7. What should I rethink? Was my position clear? Did I provide enough analysis to convince my readers?
8. How is my tone? Am I too overbearing or too firm? Do I need qualifiers?
9. Have I addressed differing points of view?
10. Does my conclusion show the significance of my essay?
11. Have I used key vocabulary words correctly to represent ideas from the article? Have I used words that refer to specific facts from the text?

Activity 22

Editing the Draft

Edit your drafts based on the information you have received from your instructor or a tutor. Use the editing checklist provided to you. The following editing guidelines will also help you edit your own work.

1. If possible, set your essay aside for 24 hours before rereading it to find errors.
2. If possible, read your essay out loud so that you can hear errors and awkward sentences.
3. Focus on individual words and sentences rather than on overall meaning. Take a sheet of paper and cover everything except the line you are reading. Then touch your pencil to each word as you read.
4. With the help of your teacher, figure out your own pattern of errors— the most serious and frequent errors you make.
5. Look for only one type of error at a time. Then go back and look for a second type and, if necessary, a third.
6. Use the dictionary to check spelling and confirm that you have chosen the right word for the context.

Activity 23

Reflecting on the Writing

Reflecting on your writing is an essential part of improving on your next assignment. When you have completed your essay, answer these six questions and submit your thought with your final draft.

1. What was most difficult about this assignment?
2. What was easiest?
3. What did you learn about debating by completing this assignment?
4. What do you think are the strengths of your argument? Place a wavy line by the parts of your essay that you feel are very good.
5. What are the weaknesses, if any, of your paper? Place an X by the parts of your essay that need help. Write any questions or concerns you have in the margin.
6. What did you learn from this assignment about your own writing process—about preparing to write, writing the first draft, revising, and editing?

Page 68 blank

Juvenile Justice

Writing Assignment

Should teenagers accused of violent crimes be tried and sentenced as adults? Why or why not?

Be sure to refer to and cite the readings and your Web-based research. You may also use examples from your personal experience or observations.

The sample student essays that follow reflect the EPT Scoring Guide's criteria.

Sample student essay with a score of 6:

The gavel plunged forcefully down as the judged uttered his verdict: guilty. Sentenced to a lifetime of imprisonment on account of murder, tears filled the eyes of the fourteen year old and his family. More and more recently minors are being charged as adults in violent crimes. What used to be considered a child is now suddenly tired as an adult. The kid who was just yesterday playing around with his friends is now suddenly a man. It is unethical and unintelligent to put an adolescent on trial as an adult and should not be happening.

There are reasons why children aren't allowed to go see an R rated movie when they are nine, or why a sixteen year old can't go down to the liquor store and buy a beer. Children are not fully matured or developed enough to handle these things. Even though, these kids that are too juvenile to smoke a cigarette or waste away their money gambling they are being put on trial as an adult for violent crimes. "Children as young as 12 and 13 are being charged as adults in America's courts" stated the Sacramento Bee's article "Kids are Kids-- until they commit crimes" (Lundstrom pg. 1). Something about that is wrong. Children do not have the full understanding and experience that the older, more mature public has been able to accumulate throughout their years of living. What I am getting at is not that these children's crimes should just be brushed off by just saying kids will be kids, but that it is not right to throw a child who doesn't even understand the enormity of the crime that they have committed, into the slammer.

The human body is a marvelous thing. When you are born you know almost nothing. Soon you pick up slight motor skills and learn a little bit of language. Everything seems to come into place as soon as you need it. The brain is the exact same way. At different periods of your life specific parts of your brain start to develop. The frontal part of the brain that is specifically design to "inhibit reckless actions" reforms itself dramatically within the teenage years (Thompson pg.2). What this means is that these young adults are unable to impulsively make decisions about their actions or decide what is right, in the same way as an adult with a fully formed brain would be able to. Given the information would you willingly put a child into court to be tried as an adult? This research clearly shows that kids are not only physically immature, but also mentally and should not be treated as if they are.

According to a Sacramento Bee article written in 2003, youth are "emotionally or intellectually unable to contribute to their own defense" when standing on trial (Krikorian pg.1). If a small child was asked to define death, most of them would not be able to do it. They see things on television and don't understand the difference between the things on their favorite show versus the real world. It may be common knowledge that a toddler doesn't understand complex situations like an adult would, but the truth is, around half of the kid in the age range of 14 to 15 don't either. A study shows that "younger individuals were less likely to recognize the risks inherent in different choices and less likely to think about the long-terms consequences of their choices" (Krikorian pg.2). Peer pressure is a well known topic in junior high. All throughout school you are hearing things like just say no and watching video's of people who used a controlled substance and are now vegetables. But for some reason kids still use drugs. This is the same reason why children commit violent crimes. They don't have the decision making skills to be able to know that it is wrong or to think, if I do this I am going to get in a lot of trouble and mess up somebody's life really bad. The Sacramento Bee states "thousands of juveniles went to adult trial when they should not have because their ability to understand the proceedings was seriously impaired." (Krikorian pg.1)

As a high school student, I am up close and personal with teens everyday of my life. Some of these kids are bright as can be and fully matured, but there are still others who it is obvious are not. I have seen a boy snort bleach up his nose to make another classmate laugh, or drink liquid dish soap in order to win ten dollars. When they were doing it they weren't thinking "oh gosh, bleach isn't supposed to go into my system," or "wow, I could get really sick if I drink this soap." All they were thinking was that they could get few kick out of it. Another thing I have seen is teenage emotion. Teenagers are the most emotional age group. I have seen brutal fights broker out over name calling, and a kid breaking down and bawling their eyes out over a failed test. Emotions are not an excuse for violent behavior, but if you mix that with low decision making skills you are definitely in for a disaster. It is in my experience and observations that teens are not fully matured and are defiantly not adults. That is why we are still in schools and our parents make up our rules. We don't have the capability to make the right decision because after all we are only kids.

You can not morally put a child on stand as an adult when you know they should not be there. They have a lack of experience in the real world, they are mentally still developing and many are ruled by emotions and peer pressure. Children are just not adults and should therefore not be treated as if they are one.

Works Cited

Marjie Lundstrom, "Kids are kids--until they commit crimes." *The Sacramento Bee* 1 March 2001.

Paul Thompson, "Startling Finds on Teenage Brains." *The Sacramento Bee.* 25 May 2001.

Greg Krikorian, "Many kids called unfit for adult trial: Those under 15 often blind to the long-term results of their choices, a study says." *The Sacramento Bee.* 3 March 2003.

6

Commentary

This essay illustrates the EPT Scoring Guide's criteria for a score of 6. The superior response indicates that this writer is very well prepared to handle college-level reading and writing.

- The writer locates her position in the context of arguments related to adolescents' lack of maturity and impaired competence.
- She demonstrates a thorough critical understanding of the readings and uses well-chosen quotations to make the argument that children should not be tried and sentenced as adults.
- The writer explores the issues thoughtfully and in depth with analysis. For example, she writes, "They don't have the decision making skills to be able to know that it is wrong or to think, if I do this I am going to get in a lot of trouble and mess up somebody's life really bad."
- The writer's response is coherent, well-focused, and logical. She uses topic sentences to guide the reader and summarizes without simply restating her argument in the conclusion.
- The essay has a pleasing colloquial style and makes excellent use of sentence variety: "The human body is a marvelous thing. When you are born you know almost nothing. Soon you pick up slight motor skills and learn a little bit of language. Everything seems to come into place as soon as you need it. The brain is the exact same way."
- Errors are rare. She uses MLA style quite accurately for her citations.

Adolescence and the death penalty, two words more commonly seen together as of late. With a growing number of young adults being tried and sentenced as adults for violent crimes; the question rises, *why did they commit these crimes"* And before this question can be answered another reveals itself, *does age matter to the jury when they are put on trial?*

According to Paul Thompson, author of the article, "Startling finds on teenage brains," it does. In his article Thompson notes a massive loss of brain tissue during the teenage years. He and his colleagues have found in their research that the cells and cell connections being lost in the brain are in areas that control impulses, risk-taking, and self-control. However, this research can not excuse teens of violent crimes, it does show that they are not yet adults and should not be treated as such (Thompson). "...juveniles being tried as adults are not competent [enough] to stand trial," quoted from Laurence Stinberg taken from the article, "Many kids called unfit for adult trial," by Greg Krikorian.

But isn't appearance also a commanding factor in the jury's decision? Adam Liptak of the New York Times, and author of the article "Supreme Court to rule on executing young killers," seems to think so. Stating in is article, "Jurors' reactions to teenagers' demeanor and appearance can be varied. The defendants they see have ages an average of two to three years between the crime and the trial." So by making the defendant look younger do they have a better chance of receiving a lighter sentence? In a case involving an 18 year-old who shot and killed two elderly neighbors, his appearance and demeanor seemed to have hurt him more that help him. The son of the murdered couple, seemed to think the young killer looked almost eight years old again with his hair combed forward, when at the time of the incident he had a "tough looking" buzz cut. So it may be safe to assume that the age, appearance, and demeanor of the defendant does take a commanding role in the jury's decision, however it is not always a helping one.

But the ever-looming question of why they even commit these crimes still has not been addressed. Thomson believes it is because the large loss of brain tissue in the frontal lobe. The frontal lobe, which helps us to regulate our emotions and control rash actions and violent passions, is very immature during the teen years. When young adults commit these crimes they will most of the time say that they made a "stupid mistake" but may prosecutors would argue that they did in fact "plan" the crime. However, does planning mean the same thing to a thirteen-year-old of a seventeen-year-old (Thompson)? In most cases you would think so but there are skeptics. Some people would say that even though they are teenagers, they should know from wrong.

But do we, as teenagers, know right from wrong? As teens we are prone to do things that are frowned upon by adults. We are in the stages of life when we are most susceptible to peer-pressure. During my own small level of research, I have found that it's the other teenagers who feel the death penalty should be strongly in-forced. Large majorities believe that if teens want to be treated as adults then we should face the consequences of our actions like adults, not say, "Well I'm just a kid and it was a stupid mistake." And when most adults were faced with this question of whether or not adolescents should be tried as adults, they said they didn't feel that they had the "power" or "right" to judge whether someone should die or not. And in my own personal opinion, derived from observations of the news and my own questioning, I feel that teenagers should face up to their actions and accept the consequences of their actions. However, the death penalty should not be enforced for any reason on any person, no body has the right to deem some-one should die.

While research is still being conducted on the reasons behind the violent crimes of young adults, there are still those teens out there who are being prosecuted for those crimes. Some of those teens are already on death row. Could all the new research that has already been published have saved the teens to unfortunate to be sentenced to death? Some people believe that this research is pointless because, the notion that teenagers are not capable of understanding what is going on is not credible. However, with the new find-ings by Paul Thompson and his colleagues about the teenage brain do put a damper on those beliefs.

Works Cited

Liptak, Adam. "Supreme Court to rule on executing young killers". The New York Times. January 3, 2005.

Thompson, Paul. "Startling findings on teenage brains". The Sacramento Bee. May 25, 2001.

Krikorian, Greg. "Many kids called unfit for adult trials". The Sacramento Bee. March 3, 2003.

5

Commentary

This essay illustrates the EPT Scoring Guide's criteria for a score of 5. The clear competence of the essay indicates that this writer is quite ready to handle college-level reading and writing.

- The essay clearly addresses the topic, making arguments based on teenagers' appearance and brain development research, drawing upon the readings, and the moral imperative against killing, which is the writer's own contribution. However, the essay lacks a clear thesis, and the conclusion does not draw the threads of the argument together.
- The essay shows some depth and complexity of thought. The apparent use of field research ("my own small level of research") is impressive although it needs more explanation.
- Paragraph organization is strong.
- The reasons and examples are an effective combination of material in the texts and the writer's own research and observations.
- The writer's control of syntax and word choice is generally strong; however, it slips in some sentences, for example: "However, the death penalty should not be enforced for any reason on any person, no body has the right to deem someone should die."
- Scattered errors are not distracting. No page numbers are given for citations and the Works Cited list does not completely adhere to MLA format.

SAMPLE STUDENT ESSAYS

Sample student essay with a score of 4:

At the age of 17, young Christopher Simmons and a friend robbed a 46 year old woman named Shirley Crook. In doing this they bound and gagged Shirley then forced her into a river where she drowned (Liptak 2). Due to despicable event like this, teenagers should be sentenced as adults because brutal times call for severe measures.

According to Greg Krikorian, a journalist for the Sacramento Bee, "juveniles tried as adults in the United States may be incompetent to stand trial." Younger individuals are said to be "seriously impaired" in understanding the judicial process (Krikorian 1). This is a ridiculous argument used to prove why teenagers shouldn't be sentenced as adults. In committing a brutal crime, not understanding the judicial process doesn't take away from the fact that a person needs to be held accountable for the severity of what they did. It has been proved that "the adolescent brain is not full developed" (Liptak 1). This is true however teenagers have a conscience. Youth are daily held accountable for making decisions that affect the rest of their lives. Another journalist for the Sacramento Bee named Marjie Lundstrom states, "the bigger the crime [adolescents commit,] the more eager we are to call them adults" (1). This statement is twisted because the justice system doesn't consider a juvenile more like an adult the bigger the crime is. The only thing is just like everything else in life, the bigger the mistake, the larger the consequence. Brutal crimes committed by juveniles deserves severe justice.

On November 8, 1994, Oregon passed Measure 11 which requires minimum sentencing for crimes committed by those under the age of 15. "The sentencing judge cannot give a lesser sentence, not can a prisoner's sentence be reduced below the minimum for parole of good behavior." Depending on the crime, criminals should have to deal with the severe consequences no matter what the age is. In doing this, teens will realize that even at a young age, choices have a life changing impact. "Proponents of the measure felt that judges were being too lenient in sentencing violent offenders. They saw the measure as critical for lowering crime rates" (Ballot Measure 1). An adolescent would be less likely to commit a crime if it knew that there would be a harsh consequence. If teen were tried with a lighter sentence, then more teens would choose to act upon their "immature" feelings knowing that they would be able to commit a crime without a harsh punishment. "Supporters credit Measure 11 for reducing crime rates" (Ballot Measure 1). It is better to have severe punishments in the judicial system for the fewer teens that commit crimes, then to have milder punishments for a greater amount of teen criminals. Because of Measure 11 less teens in Oregon are committing crimes, and more importantly, fewer amounts of innocent people are being robbed and brutally murdered by teenagers with no limits.

Thomas A. Preciado was 14 when he "stabbed to death a minimart clerk," and Nathaniel Brazil was 13 when he "shot to death an English teacher" (Lundstrom 2). Although teens are not as accountable or competent as an adult, it cannot be an excuse for vicious, life threatening behavior. Innocent people are being threatened and killed because society is so busy fighting justice for malicious criminals.

Work Cited

Krikorian, Greg. "Many kids called unfit for adult trial: Those under 15 often blind to the long-term results of their choices, a study says." The Sacramento Bee. 3 March, 2003.

Liptak, Adam. "Supreme Court to Rule on Executing Young Killers." The New York Times. 3 January, 2005.

Lundstrom, Marjie. "Kids are kids-until they commit crimes." The Sacramento Bee. 1 March, 2001.

"Oregon Ballot Measure 11." Wikipedia. 13 Sept., 2005. http://en.wikipedia.org/wiki/Oregon_Ballot_Measure_1

4

Commentary

This essay illustrates the EPT Scoring Guide's criteria for a score of 4. This adequate response to the topic suggests that the writer should be able to handle college-level reading and writing.

- The writer addresses the topic and takes the position that "brutal times call for severe measures." The writer acknowledges that teens are "not as accountable or competent as an adult" but then proceeds to argue that they should be held fully accountable. The discrepancy is never resolved in the essay; nevertheless, the writer's position is clearly maintained throughout.

- The writer misunderstands Lundstrom and makes an error about Measure 11 in Oregon; it requires minimum sentences for crimes committed by those over 15, not under 15.

- The writer generally uses examples that support his position, and Measure 11 is appropriate evidence that goes beyond the assigned texts.

- Greater development of both introduction and conclusion and the use of topic sentences would strengthen this essay.

- The writer has adequate control of syntax and word choice with some proficient parallelism; however, a variety of minor errors occur throughout: "Because of Measure 11 less teens in Oregon are committing crimes, and more importantly, fewer amounts of innocent people are being robbed and brutally murdered by teenagers with no limits." Citations are handled well.

Sample student essay with a score of 3:

Leave it to Court

Teenagers sentenced as adults may be necessary. We should not put a limit on punishments. The more the teenager is out of control, the bigger the punishment should be. You didn't get spanked for a small mistake like tripping and falling when you where little, you got spanked for being extremely rude or grounded for lying to your parents. If a child or teenager is so far from following the rules, what do you do? What will a small punishment that doesn't even faze them do? This is why we have sentenced them as adults in the pass. What do you tell the people who were threatened by a teenager, don't worry; he'll be back soon? We shouldn't take away possibilities by closing doors like adult punishment. It needs to be up to the court to choose what the punishment needs to be depending if they think the child or teenager carefully planned out the crime, and might try it again, or was pushed to it.

Greg Krikorian's article, in paragraph number one, he staits that some juveniles that are tried as adults are emotionally or intellectually unable to defend themselves. Shouldn't teenagers think of the consequences? They now it's bad, against the law, and just plain not right. The study Mr. Krikorian uses explains that sixteen and seven year olds can understand just as well as eighteen year olds, but eleven to thirteen years are "seriously impaired". If the child is not to blame, then what about parents? The law can't do too much to parents to make them better at supervising, especially when the child is extremely rebellious. When parents loose control the law does to, until taken care of.

Mr. Liptak's article in paragraph one explains how the seventeen year old shot two elderly neighbors to death, "execution style", and then stole their car. Mr. Acunda's behavior was as if he didn't show remorse. Can you imagine someone like that endangering your neighborhood?

All through Margie Lundstum's article she claims, in paragraph number three that all teenagers and children are innocent. She staits that "They can't smoke or drink or go to r movies without our "ok"." She doesn't states that teenagers and children do these things anyway, legal or not. They get older people to buy beer or to take them to movies without parents consent. It's not the laws job to supervise children that is the parent's job.

Paul Thompson has his own research group, so his article says in paragraph five. He studies the brain and found out that teenagers have loss of brain tissue. What about all of the good teenagers? Mr. Thompson also explains that if the juveniles planned their crime they had to think about it. This means it's impossible for fully thought out crimes to be unsought of. How can a genius plan be made from a boy with loss of brain tissue? What about being led the wrong way? If some one pushed or led someone to do a crime then they should be the ones with a greater punishment.

The world would be a better place with no killing teenagers on the loose. We should not let those kinds of people in public. I hope parents will punish their children so the law doesn't have to. We should keep our punishment options open, not take choices away. If we want the United States of America to be free of horrible crimes, then leave options open, we need choice of punishment. The more choices we have the better of we will be. THE END.

Work Cited

Krikorian, Greg. "Many kids called unfit for adult trial: those under 15 often blind to the long-term results of their choices, a study says." The Sacramento Bee. 3 March 2003.

Liptak, Adam. "Supreme court to Rule on Executing Young Killers." The New York Times. 3 January 2005.

Lundstrom, Marjie. "Kids are Kids Until they Commit Crimes." The Sacramento Bee. 1 March 2001.

Thompson, Paul. "Startling Finds on Teenage Brains" The Sacramento Bee. 25 May 2001.

Commentary

This essay illustrates the EPT Scoring Guide's criteria for a score of 3. Although the essay suggests developing competence, it is flawed in significant ways that suggest the writer needs additional work before being able to succeed in college-level reading and writing.

- The writer takes the position that courts should determine sentencing for teenagers. The writer tries to balance her outrage at the severity of the crimes with the idea of compulsion or peer pressure as an extenuating circumstance but is unable to clearly express her position.
- She gives a very limited summary of each article and fails to do justice to the issues they raise. For instance, in summarizing Lundstrom, she points out that teenagers ignore the legal limits that society imposes but doesn't make clear how that justifies sentencing teenagers as adults. She introduces the issue of parental responsibility but fails to show how it applies to the topic.
- The writer's control of syntax fails whenever she attempts to express complex ideas. The essay has an accumulation of errors in mechanics and usage. She attempts to give credit to her sources but does not know how to incorporate their words into her own writing.

Sample student essay with a score of 2:

Young Killers Being Killed

Ovre the past two weeks my class and i have been reading about juveniles being charged as adults. This age range for these obscured charges against children as young as 10 years old all the way to 17 almost 18 years old. Children are children, if our courts are going to trie them as adults then they should hold them as adults for every thing else including good or bad.

In one article written by Paul Thompson, he explained that at Nathaniel Brazil, a 14 year old boy who is being tried for gunning down one of his teachers. That outside his trial the crowd waved sings and posters saying "A child is not a man. "this is true seeing how the United States sees every and all children as just that, children as just that, children with the expiation of the handful children that are emancipated in this country.

Also in the article written by Marie lundstrom she said, "this is not to say that the boys ccrimes were not heinous, or that they should go unpunished " That shouldn't even be though, but the 71 children that are and have been on death row shouldn't have ever been tried as adults. But the children should have been tried as children and sentences to a stricked and emideate sentence.

In one oter article the writer, Greg Krikorian includes a little fact about Nabraska. Nabraskawas the anly state that didn't pass a new law alowing children to be tried as adults and sentenced to death row. This is right. No states should sentence 14 year old childrento death row. This is right. No states should sentence 14 year old childrento death. After all, in many of the children murder cases the children weren't on ellegal over he conter pharmasudicat drugs. Over all the controle we have over our young people is our ragous, we need to eather treat children as adults or make shure that we treat them like children.

work cited

*Krikorian, Greg-"Many kids called unfit for adult trial: Those under 15 often blind to   the long-term results of their choices ,a study says." <u>The Sacramento Bee</u>" 3march   2003.
*Liptak, Adam" Supreme Court to rule on Executing Young Killers" <u>The New York   Times</u> January 3 2005.
* Ludstrom, Marjie," kids are kids -until they commit crimes" <u>The Sacromento Bee</u>, march 1 2001.
*Thompson, Paul,"Startling finds on teenage brains" <u>The Sacramento Bee</u> May 25 2001

2

Commentary

This essay illustrates the EPT Scoring Guide's criteria for a score of 2. The serious flaws here indicate that this writer will need considerable additional work before being able to succeed in college-level reading and writing.

- The writer attempts to create a text-based essay with a thesis ("they should hold them as adults for every thing else including good or bad"), but it is severely underdeveloped.
- He has a poor understanding of the readings and is unable to maintain focus or use them to develop his response.
- The writer is unable to organize the essay, and the examples are confusing.
- The inadequate control of syntax and vocabulary overrides other considerations. An example is the sentence, ""this is true seeing how the United States sees every and all children as just that, children as just that, children with the expiation of the handful children that are emancipated in this country."
- The essay is marred with numerous errors in grammar and mechanics that interfere with meaning.

Sample student essay with a score of 1:

Juvenile Justice

Teenagers should be sentenced the death penalty because teenagers are the same as everyone else when they commit a serious crime. Teenagers aren't special. Just because they're young, doesn't mean they deserve to escape the death penalty. Teenagers' crimes are often more brutal than most adult murders. (Liptak 5)

It is ludicrous to think that <u>children</u> who commit crimes to the same degree as adults should get punished less.

Commentary

This essay illustrates the EPT Scoring Guide's criteria for a score of 1. The fundamental deficiencies of this essay clearly indicate that the writer needs much additional work to be ready to succeed at college-level reading and writing.

- The essay is too brief to allow any evaluation of the writer's ability in any area: comprehension of the readings, organizational skills, support for a thesis, or facility with the conventions of English.
- The essay's first sentence is a thesis that responds to the prompt; the second, third, and fifth (final) sentences of the essay merely restate the thesis.
- The writer could almost certainly have created an appropriate response to the prompt (note, for example, the appropriate use of the apostrophe in "Teenagers' crimes") but instead ignores the assignment parameters.

Page 80 blank

The Last Meow

Module 7

The Last Meow

Teacher Version

Reading Rhetorically
Prereading 1
   Getting Ready to Read.. 1
   Introducing Key Concepts 2
   Surveying the Text 3
   Making Predictions and Asking Questions.............. 3
   Introducing Key Vocabulary 4
Reading 6
   First Reading 6
   Rereading the Text 9
   Analyzing Stylistic Choices 10
   Looking Closely at Language 12
   Considering the Structure of the Text 13
   Using Critical Vocabulary 14
Postreading 15
   Thinking Critically 15

Connecting Reading to Writing
Writing to Learn 17
Using the Words of Others 17

Writing Rhetorically
Prewriting 18
   Reading the Assignment 18
   Getting Ready to Write...................................... 19
   Formulating a Working Thesis 21
Writing 21
   Composing a Draft... 21
   Organizing the Essay 26
   Developing the Content 27
Revising and Editing.. 27
   Revising the Draft 27
   Editing the Draft 28
   Reflecting on the Writing................................... 29
Evaluating and Responding 30
   Grading Holistically.. 30
   Responding to Student Writing 30
   Using Portfolios 31

Rubric... 32

Reading Selection
"The Last Meow"... 33

Student Version
Activity 1: Getting Ready to Read 45
Activity 2: Introducing Key Concepts 45
Activity 3: Surveying the Text 45
Activity 4: Making Predictions and Asking Questions 46
Activity 5: Introducing Key Vocabulary................... 46
Activity 6: Using Key Vocabulary 46
Activity 7: First Reading 47
Activity 8: Rereading the Text............................... 48
Activity 9: Analyzing Stylistic Choices.................... 48
Activity 10: Looking Closely at Language................. 49
Activity 11. Considering the Structure of the Text........... 49
Activity 12: Using Critical Vocabulary..................... 50
Activity 13: Thinking Critically 50
Activity 14: Reading the Assignment 51
Activity 15: Getting Ready to Write 52
Activity 16: Formulating a Working Thesis................. 52
Activity 17: Composing a Draft 53
Activity 18: Organizing the Essay 57
Activity 19: Developing the Content....................... 58
Activity 20: Revising the Draft 59
Activity 21: Editing the Draft................................ 59
Activity 22: Reflecting on the Writing 60

Sample Student Essays
On-Demand Writing Assignment and Scored
   Student Essays 61

The Last Meow

Organ transplants, chemotherapy, root canal—
how far would you go for a pet?

by Burkhard Bilger
***The New Yorker,* September 8, 2003**
Annals of Veterinary Medicine Section

Part 1

1   She arrived in Manhattan looking ravaged and ravishing, like a queen of silent film with one last swoon left in her. Her sleek ermine coat was matted and worn, her long neck so weak that it drooped to her chest. For months she had managed to hide her condition, eating full meals yet still losing weight. Now she was days away from dying, but her pale-green eyes didn't show it.

2   Shawn Levering glanced down at his cat, Lady, then cast a bewildered look around the waiting room of the Animal Medical Center (AMC), on New York's Upper East Side. He had on scuffed blue jeans and a faded Wheels of Time T-shirt, silk-screened with a picture of a custom Cadillac. His face was freckled and ruddy, his forearms thickly cabled. Standing in the middle of the room, his feet spread wide, he had the specific gravity of a man who knows exactly where to reach for his tools. Back home, in Wilmington, Delaware, Levering liked to work on old cars, taking rusted wrecks and transforming them into street rods. But this cat and her problems, and the city to which he'd been compelled to take her, were beyond him. "This place is crazy," he said. "The taxi-drivers are like demolition experts. I just hope we can find our way out again."

3   Beside him, the veterinarian, Cathy Langston, nodded, her eyes on Lady. The cat was in the throes of chronic renal failure, she said. Her kidneys weren't filtering out the toxins in her blood anymore. "I think she would definitely benefit from dialysis. It won't make her kidneys better, but it will buy her time to see if she's a good candidate for a transplant." There were risks: clotting, internal bleeding, dangerous drops in blood pressure. More than a quarter of Lady's blood would be taken out of her body each time and filtered artificially. If the dialysis was done too quickly, it could cause seizures or even a coma, but the alternative was certain death. "I've got the whole team on standby," Langston said. "We can whisk her back, put in a catheter, and take a biopsy today. If she passes all the tests, we could have her ready for transplant by next week."

4   Like many of the center's 85 veterinarians, Langston is a specialist. "Everyone has to have a passion, and the kidneys are mine," she says. But such passions are relatively new in her field. Little more than 20 years ago, all vets were general practitioners, and neutering and spaying were among

the most elaborate procedures they performed. Now the American Veterinary Medical Association has more than 7,000 specialists in 39 fields, including cardiology, radiology, ophthalmology, and oncology. As the director of the center's quarter-million-dollar kidney unit, Langston usually has one or two patients in dialysis at any given time. Some owners have chartered planes for their animals, then stayed at nearby hotels during the treatment. But not all her clients are wealthy.

5   "We're looking at spending a thousand dollars in the next 24 hours and between three and four thousand in the next week," Langston told Levering. If the dialysis was successful, Lady would have to be transferred to the University of Pennsylvania, where her condition was first diagnosed. (The university's veterinary hospital didn't yet have a dialysis unit, but its vets were more experienced in performing transplants, and Lady was a high-risk patient.) The total cost would be more than $15,000 dollars.

6   Levering sighed and shook his head. Lady was already anemic, asthmatic, and congenitally blind. She had been born on the streets of Wilmington four years earlier and dropped at a local animal clinic at the age of six months. Soon after Levering and his wife adopted her, she became allergic to her own tooth enamel. "That was a weird thing," Levering said. "Never heard of that before." But he had willingly paid $400 to have all her teeth pulled. In retrospect, it seemed like a bargain.

7   "I don't know. If it was up to me, I might not go through with it," he said. He was recovering from a bout of Lyme disease and from carpal tunnel syndrome, and he had recently had sinus surgery. His wife had been laid up for three years with back injuries, and was only now going back to work. If they were willing to go this far for a cat, it was partly out of a sense of shared misfortune. But mostly it was a matter of love. "My wife is totally wiped out about this," he said.

8   A nurse in blue scrubs came over and carefully took the cat from Levering. As she turned to go, he reached over and laid his hand on Lady's head. Then he watched as she was borne away in the nurse's arms, through a pair of swinging doors, and into another world.

Part 2

9   The AMC and the University of Pennsylvania veterinary hospital are the Mayo Clinic and the Mass General of their field. One is perhaps the world's largest private animal hospital; the other is the world's largest university veterinary center. The AMC occupies an eight-story concrete tower at the corner of 62nd Street and York Avenue, overlooking the East River, and in an average year admits 65,000 patients. The center has its own oncology, dentistry, and dermatology departments, as well as the usual surgery, emergency, and recovery wards. To insure that there is a steady supply of blood flowing to surgical patients, it keeps 13 donor greyhounds, 26 donor cats

(some of them inherited from an elderly woman who kept 70 in her apartment), and three donor ferrets. The ferrets are called Larry, Mo, and Curly.

10   New Yorkers, with their dog-averse landlords, have an unusual number and variety of exotic pets. Throughout the years, the city has been swept by vogues for potbellied pigs, Day-Glo anole lizards, and sugar gliders—a nectar-eating Australian marsupial. Most owners don't really know how to care for these animals (sugar gliders, for instance, are prone to osteoporosis in captivity), so the AMC sees a steady circus parade of patients. On a recent day, the exotics unit treated a ferret with a hair ball, an anorexic bearded dragon, a pigeon with a fracture, two wild Canada geese that had got tangled in fishing line, a four-year-old guinea pig awaiting a $5,000 surgery on a ureteral stone, and a hummingbird with a broken wing. Two X-rays hung on a light board on a wall in the corridor. One was of a duck called Nip-Nip, who had swallowed a metallic object. The other showed a long, elegant spine strung with eight perfect ovals: a corn snake with a clutch of eggs stuck in her birth canal.

11   In 1910, when the AMC was founded, animal welfare was a relative term. Officers with the American Society for the Prevention of Cruelty to Animals (ASPCA) carried guns with which to dispatch horses, several hundred of which collapsed from heat and exhaustion in the city every summer. It was considered unladylike to bear firearms, so the women's auxiliary to the ASPCA founded the New York Women's League for Animals and opened a clinic. Situated on the Lower East Side, the clinic was devoted to the city's strays and to the pets of poor immigrants and funded by charitable donations. Its first patient, carried across the Brooklyn Bridge by a young girl, was a cat whose tail had been caught in a door.

12   In 1962, when the clinic moved to the Upper East Side, veterinarians were still a utilitarian breed, and more than 90 percent of them were men. Much of their work was of the kind made famous by James Herriot in *All Creatures Great and Small:* dosing sheep, midwifing cattle. Then, gradually, women began to enter vet schools. By 1975, they represented half of all students; by 2000, nearly three-quarters—and most of them wanted to treat pets. Hospitals sold vets their outdated CAT scanners and MRI machines, making high-tech medicine more affordable. And, as the birth rate dropped, pets came to take the place of children in some families.

13   Between 1980 and 2001 alone, the number of dogs and cats in the United States grew from 98 million to 130 million. Two generations ago, fathers still gave their sons sacks of kittens to drown in the river. Today, according to a recent survey by the American Animal Hospital Association, 63 percent of pet owners say "I love you" to their pets every day. Eighty-three per cent refer to themselves as their pet's mom or dad.

14   The current director of the AMC, Guy Pidgeon, has lived through both halves of this history: He was born on a farm in western Nebraska in 1947—though you'd never guess it from the stout, Friar Tuck-ish figure he now

is—and went to the Colorado State University veterinary school, intent on becoming a country vet. "Then, at some point, I began to see an incredible dichotomy between agricultural and veterinary medicine," he told me. "One was driven by economics, the other by emotion." A sick cow could merit only a few shots before it was sent to the slaughterhouse; a sick hamster could motivate a six-hour surgery. To a veterinarian interested in cutting-edge medicine, the future lay with pets.

15   "My staff likes to tease me about the time my father came here for a visit," Pidgeon said. "He's 86 now and still lives on the farm. He tries to maintain a sense of humor about what I do, but he doesn't really understand it." The poodles getting root canals, the rabbits in radiation wards, were strange enough; but the crowning absurdity was the sight of two prairie dogs in the intensive care unit. Members of the latest exotic pet craze, they had contracted pneumonia and were having trouble breathing. "If you're a farmer in Nebraska, you've been waging holy war against prairie dogs all your life," Pidgeon said. "And here I was giving them oxygen therapy."

Part 3

16   Before I visited the AMC, I had a certain cartoonish image of its clientele: the dragon lady from Carnegie Hill kissing her lap dogs on the lips; the Wall Street power broker sending his wolfhounds to have their teeth cleaned. I thought of the German countess Carlotta Liebenstein, who in 1991 bequeathed her $80 million estate to her dog Gunther. Of J. Paul Getty, who refused to return from Europe when his twelve-year-old son died of a brain tumor but had a vet flown in when his dog developed cancer. When the disease proved fatal, he spent three days weeping in the dog's room.

17   Lady's owners were different. Like many of the rumpled, red-eyed people I sat with in the AMC waiting room, they could scarcely afford their sympathies. Shawn works with mentally disabled adults, finding them jobs and visiting them weekly at their workplaces. He recently turned forty and makes $27,000 a year. His wife, Karen, who is thirty-four, is the caregiver for a disabled teenager and is earning a degree in child psychology. They live in a three-room apartment in a plain brick building on the outskirts of Wilmington. At night, trains rumble in and out of the nearby Saturn car factory, delivering parts, and you can hear the thrum of Interstate 95 half a mile away.

18   When I visited them at home, on a Wednesday evening, Lady was scheduled for a transplant the next morning. She had made it through the dialysis treatment at the AMC and had been transferred to the University of Pennsylvania. Karen had been to Philadelphia that morning to see the kidney donor. The hospital maintains a pool of cats for the purpose, often taken from local shelters and research labs. The surgery seems to have no ill effect on the donor cats' health, and it solves the problem of having to put them to sleep: the owners of the transplantee have to agree to adopt the donor. In the Leverings' case, the new cat would bring their feline population to four.

19   As we talked, Jimmy, a fat brown tabby with a cream belly, slinked warily past Bogart, a scruffy white tom lounging on the couch. Karen had found Bogart starving in front of a 7-Eleven one night and brought him home, only to find that the cat was stone deaf and deeply irritable. The first time Shawn tried to pull Bogart and Jimmy apart, he was bitten so deeply that he had to go to the emergency room. The second time, he had to take a round of antibiotics and get a tetanus shot. Karen's asthma flared up so badly, with all the dander in the air, that she had to use her albuterol inhaler repeatedly. "But I really think my system has adjusted to them," she said.

20   Karen has strawberry-blond hair and a moon-shaped face unmarked by her relentless bad luck. When she met Shawn, in 1997, through a dating service on the local radio station, she was a teacher at a Christian school. A month before their wedding, her car was rear-ended when she stopped at a yield sign. Her injuries were serious enough to warrant visits to a chiropractor during her honeymoon, and they were compounded, three months later, when she was rear-ended again. With a fractured vertebra and several torn disks in her spine, she couldn't stand in front of a classroom anymore, so she stayed home, on constant medication. When she tried to start a family, she couldn't get pregnant.

21   "I don't know what I would have done without the cats," she said. "Shawn was working long hours, and the pain was so extreme sometimes that I would just go to the bathroom and cry." Lady seemed to sense her moods. She would leap onto the bed at night and nestle on her chest. Karen had studied enough psychology to suspect that her feelings for Lady were party misplaced mothering instincts, but she also knew that relationships like theirs could have a particular intensity. In the early 1970s, for instance, the biologist Erika Friedmann, of Brooklyn College, studied how heart-attack patients responded to social support. Patients who had a dog or cat, she found, were more than four times as likely to survive a year after a heart attack than those who didn't have a pet.

22   Research like Friedmann's has since spawned its own scholarly journal, *Anthrozoos,* and a "prescribe-a-pet" movement has sprung up among some therapies. Three years ago, Karen Allen, a psychologist at the State University of New York at Buffalo, studied two groups of hypertensive stockbrokers from Wall Street. One group was given drugs and a pet, while the other received only drugs. Six months later, the brokers took a stress test. They were asked to appease a client who pretended to have just lost $86,000, thanks to their advice. Everyone's blood pressure rose, but for those with pets it rose half as much. Allen later ran another series of tests on pet owners. This time, she had them perform stressful activities alone, in the presence of their pets, and in the presence of their spouses. The results were unequivocal: pets made people's blood pressure drop; spouses made it shoot up.

23   Sitting side-by-side on the love seat in their living room, Karen and Shawn could have passed for two of the pet lovers in Allen's study. Karen argued that her cats deserve "the respect of life." She described the prayer group that she belonged to at a Methodist church and said that the other members would be sending their blessings to Lady the next morning. Shawn reminded her that they were already in debt—"We've gone from getting by to barely scraping." He said the first time she mentioned a transplant he was tempted to have her sanity checked. The cats wound their way between them, filling the silences with their purring.

24   Late that night, Shawn and I took a drive through the deserted streets of Wilmington, past strip malls and sandwich shops to the garage where he works on his street rods. Inside, a 1940 Ford truck lay on blocks, its body sanded and primed, waiting for parts from the crippled car beside it. Shawn and his friend Eddie had bolted the truck's body to a Chevy S-10 frame. They had chopped five inches from the frame, dropped in a burly 305, and laid in a steering column and brakes from a 1987 Monte Carlo. Then the money ran out.

25   "Before Karen and I got married, I was hoping to have this car done in two years," Shawn said. He glanced around the garage and chuckled. No, he said, he wasn't imagining what $15,000 could buy. He, too, had come to depend on Lady's company. "I can't say I haven't compared this transplant to a down payment on a house," he said. "But you can't go too far down that road. If Lady comes through this thing alive, I won't think about it twice.

Part 4

26   I was reminded of the two trucks the next morning, in the operating room at the University of Pennsylvania. The donor cat, Jasper, was lying on one table, his kidney stripped out and strung from its blood vessels like an old transmission. Beside him, Lady, covered with surgical drapes, was awaiting her replacement part. An oxygenation monitor had been clipped to her tongue, an anesthesia tube was pumping Isoflurane gas down her throat, and nylon cords anchored her limbs to the corners of the table. As soon as one team of surgeons cut her open and located her renal blood vessels, aorta, and vena cava, another team would cut Jasper's kidney free. Then the transplant would begin.

27   Lillian Aronson, the head surgeon, strode in with her forearms scrubbed and dripping, her face set in an uneasy grin. She'd begun the day in good spirits, joining the nurses in the kidney chant they had made up: "K-I-D-N-E-Y, you can do it if you try! Kidney! Kidney! Kidney!" Then things began to go wrong. Every cat has two kidneys, though it needs only one to survive, but not every kidney is fit for a transplant. Jasper was Lady's second donor. The first donor, Jack, seemed to have an ideal kidney: a CT scan showed that it was neither too big nor too small, and that there was a single artery

and vein servicing it. But when Aronson opened the cat up, she found a second artery tucked behind the first. This artery would have to be sacrificed in a transplant, depriving part of the organ of blood. Luckily, Jasper—Jack's littermate—was available for surgery, and his blood type was a match for Lady's.

28   "It's all very scary," Aronson said, putting on her surgical gloves. "I ought to just open up a bed-and-breakfast and hang a 'No Vacancy' sign." Aronson, who is thirty-six, has been transplanting kidneys for 10 years. Though her success rate is high—94 percent of her patients leave the hospital, and more than half are alive after four years—the procedure still fills her with a pleasurable dread. The night before, I'd watched her practice in this room, sewing stitches into a sliced rubber glove. A cat's renal artery is only about two millimeters thick. To stitch it to another artery of the same size, Aronson has to use an enormous surgical microscope suspended above the patient's open belly, with dual eyepieces for the surgeon and for her assistant. That brings the sutures into view but throws her eye-hand coordination out of sync. Seen through the eyepiece, the most delicate forceps loom like pliers.

29   As Aronson took a scalpel and placed the tip on Lady's belly, I could see her bracing for the start as if for a pistol shot at a racetrack. Animal lovers are often accused of anthropomorphism, but after you've spent a few weeks in a veterinary hospital it's hard to resist the opposite urge: the doctors all begin to look like their patients. Aronson is unmistakably a greyhound: lean and tightly wound, with dark, downturned eyes and a disarmingly sweet nature for someone who is so single-minded. She runs marathons regularly with her husband and has wanted to be a vet almost from the time she could talk. When her oldest brother, a physicist, first heard about her transplanting a cat's kidneys, his only comment was "Why not just perform a collar transplant instead?"

30   Aronson needed only a few minutes to open Lady's belly, clamp the aorta and the vena cava, and bring over Jasper's kidney. "This cat has issues," she had warned me before the surgery. "With that asthma, I'm not sure how she'll hold up under anesthesia." So far, though, Lady's breathing was deep and even, her blood pressure steady. Using a foot pedal, Aronson steered the motorized microscope into position. She grasped the cut end of Jasper's renal artery with forceps and pressed it against a tiny hole that she had cut in Lady's aorta like a T-joint in a pipe. For the next 10 minutes, she sutured the joint together. Then, just as she was putting in the final stitch, her needle caught the back wall of the artery. As she drew in the thread, it pinched the vessel partially shut. Blood could still flow through it, but there was the possibility of a blood clot.

31   Aronson glanced up at her assistants, her features thrown into shadow by the overhead lamp. "Can anything else go wrong today?" she said. She had no choice but to take out the thread and restitch the joint, but that could irritate the arterial wall, again increasing the chance of a clot. "Her potassium

level is going up," a technician called out beside her. Aronson shook her head. "I'm worried about that artery," she said. "Very worried. I'm telling you right now this may not work."

Part 5

32   The dire choices that define a veterinarian's day aren't particularly well-compensated. The average American vet makes around $60,000 a year—$100,000 less than the average physician, though veterinary training can be just as rigorous and costly as medical school. If vet schools still have to turn applicants away, it's partly because people love to work with animals and party because they're put off by the tortured ethics of human medicine. Whatever dramas veterinarians have to face, they know that malpractice suits are rare and relatively inexpensive, and that euthanasia is always an option.

33   But that may be changing. The law has long treated pets as property, no different from a teddy bear or a windup toy. If an owner sues for the wrongful death of his cat, the most he can demand is the cost of replacing the animal. Recently, though, lawyers have begun to demand more. Two years ago in Oregon, a retired football player named Stan Brock filed a lawsuit against a man who had shot his two Labrador retrievers with arrows. (The man claimed that the dogs had been threatening stray cats near his house.) Replacing the dogs would have cost, at most, a few hundred dollars, but Brock sued for $300,000. "Pets don't depreciate; they appreciate," his attorney, Geordie Duckler, argued in court. "That's very different from what you can say about a purse or a car." The trial judge agreed.

34   Brock eventually settled out of court for an undisclosed sum, but Duckler expects a number of similar cases in coming years. In Tennessee, he says, a law that was recently passed allows owners to sue for up to $4,000 in emotional damages if their pet is killed by a negligent pet owner's dog, and several other states have comparable bills on the docket. In New York, in 1999, a housing court forced a landlord to let a woman keep a puppy in her Queens apartment when she cited research on the health benefits of pets. Elsewhere, a group called In Defense of Animals has lobbied communities to define people as "guardians" rather than owners of their pets. Seven cities and the state of Rhode Island have adopted at least a variation of the ordinance.

35   "The more people spend on their pets, the more that cost is going to be reflected in the law," Duckler says, which means that veterinarians could face million-dollar malpractice suits in the future. Each time they introduce an expensive new procedure—radiation therapy in the 1980s, MRIs in the 1990s, experimental cancer vaccines in the new millennium—they implicitly raise the value of their patients. Many vets, like doctors, are now on call at night and on weekends. When they sit at kitchen tables at four in the morn-

ing, listening patiently to owners describing their dogs' stool consistency, they suggest that a pet is worth almost any effort, any cost.

36   Vets say that rising malpractice awards will hurt both sides. "They'll just bring the insanity of the human side of the business into my profession," Pidgeon told me at the AMC. "And all those costs will be passed on to the client." But pet owners have already begun to prepare for those costs. Nearly 400,000 pets are now covered by medical insurance policies in the United States, and that number is expected to grow to 2.5 million in the next five years.

37   Not long ago, at an all-day symposium at Harvard Law School, Jane Goodall, Alan Dershowitz, and others tried to sort out the legal and ethical principles behind these issues. Should courts grant animals some human rights? If so, which animals and which rights? There was much talk of I.Q. and the theory of mind, of gorillas that can communicate in sign language and parrots that can do arithmetic. Steven Wise, an animal-rights attorney and the author of the book *Drawing the Line,* divided the animal world into four categories, based on ascending levels of intelligence. At the bottom were earthworms, bacteria, and other creatures that are notably lacking in self-knowledge or the power of deductive reasoning. At the top were the great apes, dolphins, and a few clever birds. Only this last group, Wise argued, could claim "legal personhood." Dogs, cats and most other pets hovered somewhere in category three: just a little too dim—or poorly understood—to earn our highest regard.

38   Wise knows that his categories won't convince most people. An adult chimpanzee may be smarter than most two-year-old boys, but that won't get it into day care. The rights we grant animals are, first and foremost, a function of empathy—and, on that count, no ape can compete with a pet. "The chimp is amazingly similar to us in brain structure, DNA, and behavior," Jane Goodall told me during an intermission. "But a dog can be a better friend to you than anyone else." Goodall has spent most of her life living with chimpanzees, but it was her childhood dog, Rusty, who first taught her that animals have personalities, intelligence, and feelings. If one research facility was being cruel to dogs and another was abusing primates, she said, she knew which one she would shut down first: "I'd choose the dogs."

Part 6

39   The missing voice in this debate, of course, is that of the animals. Is the agony of chemotherapy worth an extra six months of life to a dachshund? Does a parrot really want legal autonomy? Veterinarians like to talk about a pet's quality of life, but no one really knows what they mean. Injured animals no doubt experience fear and pain: the parts of their brains that process those feelings (the amygdala, the thalamus, and the hypothalamus) are similar to ours, and animals often have keener senses. Do they also feel enough

pleasure—enough joy in the sheer fact of existence—to make surviving worthwhile?

40   Two weeks before Lady's transplant, I saw a mastiff named Taberia in the intensive-care unit at the AMC. The dog was eleven years old—ancient for her breed—and barely able to stand. Her eyes were rimmed with red, and her skin draped over her bones like an old rug. She had a grapefruit-size growth hanging from her belly and a bleeding tumor on her spleen that seemed to have spread to her liver. "Surgery will probably just prolong the inevitable," a resident said. "Dogs with this kind of cancer don't respond well to chemo." The doctor gently suggested putting the dog to sleep, but the owner seemed not to have heard him. She was a bartender at Red Rock West in Manhattan, with a pale, defiant face and a voice gone smoky from years of screaming above crowds. She crouched inside the mastiff's cage and cradled its head. "Taberia used to love hanging out at the bar," she said. "I've always thought she must have been a drunken ballerina in her last life."

41   Euthanasia is one of the last dividing lines between human and animal medicine, but it has been blurred in recent years. Although Oregon legalized assisted suicide in 1997 and Jack Kevorkian and others have championed the practice for the terminally ill, veterinarians have grown more wary of the procedure. Less than 20 years ago, a pet owner could still have a healthy animal put down. Now most vets will euthanize only the very sick, and their standards continue to rise as their medicine improves. "Sometimes, in all the hoopla over what we can do, we lose sight of the fact that there are people who don't want to go that far," Pidgeon said. "And sometimes we think the pet is being forced to endure more than it should." Owners can still weigh the costs and benefits of saving a pet's life. But the more pets are treated like surrogate children, the more complicated the equation becomes.

42   In Taberia's case, under the surgical lights the doctors found exactly what they had expected: the abdomen full of blood, the spleen and the liver so engorged with purplish cancer cells that they had burst open. Even then, the owner wanted the dog sewn back up and sent home. If Taberia could just live for a few more weeks, she thought, she might be able to cure her holisti-cally.

43   The surgeons eventually persuaded Taberia's owner to let them put the mastiff to sleep. When I asked her what she planned for the body; she said that she was going to buy Taberia a plot in Hartsdale, New York, in the country's oldest and most prestigious pet cemetery. "When someone buries a dog there, you know they must have loved it to death," she said.

Part 7

44   It had been six hours since Lady's first donor was cut open. For the past 20 minutes, a brittle silence had fallen over the room. Aronson shuttled from one side of the surgical table to the other, getting the best angle on her final stitches. The replacement kidney had been without blood for about

45 minutes. Most organs can survive that long and still function, but Aron-son could never be sure. She gave her assistants a weak smile. "Pray to the urine gods," she said.

45   When the clamps came off, the renal artery and vein hung limply at first, like guy wires from a deflating zeppelin. Then, little by little, they began to stiffen. Their pale white walls stretched and expanded, until a delicate tremor ran down their length: the beating of Lady's heart. "Unbelievable," Aronson said. The sutures were holding, and the weakened artery showed no signs of collapse. Now she just had to attach the ureter: the vessel, even thinner than the artery, that carried urine from the kidney to the bladder.

46   Aronson sliced open the bladder, flipped it inside out, and cut a small hole in the side. She threaded the ureter through the hole and was preparing to attach it with a crown stitch when her hand suddenly froze. "Will you look at that?" she said. Her assistants crowded around, craning their necks. A thin stream of clear fluid was trickling from the ureter's open end. "A new kidney making urine," Aronson said, as everyone whooped and cheered around her. "There's nothing better than that."

47   Afterward, when the bladder had been stitched shut and injected with salt water to insure that it was watertight and the kidney had been sewn to the side wall of her belly to prevent it from drifting, Aronson closed up Lady's belly and rolled her to the intensive-care unit. She gave the nurse on duty the rundown: "She's blind, she's toothless, she has renal disease, and she's really sweet." Then she went out to get a Diet Coke—her first meal in more than 20 hours. Lady lay on the table, immobile. After a few minutes, she opened a single eye.

Part 8

48   Americans now spend $19 billion a year on veterinary care, up from $11 billion just seven years ago. Add to that the cost of pet food and other supplies and the number rises to $47 billion, nearly three times as much as the federal government spends on welfare grants. The figures fill even some pet owners with dismay. If society could give up on goldfish alone, the senti-ment suggests, it could fund a few dozen more Head Start programs. Cure the addiction to dogs and cats, and millions of families might be lifted out of poverty. Pets, as George Bernard Shaw wrote, "bear more than their natural burden of human love."

49   But, of course, it's not that simple. Our feelings for animals aren't eas-ily transferred, a fact best illustrated by our treatment of the pets we don't own. When Lady was recovering from her transplant, a kitten was being treated next door. His mother had died after giving birth, and his littermates, hungry for milk, had mistaken their brother's penis for a nipple, eventually giving him a bladder infection. The kitten's owners had driven in from west-ern Pennsylvania and were paying hundreds of dollars for his treatment. Yet

they could have got another kitten for free in any shelter. Every year, while pets like theirs are saved by the most elaborate means, some six million strays are put to sleep.

50   Americans are no more inconstant than other nationalities. The Chinese pamper their Pekingese and stir-fry other breeds. Polynesians used to slaughter some puppies and breastfeed others. The Inca kept hairy dogs as hunters and hairless ones as bed warmers, shielding the latter from sunburn in rooms filled with orchids. Modern veterinary medicine is either the natural culmination of these ancient relationships or their crowning folly. Spending $15,000 on a cat is an outrage, some say, yet they gladly spend four times more on a BMW.

51   The last time I saw the Leverings, Lady had been back from the hospital for a week and had a bedroom to herself. The first days of recovery are a dangerous time, Aronson says. One of her other clients tried to keep her cat from jumping down from the couch not long after its transplant. The cat shook itself free, ran downstairs, and fell over dead—its renal artery having torn free in the tussle. Even if Lady avoids such mishaps, she will have to take steroids and immunosuppressants for the rest of her life to keep her body from rejecting the new kidney. The drugs will cost about $500 a year, not counting veterinary fees for tri-monthly visits, and will leave Lady prone to infections, cancers, and diabetes.

52   Karen showed me how she prepared the doses twice a day, injecting amber cyclosporine into clear gel capsules. Two days earlier, she said, she had locked herself out of the house when it was time for the afternoon dose and had to use a rock to break in through the kitchen window. Otherwise, it had been a smooth transition. Jack, the failed kidney donor, was being adopted by a vet at the hospital. Jasper had developed a toe infection and an allergy to his plastic food bowl, but he had taken to the other cats immediately.

53   Halfway through the conversation, Shawn came back from church, propping up an elderly man with an enormous, lopsided grin. His name was Don and he worked at an auto-parts factory and sometimes helped out in the garage on weekends. He and Shawn settled on the couch across from Karen and talked about street rods for a while. Lady padded in from her room, picking her way around the furniture by memory, and joined Bogart and Jasper on the carpet. They were an oddly harmonious trio—one blind, one deaf, one allergic to plastic and missing a kidney—not unlike the people around them. Gathered there in the living room, they kept an eye on one another, the cats and the people. "It would have been hard not to have Lady around," Shawn said. The cats, as always, didn't say a word.

The Last Meow

Reading selection for this module:
Bilger, Burkhard. "The Last Meow." *New Yorker.* Sept. 8, 2003.

Reading Rhetorically

Prereading

Activity 1	### Getting Ready to Read

Write for five minutes about the following question:

> How important are pets in your life and in the lives of people you know?

With a small group of your classmates, share what you have written and talk about whether we pamper our pets too much.

Activity 2	### Introducing Key Concepts

List words that relate to pets or veterinarians, and then create a semantic map.

Activity 3	### Surveying the Text

Discuss the following questions with your class:

- The title of the article is "The Last Meow," and it was published in the category of "Annals of Veterinary Medicine." The subtitle states: "Organ transplants, chemotherapy, root canal—how far would you go for a pet?" Based on this information, what do you think the article will be about?
- What can you tell about the article by looking at its length and the lengths of its paragraphs?

Activity 4

Making Predictions and Asking Questions

Discuss the following questions with your class:

1. Read the category in which this article appears (Annals of Veterinary Medicine), the title, and the subheading. What do you think this text will be about?
2. This article appeared in *The New Yorker* magazine. What do you know about this magazine? Who do you think is the intended audience for this piece? What other audiences might be interested in this topic? How do you know?
3. Will the article take a position on the topic of veterinary care for pets? Why do you think so?
4. What is your answer to the question: How far would you go for a pet?
5. Will the article be negative or positive in relation to the cost of veterinary care? Why do you think this?

Activity 5

Introducing Key Vocabulary

Script Writing

Write a "script" using eight words from the chart shown below—two from each column. Using those eight words, design a script for a scene you might see on a TV drama or a news program. Make sure each person in your group has a speaking part and that the scene is no more than five minutes long. Use a dictionary to ensure you are using the words correctly.

unequivocal	compensated	general practitioner	dialysis
ravishing	compelled	incurable	transplant
absurdity	ravage	mercy	terminal
dichotomy	droop	suffering	donor
support	bewilder	family member	euthanasia
exotic	strays	medical treatment	lethal injection

Activity 6

Using Key Vocabulary

Complete the following sentences by changing the verb in parentheses into either an *–ed* form or an *–ing* form:

1. The patient, _____ (ravage) by the effects of diabetes, was a candidate for a kidney transplant.

2. The disease was _____ (ravage) the kidneys of the cat.

3. The _____ (droop) cat was held in the arms of her owner.

**Activity 6
(Continued)**

4. The cat _____ (droop) as the owner handed her to the veterinarian.

5. _____, (bewilder) Shawn Levering looked around the veterinary hospital.

6. He was given a _____ (bewilder) number of choices.

7. The veterinarian made a _____ (compel) argument for saving Lady's life.

8. He was _____ (compel) to choose between his hot rods and his cat.

9. The _____ (transplant) kidney was working fine.

10. The surgeon had _____ (transplant) the kidney the night before.

Reading

Activity 7

First Reading

"The Last Meow" is a fairly long and complex article. To help the reader, the author has divided it into eight parts. You are going to look at the parts separately. As you read, think about why Bilger created these divisions.

A. Your teacher has read Part 1 aloud. Now you will discuss the questions below about Part 1. Form groups and choose a recorder. Be prepared to share your answers with the class.

- What is wrong with Lady? What is the treatment? How much will it cost to treat her?
- What kind of person is Shawn Levering, her owner? How can you tell?
- What kind of person is the veterinarian, Cathy Langston? How can you tell?
- Why do you think Shawn is willing to pay for Lady's treatment? Is he the kind of person you would expect to pay for high-cost treatment for a pet?

B. For Part 2, your teacher has read the first sentence of each paragraph aloud and predicted what the paragraphs will be about. Now read Part 2 and decide if your teacher's predictions were correct.

C. Now read parts 3 through 7. Start by reading the first sentence of each paragraph in Part 3 and predict what Part 3 will be about. Then confirm your predictions or revise them if you find they are wrong. As precisely as you can, write a one-sentence summary of Part 3. Follow the same process for parts 4 through 7.

Activity 7 (Continued)	Now that you know what "The Last Meow" is about, answer the following questions:

Now that you know what "The Last Meow" is about, answer the following questions:

- Think about your original predictions. Which predictions were right? Which did you have to modify as you read "The Last Meow"?
- What is the most significant sentence in the article? Underline or highlight it. Why is it the most important sentence?
- What is the main idea of "The Last Meow"?
- How has Bilger responded to the question of whether Americans are spending too much on their pets? How do you know?

Activity 8

Rereading the Text

Now reread "The Last Meow," and annotate it as you reread. Underline, highlight, and draw arrows. In the left-hand margin, make comments about the main ideas, questions or objections, and the connections between ideas. In the right-hand margin, write your reactions to what Bilger says and what the people he writes about say.

Compare your annotations with those of a classmate. Then go back and revise your annotations if you wish.

Activity 9

Analyzing Stylistic Choices

Answer the following questions:

Words

- Reread the first paragraph of Part 1. What words does Bilger use to compare Lady to a movie star? Why does he make this comparison?
- Now read the second paragraph. What words does Bilger use to describe Shawn Levering? What point is Bilger making about Shawn?
- Now read the third paragraph. Identify the medical terminology in this paragraph. Why does Bilger use it?
- What do Lady, Shawn Levering, and Cathy Langston represent? What problem or issue do the first three paragraphs suggest that "The Last Meow" is going to explore?

Sentences

- Look at the first paragraph of Part 2. Each sentence is quite long except the last. What is the effect of ending the paragraph with, "The ferrets are called Larry, Mo, and Curly"?
- What is the purpose of the parentheses in the third sentence?
- Why does Bilger give us a long list of examples of animals treated in the exotics unit?

Paragraphs

- How are the paragraphs in this article different from paragraphs in a newspaper article?

Activity 9 (Continued)	**Essay**

Essay

- Why has Bilger divided the article into sections?
- What is the tone of "The Last Meow"?
- How would the article be different if it were a newspaper article? What if it were in a textbook for students of veterinary medicine?

Activity 10

Looking Closely at Language

Answer the following questions based on "The Last Meow."

1. According to Bilger, how has veterinary medicine changed in the last 20 years?
2. Why does Guy Pidgeon say that veterinary medicine is driven by emotion?
3. If you could own an exotic pet, what would it be?
4. How does Shawn Levering react to New York City and the veterinary hospital? Use "bewildered" in your answer.
5. What is Shawn willing to give up in order to save Lady? Use the word "sacrifice."
6. Do you feel sorry for the Leverings? Use the word "sympathetic."
7. What problem does the story of Lady and the Leverings represent?

Activity 11

Considering the Structure of the Text

Look again at the one-sentence summaries you wrote for sections 3–7. Use that information to write one-sentence summaries of parts 1, 2, and 8, and then write brief statements describing the rhetorical function of each part.

Here are some questions to answer.

- What does each part do for the reader? What is the writer trying to accomplish?
- What does each part say? What is the content?

Now look at the organization of the article. Consider these questions:

- Which part is the most developed?
- Which part is the least developed? Does it need more development?
- Which part is the most persuasive? The least persuasive?
- From your work in charting the text, what do you think is the essay's main argument? Is it explicit or is it implicit?

Activity 12

Using Critical Vocabulary

Complete the following sentences so the second part further explains the first part, clearly demonstrating your understanding of the underlined words:

1. When pet owners are willing to spend thousands of dollars on veterinary medicine, it clearly shows _____ _____ .

2. In the past, veterinarians mainly treated cows, sheep, and horses; now, however, _____ _____ .

3. Patients who have a close relationship with their pets seem more likely to recover; a reason could be _____ _____ .

4. Health care for pets is becoming comparable in many ways to health care for humans; for example, pet owners can _____ _____ .

5. People feel empathy for their pets; _____ _____ .

6. Euthanasia is an option for animals, but people _____ _____ .

7. The veterinarian persuaded the owners to have the cat put to sleep; _____ _____ .

8. People don't seem to transfer the feelings they have for their own pets to strays; in fact, _____ _____ .

Postreading

Activity 13

Thinking Critically

Questions about Logic (Logos)

1. Locate the essay's major claims and assertions and ask yourself whether you agree with the author.
2. Look at support for the major claims and ask yourself whether there is any claim that appears to be weak or unsupported. Which one, and why?

Activity 13 (Continued)	3. Can you think of counterarguments that the author does not deal with?
	4. Do you think the author has left something out on purpose? Why?

Questions about the Writer (Ethos)

1. Does this author have the right background to speak with authority on this subject? Do a Web search to find out more about Bilger.
2. Is this author knowledgeable? Smart? Successful?
3. Do you trust this author? Why or why not?
4. Do you think this author is deceptive? Why or why not?
5. Do you think this author is serious?

Questions about Emotions (Pathos)

1. Does this piece affect you emotionally? Which parts?
2. Do your emotions conflict with your logical interpretation of the arguments?
3. Does the author use humor? How does this affect your acceptance of his ideas?

Quickwrite (five minutes)

Choose one of the following topics to write about:

1. What does this writer want us to believe?
2. What is your response to one of the author's main ideas?

What did you learn from this exercise? Write for five more minutes.

Writing Rhetorically

Prewriting

Activity 14	### Reading the Assignment
	This activity gives you an opportunity to review your writing assignment.

> **On-Demand Writing Assignment**
>
> You will have 45 minutes to plan and write an essay on the topic below. Before you begin writing, read the passage carefully and plan what you will say. Your essay should be as well-organized and carefully written as you can make it.
>
> After reading the passage, explain Bilger's argument and discuss the extent to which you agree or disagree with his analysis. Support your position by providing reasons and examples from your own experience, observations, or reading.
>
> Americans now spend $19 billion a year on veterinary care for their pets, up from $11 billion just seven years ago. Add

Activity 14 (Continued)

to that the cost of pet food and other supplies, and the number rises to $47 billion, nearly three times as much as the federal government spends on welfare grants. Poodles get root canals, cats undergo chemotherapy, rabbits are treated with radiation, and prairie dogs get oxygen therapy in intensive-care units. People spend enormous amounts to pay for special diets for their pets while cities create parks for off-leash puppy play dates. For a price, we can take our dogs for day care or psychotherapy and buy them $200 cashmere sweaters and leopard-skin beds. Clearly, our love affair with our pets has gotten out of control.

Adapted from Burkhard Bilger's
"The Last Meow"
The New Yorker

Take the following steps for this exercise:

- Read the assignment carefully.
- Decide which issue you are going to discuss.
- Discuss the purpose of the assignment. What will you try to accomplish in your essay?

Activity 15

Getting Ready to Write

Answer the following questions, which will help you get ready to write:

1. What are the author's major claims?
2. Which claim is the strongest? The weakest? Has he left anything out?
3. How credible is the author on this topic?
4. How does the argument affect you emotionally?
5. Has the author tried to manipulate your emotions? How?

Activity 16

Formulating a Working Thesis

Writing down a tentative thesis at this point is a good habit to develop in your writing process. Your thesis should be a complete sentence and can be revised several times. A focused thesis statement will keep your writing on track.

Record your responses to the following questions in preparation for writing your tentative thesis statement:

- What specific question will your essay answer? What will be your response to this question? (This is your tentative thesis.)
- What support have you found for your thesis?
- What evidence have you found for this support? (Evidence can include facts, statistics, authorities, personal experience, anecdotes, stories, scenarios, examples, and so forth.)
- How much background information do your readers need to understand your topic and thesis?

Activity 16 (Continued)	• If your readers were to disagree with your thesis or the validity of your support, what would they say? How would you address their concerns? (What would you say to them?)
	Now draft a possible thesis for your essay.

Writing

Activity 17	**Composing a Draft**

When you write an argument essay, choose a subject that matters to you. If you have strong feelings, you will find it much easier to gather evidence and convince the readers of your point of view. Keep in mind, however, that your readers might feel just as strongly about the opposite side of the issue. The following guidelines will help you write a good argument essay:

1. **State your opinion on the topic in your thesis statement.** To write a thesis statement for an argument essay, you must take a stand for or against an action or an idea. In other words, your thesis statement should be debatable—a statement that can be argued or challenged and that will not be met with agreement by everyone who reads it. Your thesis statement should introduce the subject and state your opinion about that subject.

   Bilger never makes his thesis explicit. This strategy is called an implied thesis, and professional writers sometimes use this strategy because they are skilled at making the focus of their essays clear to readers without ever saying exactly what their opinion on the topic is. However, we can infer that Bilger's thesis is something like this:

   "Americans need to reassess the balance between the pleasure our pets bring us and the excessive costs of their veterinary care and the possible suffering it causes."

   Some other statements about developments in veterinary medicine would not be debatable and, therefore, would not be effective theses:

   Not debatable: In 2000, three-quarters of veterinary students were women, and most of them wanted to treat pets.

   Not debatable: According to Dr. Pidgeon, owners can still weigh the costs and benefits of saving a pet's life.

   The first example is a statistic (a fact based on research). It is not an opinion and cannot be used as a thesis. The second example is a statement about another person's opinion, not the writer's opinion.

2. **Take your audience into consideration as you write your essay.** When you write your essay, you will need to assume that your audience is generally well-informed but may not have the specific knowledge you have gained through reading and discussion

as you have moved through this module. You will need to provide your readers with information and your sources for that information, whether you are citing statistics or paraphrasing someone else's argument.

You may also want to let your readers know who you are. You can indicate, for example, that your family has two cats, a dog, and a hamster, so that when you talk about the emotional benefits of having pets, they will know that you are knowledgeable about this. On the other hand, Bilger reveals very little about himself. What we do know is that he has done fairly extensive research by observing pet owners, talking to professionals in the field of veterinary medicine, and reading research about the effects of pet ownership. In academic writing, an author's credibility is often based on the research he or she has done rather than on the writer's personal experience.

In writing an academic essay, you will usually want to take a clear stand on the issue but also acknowledge some possible alternative positions. By explaining why they are not as strong as your position, you will better respond to your readers' potential objections.

Bilger, however, does not follow this strategy. He presents arguments on both sides of the issue of providing state-of-the-art veterinary care to pets. He does not take a clear stand on either side, although you might argue that he leans toward one direction or the other. His article leaves readers wondering about another perspective on the issue—that of the pets themselves, who are unable to express their wishes.

3. **Choose evidence that supports your thesis statement.** Evidence is probably the most important factor in writing an argument essay. Without solid evidence, your essay is nothing more than opinion; with it, your essay can be powerful and persuasive. If you supply convincing evidence, your readers will not only understand your position but may agree with it.

Evidence can consist of facts, statistics, statements from authorities, and examples or personal stories. Examples and personal stories can be based on your own observations, experiences, and reading, but your opinions are not evidence. Other strategies, such as comparison/contrast, definition, and cause/effect, can be particularly useful in building an argument. Use any combination of evidence and writing strategies that supports your thesis statement.

In "The Last Meow," you can find several different types of evidence. Here are some examples:

Facts

- The Animal Medical Center has its own oncology, dentistry, and dermatology departments. (Part 2, paragraph 9)
- In 1962, veterinarians were still a utilitarian breed. (Part 2, paragraph 12)

- A group called In Defense of Animals has lobbied communities to define people as "guardians" rather than owners of their pets. (Part 5, paragraph 35)
- Oregon legalized assisted suicide in 1997. (Part 6, paragraph 41)

Statistics

- By the year 2000, women represented 75 percent of veterinary students. (Part 2, paragraph 13)
- Between 1980 and 2001, the number of dogs and cats in the United States grew from 98 million to 130 million. (Part 2, paragraph 13)
- Americans now spend $19 billion on veterinary care, up from $11 billion just seven years ago. (Part 8, paragraph 48)

Statements from Authorities

- Reference to research by Erika Friedmann on the effect of pet ownership on the recovery of heart-attack patients (part 3, paragraph 21)
- Statements by Georgie Duckler, attorney, on wrongful death suits applying to pets (part 5, paragraphs 33–35)
- Statement by Steven Wise, animal-rights attorney, about "legal personhood" for animals (part 5, paragraph 37)

Examples and Personal Stories

- The personal story of Shawn Levering, Cathy Langston, and Lady

4. **Anticipate opposing points of view.** In addition to stating and supporting your position, anticipating and responding to opposing views are important. Presenting only your side of the argument leaves half the story untold—the opposition's half. If you acknowledge that there are opposing viewpoints and answer them, your argument is stronger.

   Bilger chooses to take a stance of objectivity about the issue of providing high-cost veterinary care to pets. In order to appear objective, he is careful to balance evidence on both sides of the issue. He tells the heartrending story of Lady and her owners, which causes readers to sympathize with people who spend enormous amounts of money they may not be able to spare to keep their pets alive. And he provides evidence for the medical and psychological benefits of pet ownership. However, he also provides evidence of how extreme the spending has become at the same time that many animals are neglected. He raises the question of whether extreme measures are even in the best interests of pets like Lady. By raising these questions, Bilger challenges his readers to think more critically about these issues, but he does not provide easy answers.

5. **Maintain a reasonable tone.** Just as you probably would not win an argument by shouting or making mean or nasty comments, do not expect your readers to respond well to such tactics. Keep the "voice" of your essay calm and sensible. Your readers will be much

more open to what you have to say if they think you are a reasonable person.

Bilger maintains a reasonable tone throughout his essay. Although he provides a lot of evidence that spending on pets has gotten out of control with the example of Lady and her owners, he acknowledges the complexity of the issue when it is faced by real people with real animals. We are more ready to be thoughtful about the issue because he makes a reasonable argument rather than a strident appeal.

6. **Organize your essay in such a way that it presents your position as effectively as possible.** You want your audience to agree with you by the end of your essay; therefore, you need to organize it in a way that will make it easy for your readers to follow. The number of paragraphs will vary depending on the nature of your assignment, but the following outline shows the order in which the features of an argument essay are most effective:

Introduction
Background information
Introduction of the subject
Statement of your opinion

Body paragraphs
Common ground
Ample evidence (logical and emotional)
Opposing point of view
Response to the opposing point of view

Conclusion
Restatement of your position
A call for action or agreement

The arrangement of your evidence in an argument essay will depend to a great extent on your readers' opinions. Most arguments will be organized from general to particular, from particular to general, or from one extreme to another. When you know that your readers already agree with you, arranging your details from general to particular or from most to least important is usually the most effective strategy. Using that order, you build on your readers' agreement and loyalty as you explain your thinking on the subject.

If you suspect that your audience does not agree with you, reverse the organization of your evidence, and arrange it from particular to general or from least to most important. In that way, you will be able to take your readers step by step through your reasoning in an attempt to get them to agree with you.

| Activity 17 (Continued) | Bilger's essay follows the general outline just presented. Here is a skeleton outline of his essay: |

Introduction

Part 1: The story of Lady and her hospitalization for a kidney transplant

Body Paragraphs

Part 2: The evolution of veterinary care in the U.S.
Part 3: The medical benefits of pets
Part 4: Lady's surgery
Part 5: The evolution of the legal status of pets
Part 6: The question of quality of life for pets
Part 7: The success of Lady's surgery

Conclusion

Part 8: Revisiting the main questions:

1. Should the money spent on pets be spent on children or on other animals?
2. Are the benefits that pets provide their owners worth the costs as exemplified by the Leverings and their pets?
3. What would the animals say?

Activity 18

Organizing the Essay

The following items are traditional parts of all essays:

- An introduction (usually one or two paragraphs) that "hooks" the reader and provides a thesis statement, or roadmap, for the reader
- The body (as many paragraphs as necessary), which supports the thesis statement point by point
- A conclusion (usually only one paragraph) that summarizes the main points and explains the significance of the argument

The number of paragraphs in an essay will depend on the nature and complexity of your argument.

Here are some additional hints to help you organize your thoughts:

Introduction

- You might want to include the following in your introductory paragraph (or paragraphs):
  - A "hook" to get the reader's attention
  - Background information the audience may need
  - A thesis statement and an indication of how the essay will be developed ("forecasting"). *Note:* A thesis statement states the topic of the essay and the writer's position on that topic. You may choose to sharpen or narrow your thesis at this point.

Activity 18 (Continued)

Body

- Paragraphs that present support of the thesis statement, usually in topic sentences supported with evidence. (See "Getting Ready to Write.")
- Paragraphs that include different points of view or address counter-arguments
- Paragraphs or sentences in which you address those points of view by doing the following:
  - Refuting them
  - Acknowledging them but showing how your argument is better
  - Granting them altogether but showing that they are irrelevant
- Evidence that you have considered your own values, beliefs, and assumptions; the values, beliefs, and assumptions of your audience; and some common ground that appeals to the various points of view

Conclusion

- A final paragraph (or paragraphs) that includes a solid argument to support the thesis and indicate the significance of the argument— the "so what?" factor

Draw horizontal lines through your essay to distinguish these three parts, and label them in the margin.

Activity 19

Developing the Content

Here are few highlights about developing your essay:

- Most body paragraphs consist of a topic sentence (or an implied topic sentence) and concrete details to support that topic sentence.
- Body paragraphs give evidence in the form of examples, illustrations, statistics, and so forth and analyze the meaning of the evidence.
- Each topic sentence is usually directly related to the thesis statement.
- No set number of paragraphs makes up an essay.
- The thesis dictates and focuses the content of an essay.

Revising and Editing

Activity 20

Revising the Draft

You now need to work with the organization and development of your draft to make sure that your essay is as effective as possible.

Peer Group Work

Work in groups of three or four. Each student will read his or her essay aloud to the other members of the group. Then complete Part I of the Evaluation Form for each essay.

Paired Work

Working in pairs, decide how you will revise the problems your group members have identified.

Individual Work

Revise the draft on the basis of the feedback you have received and the decisions you have made with your partner.

Revising Guidelines for Individual Work

- Have I responded to the assignment?
- What is my purpose for this essay?
- What should I keep? What is the most effective?
- Where do I need more details, examples, and other evidence to support my point?
- What can I omit? Do I use irrelevant details? Am I repetitive?
- Are parts of my essay confusing or contradictory? Do I need to explain my ideas more fully?
- What should I rethink? Is my position clear? Do I provide enough analysis to convince my readers?
- How is my tone? Am I too overbearing or too firm? Do I need qualifiers?
- Have I addressed differing points of view?
- Does my conclusion show the significance of my essay?
- Have I used key vocabulary words correctly to represent the ideas from the article? Have I used words that refer to specific facts from the text?

Activity 21

Editing the Draft

You now need to work with the grammar and mechanics of your draft to make sure that your use of language is effective and conforms to the guidelines of standard written English.

Edit your draft on the basis of the information you have received from your teacher or a tutor. Use the editing checklist in the evaluation form provided by your teacher.

**Activity 21
(Continued)**

The suggestions below will help you edit your own work:

- If possible, set your essay aside for 24 hours before rereading it to find errors.
- If possible, read your essay aloud so you can hear errors and any rough spots.
- At this point, focus on individual words and sentences rather than on overall meaning. Take a sheet of paper and cover everything except the line you are reading. Then touch your pencil to each word as you read.
- With the help of your teacher, figure out your own pattern of errors—the most serious and frequent errors you make.
- Look for only one type of error at a time. Then go back and look for a second type and, if necessary, a third.
- Use the dictionary to check spelling and to confirm that you have chosen the right word for the context.

Activity 22

Reflecting on the Writing

When you have completed your essay, answer the following six questions:

1. What was most difficult about this assignment?
2. What was easiest?
3. By completing this assignment, what have you learned about arguing?
4. What do you think are the strengths of your argument? Place a wavy line by the parts of your essay that you feel are very good.
5. What are the weaknesses, if any, of your paper? Place an X by the parts of your essay you would like help with. Write any questions you have in the margin.
6. What have you learned from this assignment about your own writing process—about preparing to write, about writing the first draft, about revising, and about editing?

Sample Student Essays

The Last Meow

On-Demand Writing Assignment

You will have 45 minutes to plan and write an essay on the topic below. Before you begin writing, read the passage carefully and plan what you will say. Your essay should be as well-organized and carefully written as you can make it.

After reading the passage, explain Bilger's argument and discuss the extent to which you agree or disagree with his analysis. Support your position by providing reasons and examples from your own experience, observations, or reading.

Americans now spend $19 billion a year on veterinary care for their pets, up from $11 billion just seven years ago. Add to that the cost of pet food and other supplies, and the number rises to $47 billion, nearly three times as much as the federal government spends on welfare grants. Poodles get root canals, cats undergo chemotherapy, rabbits are treated with radiation, and prairie dogs get oxygen therapy in intensive-care units. People spend enormous amounts to pay for special diets for their pets while cities create parks for off-leash puppy play dates. For a price, we can take our dogs for day care or psychotherapy and buy them $200 cashmere sweaters and leopard-skin beds. Clearly, our love affair with our pets has gotten out of control.

Adapted from Burkhard Bilger's
"The Last Meow,"
The New Yorker

The sample student essays that follow reflect the EPT Scoring Guide's criteria.

Healing the Broken Heart

I thought I would never get over it when our dog Hollie died. My brother Dan and I both cried as Dad buried her under the avocado tree in our back-yard, knowing that Hollie was gone from our lives forever. We made Dad bury her very deep so no other animals could come and dig her up. Dad said that Hollie was old (we knew that) and had been sick a long time (we knew that too) and had lived a good life (we knew that too) but my heart was broken anyway.

My family also had a few pets before Hollie. For instance, we had Mous-ikins, who froze to death in the garage, and Swimmy, who went belly-up one night and got flushed down the toilet the next day. Whenever a pet dies, it is a sad thing but we did get over it. However, according to Burkhard Bilger in his essay "The Last Meow" from <u>The New Yorker</u>, Americans may be going too far to help their pets live a long time. Bilger says that "our love affair with our pets has gotten out-of-control," and I for one agree. We Americans must develop a more reasonable perspective about the role of pets in our lives.

According to Bilger, Americans are spending up to "47 billion, nearly three times as much as the federal government spends on welfare grants." Citizens who have been laid off of work or need food stamps must be discour-aged by a figure like this. In fact, I have to ask myself what a homeless person thinks when Paris Hilton's dog walks by (or is carried by Paris) in a "$200 cashmere sweater." With so many urgent needs in the world, here in Califor-nia, there in New York, and around the world, maybe we should check our pri-orities when it comes to providing dentistry and psychotherapy for dogs. My cousin has three little Yorkies, for example, and those dogs get better dental care than anyone in my family does!

Bilger's essay, I think, might be similar to something that I've noted about Americans; we love to spend our money so that everyone else can see it. As many have noted before me, this is a consumer culture, and maybe that diamond-studded cat collar is no different from that Humvee or that McMan-sion. Might Americanns simply be overdoing it in a whole lot of areas, not just with their pets?

I do understand that people have a right to spend their money as they see fit and that people greatly love their pets, however, I also wonder if their spending is a way to put on a good show or even a symptom of people's isolation. For those people who live in a major city like New York, maybe they don't have sufficiently good relationships with other humans, maybe pets replace those relationships because it's hard to have a long-term relation-ship with the doorman in your building. No wonder they are willing to spend so much money. For instance, when Hollie died, Dan and I were sad, but our parents were there to comfort us.

This issue is tough, and I have to say that I don't have the answer. How-ever, I do believe that the money we invest in pets could be better invested elsewhere, such as health care and hunger relief. That's a start, isn't it?

6

Commentary

This essay illustrates the EPT Scoring Guide's criteria for a score of 6. The superior response indicates that the writer is very well-prepared to handle college-level reading and writing.

- The essay addresses the topic completely, providing an accurate summary of Bilger's argument, offering a strong thesis that responds to the prompt, and providing evidence from Bilger and from the writer's own experience.
- The writer understands the passage thoroughly enough to avoid the simplistic (and stereotypical) reaction of most students and to acknowledge the difficulty of the issue involved.
- The essay considers the opposing viewpoint, and does so successfully, without floundering in the tension of writing a refutation. ("I do understand that people have a right to spend their money as they see fit and that people greatly love their pets, however, I also wonder if their spending is a way to put on a good show.")
- The essay uses specific, detailed examples from the writer's own experience, appropriately placed and intelligently argued (Hollie the dog, Swimmy the fish).
- Paragraphs are intelligently developed and fully fleshed-out with details; the argument does not wander away from the thesis.
- The writer uses transitions to help the reader move through the essay.
- The writer demonstrates an obvious ease with language; the essay is marked by syntactic variety, fluency of style, and a sense of fluidity and skill.
- The writer understands how to introduce the article (and author) and to quote from it appropriately, integrating quoted material smoothly into the writer's own text.
- Errors are rare, easily repaired, and unobtrusive.

Sample student essay with a score of 5:

In "The Last Meow" Burkhard Bilger argues that money spent on pets could be better spent elsewhere. Bilger explains that americans now spend eight billion dollars more than they did just seven years ago. With the cat or dog food that number rises to three times the amount the government spends on welfare. Bilger believes that a pet shouldn't have to undergo the agony of a kidney transplant, but maybe their owners should do a collar transplant instead. People are spending too much money on their animals.

Pet owners in the U.S. spend three times as much money on their pets than the government does on welfare. This shows people care more for their pets than helping people get out of poverty. If we just diverted some of the money we spend on our pets every year to charity there would be a lot less people living in poverty in the U.S. today. Furthermore, when we get medical treatment for a dying pet we are just prolonging the inevitable. Is a cat's quality of life good enough under chemotherapy to justify not ending its suffering?

More and more pet owners are treating their pets like surrogate children and will do anything to see them live just another few months, while not caring what the pet thinks. A dog senses are more refined than ours, does that mean they experience more pain than us? Just forty years ago the only reason you would own a cat was to catch mice or a dog to heard sheep, now, "we can take our dogs to day care or psychotherapy and buy them a $200 cashmere sweater and a leopard-skin bed. What happened?

A friend of my family and his wife own two dogs that they consider their children. These dogs are extremely pampered and extremely sick, they both have stomach problems. Their owner gets up every morning at the crack of dawn and feeds their cooked ground beef. My two dogs have always had out of the bag dry dog food and they are the healthiest dogs I know. This shows that pampering your pets is a waste of time and money. Dog food was made the way it was because it is healthy for them, I'm sure if ground beef were healthier, dog food would come as ground beef. This shows that you don't need to spend excess money on your pet for them to be healthy.

In conclusion, people are spending too much on their pets. They need to find a healthy medium between enough and excess. They need to do what is best for their pet, not for them.

Commentary

This essay illustrates the EPT Scoring Guide's criteria for a score of 5. The clear competence of the essay indicates that this writer is quite ready to handle college-level reading and writing.

- This essay clearly addresses the extent to which veterinary care should be provided for pets. The writer summarizes the argument in the prompt that more money is spent on pets than on welfare and suggests that this treatment is wasted when it is only "prolonging the inevitable." He or she then addresses the issue raised by the prompt of people buying luxury items for their pets, observing that pets are treated "like surrogate children." He or she supports his or her position by describing a friend whose pampered dogs have health problems in contrast to his or her own dogs, which receive no-frills dog food. The author concludes that we need to strike "a healthy medium" in taking care of our pets.

- The essay shows some depth and complexity of thought by not taking an either/or position and by considering briefly the question of how society allocates resources and the psychological aspect of Americans' relationship with pets; however, the thesis is fairly simplistic and is just repeated in the conclusion.

- Paragraph organization is strong. Rather than summarizing the passage and then responding, the writer has analyzed its assertions in two separate paragraphs and has added a third paragraph to illustrate his position.

- The example contrasting two approaches to caring for pets is effective; however, the analysis throughout the essay is minimal. The writer mainly repeats the argument of the prompt.

- Careless errors occur throughout the essay; however, the style is fluent and word choice is effective.

5

Prada shoes, gold necklaces, and lavish food are just a few of the bonuses privileged pets receive. I remember it was an ordinary day at the store when A cat suddenly appeared, with similar luxuries. Many Owner's treat their pets better than children, and many believe owner's go too far for their pets. In Burkhard Bilger's, "The Last Meow", he explains how pet owners go too far for their pets. Through my own experiences, common sense has convinced me to agree with Burkhard's argument.

Everyone has seen the rich girl with a cute little purse. Inside lurks their precious little kitten with perfect clothes and jewelry. I wonder if anyone has thought of how hot the cat gets? Even though the owner means well, the animal is probably suffering and having nightmares of the purse. Like the rich girl, I was became selfish with my first pet. The first fish I have ever gotten must have gone through hell. I didn't know anything about fish, but I had decided to buy some anyway for fun. Unfortunately, all three of them died. Most owners love their pets, but don't realize how even love can kill a life. My first day at Yosemite reminds me how someones love can literally kill a pet.

The signs at Yosemite specifically say, "Don't feed squirrels". Apparently the squirels get sick if they eat the wrong nuts. Inevitably, tourists feed squirrels because they "love" them. As it turns out, I saw a squirrel on the virge of dying on the side of the road. A chocolate bar was next to it. This situation almost parallels the previous two, because "love" had made an animals condition horrendous. It is because of situations like these that forces me to agree with Bilger's argument.

Squirrels dying were enough to convince me pet owner's go too far for their pets. If pet owner's were more considerate of the one they love, many more animal's would be alive today. I still occasionally think of the pain my fish had gone through. Three lives had been taken just because I wanted three fish. Sometimes it haunts me to think if the situation was turned around. If the fishes were the owners and killed me, they would be charged for murder.

4

Commentary

This essay illustrates the EPT Scoring Guide's criteria for a score of 4. This adequate response to the topic suggests that the writer should be able to handle college-level reading and writing.

- The writer has a general understanding of Bilger's argument that the love pet owners have for their pets may not be in their best interests; however, he or she does not analyze the topic.
- The topic is treated simplistically; the writer does not address the amount of money that Americans spend on pets. Nor does he or she address current developments in veterinary medicine. A careful analysis of the prompt could have resulted in a more thoughtful essay that would not have relied simply on personal examples.
- The essay is organized adequately around the two personal examples of fish and squirrels. However, each paragraph could have benefited from a topic sentence relating it to Bilger's argument. A strength of the essay is

its specificity and the detail with which the two examples are developed; the squirrel dying next to the fatal chocolate bar is a memorable image.

- The syntax and language of the essay is adequate. Sentences are formed correctly, and some of the word choices are especially effective. An example is the sentence, "Prada shoes, gold necklaces, and lavish food are just a few of the bonuses privileged pets receive."
- While the writer makes few grammatical errors, spelling and punctuation errors occur throughout but do not confuse meaning.

Sample student essay with a score of 3:

In the article "The Last Meow," published in The New Yorker by Burkhard Bilger describes our aggressive caringness about our pets. Veterinary care has jumped eight billion dollars over past seven years Pet surplus is worth more than "three" times the gov. spends on welfare grants. Pets get over-the-top makeovers to diminish their flaws, while some people aren't even treated with such royalty. As people become more pet friedly, the more they will treat a pet like a child, which will end up skyrocketing their annual expenses. I agree with the author, because the spending in which people conduct on their pets is truly outragous!

After working for a home development company nearby Sunset Blvd., I now know what outragous spending is. I see overpriced cars, in which everyone is driving, just to be a step up on the rest of society, but I witness daily, pets being treated like the Emperor of Rome. Have you ever hear of pet pedicures? Yes, they are out there & people spend ungodly amounts of money, just so pets can have shiny nails like a diva on the red carpet! "For a price, we can take our dogs for day care or psychotherapy & buy them a $200 cashmere sweater and a leopard-skin-bed," says Bilger. The things some people do for their pets is taking it too far, but their is always someone pushing the limit!

People spend billions of dollars more than the past years on their pets. "People spend enormous amounts to pay for special diets for their pets," describes Bilger. What do you think people of the last century would say about that? I feel horrible for pets that are locked up inside houses. "Americans now spend nineteen billion dollars a year on veterinary care for their pets," explains Bilger, "Our love affair with our pets has gotten out-of-control."

Commentary

This essay illustrates the EPT Scoring Guide's criteria for a score of 3. Although the essay suggests developing competence, it is flawed in significant ways that suggest the writer needs additional practice before being able to succeed in college-level reading and writing.

- The writer understands the general idea of the prompt, the "excessive caringness about our pets." However, he or she misinterprets the amount spent on pet supplies and does not address the issue of money spent on veterinary medicine.

- The essay lacks focus. The thesis expresses outrage at excessive spending on pets. The single body paragraph lacks a topic sentence and combines the ideas of conspicuous consumption in general (with the irrelevant example of cars), noting observations about pampering pets with pedicures. The concluding paragraph also lacks unity, mentioning pet diets, neglected pets, and a reference to Bilger.
- The essay is underdeveloped and lacks both analysis of the issues raised in the prompt and adequate specific examples. Exploring the issue of pets as a form of conspicuous consumption could have been an interesting approach, but the writer does not develop the idea.
- The writer's control of syntax and language fluctuates; some sentences are competent, but others are seriously flawed by problems with structure and word choice; the following sentence illustrates both: "I agree with the author, because the spending in which people conduct on their pets is truly outragous!"
- The essay has a variety of errors in grammar, such as "have you ever hear of," "The things . . . is taking it too far," "their is always someone." Punctuation and spelling errors occur throughout.

Sample student essay with a score of 2:

Animal Love

Burkhard Bilger's argument form "The Last Meow" in The New Yorker questions the love that Americans have for their pets. In a passage adapted from "The Last Meow," it states that Americans "spend nineteen billion dollars a year on veterinary care," added to the cost of pet food and supplies. The total is about forty-seven billion dollars a year; thats more than the amount of money the government spends on welfare grants. So, are Americans really in love with their pets? Or have they become obsesed? Well, Bilger seems to disagree with the amount of money spent on pets according to "The Last Meow." I too disagree, I believe it has become an obsesion! I say this because it has personaly become an obesesion/problem. At the begining of this year I bought a fish tank, about seventy-five gallons. At firs I just bought what was necessary but then everything got out of hand and I began to purchase many things that now aren't being used at all! It all begins when you first acquire your brand new pet(s), then you go on a shopping frenzy. You don't become aware until you have spent a fortune on you new "friends." On the other hand, pets, for some people, become a new member of the family (for any given reason). That may justify their feelings, and the money being spent on them (to a certain extent that is!)

2 Commentary

This essay illustrates the EPT Scoring Guide's criteria for a score of 2; however, it is a strong 2. The serious flaws indicate that this writer will need considerable additional practice before being able to succeed in college-level reading and writing.

- The first half of the single paragraph that forms this essay is a restatement of the prompt. The summary is accurate, but the essay itself is severely underdeveloped.
- The essay ignores the issue that resources allocated to pets could be better spent on people. Instead, the essay focuses exclusively on the "shopping frenzy" that some pet owners experience, thereby slighting aspects of the task.
- The essay lacks organization. It is a single paragraph divided into summary and example.
- The essay needs more specific examples of Americans' obsessions with their pets and more explanation and analysis of the consequences of that obsession. The author attempts to balance his or her position by also justifying the love and money that people devote to pets; this new idea, however, forms the concluding sentence and is not developed.
- The essay has relatively good control of sentence structure and language.
- Punctuation and spelling errors occur throughout the essay.

Sample student essay with a score of 1:

"For a price we can take our dogs for daycare of psychotherapy" says bilger in the EPT-type excerpt form "the last meow." This is totaly ridiculous and so are the owner's who spend this much on there pets. Burkhart bilger is totaly persuasive and I agree with he's artical in the New Yorker.

Like I said, I agree with bilger, who thinks its ok to spend nineteen billion dolars a year on care for the veterinarians? Nobodies cat is going to live that long any way, like the cat in the story who's owner got her a liver transplant. Even thought she was all ready blind with ridiculous levels of other problems and going to die any way. Pets dont live as long as people do any way, may be the people are the one's who need the psychotherapy!!!

To sum up, bigler is right, this is a major problem where dogs get root cannals. I agree with the excerpt from "the last meow."

1

Commentary

This essay illustrates the EPT Scoring Guide's criteria for a score of 1. The fundamental deficiencies here indicate that this writer will need a great deal of additional practice before being able to succeed in college-level reading and writing.

- The essay is written so weakly as to be incoherent.
- The writer moves from the essay prompt back to the original article but misremembers details from the article.
- The essay fails to respond to the prompt's instructions to provide support from the writer's own experience, observations, or reading.
- As brief as it is, the essay is repetitive; for example, the writer overuses the words "ridiculous" and "anyway."
- The writer fails to understand basic grammatical issues, such as capitalization, spelling, and usage (there/their).

Into the Wild

Module 8

Into the Wild

Teacher Version

Reading Rhetorically

Prereading 2
   Getting Ready to Read............................... 2
   Introducing Key Concepts........................... 3
   Surveying the Text 4
   Making Predictions and Asking Questions.......... 5
   Introducing Key Vocabulary 5

Reading 8
   First Reading 8
   Looking Closely at Language 12
   Rereading the Text 15
   Analyzing Stylistic Choices 19
   Considering the Structure of the Text 23

Postreading 27
   Summarizing and Responding 27
   Thinking Critically 28

Connecting Reading to Writing

Writing to Learn 31
Using the Words of Others 31

Writing Rhetorically

Prewriting.. 33
   Reading the Assignment 33
   Getting Ready to Write............................. 35
   Formulating a Working Thesis 37

Writing 38
   Composing a Draft.................................. 38
   Organizing the Essay 38
   Developing the Content 40

Revising and Editing..................................... 41
   Revising the Draft................................... 41
   Editing the Draft 43
   Reflecting on the Writing.......................... 43

Evaluating and Responding 44
   Grading Holistically................................ 44
   Responding to Student Writing 45
   Using Portfolios 45

Rubrics 46

Student Version

Activity 1: Getting Ready to Read 49
Activity 2: Introducing Key Concepts 50
Activity 3: Surveying the Text 51
Activity 4: Making Predictions and Asking Questions 51
Activity 5: Introducing Key Vocabulary........... 52
Activity 6: First Reading 52
Activity 7: Looking Closely at Language........... 54
Activity 8: Rereading the Text....................... 55
Activity 9: Analyzing Stylistic Choices 57
Activity 10: Considering the Structure of the Text 59
Activity 11. Summarizing and Responding..................... 60
Activity 12: Thinking Critically 61
Activity 13: Using the Words of Others 62
Activity 14: Reading the Assignment 64
Activity 15: Writing under Pressure 64
Activity 16: Getting Ready to Write 65
Activity 17: Formulating a Working Thesis........ 66
Activity 18: Composing a Draft 66
Activity 19: Organizing the Essay 66
Activity 20: Developing the Content............... 67
Activity 21: Revising the Draft 68
Activity 22: Editing the Draft....................... 68
Activity 23: Reflecting on the Writing 69

Prewriting Strategies.................................... 70

Evaluation Form 71

Sample Student Essays

On-Demand Writing Assignment and Scored
   Student Essays 73

Into the Wild

Reading selection for this module:
Krakauer, Jon, *Into the Wild*. Doubleday: New York, 1996.

Reading Rhetorically

Prereading

Activity 1

Getting Ready to Read

Into the Wild is a nonfiction, full-length text by Jon Krakauer. Published in 1996, it is based on an article Krakauer wrote in *Outside Magazine* about Christopher McCandless, a young college graduate who went off to Alaska and died in the woods. Because Krakauer's article drew a huge amount of mail to the magazine, he decided to write a book about this interesting character. He's a young, idealistic guy who forms a life philosophy based on his experience and his reading in college. His idealism, ironically, leads to his death by starvation. He makes choices that seem foolish as we look at them now. But McCandless genuinely loved the outdoors and wanted to live in the world without all the trappings of money and his middle-class upbringing. *Into the Wild* is, in a way, a mystery story. We're unsure as to why he rejects his family, why he's so angry with them, and why he chooses to head for Alaska.

Quickwrite:

• Think about your experience hiking, backpacking, and/or existing in the wild. What are the benefits of any one of these activities?
or

• Think about some alternative plans you might have to beginning college immediately after high school. What might you do? Why would you do it, and for how long could you see yourself doing that activity?
or

• Think about an experience you have had when you were alone and made some misjudgments that could have led to disaster but didn't (it doesn't have to be in the outdoors). What miscalculations did you make and how did you avert disaster?

Introducing Key Concepts

We know about characters from their actions, their thoughts, what they say, their appearance, and what others say about them. This book explores a character, Chris McCandless, and the actions he takes. Before reading about him, complete this prereading activity. Read the scenarios below and use specific words to describe the character in the scenario. In groups, you will compare your lists, then turn in your finalized list of descriptive words to your teacher.

Mary was from the Valley. She used the word "like" in front of most of her adjectives when she spoke and talked quite a bit. On her 16th birthday she expected to get a car. It was a given. Her friends thought she would get a pink Maserati, but she was sure her parents would buy her the candy-apple red Alfa Romeo. The day of her birthday came, and as she peered out her bedroom window, she noticed a new car in the driveway, but it was yellow—surely not hers. She thought it may have been the new cleaning woman's. She did not see any other car in the long driveway. She ran down to get a closer look. It was a new canary-colored convertible Volkswagen bug. On the front driver's-side seat was a birthday note to her. She burst into tears and ran into the house.

Words to describe **Mary:** _____

Vandana had a comfortable life. Not unlike her friends, Vandana had gone to school and done well and soon was to attend the university. She had received several scholarships and her parents had planned to pay the rest for her education. Vandana hoped to help people in her future career, but hadn't quite decided in which field she wanted to do this. She decided to take a year off before attending college. Her parents refused her this. She worked hard the summer before she was to go to college, and made enough money for a one way ticket to India. She had been interested in the life of Buddha and wanted to learn more about him. Leaving a note for her parents, she headed off to India, in hopes of discovering a spiritual and centered path for herself.

Words to describe **Vandana:** _____

Emory was very popular and made friends easily. People were drawn to his honest nature and his free spirit. It was odd when two of his classmates saw drawings he had made to build bombs in his math notebook. It was even odder when he took off one day without a word to his teachers or friends. His parents notified the police. When they did a search of his room, they found two small guns and threatening notes he had written to a former girlfriend a year earlier.

Words to describe **Emory:** _____

| Activity 3 | **Surveying the Text** |

- Count the number of chapters in the text.
- Read a few chapter titles.
- Read a few of the short epigraphs that come before a chapter begins. (An epigraph is a relevant quotation at the beginning of a book, a chapter, etc.)
- Look at the length of the book.
- Look at any maps or photographs.
- Identify the author and publication date.
- What other works has Krakauer written? Do you know of them? Have you read them?

Author's Note:

Many readers skip the author's note that begins a book, but this note by Krakauer is particularly interesting and will guide your reading of his book. Read the three-page author's note before you begin to read the work. Then form groups of three or four and discuss the following questions:

- What might have McCandless's motives have been for his behavior (paragraph 3)?
- How difficult would it be to invent a new life?
- In paragraph 4, Krakauer introduces some themes of the book. Discuss these.
- In paragraph 5, Krakauer warns us that he will not be an impartial biographer. What does this mean? Are all biographers impartial? What might we expect from Krakauer?
- In the last paragraph, Krakauer introduces the complexity of Chris McCandless. Keep in mind the following four questions as you read the text:

  1. Should we admire McCandless for his courage and noble ideas?
  2. Was he a reckless idiot?
  3. Was he crazy?
  4. Was he an arrogant and stupid narcissist?

| Activity 4 | **Making Predictions and Asking Questions** |

Find an issue of *Outside Magazine* and write a one-page report describing the magazine, its audience, the kinds of articles it publishes, and so forth. Then ask yourself these questions:

- Why do you think Krakauer wrote this particular book?
- Who do you think is the intended audience for this book?

Note that the book's roots can be found in a long article about McCandless in *Outside Magazine.*

Activity 5

Introducing Key Vocabulary

You will keep a concept dictionary as you read *Into the Wild*. Each page in the dictionary you will maintain will focus on one concept. You will gather words from the reading that seem to fit under the concept. For example, you will have one page for raw weather conditions. Words that would appear on that page would be *harsh, raw, grim, austere, stringent, severe.* You will also want to include antonyms, such as *sonorous.*

A page in the dictionary might contain the following items under the key concept heading:

- synonyms (page numbers cited)
- antonyms (page numbers cited)
- meanings of the words (in your own words)
- drawings of the word written
- plus or minus marks (denoting positive or negative), depending on the word's connotation
- other words sharing the same root or derivation if the meaning is related

The vocabulary words below are contained in the author's note. Where would they go in your concept dictionary?

- Emory University (Where is it? What kind of a university is it?)
- transcendent
- Alaska taiga
- peregrinations
- impartial biographer
- dispassionate
- authorial presence
- oblique light
- emulating
- moral rigor
- shards
- fulminated
- narcissist

Reading

Activity 6

First Reading

Because you will be given directed tasks as you read *Into the Wild,* you will need to flip back and forth in this guide. For example, you might read chapters 1 and 2, practice a reading strategy, skip to the section on vocabulary for those chapters, skip on to the section that gives you strategies for rereading, and so forth.

Reading Chapters 1 and 2: The Beginning and the End

Note the epigraphs that begin each of these chapters. One is by a friend of Chris McCandless and the other is by McCandless, followed by a

Activity 6
(Continued)

quotation from *White Fang,* by Jack London. In a notebook, keep track of the literary quotations that Krakauer uses in his epigraphs.

Make note of all the maps that begin the text.

What is your assessment of Chris McCandless so far? Keep notes as you read, ask questions of the text, and write down your reactions.

Reading Chapter 3: Home

Jot down your thoughts on the following questions:

- What was Westerberg like? What kind of character did he have?
- What was McCandless like? What kind of character did he have? Would you have liked to know him?

Reading Chapters 4–7: The Journey

Study the map that begins Chapter 4 and refer to it as you follow McCandless's journey.

Jot down answers to the following as you read these chapters:

- In your notebook, list the people McCandless met along the way.
- What was it about McCandless's personality that made an impression on people?
- Note Alex's journal. Why do you think he avoided using the first person when he talked about himself? (He did not use "I.")
- What is the purpose of Chapter 4?
- Characterize Ronald Franz. What kind of a human being was he? Did he have your sympathy? Why or why not?
- What more did you learn about Alex's relationship with his father? Do you think his anger is justified? Why or why not?

Reading Chapters 8–10: The Outcasts

- What is the function of these chapters? What is their relationship to the rest of the text?
- Why did Krakauer interrupt the McCandless story with Chapters 8 and 9?
- Were you surprised that McCandless left trails so that the authorities could find out who he was?
- What's in a name? Does it matter that we have the name we were given by our parents? How do names matter? Does your name fit you? If not, what name would you choose? Why?

Reading Chapters 11–13: Family History

These three key chapters give background information that will help you piece together the mystery of McCandless. Chapter 11 fills in his personal past; Chapter 12 fills in his family past; and Chapter 13 chronicles McCandless's family's grief.

Jot down the surprises (if any) that you encountered as you read.

- What was McCandless like as a child and as a teen? What was he like as an adult? Were there indications throughout his life as to the kind of person he would become?

STUDENT VERSION

- Do you think you are essentially the same person you were as a child? How have you changed?

Reading Chapters 14 and 15: Krakauer Interjects

- Why does Krakauer talk about himself in these two chapters?
- Do you like his interjections?
- What is your reaction to his description of his own climbing experience?
- How is Krakauer's life related to McCandless's?
- John Menlove Edwards said that climbing is a "psycho-neurotic tendency." Do you think that is so? Always?
- Do you think that Edwards defines McCandless? How is he psycho-neurotic?

Reading Chapters 16–18: Into the Alaskan Wild

Go back to the author's notes and jot down your thoughts on the questions Krakauer asks at that point:

- Was McCandless crazy?
- Was he just ignorant?
- Did he have a death wish?
- Investigate further the wild sweet peas and wild potatoes McCandless ate. Were they toxic?

Reading the Epilogue: Grief

- What was your initial sense of McCandless's mental condition compared to what you think now? Have you changed your mind?
- What was your reaction to his parents as they visited the bus?

Looking Closely at Language

Because this reading is a full-length book, there are many new words to learn. You learn most of the words you know from hearing them or reading them. Here are some clues to help you learn new words as you are reading.

1. Notice what comes before and after the word for clues as well as the parts of the word itself you may already know.
2. Link your prior knowledge with what you are reading—make connections to the word or subject.
3. Make predictions about the word's meaning.
4. Use references to find more about the word.
5. Make connections to a key concept and, if relevant, place the new word and its meaning in your concept dictionary.

Activity 8

Rereading the Text

Our first reading of a book gives us the story line, the major conflicts, and a sense of what the author intends. The second (or third) reading provides richer analyses and a deeper understanding of the text. In the author's notes, Krakauer provides a guide to our reading—especially to our subsequent reading of *Into the Wild.*

As you look at the text again, go back to the four questions he asks in his "notes."

- Was McCandless admirable for his courage and noble ideas?
- Was he a reckless idiot?
- Was he crazy?
- Was he a narcissist who perished out of arrogance and stupidity—and was he undeserving of the considerable media attention he received?

Make marginal notes as you reread the text. When you respond to the chapter questions, cite the text, if necessary, where you find evidence for your judgments.

Chapters 1 and 2

Each chapter begins with a short epigraph (a quotation that is relevant to that chapter). Now that you have a better sense of Chris McCandless's story, why do you think these epigraphs are relevant to these chapters?

Chapter 3

- How would you characterize McCandless's relationships with other people: his parents, his sister, Westerberg?
- What did his friends make of his secretive life?

Chapters 4–7

As you read, see if you can find evidence of Alex's preparation for Alaska:

Read Thoreau's "On the Duty of Civil Disobedience" and consider how Alex might have incorporated Thoreau's advice into his life philosophy.

Read some of Jack London's work that we know influenced Alex: *The Call of the Wild, White Fang,* "To Build a Fire," "An Odyssey of the North," "The Wit of Porportuk."

- Why did these works appeal to Alex?

Reread the notes Alex sent to his friends at the end of Chapter 7.

- What is his tone?
- What is his attitude?

Chapter 8–10

Reread Chapter 8 and consider the charges by others against Krakauer.

- Should they be taken seriously? Why or why not?

Study the map that begins Chapter 9 and follow Ruess's journey.

- Consider how the story of the papar (Irish monks) relates to the story of the "outcasts" that Krakauer discusses (Chapter 9).

Chapters 11–13

Consider McCandless's family history.

- Does that change your view of him?
- Characterize each of McCandless's family members. What are their strengths and weaknesses?
- Was McCandless reasonable in his reaction to his parents' past? Should he have forgiven them?
- How do you think the information about his parents affected McCandless?
- Does his anger at them explain something about McCandless's choices in life?
- Chapter 12 ends with McCandless's mother talking about a dream (nightmare?) that she had. Have you ever had such a thing happen to you? Should we take dreams such as these seriously? Why or why not?

Chapters 14 and 15

- Think about and then jot down comparisons you see between McCandless's relationship with his father and Krakauer's relationship with his.
- Do you think Krakauer understands McCandless? Why or why not?
- Do you think Krakauer reads too much into McCandless's life because he feels some sort of affinity to him?
- Respond to the following quotation at the end of Chapter 15: "It is easy, when you are young, to believe that what you desire is no less than what you deserve, to assume that if you want something badly enough, it is you God-given right to have it."

Chapters 16–18

- List the various miscalculations and mistakes McCandless made.
- Toward the end of Chapter 16, Krakauer tells us that McCandless read *Walden*. Take a look at Thoreau's text and figure out what Chris found most interesting in Thoreau's discussion of food.
- If you have worked through the module called "Politics of Food," compare Thoreau with Wendell Berry.
- Have you ever fasted? Do you know anyone who has? Do some research on fasting and report to the class what you find or write a short report.

Epilogue

The traditional definition of an epilogue is that it is a concluding part of a literary work.

- Is *Into the Wild* a "literary work"? Why or why not?
- Is the last paragraph of the book an effective ending to the book? Why or why not?

Analyzing Stylistic Choices

Precise writers make linguistic choices to create certain effects. They want to have their readers react in a certain way. Go back through the text and analyze Krakauer's use of words, sentences, and paragraphs and take note as to how effective a writer he is.

Chapters 1 and 2

Words

As you revisit these chapters, pay attention to the denotative and connotative meanings of key words. Think about the effect certain words have on you.

Krakauer describes McCandless's body in a very clinical way. Reread that description:

"Virtually no subcutaneous fat remained on the body, and the muscles had withered significantly in the days or weeks prior to death. At the time of the autopsy, McCandless's remains weighed sixty-seven pounds. Starvation was posited as the most probable cause of death."

- How are you affected by this description?
- Look again at the words in the vocabulary list that relate to the harshness of Alaska. Are you interested in traveling there sometime?
- Why does understanding the new words mater?

Sentences

Consider the sentence structure Krakauer uses.

- How varied are his sentences?
- What effects do choice of sentence structure and length have on the reader?

Chapter 3

Denotation/Connotation

Consider the connotations of some of the word choices Krakauer makes. For example, he describes Westerberg as "drawn into a scheme to build and sell 'black boxes,' which illegally unscramble satellite-television transmissions, allowing people to watch encrypted cable programming without paying for it."

- Is Krakauer sympathetic to Westerberg? How do you know?
- Compare the language and tone of the two letters that McCandless writes, one to his sister and one to his parents. What did McCandless mean when he said, " . . . they will think they have bought my respect"?

Chapters 4–7

Paragraphs

A few pages from the end of Chapter 7, Krakauer gives us an analysis of Alex's relationship with his father and mother (it begins, "Westerberg's latter conjecture . . . ").

- What is the tone of this paragraph?
- Does Krakauer cite any evidence that suggests he "knows" that his analysis is accurate?
- Does it matter?

Chapters 8–10

Paragraphs

In the first part of Chapter 8, Krakauer quotes Alaskans who had opinions about McCandless and his death.

- Why does Krakauer cite these letters? How does doing so add to the text or subtract from it?
- Choose one of these letters and respond to it, explaining the degree to which you agree or disagree.

Tone

Krakauer inserts himself into the story in Chapter 8.

- Does this give him more credibility?
- Do you find this annoying? Why or why not?

Chapters 11–13

Words

A few pages into Chapter 13, Krakauer describes McCandless's sister's behavior when she was told about her brother's death.

- Why does he use the word "keening" instead of crying?
- What are the denotations and connotations of this word? What is its history?

Sentences

Reread aloud the next-to-last paragraph in Chapter 13, where Krakauer powerfully describes Billie's grief.

- Rephrase the paragraph and simplify it in your own words.
- What makes Krakauer's description powerful?

Chapters 14 and 15

Words

The technical vocabulary in these two chapters is important. Investigate the meaning of the vocabulary and provide information for the class, using slides or drawings.

Chapters 16–18

Tone

Read aloud the last paragraph in Chapter 18.

- How does Krakauer know that McCandless "was at peace, serene as a monk gone to God"? Explain.
- Does Krakauer have the right to infer from the photograph that McCandless had the serenity of a monk?
- What is an alternative interpretation of the photograph?

| Activity 9 (Continued) | **Epilogue** |
| | Read aloud the last paragraph of the book. |

- Is the language literary? Why or why not?
- What is its effect on you?

| Activity 10 | **Considering the Structure of the Text** |

Mapping out the organizational structure of the text helps us to understand the content itself.

Chapters 1 and 2

Mapping the Organizational Structure

- Contrast the two chapters. What is the purpose of each?
- How effective is the organization?
- Draw a line where you think the introduction ends in each chapter.
- Consider the last paragraph of each chapter. What is the function of each? How does each paragraph work?

Chapter 3

- What is the point of focusing on Carthage, South Dakota, and on Westerberg in this chapter?
- How does this chapter function in terms of the organization of the whole?

Chapters 4–7

Descriptive Outlining

Write brief statements describing the function of each of these chapters. What is Krakauer trying to accomplish?

- Chapter 4:
- Chapter 5:
- Chapter 6:
- Chapter 7:
- How do these chapters work as a whole?

Chapters 8–10

Briefly outline each of these chapters and explain the function of each.

- Chapter 8:
- Chapter 9:
- Chapter 10:
- How important is it for us to compare McCandless with Rosellini, Ruess, and Waterman?
- Why did Krakauer give us these details?

Chapters 11–13

These chapters give us important background knowledge.

- Would the book have been more effective if Krakauer had used a different organizing strategy?

Activity 10
(Continued)

- What if the book had ended with McCandless's death (i.e., moved chronologically)? Argue for an organizing strategy (either Krakauer's strategy or another one).

Chapters 14 and 15

In these two chapters, we learn about Krakauer.

- Are these chapters important to the story of McCandless?
- What do they add?
- Is there an argument for dumping them?
- In the first few pages of Chapter 14, Krakauer gives his thesis for the whole book. Can you find it?
- Do you agree with Krakauer's thesis? Why or why not?

Chapters 16–18

In Chapter 16, Krakauer gives a summary of the last few months of McCandless's life.

- Do you think Krakauer admires McCandless? Cite your evidence.
- In Chapter 17, Krakauer does not arrive at the bus until after about four pages. In those first pages, he gives us the details of the equipment he carries, the river flow, and the others with him. Is this necessary? What does it add? What does it detract?
- Krakauer says that McCandless had a kind of "idiosyncratic logic." Explain what Krakauer meant and the extent to which you agree or disagree with him.

Epilogue

This part of the book is very short.

- What is the effect of having an epilogue that focuses entirely on the parents' return to the bus?

Postreading

Activity 11

Summarizing and Responding

Summarizing is a very important skill used to extract the main ideas from a text and explain what the author says about them. You have reread the text and have looked at the way in which each chapter fits into a whole. In a way, you have "mapped" the text. Now you can generate a summary from that mapping.

- Try to write a one-sentence summary of Krakauer's book (plot only).
- Try to write a five-sentence paragraph of Krakauer's book, including a bit of the plot, and offer what the book might provide to a reader in addition to a good story.
- Try to write a five-sentence summary of your favorite chapter.

Activity 12

Thinking Critically

Rhetorical appeals are the accepted ways in which we persuade or argue a case. The following questions will move you through more traditional rhetorical appeals. By focusing on logic, emotion, and the appeal of the writer, you will find yourself understanding further how Krakauer persuaded us and how you can use these techniques to persuade others when you write or speak.

Questions about Logic (Logos)

- Locate two major claims and assertions Krakauer makes in this book (e.g., I do [do not] agree with Krakauer that McCandless planned his death because . . .).

- Look at Krakauer's support for his major claims and ask yourself if there is any claim that appears to be weak and unsupported. Which one(s) and why? Respond to the claims in the quotation below:

  In Chapter 16, Krakauer says that McCandless "seemed to have moved beyond his need to assert so adamantly his autonomy, his need to separate himself from his parents. Maybe he was prepared to forgive their imperfections; maybe he was even prepared to forgive some of his own. McCandless seemed ready, perhaps, to go home."

- Look at McCandless's response to several passages in Tolstoy's "Family Happiness" toward the end of Chapter 16:

  "He was right in saying that the only certain happiness in life is to live for others. . . . I have lived through much, and now I think I have found what is needed for happiness. A quiet secluded life in the country, with the possibility of being useful to people to whom it is easy to do good, and who are not accustomed to have it done to them; then work which one hopes may be of some use; then rest, nature, books, music, love for one's neighbor—such is my idea of happiness. And then, on top of all that, you for a mate, and children, perhaps—what more can the heart of a man desire."

- Does this indicate a change in McCandless?
- Was he ready to "go home"?
- Do you think McCandless would fit into modern life—a job, a home, a mate, children? Why or why not?
- Can you think of counterarguments the author does not deal with?
- Do you think the author has left something out on purpose? Why?

Questions about the Writer (Ethos)

- Does this author have an acceptable background to speak with authority on this subject?
- Is this author knowledgeable? Smart? Successful?
- What does the author's style and language tell you about him?
- Do you trust this author? Why or why not?

Activity 12
(Continued)

- Do you think this author is deceptive? Why or why not?
- Do you think this author is serious?

Questions about Emotions (Pathos)

- Does this book affect you emotionally? Which parts?
- Do you think the author is trying to manipulate your emotions? How?
- Do your emotions conflict with your logical interpretation of the arguments?
- Does the author use humor? How does that affect your acceptance of his ideas?

Quickwrites (5 minutes)

After you finish a chapter, jot down what you think the chapter's main focus is and what the author is trying to accomplish in that chapter. Here are some other questions to ask yourself:

- What are the issues the author is discussing?
- What does the author want us to believe?

Connecting Reading to Writing

Activity 13

Using the Words of Others

One of the most important features of academic writing is the use of the words and ideas from written sources to support the writer's own points. There are essentially three ways to incorporate words and ideas from sources:

- **Direct quotation.** Jon Krakauer says, "I had been granted unusual freedom and responsibility at an early age, for which I should have been grateful in the extreme, but I wasn't" (148).
- **Paraphrase.** In Chapter 11 of *Into the Wild,* Walt, McCandless's father, remembers an early hike with twelve-year-old Chris. They made it to 13,000 feet before turning back from the 14,256-foot summit in Colorado. Chris did not want to quit, and complained all the way down (109).
- **Summary.** In *Into the Wild,* Krakauer seems to be working out his own past and his relationship with his father as well as telling the sad story of Chris McCandless. Because Krakauer, too, is a man of the outdoors, he understands something about the call of the wild.

Documentation. You will also need to learn to take notes with full citation information. For print material, you will need to record, at a minimum, the author, title, city of publication, publisher, date of publication, and page number. The two most common documentation formats used are the Modern Language Association (MLA) format, which is used mainly by English Departments, and the American Psychological Association format (APA).

MLA Format

Books. Here is the Works Cited format for a typical book in the MLA style:

> Berry, Wendell. *The Unsettling of America.* San Francisco: Sierra Club Books, 1977.

Here is the bibliographic information, in the MLA format, for the text by Krakauer:

> Krakauer, Jon. *Into the Wild.* New York: Doubleday, 1996.

Web Sites. You might also want to incorporate material from Web sites. To document a Web site, you will need to give the name of the author (if known), the title of the site (or a description, such as "Homepage," if no title is available), the date of publication or update (if known), the name of the organization that sponsors the site, the date of access, and the Web address (URL) in angle brackets. Here is an example:

> *University Writing Center.* 26 June 2003. University Writing Center, California Polytechnic University, Pomona. 26 May 2004 <http://www.csupomona.edu/uwc>.

The author for the above site is unknown, so no author name is given. This entry would appear in the Works Cited section, alphabetized by "University."

In-Text Documentation. The MLA style also requires in-text documentation for every direct quotation, indirect quotation, paraphrase, or summary. If the author is given in the text, the page number should be given in parentheses at the end of the sentence containing the material.

Practice with Sources. Choose three passages from the text that relate to a particular theme in the book. Write each passage down as a correctly punctuated direct quotation. Then paraphrase the material in your own words. Finally, respond to the idea expressed in the passage by agreeing or disagreeing with it and explaining why. Later, you can use this material in an essay.

- Direct quotation:

- Paraphrase:

- Respond to the idea expressed in a passage by agreeing or disagreeing with it and explaining why:

Writing Rhetorically

Prewriting

Activity 14

Reading the Assignment

Select a prompt from the four assignment options given below. Use your concept dictionaries to brainstorm the prompt you have chosen.

Writing Assignment

1. Investigate how someone might go about smoking game (i.e., McCandless's moose) when out in the wild. Analyze where McCandless might have gone wrong.
2. Compare and contrast your initial judgment of McCandless's parents with your judgment at the end of the epilogue.
3. Consider three people who befriended McCandless: Jan Burre, Ronald Franz, and Westerberg. Explain why McCandless left such a strong impression on each of them.
4. McCandless had certain literary heroes: Henry David Thoreau, Jack London, Leo Tolstoy, and so forth. Choose three of McCandless's literary heroes and analyze what he appreciated about their work as well as what he incorporated into his own philosophy of life.

Now you need to study the topic you chose.

Here are some strategies that will help you read assignments carefully. These strategies will help you avoid answering the wrong questions or misunderstanding the prompt:

- Read the assignment carefully.
- Decide which issue you will discuss (if it is not specified in the question itself).
- What is the purpose of the assignment? Are you informing your audience or are you reporting something? Are you going to persuade your readers to a position you hold? What will you try to accomplish in your essay?

Activity 15

Writing under Pressure

In some cases, you might be asked to write a draft of an essay in a time-pressure situation. At this point, we are using a timed writing assignment as a prewriting exercise to help you discover what you think on a related topic. Following are the writing assignment and some guidelines for approaching the timed task.

On-Demand Writing Assignment

You will have 45 minutes to plan and write an essay on the topic assigned below. Before you begin writing, read the passage carefully and plan what you will say. Your essay should be as well-organized and carefully written as you can make it.

> I think that Chris McCandless was bright and ignorant at the same time. He had no common sense, and he had no business going into Alaska with his Romantic silliness. He made a lot of mistakes based on arrogance. I don't admire him at all for his courage nor his noble ideas. Really, I think he was just plain crazy.
>
> Shaun Callarman

Explain Callarman's argument and discuss the extent to which you agree or disagree with his analysis. Support your position, providing reasons and examples from your own experience, observations, or reading.

Strategies for Writing under Pressure

1. Read and then reread the prompt. Underline the important verbs that tell you what action to perform. For example, the verbs, "explain," "discuss," and "support" are in the above prompt.
2. Find the argument in the passage.
3. Quickly jot down some ideas that come to mind. Do you agree or disagree with the author's basic position? Do you think defining terms might allow you to cushion your position?
4. Figure out the topics of your body paragraphs and what the topic sentences might be.
5. Don't worry about a smooth introduction if nothing comes to mind; begin with your point, your thesis.
6. What is the evidence that you will use to prove your position? Jot down the evidence that comes to mind in bullet form or in a few words. Fit them into your paragraph outline, after your topic sentences. Having this brief outline will remind you of what you want to say, but it won't mean that you can't change your mind.

Getting Ready to Write

Review the essay topic you selected in Activity 14, and use one or more of the prewriting techniques you have learned to generate ideas on the issue. (See Prewriting Strategies on page 70.)

Activity 17

Formulating a Working Thesis

Record your responses to the questions below in preparation for writing your tentative thesis statement.

If you are going to respond to the question that asks about your initial judgment of McCandless's parents versus your judgment after you finished the book, you might first list your initial impressions when you began the book in one column and then list your final impressions in another. Then compare the two and figure out a general statement that you can begin to outline. Your tentative thesis might then be that McCandless's parents were terrible human beings and you didn't change your mind after you read the book. Remember, if you say this, you must then go to the text to prove it.

- What specific question will your essay answer? What is your response to this question? (This is your tentative thesis.)
- What support have you found for your thesis?
- What evidence have you found for this support? For example, facts, statistics, authorities,
  personal experience, anecdotes, stories, scenarios, and examples.
- How much background information do your readers need to understand your topic and thesis?
- If readers were to disagree with your thesis or the validity of your support, what would they say? How would you address their concerns? (What would you say to them?)

Now, once again, draft a possible thesis for your essay.

Writing

Activity 18

Composing a Draft

Now write a draft of your essay. This draft is usually "writer-based," the goal of which is simply to get your ideas down on paper. You should start with your brainstorming notes, informal outlines, freewriting, or whatever other materials you have and write a rough draft of your essay.

Activity 19

Organizing the Essay

The following items are traditional parts of any essay.

Introduction (usually one or two paragraphs)

You might want to think about the following items as you compose your introductory paragraph(s).

- Use a "hook" to get the reader's attention.
- Avoid truisms—obvious statements that everyone knows: "One should always be prepared to go into the wild." Why would anyone argue with that?

| Activity 19 (Continued) | • Provide background information that the audience may need to begin reading your argument.
| | • Write a thesis statement and give some indication of how the essay will be developed. You might sharpen or narrow your thesis at this point.
| | • Write a conclusion (usually only one paragraph) that summarizes the main points and explains the significance of the argument. |

Body

The number of paragraphs in an essay depends on the nature and complexity of your argument.

- Your paragraphs should relate back to your thesis and support it.
- Your paragraphs should begin with topic sentences.
- Your paragraphs should include different points of view, and you should directly address them (e.g., refute them, show them to be irrelevant, dazzle the audience with the strength of your own argument, etc.).
- Make it clear that you have considered the values, beliefs, and assumptions of your audience as well as your own and that you have perhaps found some common ground.
- Develop the content of your argument by giving evidence in the form of examples, illustrations, statistics, and so forth.
- In addition to giving evidence, you must analyze what the evidence means to your argument and how it connects to your argument.

Conclusion

The final paragraph or paragraphs demonstrates that you have made a solid argument to support your thesis, shows the significance of your argument, and answers the question, "So what?" Your ending should be honest and elegant. It might point to a solution or tie up the ends. A good conclusion does not just stop, it ends. A mere summary of all you have said in a short essay is rather insulting to the reader.

Activity 20

Developing the Content

Understanding the following characteristics of most essays is very helpful. Read and discuss these with your classmates.

- Most body paragraphs consist of a topic sentence (or an implied topic sentence) and concrete details to support that topic sentence.
- A topic sentence is usually related directly to the thesis statement.
- No set number of paragraphs make up an essay.
- The thesis is like a contract; it dictates the content of an essay.

Revising and Editing

Activity 21

Revising the Draft

You will now need to work with the organization and development of your draft to make sure your essay is as effective as possible.

Peer Group Work

Back into groups of three or four. Each student will read his or her essay aloud to the other members of the group. Then complete Part I: Revising Checklist of the Evaluation Form for each group member's essay.

Paired Work

Work in pairs to decide how you want to revise the problems group members have identified.

Individual Work

Revise the draft on the basis of the feedback you have received and the decisions you have made with your partners. Consider these additional questions below for your individual work:

- Have I responded to the assignment?
- What is my purpose for this essay?
- What should I keep? What is most effective?
- What should I add? Where do I need more details, examples, and other evidence to support my point?
- What could I omit? Did I use irrelevant details? Was I repetitive?
- What should I change? Are parts of my essay confusing or contradictory? Do I need to explain my ideas more fully?
- What should I rethink? Is my position clear? Did I provide enough analysis to convince my readers?
- How is my tone? Am I too overbearing, too firm? Do I need qualifiers?
- Have I addressed differing points of view?
- Does my conclusion show the significance of my essay?

Activity 22

Editing the Draft

You will now need to work with the grammar, punctuation, and mechanics of your draft to make sure your essay conforms to the guidelines of standard written English.

Individual Work

Edit your draft based on the information you have received from your teacher or a tutor. See Part II: Editing Checklist of the Evaluation Form for guidelines. The suggestions below will also help you edit your own work.

Editing Guidelines for Individual Work

- If possible, set your essay aside for 24 hours before rereading it to find errors.

Activity 22 (Continued)

- If possible, read your essay aloud so you can hear your errors. Focus on individual words and sentences rather than on overall meaning. Take a sheet of paper and cover everything except the line you are reading. Then touch your pencil to each word as you read.
- With the help of your teacher, figure out your own pattern of errors—the most serious and frequent errors you make.
- Look for only one type of error at a time. Then go back and look for a second type and, if necessary, a third.
- Use the dictionary to check spelling and confirm that you have chosen the right word for the context.

Activity 23

Reflecting on the Writing

When you have completed your essay, answer these six questions in writing:

1. What was most difficult about this assignment?
2. What was easiest?
3. What did you learn about arguing by completing this assignment?
4. What do you think are the strengths of your argument? Place a wavy line by the parts of your essay you feel are very good.
5. What are the weaknesses, if any, of your paper? Place an X by the parts of your essay you would like help with. Write any questions you have in the margin.
6. What did you learn from this assignment about your own writing process—about preparing to write, about writing the first draft, about revising, and about editing?

Prewriting Strategies

Brainstorming: Based on free association, this is the act of making a list of related words and phrases.

Clustering/webbing: This is the process of "mapping" any ideas that come to mind on a specific topic. This strategy involves writing a key word or phrase in the center of the page, drawing a circle around it, then writing down and circling any related ideas that come to mind and drawing lines to the words that prompted the new words.

Discussing: This is the act of talking with another person about your subject matter and grappling aggressively with your ideas in the process.

Freewriting: Based on free association, this is the strategy of writing for a brief period of time about anything that comes to your mind.

Outlining: This is the listing of the main ideas and details related to your subject in the order in which you will probably address them.

Questioning: This is the process of asking questions that will generate new ideas and topics. This process is often based on the five Ws and one H: Who? What? Why? Where? When? and How?

Scanning: This is the process of scanning and spot reading to generate specific ideas and form opinions.

Evaluation Form

Based on the CSU English Placement Test (EPT)

Part I: Revising Checklist—Mark the appropriate categories.

	Superior	Strong	Adequate	Marginal	Weak	Very Weak	Comments
Response to the topic	Addresses the topic clearly and responds effectively to all aspects of the task.	Addresses the topic clearly but may respond to some aspects of the task more effectively than others.	Addresses the topic but may slight some aspects of the task.	Distorts or neglects aspects of the task.	Indicates confusion about the topic or neglects important aspects of the task.	Suggests an inability to comprehend the question or to respond meaningfully to the topic.	
Understanding and use of the assigned reading	Demonstrates a thorough critical understanding of the assigned reading in developing an insightful response.	Demonstrates a sound critical understanding of the assigned reading in developing a well-reasoned response.	Demonstrates a generally accurate understanding of the assigned reading in developing a sensible response.	Demonstrates some understanding of the assigned reading but may misconstrue parts of it or make limited use of it in developing a weak response.	Demonstrates very poor understanding of the main points of the assigned reading. Does not use the reading appropriately in developing a response or may not use the reading at all.	Demonstrates little or no ability to understand the assigned reading or to use it in developing a response.	
Quality and clarity of thought	Explores the issues thoughtfully and in depth.	Shows some depth and complexity of thought.	May treat the topic simplistically or repetitively.	Lacks focus or demonstrates confused or simplistic thinking.	Lacks focus and coherence and often fails to communicate ideas.	Is unfocused, illogical, or incoherent.	
Organization, development, and support	Is coherently organized and developed, with ideas supported by apt reasons and well-chosen examples.	Is well-organized and developed, with ideas supported by appropriate reasons and examples.	Is adequately organized and developed, generally supporting ideas with reasons and examples.	Is poorly organized and developed, presenting generalizations without adequate support or details without generalizations.	Has very weak organization and development, providing simplistic generalizations without support.	Is disorganized and undeveloped, providing little or no relevant support.	
Syntax and command of language	Has an effective, fluent style marked by syntactic variety and a clear command of language.	Displays some syntactic variety and facility in the use of language.	Demonstrates adequate use of syntax and language.	Has limited control of syntax and vocabulary.	Has inadequate control of syntax and vocabulary.	Lacks basic control of syntax and vocabulary.	
Grammar, usage, and mechanics (See list on next page for details)	Is generally free from errors in grammar, usage, and mechanics.	May have a few errors in grammar, usage, and mechanics.	May have some errors but generally demonstrates control of grammar, usage, and mechanics.	Has an accumulation of errors in grammar, usage, and mechanics that sometimes interfere with meaning.	Is marred by numerous errors in grammar, usage, and mechanics that frequently interfere with meaning.	Has serious and persistent errors in grammar, usage, and mechanics that severely interfere with meaning.	

Part II: Editing Checklist

Problem	Questions	Comments
Sentence boundaries	Are there fragments, comma splices, or fused sentences?	
Word choice	Are word choices appropriate in meaning, connotation, and tone?	
Subject-verb agreement	Do main verbs agree with the subject in person and number?	
Verb tense	Is the tense appropriate to the topic and style? Does the writing shift back and forth from present to past inappropriately?	
Word forms	Are any parts of verb phrases missing or incorrect? Are verb endings correct? Do other words have correct endings and forms?	
Noun plurals	Do regular plurals end in "s"? Are irregular plurals correct? Are there problems with count and non-count nouns?	
Articles	Are articles (*a, an,* and *the*) used correctly? (*Note:* Proper nouns generally don't have an article, with exceptions like "the United States" and "the Soviet Union," which are more like descriptions than names.)	
Spelling	Are words spelled correctly?	
Punctuation	Are periods, commas, and question marks used correctly? Are quotations punctuated correctly? Are capital letters used appropriately?	
Pronoun reference	Does every pronoun have a clear referent? (*Note:* Pronouns without referents or with multiple possible referents create a vague, confusing style.)	
Other problems	Are there other important problems?	

Into the Wild

On-Demand Writing Assignment

You will have 45 minutes to plan and write an essay on the topic assigned below. Before you begin writing, read the passage carefully and plan what you will say. Your essay should be as well-organized and carefully written as you can make it.

> I think that Chris McCandless was bright and ignorant at the same time. He had no common sense, and he had no business going into Alaska with his Romantic silliness. He made a lot of mistakes based on arrogance. I don't admire him at all for his courage nor his noble ideas. Really, I think he was just plain crazy.
>
> Shaun Callarman

Explain Callarman's argument and discuss the extent to which you agree or disagree with his analysis. Support your position, providing reasons and examples from your own experience, observations, or reading.

The sample student essays that follow reflect the EPT Scoring Guide's criteria for their respective scores.

Sample student essay with a score of 6:

Life: Not an Episode of "Grizzly Man"

Yes, living alone in the wilderness like Thoreau and London sounds exciting, especially if you fake a big part of your adventures or if you can pack up and go home when you get too hungry. Chris McCandless doesn't have these options, but Shaun Callarman believes that Chris is full of "Romantic silliness," and by this statement I think he means that Chris goes into Alaska seeing only the good parts of the wilderness experience. Like Callarman, I believe that Chris has a head full of "Romantic ideas" and that he lacks "common sense" although I would not call him "plain crazy."

When Chris decides to map some part of the Alaskan wilderness that's already been mapped, he is definately showing "Romantic silliness." Callarman is right about this; it doesn't seem very courageous to me to waste time doing work that someone else has already done! I would want to spend my time doing something more useful. The wilderness in Alaska is being ruined with oil pipes and spills. Chris could of taken some of his "noble ideas" and used them to better the area. By spending his energy for a good cause, he would not have seemed so arrogant and ignorant, as Callarman states. It might have felt romantic to him to draw his own map, but he was staying in a bus, so it seems pretty clear to me that somebody else had been there already.

Also, Callarman says that Chris "made a lot of mistakes base on arrogance." I agree; Chris does make a lot of errors. For instance, he brings the wrong kind of gun, the wrong kind of clothes, too many books and not enough food. What is the purpose of his reading and his library research in Alaska if he's not going to be willing to take advise? So yes, Chris's mistakes maybe coming from an arrogant brain.

On the other hand, Chris did show some "noble ideas," in contrast to what Callarman states. He tries to keep other people from getting involved with him by not letting them get too close. In addition, he really did kill a moose and not a carabou, as some people made fun of him for doing. Finally, he lives a lot longer out in the wilderness than most people could!

Chris is definately a bizarre mix of qualities, as Callarman argues, but now that I think about it Chris is not really as bad as he looks. Being young (high school and college) is suppose to be the time of our lives for Romantic silliness. Aren't we suppose to be idealists during this time? I would not want my plans and dreams to be called "arrogant" or "ignorant," because they're important to me and I want them to come true. All in all, with his bad family life and sketchy role models like London, Chris did not do too bad. I do feel sorry for his parents and sister and friends, but his life is a lesson for all of us to be careful but to follow our dreams as much as we can.

6

Commentary

This essay illustrates the EPT Scoring Guide's criteria for a score of 6. The superior response indicates that the writer is very well prepared to handle college-level reading and writing.

- The writer offers a concise and accurate explanation of the Callarman quotation and effectively addresses all aspects of the prompt.
- The essay demonstrates a thorough, critical understanding of the passage, invoking Callarman both directly and indirectly, integrating quoted material smoothly, and using the Callarman quotation to guide the writer's response.
- The essay consistently and insightfully negotiates between Callarman and the writer, even to the extent that the writing itself functions to modify the writer's position as the essay progresses.

- With a few exceptions (see the second paragraph, for example) the writer uses transitions appropriately and effectively, both within and between paragraphs, to guide the reader through the essay.
- The writer offers specific, accurate, and relevant examples (the map, the insufficient clothing and food, too many books) to support the essay's points.
- The writer concludes the essay by referring to London again at the end and bringing the essay full circle.
- The essay's paragraphs get shorter toward the end as the writer perhaps begins to rush, yet they are generally unified, focused, and well developed.
- The writer has learned to write in the literary present tense, with only some wavering of verb tense (especially toward the end of the essay).
- The essay is generally free of errors in grammar, usage, and mechanics, except for minor slips (such as "definately" and "maybe" versus "may be") that do not interfere with meaning.

Sample student essay with a score of 5:

Into the Wild Essay

Shaun Callarman does not have much good to say about Chris McCandless. He believes that he, "was bright and ignorant at the same time," meaning that Chris was smart; just smart enough to get himself killed in Alaska. Callarman also believes that Chris, "was just plain crazy," which I think is taking his argument too far. I agree that Chris was foolish and made mistakes based on arrogance, but I don't think he was crazy. Chris was just a bad combination of brains and stupidity.

A college graduate should know enough to prepare for the wilderness. Who goes to a cold and distant place like Alaska with a backpack full of books and a bag of rice? He had enough money to buy the stuff he needed, why not spend some of his savings on a $5 map? His $24,000 would of bought him a lot of equiptment and food. People kept trying to buy him equiptment but each time he denied them. Is this being independent, or is it being stupid? I vote for stupid.

Of course, Chris had a lot of problems that contributed to his decision to go into the wild. For example, his parent's marriage was awful, and his dad's double life must of been a huge shock. It seems that Chris did a lot of this to spite his parents, like lieing about his identity, ignoring letters from home, and badmouthing his Mom and Dad. There are lots of people like him that feel they have something to prove, so they go out and do something wreckless. Chris didn't prove anything by going to Alaska, besides that he was an idiot. If he hated his Mom and Dad so much, maybe he should of just gone somewhere and started a new life, maybe he should of taken his savings and bought a cabin in Alaska and been alone as long as he wanted instead of starving to death in a bus for innocent hikers to find later.

If Chris is crazy, then so are a lot of other people, but he seems more foolish and even mean. For example, what about the way he treated the old man Ron? Ron really cared about Chris and he had already lost his entire family, but Chris tried to tell him how to live. After all that, he hit the road again and left Ron behind. This example shows that he only thinks of himself throughout the book, which just makes him like many others, dumb.

Callarman lets him off too easy when he calls him "crazy". If Chris was crazy, he could of been helped, but I believe he was mostly foolish and angry. He went to Alaska in a temper tantrum to show everyone, but he paid the biggest price in his death.

5

Commentary

This essay illustrates the EPT Scoring Guide's criteria for a score of 5. The clear competence of the essay indicates that this writer is ready to handle college-level reading and writing.

- The writer provides a reasonable and clear thesis that responds to the prompt.
- The writer opens with an accurate summary of the Callarman passage, choosing to focus on the idea of whether or not Chris is crazy to develop a well-reasoned response.
- The writer shows some depth and complexity by attempting to consider opposing viewpoints in the third paragraph, although the logic wavers somewhat.
- The essay tends to overuse generalities (largely that McClandless was "dumb" or "stupid"), and some sections are underdeveloped. However, the writer does provide some specific examples (McClandless' refusal to obtain equipment, his abandonment of Ron) to back up the essay's assertions.
- The writer's personal voice is lively and consistent throughout the essay.
- Transitions are occasionally awkward or missing, but the writer generally succeeds at using transitional language to guide the reader through the essay.
- The writer is able to reiterate the essay's position in the final paragraph without being overly repetitive.
- The essay suffers from some errors of expression, such as spelling ("equiptment," "lieing"), usage ("would of," "should of"), mechanics ("his parent's marriage"), semicolon use, pronoun confusion (the use of "he" in the first paragraph), and style (overuse of "a lot"), but these concerns do not generally detract from meaning. On the strong side, this writer has learned to use a comma before coordinating conjunctions that connect independent clauses.

Sample student essay with a score of 4:

Chris McCandless was a risk-taker. He was a young man that wanted to be independent and live his life without anyone telling him what to do. Some people, such as Shaun Callarman, describe him as ignorant and arrogant. Others admire him for his ability to maintain his independence and live under his own control while maintaining his morals.

Shaun Callarman says he was "bright and ignorant at the same time." He had to have been bright. He read amazingly difficult books and followed their teachings as well. However, aside from calling him bright, Callarman also calls McCandless ignorant. Was McCandless ignorant for following the teachings of these books? No. He was just curious and obviously determined.

Callarman states, "He had no common sense, and he had no business going into Alaska with his Romantic silliness." I agree with what Callarman says in this passage. Common sense would have told him to bring the necessary supplies with him before attempting to go into the wilderness of Alaska. I have been taught from a very young age to not go anywhere without my necessities, whether it be money, food, or water. I also have been taught to not go anywhere alone, especially if it is a huge risk. Chris McCandless ignored, or showed absolutely no common sense.

I do not however think he was crazy. I do admire him for his ability to retain his morals and live his dreams out to their fullest potential. He took risks and in doing so was able to achieve what he most wanted. Independence.

4

Commentary

This essay illustrates the EPT Scoring Guide's criteria for a score of 4. This adequate response to the topic suggests that the writer should be able to handle college-level reading and writing.

- The writer demonstrates a generally accurate understanding of the passage, although the writer struggles to understand some of Callarman's points (i.e., how McCandless could be "bright and ignorant at the same time").
- The essay delivers its thesis in the first sentence; this thesis is succinct and responds to the prompt.
- The first paragraph is brief but adequately set up, with the question, Was Chris independent or arrogant? posed through logic and transitional language (e.g., "Some people . . ." in the third sentence, followed by "Others . . ." in the fourth).
- The writer quotes Callarman both directly and indirectly and attempts to incorporate quoted material smoothly with tag phrases, introductions, and other markers, although the quotations after the first paragraph are repetitive in terms of structure and logic.
- The essay as a whole is somewhat simplistic and repetitive. The final paragraph, for example, basically restates the thesis paragraph (first paragraph), and the body paragraphs tend to repeat their points as well.
- The logic in the essay is uneven, particularly in the third paragraph, where the essay seems to argue against its own thesis when the writer attempts to acknowledge Callarman's "Romantic silliness" comment.
- The writer offers transitional language, although somewhat simplistic, within paragraphs ("however" is a prominent transition) but does not provide similar guidance for the reader between paragraphs.
- The examples from the text (reading hard books, leaving without necessities) are relevant but are general and underdeveloped.

- The essay generally demonstrates control of grammar, usage, and mechanics; in fact, this essay is a prime example of a paper that handles the English language quite competently but that struggles in other areas, such as organization and development.

Sample student essay with a score of 3:

Chris McCandless was an adventourous man. Chris McCandless wanted to live his life to the fullest. Chris had changed his name to Alex the Supertramp. Alex wanted to live on the 'road'. So he packed up all his belongings and burned his money. He unfortunaly died hundred and twelve days after he 'hit the road'. Many people think of him as inspiration. While Others belived he was Crazy.

I personally believe that Alex was an inspiration. An man by the name of Shawn Callarman had written a passage about Alex. Callarman writes "I think that Chris McCandless was bright and ignorant." Callarman goes on to say that "I think he was just plain Crazy." I disagree I believe Alex had a purpose in life.

I believe that Alex had taken some time to think about his journey. Alex had a purpose in his life. I believe he wanted to show people how they can have goals and still acheive them. Even though he died on his Journey he left a 'track' behind. Alex had many pals along the way and he made a difference in their lives.

Chris McCandless was an inspiration to me. Many people have their opinions of Chris. Chris's story could lean towards both ways. I believe that Chris MaCandless made a difference in a least one person's life on his Journey. Chris McCandless was Crazy but he was not just a regular man. Chris McCandless was an inspiration to us all.

3

Commentary

This essay illustrates the EPT Scoring Guide's criteria for a score of 3; however, it is a weak 3. Although the essay suggests developing competence, it is flawed in significant ways that suggest the writer needs additional practice before being able to succeed in college-level reading and writing.

- The writer makes limited use of the passage, focusing solely on the idea of McClandless's potential craziness.
- The essay quotes Callarman by implication and without attribution in the final sentence of the first paragraph. It mentions Callarman directly only in the second paragraph by providing two quotations, the first of which is simply dropped in, then left unaddressed.
- The writer struggles to choose between two potential thesis statements ("I personally believe that Alex was an inspiration" and "I believe Alex had a purpose in life"), both contained in the second paragraph and reiterated but not supported elsewhere in the essay.
- The body paragraphs are a series of assertions that lack effective transitions.

- The writer has limited control of syntax and vocabulary, using a highly repetitive sentence structure throughout the essay, with constructions of similar length, grammatical structure, and simplicity (e.g., the first three sentences of the first paragraph open with the word "Chris").
- The writer offers examples from the text that are accurate (McClandless's changing his name, burning the money, making friends along the way), but these examples are often unspecific and are generally underdeveloped and undersupported.
- The writer struggles to maintain a consistent and appropriate verb tense throughout the essay.
- The essay suffers from an accumulation of errors, especially errors in spelling ("unfortunaly" and "belived"), punctuation (missing commas and misused single quotation marks), and erratic capitalization ("Others" and "Crazy").

Sample student essay with a score of 2:

Into the Wild Essay

Callarman's argument is that he thinks that McCandless was bright but a the same time ignorant. He tries to said that he was dum by saying he was ignorant. Also he try to said that McCandless didn't have no business to go to Alaska. That he made Mistakes based on Pride. That he was just going there because he was Crazy he didn't know why he was going there.

I also agree with him because why he wanted to go to Alaska. Specialy when he didn't have the right things to live in a place like that. He also was acting crazy that he didn't even know what he was doing. He even die because he didn't have no Food to eat. And he was acting weird with his parents and his brother and sister.

Callamar made a good opinion about McCandless by saying that because he didn't act like a normal person. I think he didn't act like an adult. Specialy when he sent the Letters to his Family and his Friends. I think he did Miss his people he didn't wanted to assume he Miss them. He should to stay with his parents and never went to Alaska.

McCandless did it wrong because he went to Alaska just because of his Romantic illness. That was not a good reason to just go away and live to another place were he would not live in good conditions. I think he could Forget about his Romantic illness and he could even get another person. But he even kill his own life which is not a good thing.

2 Commentary

This essay illustrates the EPT Scoring Guide's criteria for a score of 2. The serious flaws here indicate that this writer will need considerable additional practice before being able to succeed in college-level reading and writing. This piece provides a good picture of a student whose ESL writing features are profoundly obscuring what would otherwise be a stronger (that is, a 3-level) essay.

- The writer demonstrates a basic understanding of the passage but focuses on repeating Callarman's points without establishing a clear direction for the essay.
- The writer fails to respond to the prompt with a focused thesis. The first sentence of the second paragraph, "I also agree with him . . . " alludes to a potential thesis that has not yet been offered and that never appears explicitly in the essay.
- Although the writer attempts four body paragraphs, the paragraphs are not logically linked to one another.
- The writer attempts in the second paragraph to use transitional language to guide the reader through that particular paragraph, but the essay's organization both within and between paragraphs is left largely to the reader to discern.
- The essay offers generalizations ("he was acting weird with his parents") without providing specific support.
- The writer lacks basic control of syntax (see the first sentence of the third paragraph) and vocabulary ("Romantic illness"), and some statements make no logical or syntactic sense at all (see the third sentence of the second paragraph and the first sentence of the third paragraph).
- The writer has serious and persistent errors in grammar, usage, and mechanics (spelling, erratic capitalization) that severely interfere with meaning. The problems many English learners have with idioms ("because why he wanted to go"), verb tenses ("he tries to said"), and verb forms ("he even kill his own life") are pervasive and profoundly obscure meaning.

Sample student essay with a score of 1:

I sure do agree with Callarmans argument. She is absolutely right McCandless was bright and ignorant. And He defenatly had no common sense, he was one of those weird people you won't expect. For my observation she gots the same thoughts as I do. I shure think defining terms allows me to cushion my position. The evidence that I will use is that He was writing all his up and down pants.

In my point of view I think that McCnadless was avery unique guy. He even did things that no one would do. An example, work everywhere he stop use his name and give out half of his idenity. That is my point and answere for this paragraph.

1

Commentary

This essay illustrates the EPT Scoring Guide's criteria for a score of 1. The fundamental deficiencies of this essay clearly indicate that the writer needs much additional practice in order to be ready to succeed at college-level reading and writing.

- The writer agrees with the Callarman quotation without demonstrating any understanding of the passage.
- The writer fails to use the Callarman passage to develop a meaningful response to the prompt.
- The essay, at approximately 120 words, is seriously underdeveloped; statements of agreement with Callarman make up a considerable portion of the text.
- The digression about "cushion[ing] my position" contributes nothing to the minimal text the writer provides. The writer's reflective statements about purpose are similarly wasted.
- The only evidence provided by the writer is McCandless's evasive attitude toward self-identification at work, but even this example is so poorly expressed as to be nearly incoherent.
- The writer lacks basic control of syntax and vocabulary.
- The writer has serious and persistent errors in mechanics that severely interfere with meaning. Spelling and verb form errors are pervasive.

pg. 82 blank

Appendix

APPENDIX E: EVALUATION FORM
Based on the CSU English Placement Test (EPT)

Part I: Revising Checklist—Circle the appropriate categories.

	Superior	Strong	Adequate	Marginal	Weak	Very Weak	Comments
Response to the topic	Addresses the topic clearly and responds effectively to all aspects of the task.	Addresses the topic clearly, but may respond to some aspects of the task more effectively than others.	Addresses the topic, but may slight some aspects of the task.	Distorts or neglects aspects of the task.	Indicates confusion about the topic or neglects important aspects of the task.	Suggests an inability to comprehend the question or to respond meaningfully to the topic.	
Understanding and use of the assigned reading	Demonstrates a thorough critical understanding of the assigned reading in developing an insightful response.	Demonstrates a sound critical understanding of the assigned reading in developing a well-reasoned response.	Demonstrates a generally accurate understanding of the assigned reading in developing a sensible response.	Demonstrates some understanding of the assigned reading, but may misconstrue parts of it or make limited use of it in developing a weak response.	Demonstrates very poor understanding of the main points of the assigned reading, does not use the reading appropriately in developing a response, or may not use the reading at all.	Demonstrates little or no ability to understand the assigned reading or to use it in developing a response.	
Quality and clarity of thought	Explores the issues thoughtfully and in depth.	Shows some depth and complexity of thought.	May treat the topic simplistically or repetitively.	Lacks focus or demonstrates confused or simplistic thinking.	Lacks focus and coherence, and often fails to communicate its ideas.	Is unfocused, illogical, or incoherent.	
Organization, development, and support	Is coherently organized and developed, with ideas supported by apt reasons and well-chosen examples.	Is well organized and developed, with ideas supported by appropriate reasons and examples.	Is adequately organized and developed, generally supporting ideas with reasons and examples.	Is poorly organized and developed, presenting generalizations without adequate support, or details without generalizations.	Has very weak organization and development, providing simplistic generalizations without support.	Is disorganized and undeveloped, providing little or no relevant support.	
Syntax and command of language	Has an effective, fluent style marked by syntactic variety and a clear command of language.	Displays some syntactic variety and facility in the use of language.	Demonstrates adequate use of syntax and language.	Has limited control of syntax and vocabulary.	Has inadequate control of syntax and vocabulary.	Lacks basic control of syntax and vocabulary.	
Grammar, usage, and mechanics (See list on back for details)	Is generally free from errors in grammar, usage, and mechanics.	May have a few errors in grammar, usage, and mechanics.	May have some errors, but generally demonstrates control of grammar, usage, and mechanics.	Has an accumulation of errors in grammar, usage, and mechanics that sometimes interfere with meaning.	Is marred by numerous errors in grammar, usage, and mechanics that frequently interfere with meaning.	Has serious and persistent errors in grammar, usage, and mechanics that severely interfere with meaning.	

Part II: Editing Checklist

Problem	Questions	Comments
Sentence Boundaries	Are there fragments, comma splices, or fused sentences?	
Word Choice	Are word choices appropriate in meaning, connotation, and tone?	
Verb/Subject Agreement	Do main verbs agree with the subject in person and number?	
Verb Tense	Is the tense appropriate to the topic and style? Does the writing shift back and forth from present to past inappropriately?	
Word Forms	Are any parts of verb phrases missing or incorrect? Are verb endings correct? Do other words have correct endings and forms?	
Noun Plurals	Do regular plurals end in "s"? Are irregular plurals correct? Are there problems with count and non-count nouns?	
Articles	Are articles (a, an, and the) used correctly? (Note: Proper nouns generally don't have an article, with exceptions like "the United States" and "the Soviet Union," which are more like descriptions than names.)	
Prepositions	Are prepositions used the way a native-speaker of English would naturally use them? (Note: It is difficult to learn prepositions through definitions or rules. They have to be acquired through seeing or hearing them in use.)	
Spelling	Are words spelled correctly?	
Punctuation	Are periods, commas, and question marks used correctly? Are quotations punctuated correctly? Are capital letters used appropriately?	
Pronoun Reference	Does every pronoun have a clear referent? (Note: Pronouns without referents, or with multiple possible referents, create a vague, confusing style.	
Other Problems	Are there other important problems not on the list?	

Expository Reading and Writing Course

APPENDIX F: HOLISTIC SCORING GUIDE
(Based on the English Placement Test criteria)

The categories of each score are consistent with the following legend:
- a. = response to the topic
- b. = understanding and use of the passage
- c. = quality and clarity of thought
- d. = organization, development, and support
- e. = syntax and command of language
- f. = grammar, usage, and mechanics

Score of 6: Superior
A 6 essay is superior writing, but may have minor flaws.
A typical essay at this level is characterized by these features:
- a. addresses the topic clearly and responds effectively to all aspects of the task
- b. demonstrates a thorough critical understanding of the passage in developing an insightful response
- c. explores the issues thoughtfully and in depth
- d. is coherently organized and developed, with ideas supported by apt reasons and well-chosen examples
- e. has an effective, fluent style marked by syntactic variety and a clear command of language
- f. is generally free from errors in grammar, usage, and mechanics

Score of 5: Strong
A 5 essay demonstrates clear competence in writing. It may have some errors, but they are not serious enough to distract or confuse the reader.
A typical essay at this level is characterized by these features:
- a. addresses the topic clearly, but may respond to some aspects of the task more effectively than others
- b. demonstrates a sound critical understanding of the passage in developing a well-reasoned response
- c. shows some depth and complexity of thought
- d. is well organized and developed, with ideas supported by appropriate reasons and examples
- e. displays some syntactic variety and facility in the use of language
- f. may have a few errors in grammar, usage, and mechanics

Score of 4: Adequate
A 4 essay demonstrates adequate writing. It may have some errors that distract the reader, but they do not significantly obscure meaning.
A typical essay at this level is characterized by these features:
- a. addresses the topic, but may slight some aspects of the task
- b. demonstrates a generally accurate understanding of the passage in developing a sensible response
- c. may treat the topic simplistically or repetitively
- d. is adequately organized and developed, generally supporting ideas with reasons and examples
- e. demonstrates adequate use of syntax and language
- f. may have some errors, but generally demonstrates control of grammar, usage, and mechanics

Score of 3: Marginal

A **3** essay demonstrates developing competence, but is flawed in some significant way(s).

A typical essay at this level reveals *one or more* of the following weaknesses

a. distorts or neglects aspects of the task
b. demonstrates some understanding of the passage, but may misconstrue parts of it or make limited use of it in developing a weak response
c. lacks focus, or demonstrates confused or simplistic thinking
d. is poorly organized and developed, presenting generalizations without adequate and appropriate support or presenting details without generalizations
e. has limited control of syntax and vocabulary
f. has an accumulation of errors in grammar, usage, and mechanics that sometimes interfere with meaning

Score of 2: Very Weak

A **2** essay is seriously flawed.

A typical essay at this level reveals *one or more* of the following weaknesses:

a. indicates confusion about the topic or neglects important aspects of the task
b. demonstrates very poor understanding of the main points of the passage, does not use the passage appropriately in developing a response, or may not use the passage at all
c. lacks focus and coherence, and often fails to communicate its ideas
d. has very weak organization and development, providing simplistic generalizations without support
e. has inadequate control of syntax and vocabulary
f. is marred by numerous errors in grammar, usage, and mechanics that frequently interfere with meaning

Score of 1: Incompetent

A **1** essay demonstrates fundamental deficiencies in writing skills.

A typical essay at this level reveals *one or more* of the following weaknesses:

a. suggests an inability to comprehend the question or to respond meaningfully to the topic
b. demonstrates little or no ability to understand the passage or to use it in developing a response
c. is unfocused, illogical, or incoherent
d. is disorganized and undeveloped, providing little or no relevant support
e. lacks basic control of syntax and vocabulary
f. has serious and persistent errors in grammar, usage, and mechanics that severely interfere with meaning

Readers should not penalize ESL writers excessively for slight shifts in idiom, problems with articles, confusion over prepositions, and *occasional* misuse of verb tense and verb forms, so long as such features do not obscure meaning.

THE CALIFORNIA STATE UNIVERSITY
Focus on English

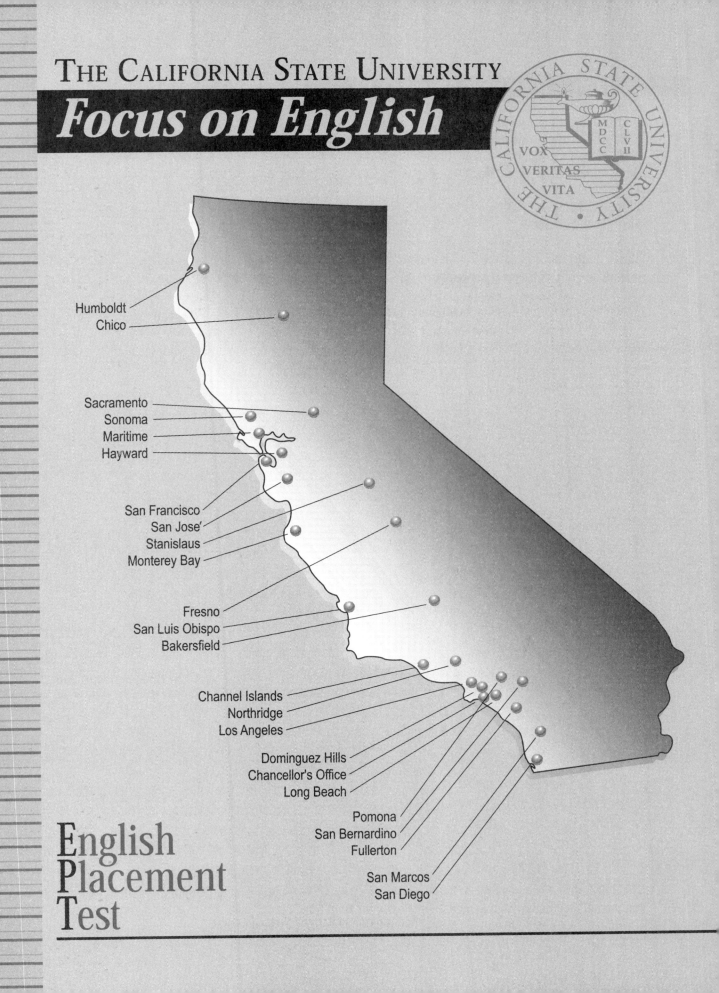

Humboldt
Chico

Sacramento
Sonoma
Maritime
Hayward

San Francisco
San Jose'
Stanislaus
Monterey Bay

Fresno
San Luis Obispo
Bakersfield

Channel Islands
Northridge
Los Angeles

Dominguez Hills
Chancellor's Office
Long Beach

Pomona
San Bernardino
Fullerton

San Marcos
San Diego

English
Placement
Test

For further information, please contact:

Testing Coordinator
California State University
Office of the Chancellor
401 Golden Shore, Sixth Floor
Long Beach, CA 90802
Phone: (562) 951-4731
Fax: (562) 951-4867

While additional copies of Focus on English may not be available, the publication may be downloaded from the web for duplication. The URL for Focus on English is:

http:www.calstate.edu/ar/ept.pdf

The 2002 edition was prepared by Mary Kay Harrington, CSU Faculty English Consultant; and members of the English Placement Test Development Committee.

Table of Contents

Nature and purpose of Basic Skills Assessment at CSU 2

EPT exemptions 2

The specifics of the English Placement Test (sample test items) 3- 10

EPT score reporting 11

How a teacher can help prepare students for the EPT 12

EPT online & the Diagnostic Writing Service 12

Sample essay topic, EPT Scoring Guide, sample essays & commentaries 13- 20

More sample essay topics 21

Appendix A: Alignment of EPT and Content Standards 22

Appendix B: Interpretation of individual score reports 23- 25

Basic Skills Assessment at the California State University

New students enrolling at the 23 campuses of the California State University (CSU) will be joining more than 390,000 students and 22,000 faculty members in an academic program requiring college-level skills in reading, writing, and computation. Students need to master these basic skills not only to accomplish college-level work but also to meet society's need for a literate, educated citizenry. Because some students admitted to the California State University lack the necessary proficiency in reading, writing, or math to succeed in college, the CSU has designed tests in English and mathematics to identify those students who could benefit from additional pre-baccalaureate study in these areas. Students who cannot demonstrate the level of proficiency in English and mathematics expected by faculty of entering freshmen will be placed in special courses or programs during their first term of enrollment to increase that proficiency and mastery.

This brochure provides information about the English Placement Test (EPT). Another brochure, called *Focus on Mathematics,* available from the CSU Chancellor's Office or online at **http://www.calstate.edu/ar/fom.pdf,** provides information about the math assessment test, the Entry Level Mathematics Test (ELM).

Nature and Purpose of the English Placement Test

The English Placement Test, developed cooperatively by the CSU faculty and Educational Testing Service (ETS), is designed to assess the level of analytical reading and writing skills of students entering the California State University. The test has no effect on admissions decisions.

The CSU English Placement Test must be completed by all non-exempt undergraduates prior to enrollment in the CSU. Entering students have one year to complete required developmental courses.

EPT Exemptions

Students are exempt if they can present proof of one of the following:

* a score of 550 or above on the verbal section of the college Board SAT I Reasoning Test taken April 1995 or after*

* a score of 24 or above on the enhanced ACT English Test taken October 1989 or later

* a score of 680 or above on the College Board SAT II Writing Test taken May 1998 or after*

* a score of 3, 4, or 5 on either the Language and Composition or Literature and Composition examination of the College Board Advanced Placement Program

* completion and transfer to the CSU of a college course that satisfies the requirement in English Composition, provided such course was completed with a grade of C or better

*Students who took the SAT I Reasoning Test before April 1995 or the SAT II Writing Test before May 1998 should contact the campus Admissions and Records Office or Test Office for appropriate exemption scores.

- Note 1: The College Board SAT and Achievement Tests were replaced by SAT I and SAT II, respectively, beginning March 1994. Since April 1, 1995, the SAT I and SAT II exams have been scored on a new scale.

- Note 2: Beginning in May 1998, SAT II: Writing Test scores increased about 10-20 points. The adjustment was made to make Writing Test scores more comparable to scores on other SAT II subject tests. Although scores are higher, their relative rank compared to scores for tests taken before May 1998 remains the same.

About 27 percent of regularly admitted students are exempt from taking the EPT based on the above criteria. All other admitted students must take the test.

EPT Placement and Design

Once admitted, students required to take the test must take it at their earliest opportunity. The test must be taken before enrollment in any classes at the CSU. At present, there is no charge to the student to take the EPT. Students may take the EPT only once. It may not be repeated. Students will receive necessary information and registration materials by mail, usually from the admission office of the campus they plan to attend. The test is offered on all CSU campuses three times a year. Special demand test dates may be scheduled on some campuses during other months of the year, but students should not rely on such dates being scheduled. Students who do not demonstrate requisite competence on the English Placement Test are required to enroll in appropriate remedial or developmental programs/activities during the first term of enrollment and each subsequent term until such time as they demonstrate competence. Such courses or programs do not convey credit toward the baccalaureate degree. Students *must* complete and pass all remedial work during the first year of enrollment in the CSU.

Once a year, summaries of EPT aggregate student performance by high school are provided on the World Wide Web (**http://www.asd.calstate.edu/performance**) for those students who took the test and enrolled in the CSU for the fall term. Companion data for the ELM are also provided in the same place.

Since its beginning in 1977, the EPT has been given to more than 575,000 students. Approximately 40,000 first-time freshmen are tested each year. Of those students enrolling in the fall of 2001, approximately 54 percent demonstrated proficiency in reading and/or writing skills needed to succeed in college-level work. The remaining 46 percent were placed in appropriate remedial courses. The California legislature provides funding for EPT testing and also provides funding for campuses to establish developmental reading/writing programs.

Because the EPT is designed to place students in appropriate classes that will help them succeed in college-level work, it is not as difficult as some other English tests. The EPT is a placement test, not an admission or achievement test. Ongoing evaluation of the EPT shows that it measures students' abilities accurately, and that it is useful to students and their advisers in selecting appropriate courses and programs.

The EPT consists of a 45-minute essay and two 30-minute multiple-choice subsections: Reading Skills and Composing Skills.

The essay portion of the test requires students to read a brief passage in which an argument is made or a position is taken.

Students are asked to analyze and explain the ideas presented in the passage, and then take a position that they support by providing reasons and examples from their own experience, observations, or reading.

Because the writing assignment requires students to analyze the passage's ideas in developing their own position on the subject, it integrates the critical reading and expository writing skills that are both essential to college-level work.

For example, students might first read a passage on how tobacco companies have agreed to settle a lawsuit and give millions of dollars to the state. Students are then asked to explain how they would choose to spend the money (for example, on health care for smokers or on an anti-smoking campaign) and to support that position.

Students who cannot read effectively will not be able to write an appropriate essay; they may misunderstand or misread the passage.

Students are now able to have their writing skills diagnosed through the CSU/EPT Diagnostic Writing Service. For more information, please turn to page 12.

Please turn to page 13 for the EPT scoring guide, an EPT topic with sample essays, and commentaries.

Assessment of Reading Skills—30 minutes

Part A: Reading Comprehension

Students will be asked to analyze the ideas presented in brief passages (typically 100-150 words).

Students should be able to read closely in order to

- identify important ideas
- understand direct statements
- draw inferences and conclusions
- detect underlying assumptions
- recognize word meanings in context
- respond to tone and connotation

Students may be asked to select the answer choice that best summarizes a passage, explains the purpose of a passage, focuses on a specific detail, explains a word in context, compares/contrasts two aspects of a passage, explains the implications or suggestions made in a passage, identifies causal relationships, etc.

Directions: Each passage below is followed by questions based on its content. Answer all questions following a passage on the basis of what is stated or implied in that passage.

Questions 1-3 are based on the following passage.

The search for a workable panacea is not new. Spanish explorers sought the Fountain of Youth. Millions of Americans used to seek health and contentment in a patent medicine called Hadacol. During the past two decades, however, more and more people have been turning to various branches of psychology for magic solutions, hoping that psychology can take care of any problem, cure the common cold, or solve the riddle of existence.

1. From the passage one can infer that the word "panacea" means

    (A) utopia
    (B) religion
    (C) cure-all
    (D) life style

2. According to the passage, what do the Fountain of Youth and Hadacol have in common?

    (A) Neither really existed.
    (B) Both brought their discoverers great fortunes.
    (C) Both helped to end the search for magic solutions.
    (D) Both were thought to have great power.

3. What does the passage call into question?

    (A) People's expectations of psychology
    (B) People's use of the lessons of history.
    (C) The relationship between psychology and medicine.
    (D) The legitimacy of the field of psychology.

Answer key: 1.C 2.D 3.A

Part B: Vocabulary in Context

Students should be able to understand the meaning of a particular word or phrase in the context of a sentence.

Students will be asked to consider grammatically similar words and choose the one that fits most logically into each sentence in place of a nonsense word, "gliff."

Directions: For each of the following questions, choose the best word or phrase to substitute for the underlined portion containing gliff, a nonsense word.

4. Though Mr. Rivera is a gliff man and could live anywhere he chooses, he still lives in the small house in which he was born.

    (A) an unhappy
    (B) a wealthy
    (C) an ambitious
    (D) a strong

5. The water looked fine for swimming but, in fact, the currents in the river were gliff.

    (A) contaminated
    (B) soothing
    (C) treacherous
    (D) unnoticeable

6. Many of the problems we have with our natural resources could be gliffed if all of us did what we could to conserve those resources.

    (A) avoided
    (B) defined
    (C) publicized
    (D) understated

Answer key: 4.B 5.C 6.A

Part C: Logical Relationships

Students should be able to read two related statements and understand the relationship between them to see how

- they may contrast
- they may illustrate cause and effect
- they may contradict each other
- they may show cause and effect
- one may explain the other
- one may provide a more specific example to illustrate the other
- one may explain consequence
- one may clarify something implied by the other

Students will be asked to find exactly what the second sentence does in relation to the first and/or how the two sentences relate to each other.

Directions: In each of the following questions, two underlined sentences have an implied logical relationship. Read each pair of sentences and the question that follows, and then choose the answer that identifies the relationship.

7. The Historic Dominguez Rancho Adobe, usually visited by those in search of tranquility, became a political battleground.

   The cities of Compton and Carson each claimed ownership of the estate.

   In relation to the first sentence, what does the second sentence do?
   - (A) It makes a comparison.
   - (B) It provides factual support.
   - (C) It describes an inevitable result.
   - (D) It introduces a different point of view.

8. Harry typically vacations in Tahoe.
   Two years ago, Harry spent his vacation in Madrid.

   In relation to the first sentence, what does the second sentence do?
   - (A) It clarifies an assumption.
   - (B) It notes an exception.
   - (C) It adds emphasis.
   - (D) It draws a conclusion.

9. Teresa has missed the last three practices of the dance step.
   She cannot perform the maneuver.

   In relation to the first sentence, what does the second sentence do?
   - (A) It states a consequence.
   - (B) It suggests a cause.
   - (C) It offers proof.
   - (D) It limits a preceding idea.

Answer key: 7.B   8.B   9.A

6 · English Placement Test

Part A: Construction Shift

Students should be able to rephrase a sentence by beginning with a different construction and producing a new sentence that does not change the meaning of the original. These questions ask students to

- find a more economical or effective way of phrasing a sentence
- find a more logical way of presenting a fact or idea
- provide appropriate emphasis
- achieve sentence variety

Students may be asked to spin out a sentence using an introductory phrase beginning with a gerund or an adverb, etc; or to avoid slow starts, they may be asked to consider a more appropriate noun phrase, or to consider a phrase that includes parenthetical information.

Directions: The following questions require you to rewrite sentences in your head. Each question tells you exactly how to begin your new sentence. Your new sentence should have the same meaning and contain the same information as the original sentence.

10. The student senate debated the issue for two hours and finally voted down the resolution.

    Rewrite, beginning with <u>Having debated the issue for two hours,</u> . . .

    The next word or words will be

    (A) the issue
    (B) it
    (C) the student senate
    (D) a vote

11. The tree fell away from the house when it was struck by lightning.

    Rewrite, beginning with <u>Struck by lightning,</u> . . .

    The next words will be

    (A) It was when
    (B) it fell when
    (C) the tree fell
    (D) and falling

12. Watson maintains that the worsening economic plight of the poor is reflected in the rising unemployment rate.

    Rewrite, beginning with <u>Watson maintains that the rising unemployment rate</u> . . .

    The next words will be

    (A) reflects the
    (B) and the plight of
    (C) is what worsens
    (D) is worse

Answer key: 10.C 11.C 12.A

Part B: Sentence Correction

Students should be able to find the best way of correcting a sentence in order to resolve problems of

- clarity
- sentence predication
- parallel structure
- subordination and coordination
- modification
- sentence boundaries

Students are asked to select the best way to phrase an underlined portion of a sentence. This question type tests the students' understanding of syntax, usage, and idiom rather than specific knowledge of grammatical rules.

Directions: In each of the following questions, select the best version of the underlined part of the sentence. Choice (A) is the same as the underlined portion of the original sentence. If you think the original sentence is best, choose answer (A).

13. Ancient Greeks ate with their fingers, wiped them on pieces of bread, and <u>tossed them</u> to the dogs lying under the table.

   (A) tossed them
   (B) tossing them
   (C) tossed the bread
   (D) they tossed

14. Many doctors are now convinced <u>of a fiber-rich diet reducing the risk of colon and heart diseases.</u>

   (A) of a fiber-rich diet reducing the risk of colon and heart diseases.
   (B) of the risk of colon and heart diseases caused by a fiber-rich diet.
   (C) that the reduction of the risk of colon and heart diseases caused by a fiber-rich diet.
   (D) that a fiber-rich diet reduces the risk of colon and heart diseases.

15. Painters studied in Florence for the opportunity both to live in Italy <u>and for seeing the art treasures.</u>

   (A) and for seeing the art treasures.
   (B) and to see the art treasures.
   (C) as well as the art treasures to be seen.
   (D) as well as seeing the art treasures.

Answer key: 13.C 14.D 15.B

Part C: Missing Sentence

Students should be able to select an appropriate sentence that most logically

- begins a paragraph

- fits in the middle of a paragraph

- ends a paragraph

Students may be asked to find the most appropriate topic sentence (one that most successfully generalizes what follows); to find the most appropriate middle sentence (adds specifics or carries the paragraph forward in some way); or to find the sentence that logically concludes the paragraph.

Directions: Each of the following questions presents a passage with a missing sentence indicated by a series of dashes. Read each passage and the four sentences that follow it. Then choose the sentence that can best be inserted in place of the long dash (———).

16. - - - . Scholars hold differing opinions. Some trace the roots of Mexicans in the United States all the way back to the earliest migrations across the Bering Strait. Others start with Aztec society to demonstrate the historical continuities between contemporary Chicanos and their Aztec ancestors. A third group identifies the "Spanish Borderlands" period (1540-1820) as the earliest phase of Chicano history.

   (A) When does Chicano history begin?
   (B) There is continuing interest in Chicano history.
   (C) Chicano history has fascinated scholars for many years.
   (D) Few are concerned about setting a precise date for the origin of Chicano history.

17. Many Easterners think that all California college students surf every day, wear sunglasses indoors as well as outdoors (even on rainy days), and mingle with the superstars daily. - - - . A recent survey of students on a large, urban CSU campus revealed that only 2 percent had surfed, and although 40 percent did wear sunglasses, 15 percent of those were doing so on their doctors' recommendations. As for the superstars, barely 10 percent had met a Hollywood actor.

   (A) The possibilities of such stereotypes are endless.
   (B) Stereotypes, however, are often misleading.
   (C) Probably both Easterners and Californians would like to fit all of those stereotypes.
   (D) Most California students do live up to those enviable stereotypes.

18. Accompanying the article on humor were pictures of a leering Groucho Marx and a grinning Sigmund Freud, one a brilliant humorist and the other a brilliant analyst whose own study of humor has been largely ignored. The unlikely pair attracted readers to the article, whose author made two major points. Serious studies of humor are rarely undertaken. - - - .

   (A) Comics would urge us to laugh, not soberly to study laughter.
   (B) What a joke a Freudian analysis of the Marx Brothers would have been.
   (C) The studies that are made are rarely taken seriously.
   (D) Freud was interested in all aspects of the human mind.

Answer key: 16.A 17.B 18.C

Part D: Supporting Sentence

Students should be able to read a sentence and decide which of four subsequent sentences will give appropriate logical support by

- adding relevant detail
- stating a probable cause or explanation
- providing a supporting example

Students will be asked to discriminate among sentences that might all seem related to the original sentence, but only one of which provides logical support for the original.

Directions: Each of the following questions presents a topic and four sentences. Select the sentence that provides the best support for the topic presented.

19. Chester Nakamura is an expert on Samurai swords.

(A) The swords are richly decorated, and their engravings have meaning to the collector.
(B) Collectors around the world seek his advice about swords they plan to buy.
(C) Each Samurai took pride in his sword.
(D) Many people in the United States have extensive collections of such swords.

20. It is not true that intellectual development stops after age 17.

(A) Older people commonly complain of poor memory.
(B) Many older people can learn at least as well as young people can.
(C) People in their 60s, 70s, and 80s have been studied.
(D) Sometimes depression can cause what is assumed to be mental deterioration.

Answer key: 19.B 20.B

Test Score Reporting

Essay Score

Each essay is read independently and scored holistically by two faculty members who use a scoring guide that defines levels of performance on the essay. The two readers' scores are totaled to give the student's reported Essay score, which falls between scores of 2 (low) and 12 (high). (See page 13 for a scoring guide and sample essays.) Students must write on the assigned topic, demonstrate an understanding of the reading passage, and support their generalizations with specific reasons and examples. Such matters as clarity of thought, fluency, careful organization, development of ideas, and the use of clear and precise language all have an important influence upon the score given by each reader.

A different topic is used each time the test is given; all students taking the test at the same time write on the same topic. Topics are designed to allow all students to display their best writing. The topics selected are of general interest and should be accessible to all groups of EPT candidates. All essay topics are pretested at CSU campuses and are given final approval by the English Placement Test Development Committee.

A total Essay score of 6 or below strongly suggests that a student is not prepared for college-level writing. An Essay score of 7 is borderline. A low Essay score, combined with a Composing Skills score below 146, suggests that a student should have at least a one-semester (or quarter equivalent) pre-college writing course. A low Essay score combined with a Reading Skills score that is below 141 suggests that a student needs a year of developmental work before taking freshman English.

Reading Skills Score

This portion of the test presupposes a close relationship between reading and writing, and assumes that some students may best profit from special instruction in writing when their skill in reading is also strengthened. All of the reading material is accessible to and appropriate for college-bound students. Much of the content is of special interest to Californians and reflects the diversity of cultural experience in the state.

A Reading Skills score below 151 suggests that the student is not prepared for the demands of college-level reading and would benefit from a developmental course that includes analytical reading and writing.

The lower the Reading Skills score the more likely it is that the student should take two semesters of developmental reading and writing before enrolling in freshman English.

Composing Skills Score

Lack of skill in sentence construction and paragraph development seriously undermines a student's ability to succeed at college-level work. This section of the test presents sentence- and paragraph-level problems that commonly occur in the writing of students not yet prepared for college-level work.

This portion of the test requires that the student understands the conventions of academic writing. The EPT is designed to assess how well students can handle the kind of language that they will encounter as college students. For this reason, the conventions of standard written English that serve as criteria for the judgment of performance on this section of the test are those found in most college reading and required of students on papers and examinations.

How a Teacher Can Help Prepare Students for the EPT

To enhance students' performance on the **Reading Skills** portion of the test, course work should encourage and require analytical reading of nonfiction as well as fiction. Many students are placed in remedial coursework because of low Reading Skills scores.

While there are many ways to teach the skills measured by the **Composing Skills** section of the test, one of the most effective methods is to ask for revision of student written work.

Preparation for the essay portion of the test requires that students practice essay writing by reading arguments and responding to another's position. Evidence suggests that the greatest improvement in student writing comes about when careful and sensitive evaluation of essays is followed by revision in the light of that criticism. Some teachers have experimented successfully with student scoring of essays in accordance with scoring guides as a way of helping students to evaluate their own and others' work. The scoring guides and sample papers in this book may be of use to classroom teachers who wish to help students understand how their EPT essays will be scored. Teachers may also want to encourage their students to use the Diagnostic Writing Service (DWS) described below. DWS provides practice both in the multiple-choice part of the EPT and in the essay.

The English Placement Test Online

Students can have their reading, composing, and essay writing skills diagnosed through the CSU/EPT Diagnostic Writing Service (DWS). To reach this service, go online at **http://www.essayeval.org**.

For the reading and composing skills sections of the test, students may take a free, self-correcting practice exam which is made up from questions on previous EPT statewide exams. Once they submit the test, the tests are scored instantly and students are provided with explanations of any questions they miss.

For the essay portion of the test, students can have their writing diagnosed by CSU faculty for a small fee. Through this service, individual students, or entire classes of students, can submit essays responding to EPT essay questions and have their essays read by CSU faculty. Within 10 business days, students should receive their essays back online, with diagnostic comments. DSW is also available as a paper-and-pencil service. Students using the paper service must wait about three to four weeks to receive their reader feedback.

The DWS Comments

The comprehensive DWS comments provide specific diagnostic help to the students and to their teachers. Specifically, the DWS comments explain to students

- how fully and effectively they have responded to the essay task
- how well they have developed and supported their argument
- how well-chosen their examples are
- how sound their reasoning is
- how well they have organized and connected their ideas
- how well they have maintained control of sentences, of diction, and of syntax
- how well they have shown command of standard written English

CSU English Placement Test Scoring Guide

At each of the six score points for on-topic papers, descriptors of writing performance are lettered so that:

a. = response to the topic
b. = understanding and use of the passage
c. = quality and clarity of thought
d. = organization, development, and support
e. = syntax and command of language
f. = grammar, usage, and mechanics

Score of 6: Superior

A **6** essay is superior writing, but may have minor flaws.

A typical essay in this category:

a. addresses the topic clearly and responds effectively to all aspects of the task
b. demonstrates a thorough critical understanding of the passage in developing an insightful response
c. explores the issues thoughtfully and in depth
d. is coherently organized and developed, with ideas supported by apt reasons and well-chosen examples
e. has an effective, fluent style marked by syntactic variety and a clear command of language
f. is generally free from errors in grammar, usage, and mechanics

Score of 5: Strong

A **5** essay demonstrates clear competence in writing. It may have some errors, but they are not serious enough to distract or confuse the reader.

A typical essay in this category:

a. addresses the topic clearly, but may respond to some aspects of the task more effectively than others
b. demonstrates a sound critical understanding of the passage in developing a well-reasoned response
c. shows some depth and complexity of thought
d. is well organized and developed, with ideas supported by appropriate reasons and examples
e. displays some syntactic variety and facility in the use of language
f. may have a few errors in grammar, usage, and mechanics

Score of 4: Adequate

A **4** essay demonstrates adequate writing. It may have some errors that distract the reader, but they do not significantly obscure meaning.

A typical essay in this category:

a. addresses the topic, but may slight some aspects of the task
b. demonstrates a generally accurate understanding of the passage in developing a sensible response
c. may treat the topic simplistically or repetitively
d. is adequately organized and developed, generally supporting ideas with reasons and examples
e. demonstrates adequate use of syntax and language
f. may have some errors, but generally demonstrates control of grammar, usage, and mechanics

Score of 3: Marginal

A **3** essay demonstrates developing competence, but is flawed in some significant way(s).

A typical essay in this category reveals *one or more* of the following weaknesses:

a. distorts or neglects aspects of the task
b. demonstrates some understanding of the passage, but may misconstrue parts of it or make limited use of it in developing a weak response
c. lacks focus, or demonstrates confused or simplistic thinking
d. is poorly organized and developed, presenting generalizations without adequate and appropriate support or presenting details without generalizations
e. has limited control of syntax and vocabulary
f. has an accumulation of errors in grammar, usage, and mechanics that sometimes interfere with meaning

Score of 2: Very Weak

A **2** essay is seriously flawed.

A typical essay in this category reveals *one or more* of the following weaknesses:

a. indicates confusion about the topic or neglects important aspects of the task
b. demonstrates very poor understanding of the main points of the passage, does not use the passage appropriately in developing a response, or may not use the passage at all
c. lacks focus and coherence, and often fails to communicate its ideas
d. has very weak organization and development, providing simplistic generalizations without support
e. has inadequate control of syntax and vocabulary
f. is marred by numerous errors in grammar, usage, and mechanics that frequently interfere with meaning

Score of 1: Incompetent

A **1** essay demonstrates fundamental deficiencies in writing skills.

A typical essay in this category reveals *one or more* of the following weaknesses:

a. suggests an inability to comprehend the question or to respond meaningfully to the topic
b. demonstrates little or no ability to understand the passage or to use it in developing a response
c. is unfocused, illogical, or incoherent
d. is disorganized and undeveloped, providing little or no relevant support
e. lacks basic control of syntax and vocabulary
f. has serious and persistent errors in grammar, usage, and mechanics that severely interfere with meaning

Readers should not penalize ESL writers excessively for slight shifts in idiom, problems with articles, confusion over prepositions, and *occasional* misuse of verb tense and verb forms, so long as such features do not obscure meaning.

The sample topic below is similar to the topic students will be assigned in the Essay Section of the test. Other topics are listed on page 21. The topic is followed by six sample student essays at every score point (1-6). Each essay is followed by comments on the scoring.

Directions: You will have 45 minutes to plan and write an essay on the topic assigned below. Before you begin writing, read the passage carefully and plan what you will say. Your essay should be as well organized and as carefully written as you can make it.

"For many Americans, the concept of success is a source of confusion. As a people, we Americans greatly prize success. We are taught to celebrate and admire the one who gets the highest grades, the one voted most attractive or most likely to succeed. But while we often rejoice in the success of people far removed from ourselves- people who work in another profession, live in another community, or are endowed with a talent that we do not especially want for ourselves- we tend to regard the success of people close at hand, within our own small group, as a threat."

Explain Mead's argument and discuss the extent to which you agree or disagree with her analysis. Support your position, providing reasons and examples from your own experience, observations, or reading.

Student Essays and Commentaries (Scores 6-1)

Score of 6: Superior

"He Who Dies with the Most Toys Wins"

In her book *The Egalitarian Error,* Margaret Mead states, "We are taught to celebrate and admire the one who gets the highest grades, the one voted most attractive or most likely to succeed. But while we often rejoice in the success of people far removed from ourselves- we tend to regard the success of people close at hand, within our small group, as a threat." It is this occurrence, she says, that makes the "concept of success" complicated, seemingly contra- dictory, and thus often "a source of confusion." But is this the case in society? Success is seen as a source of happiness and security, a source of pride. It is thought of as a good thing to be successful. But success can become threatening when your classmates, neighbors, or coworkers are more successful than you. Then your pride is hurt. Though success itself is a good and positive thing, it creates competition that can foster negative interactions.

In this society, we are taught to look to those people who are far out of reach as role models. We should strive to achieve the degree of success that they have. We should strive for greatness displayed in public so that, in the future, young children will be striving in turn to be like us. We look to famous actors, computer moguls, and people famous for being rich as the distant but maybe attainable goal that we should always work toward. We celebrate them when they turn out another great movie or another great computer program. They illustrate Mead's statement that we celebrate the success of those far away from us. But more locally, things could not be more different.

How many times have you been compared to your older brother or sister? Or, how many times have your younger siblings been compared to you? Instead of giving them a brotherly pat on the back for doing a good job in school, or getting a raise at work, this comparison created hostile feelings. Also, teachers that grade on the curve constantly put students in direct competition with each other. So instead of congratulating your successful classmates on a job well done, you feel threatened because you are being graded against them. On the other hand, if some stranger in a different school gets an A, why should you care? Sports teams are also a prime example of how success of others nearby can become threatening. Schools have forgotten the meaning of good sportsmanship and have replaced it with a desire to win, fueled by the fear that an opponent's success might mean that they are better than you. Even youngsters can't play a friendly soccer game without such worries looming over them. But this time it is the parents who are threatened by the success of the other side. This idea of others' success being threatening is still present when you leave the soccer field and go back to your neighborhood. Cars, yard appearance, and satellite dishes represent success and create posturing among neighbors, as I have seen in my very own neighborhood.

I believe that success of people nearby is seen as threatening because it directly affects us. It affects how we feel about ourselves and what others think of us. This is not so much true when the image of success is far removed. Becoming an actor is seen as an impossible achievement, so we look up to anyone that has accomplished it. But it is not quite so close to home, and so it is more personally meaningful to be beaten out by people that you know in some activity that you take pride in. This is where success creates competitiveness and envy.

Commentary for 6 essay

This essay illustrates the scoring guide's criteria for a score of 6. The superior response indicates that the writer is very well prepared to handle college-level reading and writing.

- The writer demonstrates a thorough critical understanding of the passage in developing an insightful response.

- The summary of Mead is complete and accurate, although paraphrase may have been preferable to lengthy quotation in the first sentence.

- The writer explores the issues of success and jealousy thoughtfully and in depth, and has a clear sense of how to write and where to place the thesis: "Though success itself is a good and positive thing, it creates competition that can foster negative interactions."

- The writer understands how to organize a coherent, well-focused, logical response.

- The use of examples for support is more than a list; this writer also explains the relevance of these cogent examples (e.g. paragraph 3).

- Although there are occasional grammatical errors ("Instead of giving them a brotherly pat on the back . . . this comparison created hostile feelings"), they do not obscure intended meaning and represent the exception in a fluent response.

• •

Score of 5: Strong

I think that what Mead is trying to say is that we admire other people's success and accomplishments only when we don't know those people and if they succeed at things that don't matter to us. For example, you might admire someone who can play classical piano because you don't play and aren't really into classical music all that much. But if you want to be a great blues guitarist and the guy next door is a lot better than you, then it's different. When it's someone close to you that you associate with all the time, instead of admiration you feel threatened.

I think the first part of what Mead is saying is true. We admire people we don't know all the time. When we watch television we see actors, musicians, and models that we admire because of their success. We read in the newspapers and magazines about people who are really smart or are super athletes who made it to the Olympics. We all look up to other people we don't know and admire their success.

I think the second part of her statement is somewhat true but at the same time somewhat false. I do think that sometimes people allow themselves to get so caught up with being the best that they start to compete with their close friends or family members. If someone in that group happens to do something better you might feel a bit threatened.

For example, both me and my sister started to take horseback riding lessons. At first she was a lot better than I was. But once I got the hang of things I gradually became better than her. She was so upset that I had succeeded in horseback riding that she quit. She didn't see that she too had succeeded. I was just a better rider. She didn't see that even if I had succeeded more, the activity could still be fun for her.

I do believe, though, that people close to you can succeed and you won't feel threatened by it. I have played the violin for eight years and my best friend has only played for three. We both did orchestra through school and both of us had no private lessons. I happened to be better and had more success than she in playing. But she never held it against me. She never once felt threatened by my talent for playing the violin. She might have felt different if we were actually in the same family and had been playing the same amount of time, but probably not. She isn't a competitive person.

I do know that some people, instead of admiring a person's success, take it as a threat. But I do think for the most part people, especially true friends, will be happy and admire all your success and accomplishments if you do the same for them. Mead is only part right. Whether you feel threatened by a successful person or not doesn't just depend on how far away the person is, but on how you choose to view things.

Commentary for 5 paper: Strong

This essay illustrates the scoring guide's criteria for a score of 5. The clear competence indicates that this writer is quite ready to handle college-level reading and writing.

- The essay clearly addresses the topic and demonstrates a sound critical understanding of the passage in developing a well-reasoned response. The first paragraph accurately para-phrases Mead's main point and nicely uses the examples of the piano and guitar players to illustrate it. Unlike less able writers, this writer does not repeat the word "confusion" but summarizes the ideas in her own words "instead of admiration you feel threatened."

- The essay shows some depth and complexity of thought.

- Paragraph organization could be stronger. The writer needs to pay attention to writing more focused topic sentences.

- The reasons and examples are appropriate although the examples sometimes serve to support a point already adequately made (paragraph 2).

- Despite a few distracting errors (e.g., "both me and my sister"), a preference for colloquial diction, and a tendency to begin sentences with "I think" (see openings of first three paragraphs), the writer displays good control of language and some variety in sentence structure.

• •

Score of 4: Adequate

"Source of Confusion"

The concept of success is often misunderstood by many people. When someone succeeds we are suppose to praise and admire them for what they have done or accomplished. Instead, we see them as a threat and try to overpower or outdo them. For this reason, I agree with Margaret Mead that "the concept of success is a source of confusion."

Imagine you are competing with other classmates to be the top student in your class. If someone succeeds over you, you will most likely be jealous of their success, rather than praise them. Part of being human is that we desire what we don't have. We desire someone else's accomplishments and want to succeed over others. Our will to succeed overpowers our will to admire, therefore, we want what other people have.

Society competes in almost everything. We compete in jobs, school, social status, and power. For example, if another country invented a bomb that the United States did not have, we would do everything in our power to invent one. In order to stay in control, we must not let others succeed. For them to succeed would mean that we fail.

No one wants to fail and no one likes to fail. This forces us to have the desire to succeed. We become threatened when we fail and another accomplishes what we cannot. Confusion sets in because many emotions are replaced with fear. We may admire someone for succeeding but we also feel anger and jealousy towards them. With these mixed emotions we cannot praise nor admire those that have succeeded over us. With this, success becomes "a source of confusion."

Commentary for 4 paper—Adequate
This essay illustrates the scoring guide's criteria for a score of 4. The adequate response to the topic suggests that this writer should be able to handle college-level reading and writing.

- The writer demonstrates a generally accurate understanding of the passage and develops a sensible response. The writer seems to discover what she thinks in the final paragraph. A quick plan would probably have resulted in a more focused reply.

- The topic is treated somewhat simplistically, for the writer never recognizes or explores Mead's point that our feelings about success vary with its proximity to us.

- The essay is organized and developed adequately, but it would have benefited from more and better examples: The example of students competing for grades is taken from Mead and extended no further, and that of the bomb is not especially relevant to Mead's point about the American attitude toward success.

- In place of more specific support, the writer provides generalities that are sometimes vague or imprecisely phrased: For example, "Society competes in almost everything."

- The essay does have some errors (pronoun/antecedent agreement- "someone . . . they" and "suppose to" for "supposed to") but generally demonstrates control of mechanics, usage, and sentence structure.

• •

Score of 3: Marginal

I think Mead means in calling the concept of success "a source of confusion" because we are not all the same and we do not think the same. Some of us might think that having alot of money is being successful, while others think that being successful is being happy with you and your family. I think Mead is also saying that we consider people to be successful when they are not close to us or when they are from another community because we do not want people that are within our group to be considered successful.

In a way I think we are selfish because we want to be the only one who is successful in a group. Because we want to get all the admirations and attentions. If anybody else that is in our group is considered successful we take it as a threat because we want to be the only ones that are successful.

I agree with Mead because not always are the right people recognized for being successful. In my family I am the "successful one" because I'm going to go to college and work and get good grades. On the other hand there's my brother who does not get good grades and by parents do not consider him to be successful. In my opinion he is successful because he is trying to do better and he is not giving up eventhough he does not get the good grades.

People often define success as different things. I define success as a person who does not give up eventhough they are not doing well. They are successful because they are still trying and not giving up. It is true what Mead said about considering a threat people that are successful that are near you because you do not want to feel inferior to people that are said to be successful.

Commentary for 3 paper—Marginal

This essay illustrates the scoring guide's criteria for a score of 3. Although the essay suggests some developing competence, it is flawed in significant ways which suggest that the writer needs remedial work before succeeding in college-level reading and writing.

- The writer demonstrates a limited understanding of Mead's passage, and because of this misunderstanding, the response is weak.

- The thesis is never clearly stated.

- The overall essay has problems with focus and organization, suggesting that the writer did not have a plan before beginning.

- Although there is an attempt at development in this four-paragraph essay, the examples are often confusing and tangential; for example, the second paragraph attempts development, but it merely repeats a previous point ("In a way I think we are selfish . . ..").

- Most of the final paragraph is tangential, as it concerns the writer's- not Mead's- notions of success.

- The sentence-level problems are not as severe as those in some essays in the 3 range; however, moments of confusion and circular reasoning confound the reader. For example, the final sentence says, "It is true what Mead said about considering a threat people that are successful that are near you because you do not want to feel inferior to people that are said to be successful."

- The essay has an accumulation of errors in mechanics and usage ("admirations and attentions").

● ●

Score of 2: Very Weak

Some people see the concept of success as a source of confusion, even if they don't realize it. Margaret Mead, the author of *Egalitarian Error*, quotes, "For many Americans the concept of success is a source of confusion." I think what she means is that success is something people don't see and they confuse themselves in trying to see if they really succeeded in what they wanted to do. I agree with Mead because people get confused when he or she has succeeded or not.

Sure some people know that when he or she gets a good grade or when he or she wins a prize that he or she has succeeded. But do people realize what succeeding in life really is? It seems that when a person wins a contest, other people often say that he has succeeded. What are the people really celebrating? Are they celebrating his or her accomplishments or are they just celebrating because he or she beat the other contestants and he or she was the best in the game? I think it is because he or she beat the other contestants. No one ever say, "Congratulations you have succeeded in winning the game."

A lot of people tend to keep going at their job or school and not even know that he or she has succeeded in something throughout his or her life. Confusion makes the person keep trying harder and makes he or she climb more steps in life. Confusion can be good.

Commentary for 2 paper—Very Weak

This essay illustrates the scoring guide's criteria for a score of 2. The serious flaws here indicate that this writer will need some considerable help before succeeding at college-level reading and writing.

- The writer demonstrates a very poor understanding of the passage and, specifically, does not understand what Mead means by "confusion," nor that the "confusion" has to do with ambivalence- in this case, having more than one emotion or attitude at one time.

- Because the writer misunderstands the passage, she is unable to use it in responding to the prompt.

- The essay lacks focus and coherence, and it often fails to communicate its ideas: For example, in the third paragraph, the writer says, "Confusion makes the person keep trying harder and makes he or she climb more steps in life."

- This three-paragraph essay is undeveloped and shows little organization within paragraphs.

- The simplistic generalizations ("Confusion can be good.") exist without support.

- The sentence control is often inadequate: For example, in the first paragraph, the writer states, "I agree with Mead because people get confused when he or she has succeeded or not."

- Because the writer misuses "confusion" and the essay's point seems to turn on that word, the essay fails to make sense.

• •

Score of 1: Incompetent

After reading a small paragraph of The Egalitarian Error by Margaret Mead, she states that success is "a source of confusion." I have to disagree with that. I think everyone in their own way celebrate success some may celebrate bigger than other. That is true because if you get good grades in high school your parents would give money instead of buying you a car. But say you win the biggest game in college football then you get a party and people will know who you are. I think it is the way you see life.

In a way I do know why Margaret Mead may have stated that is because when you know if you successed, or when do you know that someone or your self succeed. Take myself I have never so I think have success. The only think is my grade but to me that is not success. When your in school your teachers, parents, and yourself think that you are too be getting good grades. When I was high school my friends would get money for every A or B on their report card. I wouldn't, I thought why are my friends succeed but not me because I never got money. So I was confused. I think when people get older they realize it wasn't confusion you were just enjoying your success different.

Success can mean any different to people. To some it may be confusing or not but it is up to that person to make that choice. Success to me can be very different to the person next to me.

Commentary for 1 paper—Incompetent

This essay illustrates the scoring guide's criteria for a score of 1. The fundamental deficiencies here clearly indicate that this writer is not yet ready to succeed at college-level reading and writing.

- The writer seems unable to understand the passage and does not use it to produce a meaningful response.

- The essay does not have a clear thesis early in the paper.

- The essay is illogical, unfocused, and disorganized.

- At the paragraph level, the writer has no sense of topic sentences or of how to use specific examples to support a statement.

- A series of disconnected thoughts about success appear in place of argument and support.

- Most sentences show serious problems with usage, word choice, sentence construction, and idioms: for example, ". . . that is because . . . . (first sentence of paragraph 2); or "Success can mean any different to people" (first sentence of paragraph 3).

- The writing suggests second-language interference.

1. "Because of cell phones, hiking in wilderness areas may be safer than before, but it is also noisier than ever. Although people might bring cell phones with them to use in case of an emergency, emergencies are rare. More often, people receive incoming business and even social calls. Technology seems to be following us everywhere: into the wilderness, and then back into civilization. Anywhere at any time, everyone else present can be disturbed by one person's call. Because more people in these circumstances are bothered by cell phones than are helped, these gadgets should not be permitted in certain public places or designated natural areas."

- Lois Quaide

Explain Quaide's argument and discuss the extent to which you agree or disagree with her analysis. Support your position, providing reasons and examples from your own experience, observations, or reading.

2. "The purpose of public universities should be to train the appropriate number of people for the professions. In order to fulfill this purpose, the number of students admitted to each field of study should be pre-set, as in Sweden, so that no more people are trained than will be needed to fill the estimated number of openings in each profession."

- Phyllis Stein

Explain Stein's argument and discuss the extent to which you agree or disagree with her analysis. Support your position, providing reasons and examples from your own experience, observations, or reading.

3. "Two-thirds of adolescent and adult Americans drink alcohol, and of those, 8 to 12 percent will become alcoholics or problem drinkers. To combat this huge public-health crisis, we should begin a national system of licensing, with appropriate penalties. Applicants for a drinking license would first be required to study a manual containing basic information about alcohol and the law, much like the driver's manual we all memorized in high school. Next they would have to pass a written test, after which they would receive a drinking license. License holders, and only license holders, would then be able to buy alcoholic beverages (including beer). Most of the problem drinkers would, at some point, probably face arrest on alcohol-related offenses. If convicted, they would lose their license. A liquor store or bar caught selling to an unlicensed drinker would lose its license as well."

- Earl Rochester

Explain Rochester's argument and discuss the extent to which you agree or disagree with his analysis. Support your position, providing reasons and examples from your own experience, observations, or reading.

4. "Ours is an open, fast-moving society- equipped with cars, trains, planes- that makes it too easy for us to move away from the people and places of our past. Not too many families live together in the same neighborhood; generally, we travel long distances in order for grandchildren and grandparents to spend time together, and often we lose track of old friends we never see again. As a result, we tend to lack the close, supportive relationships that people in former generations enjoyed. The advantages to living in such a highly mobile society are thus outweighed by the disadvantages."

- Perry Patetic

Explain Patetic's argument and discuss the extent to which you agree or disagree with his analysis. Support your position, providing reasons and examples from your own experience, observations, or reading.

Comparison of State Board of Education English Standards and The CSU Multiple-Choice Section of The EPT and DWS

State Board English-Language Arts Content Standards		CSU EPT/DWS (Multiple-Choice)
Reading (Word Analysis)	1.0 and 1.1 and 1.2 and 1.3	Reading Skills Section I A This section tests the ability to understand and analyze prose (non-fiction) reading passages.
Reading Comprehension	2.0 and 2.1 and 2.2 and 2.4	
Reading (Word Analysis)	1.0 and 1.2	Reading Skills Section I B Gliff This section tests the ability to choose the best word or phrase to substitute into a sentence.
Reading (Word Analysis)	1.0 and 1.2	Reading Skills Section I C This section tests the ability to see logical relationships between sentences.
Reading Comprehension	2.0 and 2.2	
Reading (Word Analysis)	1.0 and 1.3	Composing Skills Section II A This section tests the ability to rewrite a sentence.
Reading Comprehension	2.0 and 2.2	
Writing Strategies	1.9	
English Language Conventions	1.0 and 1.1	
Reading (Word Analysis)	1	Composing Skills Section II B This section tests the ability to choose the best version of a given sentence.
Writing Strategies	1.9	
English Language Conventions	1.0 and 1.1	
Reading (Word Analysis)	1.0 and 1.2	Composing Skills Section II C This section tests the ability to understand sentence relationships within a passage and to provide a necessary missing sentence.
Reading Comprehension	2.0 and 2.2	
English Language Conventions	1.1	
Reading (Word Analysis)	1.0 and 1.2	Composing Skills Section II D This section tests the ability to select a sentence that provides the best support for the topic presented.
Reading Comprehension	2.0 and 2.2	
English Language Conventions	1.1	

Comparison of State Board of Education English Standards and The CSU Essay Section of The EPT and DWS

State Board English-Language Arts Content Standards		CSU EPT/DWS (Essay)
Reading/Word Analysis, Fluency, Systematic Vocab Development	1.0	Response to Writing Task
Reading Comprehension If a short reading passage:	2.0, 2.2 2.4, 2.5	
Writing Strategies	1.0, 1.1, 1.2, 1.3, 1.4, 1.5	Development
Writing Applications	2.1 a,b,c,d,e; 2.3 a,b,c; 2.4c	
Writing Strategies	1.1, 1.2, 1.3, 1.4	Organization
Writing Applications	2.1, a,b,c,d,e; 2.3 a,b,c; 2.4 a,b,c,d	
Writing Strategies	1.5, 1.9	Sentence Control
Written English Language Conventions	1.0, 1.1, 1.2, 1.3	
Written English Language Conventions	1.0, 1.1, 1.2, 1.3	Grammar, Usage, and Diction

The alignment is both direct and indirect in the case of reading prompts; the standards do not mention any emphasis on understanding a task.

Some areas in the EPT repeat the Content Standards more than once.

TEST DATE: MARCH 2002

Scores Reported to: BAKERSFIELD
                        POMONA

English Placement Test

Form:	Y1
Total Score:	151
Subscores	
Essay (raw score):	008
Reading Skills:	152
Composing Skills:	147

Entry Level Mathematics Test

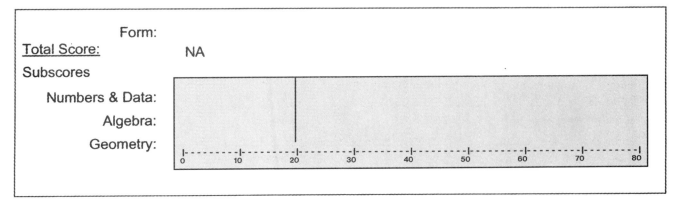

Form:
Total Score: NA
Subscores
    Numbers & Data:
    Algebra:
    Geometry:

0   10   20   30   40   50   60   70   80

SEE OTHER SIDE FOR SCORE EXPLANATIONS.

English Placement Test

What do my English Placement Test (EPT) scores mean?

The EPT Total Score is reported on a scale of 120-180. The CSU has determined that a Total Score of 151 or higher indicates that you are ready to undertake coursework that requires college-level writing. However, there may be some slight variation in the way campuses use scores to establish preparedness for college-level course work. You can find out what the campus of your choice does by consulting the campus catalog or course schedule.

Your EPT subscores may help your campus's writing faculty focus instruction where it is most needed. Essay subscores range from 2, the lowest score, to 12, the highest. A score of 0 means the essay did not address the assigned topic. Subscores in Reading Skills and Composing Skills are reported on the same scale (120-180) as the EPT Total Score.

Entry Level Mathematics Test

What do my Entry Level Mathematics (ELM) scores mean?

The ELM Total Score is reported on a scale of 0-80. The CSU has determined that a Total Score of 50 or higher indicates that you are ready to undertake college-level coursework in mathematics. However, there may be some slight variation in the way campuses use scores to establish preparedness for college-level coursework. You can find out what the campus of your choice does by consulting the campus catalog or course schedule.

Your ELM subscores may help your campus's mathematics faculty focus instruction where it is most needed. ELM subscores are shown graphically as ranges in relation to the "cut score" of 50. These ranges indicate your level of proficiency in the three content areas the test covers.

For more information about EPT and ELM scores and what they mean, you can consult the EPT/ELM *Information Bulletin.* You can obtain the *Information Bulletin* from your campus Admissions and Records Office or Test Office. You can also consult the *Information Bulletin* on-line at www.ets.org/csu.

Interpretation of Test Results

Individual test results are sent to each student and to the campus where the student intends to enroll. On each campus, students are placed into appropriate classes on the basis of their test scores.

The Total (T) score shows how well the student did on all three sections of the test. The T score is reported on a scale ranging from a low of 120 to a high of 180. Students scoring below 151 may experience some problems in regular college work; those scoring 145 or below are likely to have such problems. Scores lower than 140 indicate the probability of real difficulty for the student unless considerable help is made available.

The Reading Skills (R) and the Composing Skills (C) scores indicate performance on those sections of the EPT. Scores on these two sections of the test are also distributed on the 120-180 scale, and score levels for these skills may be interpreted in approximately the same way as is the T score. The Essay (E) score is a sum of two independent judgments on a scoring scale from 0-6; hence, the best possible score is 12. The essay score is reported as a raw score, and separated from the other scores to minimize confusion.

Each score report for the EPT thus provides the following scores:

Reading Skills .. .. .R120 to R180
Composing Skills .. .. C120 to C180
Essay .. .. E 0 to E 12
Total Score .. ..T120 to T180

At the request of the California Legislature, summary information about the performance of students from each high school is provided annually to school districts. While these reports should be seen only as a score distribution for those who have taken the test (not, for instance, an evaluation of all students, or even all college-bound students), the information should be useful to administrators and faculty assessing high school English programs.

The following sample score reports, with some interpretive comments, show the usefulness of the information provided by the EPT.

The California State University
Office of the Chancellor
Student Academic Support
www.calstate.edu